THE
COVENANT

ONE NATION UNDER GOD

AMERICA'S SACRED & IMMUTABLE
CONNECTION TO ANCIENT ISRAEL

Legends Library

New York

To see the complete Legends Library, visit www.legendslibrary.org

For info or permissions write to: info@digitalegend.com or call toll free: 877-222-1960

ISBN: 978-1-937735-20-3

Printed in the United States of America: Updated 2018 (V4)

Cover design and book interior layout by Alisha Bishop

THE
COVENANT

ONE NATION UNDER GOD

AMERICA'S SACRED & IMMUTABLE CONNECTION TO ANCIENT ISRAEL

Timothy Ballard

LEGENDS Library

New York

CONTENTS

For Katherine

Covenant: *noun: an agreement between God and his people in which God makes certain promises and requires certain behavior from them in return.*

—Webster's Revised Unabridged Dictionary, (1913)

Prologue

Summer 1776

Following the British evacuation of Boston in March 1776, the American colonists were encouraged. However, as the British fleet headed southward down the eastern coastline, it became clear to everyone that the British general, William Howe, would begin preparations for a military strike against the commercial and cultural hub of America—New York City. New York would make an ideal headquarters for Howe, as it was crawling with loyalists in support of Britain. The city was also surrounded by rivers and harbors, making it an easy target for the world's most powerful navy. In anticipation, Washington immediately sent his forces to defend New York City. By April 1776, the Continental Army had arrived and began making its preparations to defend the city.

The situation for Washington was next to hopeless. In addition to the large amount of loyalists in New York, and the many bays, rivers, and waterways conducive to a British naval attack there, a fresh and enormous British fleet had recently arrived and joined with Howe's already powerful forces. By the end of June, this reinforced British fleet began its impressive advent into New York Harbor. With some four hundred ships, at least seventy of which were state-of-the-art war ships with fifty guns or more, it was—at that time—the largest naval force ever sent forth by any one nation against another. One of Washington's men recorded, "I do declare that I thought all London was afloat."[1] Furthermore, upon the

1

decks of these ships were close to thirty thousand armed troops—more soldiers than the entire civilian population of New York or Philadelphia. With New York completely surrounded by water, the British could advance on land with these troops wherever and whenever they desired.

Washington, on the other hand—himself never having commanded a significant battle— led only a rag-tag group of civilian soldiers, who counted well under half the number of British troops; and most of these American volunteers had never even seen a battle, let alone fought in one. Worse yet, the American General did not have even a single warship at his disposal.[2] But what he *did* have was more powerful than any warship and more reliable than any cannon. He had access to a divine covenant that offered the embryonic American nation certain blessings, including protection from its enemies. At this particular moment in history, even more important than the existence of such a covenant was the fact that *Washington knew how to invoke it.*

Washington and Staff Watching the Battle of Long Island, circa 1920. Collection of Fraunces Tavern Museum.

As is the case with all covenants, both parties have certain obligations to each other. Washington knew that Providential protection came only as his soldiers and the American people were worthy of it. This was especially worrisome as, with the increase of sinful opportunity in New York City, immorality among the troops was on the rise. Washington recognized it. And so, in addition to leading the physical preparations for battle, Washington also led the spiritual ones. On May 15, shortly after the Continental Army's arrival at New York, Washington issued a General Order to all under his command, which read:

> Instant to be observed [on Friday the 17th] as a day of fasting, humiliation and prayer, humbly to supplicate the mercy of Almighty God, that it would please him to pardon all our manifold sins and transgressions, and to prosper the Arms of the United Colonies, and finally establish the peace and freedom of America, upon a solid and lasting foundation.[3]

Then again on July 2, Washington in another General Order would remind his men that "the fate of unborn Millions will now depend, under God, on the courage and conduct of this army...Let us therefore rely upon the goodness of the Cause, and the aid of the Supreme Being, in whose hands Victory is."[4] Two days later, in Philadelphia, these same sentiments would be immortalized by the Continental Congress in the Declaration of Independence, which concludes, "And for support of this Declaration, *with firm reliance on the protection of divine Providence*, we mutually pledge to each other our Lives, our Fortunes, and our sacred Honor."

Washington was so convinced of his utter dependence upon this covenant relationship with God that he would continue to extend reminders and calls to repentance. On July 9, Washington issued another General Order in which he called for chaplains in each regiment to ensure that the soldiers "attend carefully upon religious exercises." The order concluded with the following: "The blessing and protection of Heaven are at all times necessary but especially so in times of public distress and danger—the General hopes and trusts, that every officer and man, will endeavor so to live, and act, as becomes a good Christian soldier defending the dearest Rights and Liberties of his country."[5] Just days before battle would commence, Washington issued yet another General Order in which he recommended the keeping of the Sabbath and pleaded with his men to shun the immoral temptations that abounded in the city, exhorting them to "endeavor to check [such behavior] and

...reflect, that we can have little hopes of the blessing of Heaven on our Arms, if we insult it by our impiety and folly."[6] Such a covenant relationship is reminiscent of the Lord's relationship with Moses, Joshua, and the children of Israel, as read in the Old Testament account.

That Washington was assured the Lord would provide in the upcoming battle is evidenced by the army's positive response to their commander-in-chief's spiritual encouragements. One observant New Yorker, unaccustomed to seeing a pious group of soldiers, wrote of his surprise to see how Washington's men attended prayers "evening and morning regularly." "On the Lord's day," commented the observer, "they attend public worship twice, and their deportment in the house of God is such as becomes the place." Washington's trusted officer, Henry Knox, wrote to his wife that he would daily "rise with or a little before the sun and immediately, with part of the regiment attend prayers, sing a psalm or read a chapter [from the Bible]."[7] They were trying diligently to keep their end of the covenant.

The faith and influence of Washington was extended through other revolutionary leaders who caught his vision and acted upon it. One such leader, Connecticut Governor Jonathon Trumbull, upon learning of Washington's impending battle, called for nine fresh regiments to march in support of Washington (and this was in addition to the five regiments he had already sent). Trumbull's call to arms sounded much like something Joshua might have said in the camp of Israel: "Be roused and alarmed to stand forth in our just and glorious cause. Join...march on; this shall be your warrant: play the man for God, and for the cities of our God! May the Lord of Hosts, the God of the armies of Israel, be your leader."[8]

On July 2, 1776, the same day the Congress had officially voted for the Declaration of Independence, the British landed on the southern shores of Long Island, New York. Long Island is located to the east of Manhattan Island (home of New York City and Washington's headquarters), separated by the mile-wide East River. Having anticipated such advancements,

Washington had already begun sending his troops from Manhattan over the East River to the western shores of Long Island at Brooklyn. Over the next several weeks, the two forces inched their way toward each other—the first great battle of the war was imminent.

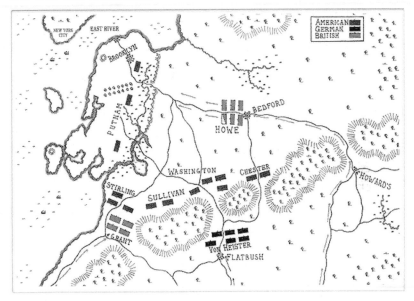

Battle of Long Island Map

On August 27, several miles inland from Brooklyn's shores, the Battle of Long Island commenced. The Americans were devastatingly defeated. Almost immediately, Washington lost over one thousand men, while the British lost less than one hundred.[9] All the Americans could do was run back toward the western shores of Brooklyn, Long Island, in hopes of escaping over the East River back into New York City before the advancing enemy could catch up to them. The British responded by sending their fastest ships up the East River to cut off Washington's escape route with the intention of surrounding the rebels from all sides. Howe knew that such action would compel an American surrender, as Washington's entire Continental Army would be trapped. This would be the end of America's hope for independence. As one prominent historian stated, "If Washington and his army had been trapped in Brooklyn...the war would have ended quickly."[10] After giving their all, the Americans were now in a devastatingly hopeless state, which is often when the Lord enters the scene—and enter He did!

As the British fleet raced northward and entered the mouth of the East River in order to block Washington's retreat and crush his rebel army, a ferocious wind from the north began pushing the British back down. A total of five ships carrying over seventy-two guns attempted—but failed—to advance up the river to cut off the Americans.[11] Washington would have a small window of opportunity to evacuate his troops from this would-be British trap.

On the night of August 29, under the cover of darkness, Washington began gathering every boat that could be acquired, and prepared to secretly ferry his men back across the East River and back into New York City. Knowing that the British would respond to such an evacuation with a swift land assault, Washington ordered his men to continue firing long-range guns through the night at the British land troops. He further ordered a few soldiers to maintain the noise and campfires indicative of a busy campsite, thus making the British believe the Americans were anything but on the move.

In the meantime, these British land forces would wait until the advancing British fleet made its way up the river, thus enabling them to surround Washington from all sides. Until this happened the British land troops, convinced that the rebels were bedding down for the night, would wait patiently. (Fortunately for the Americans, there were no means of communication that would permit the British naval officers to alert the British land officers that the ships could not get up the river.)

Convinced that his ruse was working on the British land troops, and with the blessed storm holding back the British navy, Washington would attempt the impossible—to secretly ferry over nine thousand troops, along with their baggage, guns, horses, etc, across the mile-wide river, and all before the light of day exposed his daring scheme. If the British land troops were to discover what was happening, it would be over for the Americans.

Shortly after the evacuation began, the Americans again fell into despair, as the same wind that kept Howe's ships from advancing up river, was also making it impossible for them to manage their over-crowded rowboats and advance their army westward to safety. Then, a little after nine, the wind miraculously shifted to a westerly direction, facilitating the exodus with most favorable conditions.[12]

But even with the favorable wind, the night was dying fast. The rising sun would soon expose Washington's scheme to the full view of the British. Another miracle was needed. Pulitzer Prize-winning historian, David McCullough, explains:

> Troops in substantial number had still to be evacuated and at the rate things were going, it appeared day would dawn before everyone was safely removed. But again the "elements" interceded, this time in the form of pea-soup fog. It was called "a peculiar providential occurrence," "manifestly providential," "very favorable to the design," "an unusual fog," "a friendly fog," "an American fog." "So very dense was the atmosphere," remembers Benjamin Tallmadge, "that I could scarcely discern a man at six yards' distance." And as daylight came, the fog held, covering the entire operation no less than had the night…while over on the New York side of the river there was no fog at all.[13]

Washington waited until the last man evacuated Long Island before boarding the final ferry boat. The escape was a success, and without a single casualty. Washington and his men would live to fight another day.

Alexander Graydon, an eyewitness to the event, commented that "in less than an hour after [the complete evacuation], the fog having dispersed, the enemy was visible on the shore we had left." The British were bewildered. "That the rebel army had silently vanished in the night right under their very noses," according to McCullough, "was almost inconceivable." British Major Stephen Kemble wrote in his diary that "[i]n the morning, to our great astonishment, [we] found they had evacuated...and the whole escaped to...New York." British General James Grant wrote, "We cannot yet account for their precipitate retreat."[14]

McCullough summed up the entire event:

> But what a close call it had been. How readily it could have gone all wrong—had there been no northeast wind to hold the British fleet in check through the day the Battle of Long Island was fought, not to say the days immediately afterward. Or had the wind not turned southwest the night of August 29. Or had there been no fortuitous fog as a final safeguard when day broke....Incredibly, yet again—fate, luck, Providence, the hand of God, as would be said so often—intervened. [15]

This miracle at Long Island would cause many to think twice about the seemingly prophetic words spoken three months earlier by the very influential Reverend John Witherspoon, who presided over the College of New Jersey (what is now Princeton University) and thus was mentor to one vice president, over fifteen delegates to the Continental Congress and Constitutional Convention, forty-nine members of the House of Representatives, twenty-eight senators, three Supreme Court Justices, and scores of other government officers and patriots. A signer of the Declaration of Independence, Witherspoon would prophetically describe how God would secure America's victory: "The armies of the enemy...are rendered irresolute when...rains make the terrain of the final charge impossible; [and] an unforeseen fog brings operations to a halt. Nature affords countless chinks in its regular workings through which the Divine Artist...can govern events."[16]

Witherspoon revealed this prophesy on May 17th 1776, even the very day Washington and his men were praying and covenanting with God Almighty (as described above). That Witherspoon prophesied of an "unforeseen fog" as the godly solution for the army, and that he did so the same hour the army was seeking such a miracle is astonishing. That their joint prayers of that day were answered weeks later in the precise manner projected by Witherspoon, is almost unbelievable.

Washington himself made an independent yet concurring prophetic statement in January 1776, also many months before Long Island, when he expressed that victory could only come if "the finger of Providence is in it, to blind the eyes of our enemies." [17]

God heard America's plea and honored the army's efforts to invoke the ancient covenant relationship. In His wisdom, He allowed Washington and his band of inexperienced men to engage the enemy at Long Island, thus acquiring the much needed taste of battle that would serve them in the future, while at the same time miraculously extricating them from the grips of destruction. The Revolution would live on!

★ ★ ★ ★

Sadly, most Americans don't know anything about the Battle of Long Island, let alone the desperate importuning of General Washington and God's miraculous and prescient response. The truth is that much of our nation's history has been trimmed to the point where God is no longer a part. For instance, what if we hadn't known that General Washington and his commanders ordered and begged their soldiers to keep the commandments and check their behavior, so that they might merit the protection and aid of God? As we fail to see these truths belonging to our history, we will (as secularists desire) fail to learn the lessons God has left behind for us. We

9

will fail to see the evidence that God lives and governs in the affairs of man. And, most alarmingly, we as a people will fail to find reason to orient our individual behavior and national policy toward any core set of values.

The fact is there IS a God! He DID make a covenant with an ancient nation, which produced the exact same set of blessings we have enjoyed in America for over two hundred years. Those blessings are contingent upon specific obligations, just as they were for the children of Israel in the days of Moses. That very covenant was passed down through the generations of time and found its way (by no accident) to America. Columbus sailed, Bradford settled, Winthrop built, Washington fought, Madison wrote, and Americans endure—all under the influence and direction of this national covenant. As we explore the history of the United States of America, we will refer to, and give evidence of, the relationship between God and the citizenry of this chosen nation. This relationship we call "The American Covenant."

We are fortunate to have a few accomplished historians who are still willing to fight the growing secularist movement and recognize God's miracles in our history. But even then, how many of these inspired historians have really connected these miracles to a covenant? For example, how many have revealed the truth about how Washington and his people clearly understood that their success—and God's miracles in their cause—were contingent upon national righteousness? As we will see in the coming chapters, the miracle at Long Island is but one of many examples that *prove* early Americans believed—that *prove* they lived and died by *The Covenant*.

ENDNOTES

[1] McCullough, *1776*, 134, 148.

[2] McCullough, *1776*, 131-132, 163.

[3] Bennett, *The Spirit of America*, 393.

[4] Novak, *Washington's God*, 71.

[5] Bennett, *The Spirit of America*, 390.

[6] Novak, *Washington's God*, 89.

[7] McCullough, *1776*, 123, 147.

[8] Jonathon Trumbull, as quoted in Marshall and Manuel, 394.

[9] McCullough, *1776*, 179-180.

[10] Thomas Fleming, "Unlikely Victory," *What If? The World's Foremost Military Historians Imagine What Might Have Been*, James Cowley, ed., 165.

[11] McCullough, *1776*, 184.

[12] David McCullough, "What the Fog Wrought," *What If? The World's Foremost Military Authorities Imagine What Might Have Been*, James Cowley, ed., 197.

[13] McCullough, "What the Fog Wrought," 198; McCullough, *1776*, 191.

[14] McCullough, *1776*, 191-192.

[15] McCullough, "What the Fog Wrought," 199; McCullough, *1776*, 191.

[16] John Witherspoon, as quoted in Novak, *On Two Wings*, 15.

[17] Washington, as quoted in Novak, *On Two Wings*, 79.

11

PART I

*Defining the American
Covenant*

CHAPTER 1

THE COVENANT

*For I will have respect unto you, and make you
fruitful, and multiply you, and establish my
covenant with you… And I will walk among you,
and will be your God, and ye shall be my people.*

—Leviticus 26:9, 12

There is purpose to life. This purpose revolves around
bridging the gap between mankind and its Maker. It revolves
around the ability of God's children to reach out and find
salvation through the grace and mediation of a saving
"Messiah." But there is evil lurking about—evil that will do all
it can to obstruct the process of salvation. This evil will attack
the one thing mankind needs to fully gain access to the
principles that lead to God and salvation. It will attack liberty.
For this reason, the Almighty God has raised up nations and
made covenants with them, so that they might serve to fight
this evil, preserve His liberty, and make available salvation to
all who will receive it. One such nation is the United States of
America.

If we are to discover this covenant relationship within
the history of our land, there are certain questions we must

15

first address. For example, what is a "national covenant"? How does such a covenant really help us today? And why should we think to apply this covenant to America? Though it will take the length of this book to fully answer these questions and flesh out these concepts, it is the purpose of this chapter to introduce the discussion.

What is a National Covenant?

In the legal sense, a covenant is a formal agreement between two entities. For example, a loan covenant between a bank and a borrower describes a promise by the borrower upon which the loan is contingent. If the borrower fails to keep the covenant, the loan can be called and the original agreement nullified. In a biblical sense, a covenant refers to the relationship between God and His children. Throughout the New Testament we learn of these *individual* covenants. Promised blessings are contingent upon prescribed behavior. We promise to love and serve our neighbors and He promises the fruits of the Spirit (see Galatians 5:22). We promise to be reborn of the Spirit and He promises the kingdom of God (see John 3). These *individual* obligations and blessings are far and away the most significant covenants, as they directly fulfill the purposes of God by assisting His children to fill the measure of their creation. These sacred covenants are spiritual in nature.

National covenants are different. They are made with nations, not individuals, and exist as a support mechanism to the more important *individual/spiritual* covenants. National covenants provide the framework, foundation, and environment in which these individual covenants might be made and lived unto eternal life. And so, though national covenants serve as lesser covenants—and certainly are not requisite for individual salvation—they do carry the same eternal purposes of God. The Old Testament focuses heavily on national covenants.

Biblical scholars have pointed out that the Old Testament "is a book directed to, and recorded for, the Israelite nation in general—not the worthy [followers of God] who may have been among them. The words of the prophets in it are public pronouncements to their wayward society, not their private teachings to those who had risen above the sins of their generation."[1] This, accordingly, explains why the Old Testament perhaps seems less applicable to our personal lives than is the New Testament, which overflows with personal and individualized messages from the Christ. However, the Old Testament speaks to our *national* life in a way no other book does. It lays out the national covenant. It is therefore no less important than the New Testament. The Founding Fathers understood this. In fact, the Founders of America quoted from the Old Testament more than any other literary source. More particularly, the Founders' most quoted book of scripture was Deuteronomy (which does more to lay out the covenant law and obligation, as connected to the "Promised Land," than any other).[2]

Indeed, in their effort to make a covenant land of America, the Founders relied upon the example of the Hebrew nation. The Hebrew's covenant is detailed throughout the Old Testament: "For I will have respect unto you...and establish my covenant with you...And I will walk among you and will be your God and ye shall be my people" (Leviticus 26:9, 12). This is but one of many such Old Testament verses which describe this national covenant made, not with an individual, but with an entire people (known as Israel). The familiar blessings offered to Israel as part of this covenant were liberty, protection, and prosperity. We see the blessings of *liberty*, for example, dispensed when the Lord liberates Israel from Egyptian slavery, as manifested in part by the miracle of the parting of the Red Sea (Exodus 14:13-16). We further witness these blessings when God establishes this chosen people under a sound system of government that protects these liberties.[3] We see the blessings of *prosperity* dispensed when the Lord provides Israel with a promised land in which it could thrive economically, even a land "flowing with milk and honey" (Exodus 3:8). And we see the blessings of physical *protection* dispensed when the Lord provides defenses against foreign powers, such as the Philistines, who sought to destroy God's work among Israel (1 Samuel 17:45-47). If His people would but listen and obey, all this would be theirs.*

Moses Parts the Red Sea, by Robert T. Barrett

Though we accept this covenant relationship, we often fail to ponder why it was, exactly, that the Lord provided these temporal blessings of *liberty, protection,* and *prosperity* to ancient Israel. Did He do this solely because He wanted to help a group of people overcome the hardships of mortality? If so, what about the millions of others at this time, and at other times, who never received such an offer? The truth is, there

---

* See Leviticus 26 for a detailed description of Israel's national covenant, complete with obligations of obedience, and blessings of liberty, protection, and prosperity.

was and is much more to it. From the day God covenanted with Abraham, God has continually offered Abraham's posterity this national covenant (see Genesis 17:1-10; 26:1-5, 24; 28:1-4, 10-14; 35:9-13; 48:3-4; Leviticus 26:42; Acts 3:25). He did so because it was through the blessings of this national covenant (*liberty, protection,* and *prosperity*) that the greater gospel purposes and individual covenants could be secure enough to thrive in the world. Would the Lord have, for example, set up his sacred law and temple for His people of Israel while they suffered under the distrustful eye and brutal tyranny of the Egyptians? Could His temple have remained undefiled in a land of overwhelming poverty and crime? Or in a land riddled with conquering invasions? Could God trust that His Gospel and His church would be secure in a land of overbearing oppression and wickedness? Trying to establish God's work on earth without a national covenant to fight against the influence of evil and oppression would be like tossing a handful of seeds into a pot filled only with concrete—doomed from the start. Conversely, instituting a binding covenant that carried protective promises would be like filling the pot with rich soil, so that the seeds of the gospel could be carefully planted.

In sum, national covenants serve to secure and enhance the social, economic, and political situation of God's children, thus maximizing their ability to safely, securely, and freely access His greater individual covenants unto eternal life.

Why a National Covenant Today?

Without the social, political, and economic security provided by national covenants, the gospel would struggle to survive. Had ancient Israel been faithful until the end, their national covenant might have remained unscathed until the present day. This would have allowed God's eternal purpose for His children to thrive continuously through Israel, from their day to ours. However, as a result of man's (not God's) broken covenants, not the least of which was man's failure to worship the one true God, Israel temporarily lost the covenant blessings of its promised land. Slowly but surely, Israel's *liberty, protection,* and *prosperity* faded away, resulting in the nation being destroyed, swept off, and scattered throughout the world. A tragic loss of truth and salvation then pervaded the earth (Deut. 4:26-27; Ezekiel 11:16; Amos 8:11).

It was during this dark period that the Savior came into mortality. Clearly, there was enough freedom still left in Israel to allow Christ to teach the people, establish His Gospel as a fulfillment of the Law of Moses, and organize His church. (This was mostly due to Rome's initially tolerant stance on religious freedom within its commonwealth, of which Israel was a part.) But after He completed His mortal mission, the most important part of which was His atoning sacrifice, His church had little time to develop and congeal. For, with the lack of any strong national covenant that would support the existence of Christ's Gospel, the church began suffering greatly by the end of the first century AD. The forecast for the early church, of course, was especially gloomy after Christ's own nation sponsored His execution. The political foundations (both Roman and Israelite) that could have and should have protected the upstart church, ultimately came down upon it and displayed utter disregard for the preservation of precious truths bearing the gospel of salvation. Christ Himself, along with the apostolic writers, recognized in mortality that the nation they lived in would not adhere to its national covenant and that the gospel fullness would, as a consequence, suffer.

Christ declared, "Oh Jerusalem, Jerusalem, thou that killest the prophets, and stoneth them which are sent unto thee, how often would I have gathered thy children together, even as a hen gathereth her chickens under her wings, and ye would not! Behold, your house is left unto you desolate" (Matthew 23:37-38). Similarly, Paul prophesied, "For I know this, that after my departing shall grievous wolves enter in among you, not sparing the flock" (Acts 20:29-30).*

Early Christians, who witnessed this attack on the church, referenced these earlier prophecies and wrote clearly about them. Justin Martyr (A.D. 110-165), a great defender of Christianity who ultimately gave his life for the cause, explained:

> For what things He [Christ] predicted would take place in His name, these we do see actually accomplished in our sight. For he said, "Many shall come in My name, clothed outwardly in sheep's clothing, but inwardly they are ravening wolves." And "There shall be schisms and heresies." And "Beware of false prophets."...There are, therefore, and there were many, my friends, who, coming forward in the name of Jesus, taught both to speak and act impious and blasphemous things...So that, in consequence of these events, we know that Jesus foreknew what would happen after Him.[4]

A scholar of early Christianity, A. Cleveland Coxe, summed it up succinctly: "If it shocks the young student of the virgin years of Christianity to find such a state of things [the successful attacks upon the church], let him reflect that it was also foretold by Christ himself, and demonstrates the malice and power of the adversary."[5]

Fortunately, the light of Christianity would never be snuffed out, as good men and women fought to keep holy principles alive and miraculously preserved the biblical texts. At the same time, however, a fullness of religious liberty was no hallmark during the next fourteen centuries after Christ— commonly known as the Dark Ages. Christians often found themselves on the run, or found that their precious doctrines were being exploited for political gain. Even in "Christian"

---

* See also Matthew 21:43; 24:4-5; 2 Tim. 3:1-6; 2 Peter 2:1-3; 2 Thes. 2:1-5.

lands, governments often served as obstructions to personal salvation. In 1401, for example, the king of England issued a national edict, which called for the immediate arrest and punishment of anyone who preached religious thought contrary to the king's religion. If found guilty of a second offense of the same, the decree called for immediate death by hanging.[6] Then, of course, there were the similarly violent and seemingly endless atrocities surrounding the Inquisition, which was responsible for the torture and death of tens of thousands of "non-believers" from Spain to Asia and from Central to South America.[7] So successful were the adversary's efforts to deny a fullness of liberty in the Old World, that even the "faithful" adherents of the state church had to risk life and limb just to pick up a Bible and read it. Such was forbidden by the clergy, who desired to control "God's law."[8] Furthermore, by 1685, the king of France, in the same evil spirit, demanded that all those unwilling to accept French Catholicism were to be immediately exiled or put to death.[9] Sadly, these examples represent only a portion of the religious intolerance that permeated the world during this dark era.

Unless and until a "promised land" could be reestablished, fully equipped with the national covenant blessings of *liberty, protection,* and *prosperity,* Christian principles would continue to struggle to find their zenith. Until a land could be established in which all religions were safe—even a land where the most obscure, minority religion or sect could thrive unmolested—then Christianity in its fullness could never claim complete victory over the Devil and his assault on liberty and salvation. For, unless the lowliest of religionists are safe in worshipping according to the dictates of conscience, none of us are truly safe. We will later learn how the Founding Fathers anticipated and dreamed that the nation they were creating "under God" would result in just the sort of tool God needed to bring about such liberty unto eternal salvation. There is, after all, a reason the Founders called their land and their people the "New Israel."[10]

Though this glimpse into history reveals our need for a national covenant today, to fully understand the most significant reasons such a national covenant would be needed in the modern-day era (or any other era), requires us to look to a point in time, way outside the establishment and failures of ancient Israel. We must look to the heavenly realm. The Scripture teaches that "there was war in heaven:

> Michael and his angels fought against the dragon; and the dragon fought and his angels, And prevailed not; neither was their place found any more in heaven. And the great dragon was cast out, that old serpent, called the Devil, and Satan, which deceiveth the whole word: he was cast out into the earth, and his angels were cast out with him" (Revelation 12:7-9).

With Satan and his angels here upon the earth, the war in heaven has spilled over onto the earth. And it is being fought over the same idea. "And the dragon was wroth...and went to make war with [God's children], which keep the commandments of God, and have the testimony of Jesus Christ" (Revelation 12:17).

If the Devil desires that mankind be obstructed from gaining a testimony of Jesus Christ, what better tactic than to deny mankind freedom and personal liberty? What better tactic than to buy up armies and navies, to employ tyrants that rule with blood and horror upon the earth? If Satan can deny us any amount of liberty, he inches closer to winning the war over the souls of men. He understands that liberty in its fullness is the only mechanism by which God's children can achieve the highest heavenly reward. He knows the value of the human experience. And so he fights for a system of governance that oppresses, compels, and makes choices *for* its subjects, thus making the true steps toward our heavenly reward more difficult to find and receive. Indeed, his system would deny us the liberty to find and employ faith, to fully repent, to seek and find truth, to be reborn through Christ's

23

atonement, to longingly make and keep covenants, to struggle, fail, succeed, then grow, and thus "work out [our] salvation" (Philip 2:12) through the grace of the Father and His Son. If Satan utilized wicked governments to remove our ability to choose to take those necessary steps, our salvation would be in jeopardy. If he used these compromised governments to block the knowledge of true principles, such as faith in and repentance through Christ, the effect would be the same. If he tempted the world into complete and total subjugation, God's work would be severely hampered. In any case, as he destroys liberty in any degree, he withholds from us our fullest potential as God's children.

Satan and his followers, once "cast down" to earth, would certainly continue to employ their *modus operandi* and do all in their power to influence those they could—from kings and their armies to tyrants and their navies—to stifle and oppress. They would attempt to control man, thus limiting his choices and thwarting his God-given freedoms. This form of physical oppression would and does frustrate man's ability to reunite with Deity. Of course, Satan would disguise his evil intentions, even permitting the use of some semblance of truth and scripture; but this scripture would merely be mingled with the dominating and oppressive philosophies of men. For, no matter how he presents it, his evil designs will always have at their root a malicious attempt to destroy liberty.

Commenting on such adversarial ploys, a Christian leader made the following commentary during World War II: "Think of it now—the value of freedom of choice! That was the great principle involved when the war arose in Heaven when Lucifer would have deprived God's children the right to choose. Your sons and mine are out fighting for that principle [of freedom]. In the last analysis that is the great question in this war so far as the Allies are concerned—whether we shall have the right to think as we please."[11]

Today we stand on earth, witnessing Satan's efforts in the war against God and His children. A mere glimpse into modern history (say, the last couple hundred years) reveals the Evil One's influence over governments. Backed by armies and navies, men susceptible to Satan's influence have repeatedly turned to tyranny and attacked precious freedom and liberty. Such attacks have invited ignorance, violence, and the near destruction of personal liberty, and thus the near destruction of personal progression towards eternal salvation. Consider, for example, the monarchical systems of Europe, the oppressive Confederate system (sponsor of human slavery) that once existed in the United States, fascist regimes like Nazi Germany, dictatorial regimes such as those the world witnessed under the Soviet Union, or the tyrannical systems of the Middle East we still see today. Though, admittedly, no such system of wicked governance could ever completely destroy freedom and spiritual growth (man does, after all, always maintain his thoughts and intentions, which allow for at least limited progression), these examples of bad government come dangerously close. For they have allowed Satan to have his way. Depending on the firmness of his evil grasp, sometimes this means the ability to control and oppress almost every aspect of man's life. Other times, it means less control over man's every choice, but still a full ability to deny the freedom required for Christianity to establish itself within the borders of the infected nation-state. Either way, through denying a fullness of liberty, the adversary has, through time, maintained a choke-hold on mankind's spiritual progression.

And this is where the national covenant comes in. For, as this adversarial influence created a very real and *physical* affront to God's plan for the full salvation of His children (again, we are talking about the adversary's influence over literal armies and navies, etc.), a very real and *physical* response from Heaven would be required. If God could counter Satan in modern days, as He did in ancient days with Israel, by forming a government built upon a new national covenant complete with the necessary *liberty*, *protection*, and *prosperity*, then this new nation could, under the guidance of Heaven, fight against these evil tyrants, these armies and navies, and thus protect and maximize the divine liberty of man. Only then could all mankind receive the opportunity to fully and freely worship according to the dictates of their conscience. *Individual adherents* of Christ's church, mere people who would live and minister the gospel upon the earth, could not alone defeat such a physical threat. But a righteous *nation* blessed with abundant resources, of which they were a part, certainly could! Once such a nation and government under God was in place, with liberty unto salvation enhanced, the spiritual work and progression of God's children would be facilitated and the "Kingdom of God" could finally thrive and grow. Freedom could spread, allowing more and more of God's children to find the truths of Christ's Gospel.

It should be noted, however, that though the gospel is the crowning purpose of God's national covenants, this does not preclude non-Christians or anyone else from being beneficiaries of them. As implied above, these national covenants, which provide and enhance liberty, benefit *all* children of God by allowing them to choose freely, employ personal responsibility, and thus learn and grow from their successes and failures—whether in or out of any particular belief system. As any spiritual enlightenment brings men and women closer to God and His eternal plan, they too have claim and interest in the national covenant. Indeed, the eternal outcome of *all* God's children is attached to this national covenant, which is why we need a national covenant today and always.

Why the United States of America?

Though we might acknowledge our need for a national covenant today, why the United States of America? What proof exists that the United States is the modern nation God has established and set apart under this covenant? What evidence is there that America is His instrument in developing, defending, and distributing the socio-political system that would promote a fullness of liberty? Answering these questions in full will require the length of this book. However, there are certain immediate evidences that suggest that the United States might, indeed, be a nation under God's covenant.

We might consider how a cursory review of American history reveals a consistent pattern: where go the adversary's political and military tools of oppression unto spiritual obstruction, there goes America to confront and defeat it; and where goes America to confront and defeat it, there follow the divinely inspired constitutional principles of liberty and personal agency; and where go these divine principles, there follows a proliferation of enlightenment and human rights, along with increased opportunity for personal and spiritual progression in one's religion of choice. Freedom and happiness become more accessible. Salvation becomes more accessible.

We recently identified several such adversarial regime-types in modern times that have thwarted or at least severely hampered liberty and have thus been responsible for obstructing the spiritual progression of millions upon millions of God's children. And in every case, it was America who led the fight back at them. It was America who first took on the monarchical system of the Old World by defeating Great Britain and thus securing the freedom that would become the fertile ground for a restoration of the national covenant and the subsequent proliferation of Judeo-Christian ideals. The American Union would likewise take on wicked elements from within (like the Southern Confederacy/slavery), thus purifying this fertile ground in furtherance of Judeo-Christian principles. America has also successfully attacked both fascist and communist dictatorships (e.g. Nazi Germany and Soviet Russia), along with Middle Eastern tyrants and other wicked regimes. As liberty has thus spread, so have the effects of enhanced freedom. And in almost every instance, once America's victory is secured, whether at home or abroad, America moves on, leaving constitutional principles in its wake—principles which facilitate the proliferation of religious liberty and thus salvation. So it has been, and so it shall be. Indeed, that great war in heaven has spilled over upon the earth. It rages today. As a covenant nation, America has been (and continues to have the opportunity to be) a positive force, under God, in this eternal struggle.

In light of this historical glimpse, it should be of little surprise that God is such a prominent part of America's founding documents, which, as we will discuss later, are the first of their kind, in both their inspired content and the miraculous manner in which they came to exist. The documents referred to, of course, are the Declaration of Independence and the Constitution, which declare that it is the responsibility of America to "secure" certain "inalienable rights," which have been "endowed [to man] by their Creator," and which include the gifts of "Life, Liberty, and the Pursuit of Happiness," and promote as their ultimate goal, "the blessings of liberty."

Raising the Flag on Iwo Jima, Joe Rosenthal, 1945

Furthermore, the United States has, for reasons not fully explicable to the secular mind, developed into perhaps the only nation in world history blessed with the resources necessary to fulfill this divine purpose. What other nation has possessed the ability to not only provide and enforce such liberty at home, but also—through example, diplomacy, economic incentive, and even war (when necessary)—provide and enforce this same liberty abroad? It is certainly interesting that the Founding Fathers prophetically declared this "freedom promoting" intention for America, and then America proceeded to fulfill that prophecy in ways no other nation could. And the fact that America, one of the youngest nations on the planet, has grown, in such a short period, into the greatest superpower the world has ever known, only adds to the miracle of it all. Indeed, God has been behind this movement.

If the fruit of the national covenant is full religious freedom—that mankind might access eternal salvation—then, again, America fits the bill like no other. For the type of liberty that America has graciously and miraculously received is precisely that type of liberty required for God's work to progress. To be sure, America provided the fertile ground of religious freedom (in contrast to the hard, stubborn ground of the Old World). This has allowed Christianity (as well as a multitude of other religions, sects, creeds, etc.) to flourish like never before. A recent report produced by the Pew Research Center concluded that the United States of America has more Christians than any other nation in the world. In fact, the second largest Christian nation (Brazil) trails the United States by more than seventy million.

Studies further conclude that Americans—in addition to representing the largest Christian nation—actually *live* their religion. Almost 80 percent of the American population claims to be Christian. But their actions speak even louder than their words. Charitable donations in the United States (not including the colossal amount of service hours offered by

Americans) is twice as much as the next most charitable nation (the United Kingdom).[12] Eighty-three percent of Americans belong to a religion, 59 percent pray regularly, 80 percent are absolutely sure there is a God, and 60 percent are absolutely sure there is a heaven.[13] America is not perfect and must fight harder to increase its righteousness. But, it has been, and continues to be, the preeminent safe-haven for Christian principles.

Other nations of the world also promote much good and provide fertile ground for Christianity to expand. However, let us never lose sight of the truth that America was *first* to receive and promote this liberty. The greatest export of America has been the constitutional principles that have paved the way for God and gospel to make entry in other lands. This exportation of freedom, and the sacrifices made by Americans to make it happen, is yet one more testimony of the goodness that exists in the land. It is also a testimony of the inspiration Americans have felt and followed from above. God has been the driving force behind America and the liberty America has brought in furtherance of His plan for His children.

Good Christians everywhere should ask themselves where Christianity would be today without America and her covenant blessings bestowed by the grace of God. As Christ Himself taught, "by their fruits ye shall know them" (Matthew 7:20). These are America's fruits. It is a covenant land.

Like ancient Israel, America's God-given abundance of *liberty, protection,* and *prosperity* has certainly been put to effective use for the divine purposes of Heaven. America may ask, *Why me?* The reply: *Because God created and prepared you specifically for this mission at this time; this is your burden and your blessing. Now, you must keep the covenant!*

Notwithstanding the obvious notion that America has been a blessed nation that has promoted the freedoms for faith and salvation to expand, is it really a *covenant land*? Is it really worthy of such a distinction—even the same distinction given to the chosen Israelites of old? Many religious scholars would balk at the suggestion. They have, after all, claimed for years that America is nowhere to be found in the biblical account. America, therefore, cannot reach to those heights reserved for biblical peoples.

But what if America *is* mentioned in the Scripture? What if its mission in these modern times is so important to God, that He revealed it to His ancient prophets? What if we have just been failing to see such biblical prophecies and how these prophecies have been so clearly fulfilled in American history? While rebuking the Old World for its inability to follow Him in righteousness, what if Christ had *America* in mind when he declared the following prophetic warning?

"The Kingdom of God shall be taken
*from you, and given to a **nation***
bringing forth the fruits thereof."

(Matthew 21:43)

Was Christ speaking of America? Perhaps the Bible itself has the answer....

ENDNOTES

1 Kent P. Jackson, "Foretelling the Coming of Jesus," Richard Neitzel Holzapfel and Thomas Wayment, ed, *The Life and Teachings of Jesus Christ, Volume I* (Salt Lake City: Deseret Book, 2005) 8.

2 Bruce Feiler, *America's Prophet, Moses and the American Story* (New York: HarperCollins Publishers, 2009) 92-93.

3 Ancient Israel's government promoted policies such as "Proclaim liberty throughout out the land" (see Leviticus 25:20). Small, manageable units of government were also established, allowing participation amongst the citizenry (see Exodus 18: 13-26). Furthermore, leaders were elected and laws were approved by consent of the people (see Samuel 2:4; 1 Chr. 29:22; 2 Chr. 10-16; Exodus 19:8). For more, see W. Cleon Skousen, *The Five Thousand Year Leap* (Washington D.C.: The National Center for Constitutional Studies, 1981), 15-17.

4 Justine Martyr, as quoted in Alexander Roberts, and James Robertson, eds., *The Ante-Nicene Fathers*. 10 Volumes. (Grand Rapids: Wm. B. Eerdmans Publishing Company, 1885, reprinted in 1980-1985), 1: 212.

5 A. Cleveland Coxe, as quoted in Alexander Roberts and James Robertson, eds, *The Ante-Nicene Fathers*, 1:309.

6 Bobrick Benson, *Wide as the Waters: The Story of the English Bible and the Revolution it Inspired* (New York: Simon and Schuster, 2001), 67; John Foxe, *Foxe's Book of Martyrs*, ed. W. Grinton Berry (Grand Rapids, Mich,: Baker Book House, 2000), 86-87.

7 Paul Kengor, *God and Ronald Reagan* (New York: Regan Books, 2004), 147.

8 Harry Emerson Fosdick, ed. *Great Voices of the Reformation: An Anthology* (New York: Random House, 1952), 41, 242.

9 Philip P. Weiner, ed., *Dictionary of the History of Ideas* (New York: Scribner's, 1973), 4:112-113.

10 Bennett, *Spirit of America*, 366.

11 David O McKay, "Freedom of Choice," *Relief Society Magazine* 31 (July 1944): 355-59.

12 See "Global Christianity: A Report on the Size and Distribution of the World's Christian Population," The Pew Research Center, December 2011. Available at www.pewforum.org/Christian/Global-Christianity-americas.aspx. See also Chris Stewart and Ted Stewart, *Seven Miracles That Saved America*, 290.

13 Robert Putnam and David Campbell, *American Grace* (New York: Simon and Schuster, 2010), 7.

CHAPTER 2

THE COVENANT-MAKERS

*Joseph is a fruitful bough, even a fruitful bough by
a well; whose branches run over the wall....*

—Genesis 49:22

Who are "God's people"—Adam's family, Noah's family, Abraham's family, Israel's family, Judah's family, Joseph's family? We are all children of God (our Heavenly Father), of course. But, there have definitively been specific groups of people throughout the history of the world who lay claim to such a title in behalf of a group (i.e. a nation). What qualifies a nation-family as "God's"? It is true that each and every person on this earth can have a personal, individual, and intimate relationship with God and is subject to eternal salvation. However, the Old Testament teaches us that God worked through His relationship with the aggregate, as well as with the individual, to accomplish His purposes. If that was His pattern in the ancient world, doesn't it make sense that it would be His pattern today? There are at least three elements among the families listed above that may serve as qualifying characteristics of "God's people": 1) genealogical linkage one to another, 2) scriptural confirmation, and 3) a covenant relationship between the family-nation and God, in which the blessings of *liberty, protection,* and *prosperity* are delivered to the family-nation for God's eternal purposes. Besides the nation-state of Israel, is there another nation today that possesses these three elements? Could America fit this description?

The story of America and its profound relationship with the Almighty begins in Genesis 49 when Abraham's grandson, Jacob (or Israel) is giving patriarchal blessings to his twelve sons. It is here we first read of the prophetic blessings given to Joseph and his family. (This is the same Joseph that was sold into slavery by his brothers.) It is here where we first learn about the American Covenant.

Judah, Joseph, and the House of Israel

Before discussing how America might actually be a foreordained land according to the ancient Scripture, we must first understand certain concepts about God's ancient peoples. Too many biblical students today overlook the significance of the Old Testament and its treatment of the House of Israel simply because they assume this record pertains only to the Jewish people and not to them. Such students opt, instead, to focus only on the New Testament. However, the Old Testament prophets knew much more about our day than many give them credit for. They knew that the House of Israel was actually much larger than the Jews alone.

Much of the Christian confusion today about who Israel actually is stems from a single and highly significant event that occurred in 1948. The Jews, having reclaimed their homeland after World War II, established a nation-state. They called it Israel. This moment represented a climax of sorts in the long and fascinating history of the Jewish people. The telling of their history often begins with Moses leading the twelve tribes of Israel (the Hebrew nation) out of Egypt. They eventually inherited the promised land (known as Canaan, Palestine, or Israel). The tribes lived in this promised land as a united group that kept their tribal identities—the two most prominent tribes being Judah and Joseph. Joseph's preeminent heir, Ephraim, was a predominate namesake for Joseph's people. The tribes were collectively known as Israel.

After over four hundred years, the northern tribes of Israel, led by Joseph and Ephraim, began to be troubled by what they perceived as oppressive politics being forced upon them by the southern tribes, led by Judah. The northern tribes, known alternatively as "Joseph," "Ephraim," or "Israel," created their own kingdom. They became the Northern Kingdom and they consisted of the ten tribes of Israel, led by Joseph/Ephraim. The Southern Kingdom, known as "Judah," retained their own land and government (see 1 Kings 12). (Though Judah was the leader, and thus the namesake of the Southern Kingdom, the tribe of Benjamin, along with remnants of Levi and perhaps other tribes, mingled with them. According to 2 Chronicles 11: 13-16, after the northern ten tribes declared independence, certain members from these northern tribes feared they would not be able to appropriately worship God unless they lived in the Southern Kingdom, wherein stood the temple. These few then migrated and joined with the Southern Kingdom. But the main bodies of the ten tribes stayed in the Northern Kingdom.) The Northern Kingdom and the Southern Kingdom *never fully* reunited.

Beginning in 587 B.C., Judah/the Southern Kingdom was sufficiently wicked so as to lose the covenant blessings. This resulted in the tragic takedown of the Southern Kingdom by the foreign nation-state of Babylon, led by King Nebuchadnezzar. Indeed, Nebuchadnezzar attacked Jerusalem, destroyed the temple, and carried Judah away into Babylonian captivity. After seventy years, Cyrus of Persia, who had wrested control of Judah from the Babylonians, allowed Judah to return to Jerusalem and rebuild the temple.

From that point, Judah occupied Jerusalem and the promised land for hundreds of years, even up until and during the time when Judah's greatest heir, even the prophesied Messiah (Jesus Christ), entered mortality. His own people rejected Him. With the covenant now in breach like never before, God could not protect Judah from the Romans, who sacked Jerusalem in 70 A.D., thus causing Judah to be scattered throughout the world. Judah, however, never lost its identity. They became known as the Jews. They kept their traditions, their religion, and their affinity for the promised land they had lost. Then, as mentioned above, by the grace of God Almighty, who loved His chosen ones, after World War II, they came home. They then established a nation-state in 1948. And they called it Israel, after the father of the twelve tribes, whose name was Jacob, or Israel. Some Christians believe in "Replacement Theology"—that the Jews lost their covenant and blessings. They believe the Jews were replaced. Not so. The promises remain, which explains why the nation-state of Israel was able to be established and maintained, even until the present-day, against all odds.

But does this tell the whole story of Israel? The Jews of 1948 were well within reason to call their homeland Israel, though this decision has caused much confusion for some Christians today. For the Jews, or Judah, represented only a portion of Israel. Their story, therefore, is *not* the whole story. Perhaps if they had called their land Judah (a more precise description), then more Christians today would be asking about the other tribes. What of Joseph? Ephraim? The others?

While we often recount the story of Judah being torn from their land, returning to their land, being scattered again, then returning again, we seldom remember that there was also a Northern Kingdom led by Joseph/Ephraim. Too often we discount their story. We fail to recognize that they, too, were Israel. Almost 150 years before Judah and the Southern Kingdom were carried into Babylon, Joseph/Ephraim and the Northern Kingdom were carried away northward by the

Assyrians. This occurred around 721 B.C. (see 2 Kings 17). Through wickedness, they too had lost the covenant blessings in the land. They too were scattered among the nations. When this happened, so the Scripture states, "There was none left but the tribe of Judah only" (2 Kings 17:18). Indeed, they were two distinct factions of Israel, each with a separate story.

But, like their kinfolk Judah, God would not forget Joseph/Ephraim. He would bring them to the promised land to fulfill His purposes. They were, after all, children of the covenant. But they would not return to the promised land we traditionally think of. They would not return to the promised land that Judah would return to. When the Jews returned from Babylon to Palestine, it was Judah (along with Benjamin, parts of Levi, and perhaps remnants of the other tribes who had remained with the Southern Kingdom), that returned (see Ezra 2:1; Ezra 1:5). Some biblical students just assume that somehow the main and whole body of Joseph/Ephraim returned with Judah at this time. But remember, Joseph/Ephraim had been carried away by the Assyrians some 150 years before Judah ever even left for Babylon. Throughout the books of Ezra and Nehemiah, genealogies are given for those who returned to Palestine at this time. The ten tribes of the Northern Kingdom were not in Babylon and are, therefore, not listed among those that returned.[1] By the time of Judah's return, the Northern Kingdom (led by Joseph/Ephraim) had left the land never to return. They were the "Lost tribes of Israel." The Bible and history confirm nothing about their return to Jerusalem. In fact, as we shall see below, the Bible and history perhaps testify that Joseph/Ephraim and the ten lost tribes were led in a very different direction—a direction that deeply affects Americans even today.

The renowned Christian pastor/author, Herbert Armstrong, has perhaps studied this issue as much as any other Christian writer. His conclusion:

> [Many] assume, in error, that *all* Israelites were Jews and that...Jews in the world today constitute the

entire population of Israelites remaining alive at this time. Some theologians falsely claim that all of the ten tribes who went into Assyrian captivity in 721-718 B.C. returned to Jerusalem with the Jews who returned to build the Temple there seventy years after Judah's captivity…But that is in total error. Only part of Judah went back. And those who returned were *all* of the three tribes of Judah, Benjamin, and Levi. Check the genealogies in Ezra and Nehemiah.[2]

In her book, *Ye Have Been Hid: Finding the Lost Tribes of Israel*, author Leslie Rees confirms the same:

Many Old Testament commentaries deal with [the Scripture] by recounting the history of the Jewish people and showing the fulfillment of prophecy. They do so correctly, but leave out the larger portion of the House of Israel, the northern tribes who were conquered and scattered and carried in large bodies into captivity.[3]

The biblical/historical proofs (which we will detail in the pages to come), certainly corroborate the conclusions of these authors/historians. Indeed, as Pastor Armstrong noted, Joseph/Ephraim "never returned to Jerusalem from Assyria, where they were driven with the ten tribes after 721 B.C., and were never again mixed with the Jews from that time!"[4] Instead, they would become completely independent and inherit a new promised land. They would inherit America.

As we now enter a discussion concerning America's literal connection to ancient Israel, certain things must be understood. First and foremost, what follows in this chapter is *theory*. There simply is not enough available data to definitively prove (or disprove) this literal connection.

The main evidence in this book (as put forth in Part II) *does* prove America's covenant relationship with the Almighty. The proof is in the details of America's sacred and real history. This history and its message concerning God and country stand independent of the theory put forth in this chapter. Indeed, America's deep spiritual roots are in *no way* reliant upon the veracity of this theory.

That said, we will still open the discussion here on this theory, as it does have relevancy. For, notwithstanding its problems, it does present evidence that should make the honest reader at least ponder the deeper meanings of America —especially as this theory is coupled with the historical facts of America (to be detailed in Part II of this book).

It should also be noted that the following theory is based in long-standing research dating back hundreds of years. As such, many offshoots of this theory have been born. Some of these offshoots make despicable and racist claims against certain populations. The theory, as put forth here, wholly rejects such bigotry.

Finally, it should be recognized that the theory here presented has been developed, maintained, and taught (in one form or another) by very accomplished scholars, as well as by honest, God-fearing theologians from various Christian denominations and religious sects, as will be seen by the many citations and references documented in the pages below.[5]

From Abraham to America

Having introduced the idea that the House of Israel is much larger than just Judah and the promised land in the Middle East, we are at last prepared to delve into the biblical references that support this—references that also suggest an Israelite connection to the promised land of America. To do this, we must begin the story at the sacred and historic point when the House of Israel was first created by the Almighty—to a time long before Moses led the twelve tribes toward the promised land. We must begin with the great father of the House. We must begin with Abraham.

39

God Almighty made powerful and wonderful promises to Abraham. He made a covenant with Abraham. As this covenant (which the title of this book is named for) began with this great prophet and leader, many appropriately call it the Abrahamic Covenant. God promised Abraham that his descendants would become "a great *nation*" (Genesis 12:2). God told Abraham that, if he would be righteous, "I will make my covenant between me and thee, and will multiply thee exceedingly" (Genesis 17:1-2). The Almighty further promised that Abraham "shalt be a father of *many nations*" (Genesis 17:4). "I will make thee exceedingly fruitful, and I will make *nations* of thee" (Genesis 17:6) declared God to Father Abraham.

Purely spiritual blessings that reach out and touch the individual, one by one, were also bestowed upon Abraham and his posterity. However, too often we forget about the *national* blessings, those dealing with the land and with prosperity. As noted in the previous chapter, national blessings and national covenants must, by necessity, accompany the more individual/spiritual blessings in order to preserve and protect those spiritual blessings. The portions of God's promises to Abraham that deal with lands and nations are indeed profound and should never be sidelined.

The covenant, of course, would not die with Abraham. Said God to Abraham: "And I will establish my covenant between me and thee and thy seed after thee in their generations for an everlasting covenant, to be a God unto thee, and to thy seed after thee" (Genesis 17:7). Abraham's son, Isaac, carried this covenant and naturally passed it on to his son Jacob. Said Isaac to Jacob, "And God Almighty bless thee... And give thee the blessing of Abraham, to thee, and to thy seed with thee....And thy seed shall be as the dust of the earth, and thou shalt spread abroad to the west, and to the east, and to the north, and to the south: and in thee and in thy seed shall all the families of the earth be blessed" (Genesis 28: 4, 14). Jacob, the covenant carrier, would later be divinely bestowed with the name *Israel* (see Genesis 35:10). The covenant would continue to go forth under that powerful name.

Jacob-Israel's children would subsequently be taught that the covenant blessings would consist of *liberty*, *protection* and *prosperity*, and that the covenant obligations would consist of righteousness and obedience to the God of the land, as defined (among other places) in Leviticus 26. If they would but obey and be humble before God, "Then will I remember my covenant with Jacob, and also my covenant with Isaac, and also my covenant with Abraham will I remember; *and I will remember the land*" (Leviticus 26:42).

Do the covenant prophecies indicate only one land, only one nation? Absolutely not! There were to be multitudes of people under the covenant, and there were to be *nations* under the covenant. Yet Judah was only given but one land and nation. Indeed, the blessings are far more extensive than many have realized. They reach out and touch many other nations in addition to Judah.

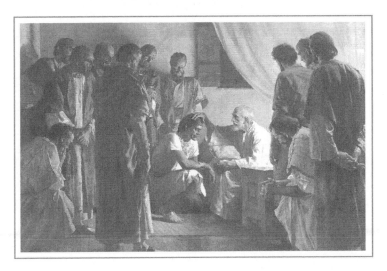

Jacob Blessing His Sons, by Harry Anderson

41

But where else would Israel go? Where else would they establish a covenant nation? Before Jacob-Israel died, he gathered his twelve sons—twelve carriers of the covenant— around him. There, he gave answers to these questions. To Judah, he promised that the Messiah would come through his tribe—a prophecy fulfilled in the New Testament. And to Joseph he promised a land where the covenant would be restored. He promised a nation that God would raise up for His purposes in the last days. He promised America.

Listen to the words of Jacob-Israel to Joseph:

> Joseph is a fruitful bough, even a fruitful bough by a well; whose branches run over the wall. The archers have sorely grieved him, and shot at him and hated him: But his bow abode in strength, and the arms of his hands were made strong by the hands of the mighty God of Jacob...[T]he Almighty...shall bless thee with blessings from heaven above, blessings of the deep that lieth under, blessings of the breasts and of the womb: The blessings of thy father have prevailed above the blessings of my progenitors unto the utmost bound of the everlasting hills: they shall be on the head of Joseph, and on the head of him who was separate from his brethren (Gen. 49: 1, 22-26).

So important are these blessings that they are repeated in almost identical language in a similar blessing given by the Prophet Moses to the same family of Joseph. "And of Joseph he said, blessed of the Lord be *his land*..." (See Deuteronomy 33:13-17).

So what does this blessing imply? To begin with, it clearly prophesies of several blessings that are to accompany Joseph's posterity. First, it speaks of Joseph's ability to thwart his enemies, even "the archers" that "shot at him and hated him," and suggests that Joseph would defeat them with his "bow [abiding] in strength." This promise implies that Joseph will possess effective machines of war and defense.

Furthermore, it is made clear that this defense is made possible through the strength provided "by the hands of the mighty God of Jacob." And so we see that Joseph's posterity would defeat its enemies through the *protection* of the Lord.

The second blessing mentioned are those things connected to being "fruitful," even blessings of the "breasts" and "the womb" (a strong posterity) and "blessings of the deep that lieth under." Moses' version of this particular blessing includes the promise of "precious fruits brought forth of the sun," and for "the chief things of the ancient mountains," implying the richness of resources to be made available (Deuteronomy 33:14-16). It appears Joseph's posterity would be offered a blessed land. So great and abundant would be the blessings of "his land" (Deut. 33:13) that Jacob describes them as having "prevailed above the blessings" of his own powerful ancestry. It is clear in Genesis 49 then, that Joseph's posterity would be large, enduring, and would not want materially in their promised land. They would enjoy an abundance of capital and labor, which are the two primary inputs for a nation's gross domestic product (GDP). They would for certain enjoy *prosperity*.

With an abundance of divine *protection* and *prosperity*, Joseph's people would naturally enjoy the fruit of such blessings—a fullness of *liberty*.

Jacob's blessing also indicates that Joseph's "branches" (posterity) would "run over the wall." Exodus 14:22 uses the word "wall" to mean great waters (it is a reference to the Red Sea). As such, it can be inferred that the above-referenced promises to Joseph's posterity were connected to a land across the seas from the Old World. Or (even if the reference to Exodus 14:22 is not a hint), at the very least "the wall" over which Joseph's posterity would run, certainly implies that some great obstruction stands between the land of Joseph's old world and the promised land of his new world. Either way, great waters certainly fit the description. Jacob's concluding words to his son substantiate this by indicating that

Joseph's people would be "separate from [their] brethren." We are also told that this land would extend to "the utmost bound" (to a distant place?).

In addition to being located far away, (perhaps across the sea), the blessing suggests that the land would also contain "everlasting hills." The longest mountain range in the world—the Andes—stretches 4,300 miles and resides in the Americas. The second longest mountain range in the world—the Rockies—stretches more than 3,000 miles through North America, boasting widths of up to 300 miles and ages of up to 3.3 billion years. Looking down, through satellite imagery, upon the geography of these ranges, which almost appear to the eye to be extensions of one another, "everlasting hills" certainly comes to mind. In fact, there is no other place on earth that more accurately fits the description of "everlasting hills." Did Jacob-Israel see a geographically-based vision of the New World as he blessed his son Joseph?

Finally, it should be noted that when Jacob brought Joseph and his other sons to pronounce these blessings, he clearly stated that these blessings would "tell you that which shall befall you in the *last days*" (Gen. 49:1).

This, of course, leads us to the following questions: Is there a nation in the world that has, in these "last days," received divine protection and remarkable prosperity? Does that nation enjoy liberty, even freedoms sufficient to fully exercise personal agency in choosing Christ and His Gospel as a means of eternal salvation and happiness? Is there a nation in the world whose founders and nation-builders understood their land to be a covenant land? Did they associate this land with Israel, even calling themselves "Israel"? Did they invoke, before God and man, the same national covenant the ancient Israelites did? If there is such a land today, is it separated from the Old World by a great distance and by great waters? Does it contain anything that might be described as "everlasting hills"? Does any nation-state fit every one of these requirements? Perhaps only the United States of America.

To be sure, the Tribe of Joseph perhaps was foreordained thousands of years ago to eventually house God's national covenant in America. This is especially significant in light of the fact that the national covenant originally given to the ancient Hebrew nation would severely stumble, thus leaving a void that would need to be filled by some nation, somewhere, at some point in time. Indeed, the damaged covenant would need to be restored so that Christianity might find a safe-haven where it could flourish. Perhaps it is no coincidence that in the Samarian tongue (Samaria being a onetime capitol of ancient Israel), the name/title "Joseph" is Taheb, or "The Restorer."[6]

Though it is plainly asserted that through Abraham, the Lord would "make and bless many nations," many biblical scholars would admittedly scoff at the idea that Abraham's covenant—extended through the posterity of his great-grandson Joseph—included America as one of these nations. However, as discussed above, Genesis 49 seems to point to America as this God-inspired nation. Joseph's seed would cross great waters to a land of "everlasting hills" and inherit blessings of *liberty, protection,* and *prosperity* that were greater than—or "above the blessings"—that were given to Jacob's progenitors (Genesis 49:26). If not America, where could that be? What other nation superseded the recorded blessings given to the ancient Hebrews? As Joseph was clearly to be the predominant bearer of this covenant, his posterity naturally would be the predominant American Covenant-makers.

But besides these sometimes vague clues above, how else might we link Joseph's seed to America? For if we can make that connection, it would be further evidence that God has established America as a covenant nation. Indeed, if this connection is true, it would serve as a wake-up call to Americans to restore the covenant and live it in the land!

American history does much to corroborate this scriptural suggestion, as we will see in Part II of this book. However, before entering that remarkable history, more scriptural evidence is required for this rather bold claim.

Beginning Down the Biblical Trail

If the Bible promises that Joseph is to receive such profound blessings from the Almighty—even a land across the sea ringing with *liberty, protection* and *prosperity*—where can we read about the fulfillment of this promise? The Bible does not tell the details of how this story ends. It does not fulfill the prophecies given to Joseph. However, clues do exist. We will first turn to the Old Testament prophet Ezekiel. For Ezekiel makes reference to a separate book which would certainly contain the answers we're looking for.

> Moreover, thou son of man, take thee one stick, and write upon it, For Judah, and for the children of Israel his companions: then take another stick, and write upon it, For Joseph, the stick of Ephraim, and for all the house of Israel his companions: And join them one to another into one stick; and they shall become one in thy hand (Ezekiel. 37:16-17).

It seems clear from this passage that the posterity of Joseph will have a separate record or "stick" (scroll or tablet upon which the ancients wrote)* from that of Judah, or the Jews. Judah/the Jews offered us "the stick" we call the Bible. There is no consensus among modern Christian scholars as to whether a stick of Joseph exists, but it can be assumed that if Joseph's record existed it would certainly include a fulfillment of these great promises. Whether there is another book or not, the indication is that there exists another story. It is a story of Abraham's posterity, through the line of his great-grandson Joseph, leaving the Old World, crossing "over the wall," discovering a new land with "everlasting hills," and enjoying the blessings of *liberty, protection,* and *prosperity*—all for the

---

*Many biblical scholars believe that the word "stick" in this passage refers to the ancient wax-filled tablets utilized in the Near East during the days of Ezekiel to keep records. After the discovery of these tablets in 1953, the New English Bible changed the word "stick" in this passage to "wooden tablet." See Matt Brown, *All Things Restored* (American Fork: Covenant Communications, 2000), 187-188.

purposes of God. (Some commentators believe that Ezekiel's reference to Judah and Joseph becoming "one in thy hand" is a reference to an ancient reunion of the estranged tribes. This theory puts forth the idea that this prophetic reunion would be manifested at a much later time period.)

The clue we need to derive from Ezekiel is the reference to Ephraim.

Joseph had two sons inducted into the House of Israel: Ephraim and Manasseh. So important was their induction, that Jacob also laid his hands upon them and transferred the blessings to them and their posterity, declaring that their seed shall become a great people and "a multitude of nations" (see Genesis 48:9-20). As they were both direct descendants of Joseph, it follows that they both were to carry the same general responsibilities regarding the American Covenant. Ephraim, it should be noted, was the principal heir of this covenant (see Genesis 4:19), and so we shall follow him closely.

Do the scriptures indicate that Ephraim might be the people God sent to carry the national covenant into America for the purposes of the Almighty?

Ezekiel's reference to Joseph/Ephraim is only one of many reasons we should take a good look at this family line. We should also recall the preferential treatment Joseph was always given in the Old Testament account. "Now, Israel loved Joseph more than all his children" (Genesis 37:3). So much of the early history of the House Israel revolves around Joseph. As recently noted, per the prophecies in Genesis 49, the greatest national blessings Jacob-Israel bestowed upon the tribes went to Joseph and his posterity. "But the birthright was Joseph's," so we are told (I Chronicles 5:2).

As Jacob-Israel placed his hands upon Joseph's two sons, Ephraim being the prominent heir, he proclaimed, "bless the lads; and let *my name* be named upon them" (Genesis 48:16). Indeed, at that point they were given, by priesthood and patriarchal authority, and in the name of God, the name/

title for Jacob, which is *Israel*. (Again, we should not place the title of "Israel" *only* upon Judah, though Judah is admittedly referred to alternatively as "Israel." The ancients understood the significance of this title-transfer to Joseph/Ephraim so much so that they began, at times, to distinguish Joseph/ Ephraim as "Israel," while leaving the Southern Kingdom with their original title of "Judah." For example, in Jeremiah 31:31 the Lord declared, "I will make a new covenant with the house of Israel, and with the house of Judah.") After he distinguished Joseph's heirs as "Israel," Jacob-Israel declared, "let them grow into a multitude in the midst of the earth" (Genesis 48:16).

Based on all of the above, how can we ignore Joseph/ Ephraim? How can we possibly think that somehow their story was simply consumed in Judah? And so, let us follow Joseph/ Ephraim to their prophetic end.

Jacob Blessing the Sons of Joseph, Rembrandt, 1656.
Displayed in Staatliche Museen Kassel, Germany

★ ★ ★ ★

As already discussed, the last time we really hear from the Tribe of Ephraim in the Scripture is when it leads a rebellion against Judah and separates itself. Ephraim and his companions thereafter become known as the Northern Kingdom, or "Israel" (remember, it was Jacob-Israel who bestowed that sacred name on Ephraim). The Southern Kingdom, as noted above, becomes known as Judah. Ephraim and his ally tribes live independently until their wickedness and disobedience allows the Assyrians to conquer them and carry them off to a land north of Nineveh.[7] But then what? Is that the end?

When Ezekiel spoke of Joseph/Ephraim having a story to be told, he was projecting to a time *after* Joseph/Ephraim's northward migration. How do we know this? Because Ezekiel lived and prophesied well *after* Joseph/Ephraim had been lost to the north. And so, the implication is that their story—as Jacob-Israel also implied—would be fulfilled in "the last days."

Other Old Testament prophets seemed to have testified of the same. The only other ancient references that are made about Joseph/Ephraim reveal something about the prophecies and promises of their ultimate destiny. For example, whereas the Lord could have completely destroyed them for their wickedness, He instead chose to hide them away and preserve them for a later mission in a later day. As the prophet declared, though "Ephraim is smitten," the Lord would only "cast them away" to be "wanderers among the nations" (Hosea 9:17). Furthermore, and in spite of their wandering state, they were to strongly present themselves again. Said the Lord: "I will save the house of Joseph, and I will bring them again to place them...and they shall be as though I had not cast them off... And they of Ephraim shall be like a mighty man, and their heart shall rejoice...And I will sow them among the people: and they shall remember me in far countries" (Zechariah 10:6-9). "Is Ephraim my dear son?" declared the Lord, "I will surely have mercy upon him" (Jeremiah 31:20). In light of these and related prophecies, one might surmise that Ephraim was carried to "far countries" in order to support and build up such lands unto God. After all, it was given anciently to Ephraim, through his lineage from Abraham and Joseph, to "make" and "bless" nations (Genesis 17:6; 22:18). There certainly was a reason God had promised to "sift the house of Israel among all nations" (Amos 9:9). There is a reason His prophet Isaiah prophesied (as he did on multiple occasions) that "Israel shall blossom and bud, and fill the face of the world with fruit" (Isaiah 27:6).

So, after migrating to the north, where did Joseph/ Ephraim go to build the covenant nations? "For, lo, I will command, and I will sift the house of Israel among all nations, like as corn is sifted in a sieve, yet shall not the least grain fall upon the earth" (Amos 9:8-9). That they were heading north is clear not only from the fact that Assyria is in that direction, but also from the words of the prophets. When the Lord called on Israel to return from its lost state, it was clear where the messengers would find them: "Go and proclaim these words toward the North and say, return, thou backsliding Israel" (Jeremiah 3: 11-12). Some may argue that the Lord is speaking here to Israel in the Northern Kingdom within Palestine (they were always north of Judah, after all). However, Jeremiah, who recorded these words, lived well after Joseph/ Ephraim had abandoned Palestine all together. They had already migrated north of the ancient promised land. In later chapters, Jeremiah again refers to the land of the lost tribes as the "land of the north" (Jeremiah 3:18; 16:15).

But it was not just a northern migration. According to Hosea 12:1, "Ephraim...followeth after the east wind." As an east wind travels west, we might consider that Ephraim, in addition to being carried to the north, predominately traveled also to the west. Some scholars believe that Isaiah also provided clues as to Joseph/Ephraim's coordinates when he declared that they would be called "from the north and from the west" (Isaiah 49:12). According to some scholars, ancient Hebrew has no distinct word for the coordinate "northwest." Accordingly, the thought is that Isaiah was doing his best, in these verses, to convey that lost Israel had migrated to a northwestern location—that Isaiah's use of "the north and the west," was simply his designation for what we would call "northwest." Hosea perhaps indicated the same when speaking specifically about Ephraim. Said Hosea: "The children [referring to Ephraim] shall tremble from the west" (see Hosea 11:8,10).

If Joseph/Ephraim and the lost tribes had followed this general northwesterly direction, they would have landed squarely in Western Europe. Theoretically, Joseph/Ephraim might have ended up in the nation-state known today as Great Britain. From there, the Lord might have called them "over the wall" to America. After all, Jacob-Israel, when describing the blessed land of "everlasting hills" (America) to be inherited by Joseph/Ephraim, prophesied that Joseph was a "fruitful bough by a *well*." This perhaps indicates that Joseph/Ephraim would migrate to the coast in preparation for the discovery, settlement, and establishment of America and her covenant.

More on Joseph's prophetic destiny was revealed in the Scripture. "Moreover I will appoint a place for my people Israel, and will *plant* them, that they may dwell in a place of their own, and move no more" (see 2 Samuel 7:10 and Chronicles 17:9). It seems that perhaps this refers to a different land than Palestine, one that would be "their own," and one (unlike Palestine) where they would be "planted" and "move no more." Could this be America?

Jeremiah, who, as recently noted, indicated a northern migration of Israel, added more to the geographic location: "Behold, I will bring them from the north country, and gather them *from the coasts* of the earth" (Jeremiah 31:8). Again, it appears Ephraim would be brought to the water's edge of the north country in order to cross "over the wall," to be a colonizing people God would "plant" abroad. Isaiah (in Isaiah 49), also speaking *after* Israel had already been scattered, calls Israel to "gather" in order "to restore the preserved of Israel" (verses 5-6). He refers to them alternatively as "Israel" *and* as the "isles." "Listen, O isles, unto me," he declares (see 1-3). Later, Isaiah again addresses Israel, stating, "Keep silence before me, O islands; and let the people renew their strength" (Isaiah 41:1). Is it possible that Isaiah is calling Israel to America—to a place where they can be "gathered" and "restored"—and that he is calling them *from* the British isles, where they await in "silence," and where they "renew their strength"?

If the clues above indicate that Joseph/Ephraim would travel from Palestine in a *northwest* direction until they landed on a *coastline*, their destination becomes very clear. If one were to take a straight-edged ruler and place it over a world map, with a starting point of Palestine/Israel, and direct it *precisely* in a northwest direction, the ruler would end squarely in the British isles.

Another clue of Joseph/Ephraim's geographic destiny comes from the ancient apocryphal prophet/writer Esdras. Esdras describes Joseph/Ephraim's northern migration, which leaves us wondering how, by geographic necessity, they did not at some point swing near or through what is modern-day Europe.[8] Having studied the words of Esdras, a Christian scholar (and Mormon Elder), George Reynolds, explains how these ancient writings indicate that a large portion of the Lost Tribes of Israel, particularly the Tribe of Ephraim, might have settled in what is now Europe. Summarizing Esdras' description, Reynolds opines:

> Is it altogether improbable that in that long journey of one and a half years, as Esdras states it, that from Media the land of their captivity to the frozen north, some of the backsliding Israel rebelled, turned aside from the main body, forgot their God, [and] by and by mingled with the Gentiles? And who so likely to rebel as stubborn, impetuous, proud and warlike Ephraim? Rebellion and backsliding have been so characteristically the story of Ephraim's career that we can scarcely

conceive that it could be otherwise...Can it be any wonder then that so much of the blood of Ephraim has been found hidden and unknown in the midst of the nations of northern Europe?[9]

The implications, from all the evidence above, are quite stunning. Could this be true? Is it possible that the Europeans who established North America, and that represent a vast majority of the early U.S. population, actually descended from the Tribe of Ephraim? Could the blood and covenants of Israel be deeply attached to our explorers, to our settlers, to our revolutionaries, founders, and patriots?

Prophecies of Jeremiah Reconsidered

The Old Testament prophets cited above, who revealed the geographic location and spiritual destiny of Ephraim—to include Ezekiel, Hosea, Zechariah, Isaiah, and Esdras—all lived during or after the northern migration of Joseph/Ephraim and the lost tribes. This is important, as it reveals to us that their prophecies related to Joseph/Ephraim have to do with some future time—a time the Bible account does not fully cover. Indeed, they leave us with great prospects for Joseph/Ephraim, but then the Bible account of this family ends. And so, it is incumbent upon us, in these modern days, to seek these biblical fulfillments in our known histories.

The suggestion thus far is that Joseph/Ephraim landed in Western Europe, occupied the British Isles, then migrated to the promised land of America. The prophet Jeremiah, who also lived and spoke *after* Joseph/Ephraim had abandoned Palestine, leaves us with one of the strongest witnesses of the truthfulness of this theory.

Indeed, in his famous Old Testament prophecies regarding the gathering of Israel, it seems Jeremiah foresaw the American Covenant and its participants. For Jeremiah speaks of the "Children of Israel" being brought by the Lord from the "land of the north and from all the lands whither he had driven them" into "their land that I gave their fathers" (Jeremiah 16:15). (Recall that their father Joseph was perhaps given the land America, per his blessing in Genesis 49.) He declares that they will be gathered from "the coasts of the earth" (Jeremiah 31:8). (Recall that Joseph's posterity was given a land "over the wall" of water and separate from the rest of the tribes of Israel. If they were to travel over this *wall*, of course they would begin at "the coasts of the earth.") He further details this migration, stating that "Ephraim shall cry, Arise ye, and let us go up to Zion." Jeremiah foresees them traveling from the "north country" (Europe?), being gathered from "the coasts" (the British Isles?), and delivered into this new land of its inheritance (America?), saying they will come "with weeping, and with supplication" (the historical record is clear on the difficulties faced by our American founders' early migration and settlement).*

But, as Jeremiah points out, the Lord would also bless them with the very blessings of the national covenant. God would indeed "lead them" and protect them "from the hand of him that was stronger than [them]." The Lord further promised to provide for them that they might "come and sing in the height of Zion" and receive "the goodness of the Lord," even "wheat", "wine", "oil", "the young of the flock and of the herd," and thus sayeth the Lord, "my people shall be satisfied with my goodness" (Jeremiah 31:6-14). It should be emphasized once again that at the time Jeremiah made these prophecies, Israel, to include Ephraim, was in Assyrian captivity and had been for well over one hundred years. This would suggest that these blessings would be restored to Ephraim at some future date.

---

* The obvious perils the early American settlers faced—from sea travel, to disease, to attacks from the Native Americans—is reflected in the fact that during the first decade or so of certain American colonies, the mortality rate approached 80 percent. See Matthew S. Holland, *Bonds of Affection* (Washington D.C.: Georgetown University Press, 2007), 29.

In summation, and in light of all the evidences put forth in this chapter, these references about Ephraim migrating during a time that points to a later setting, to a land that provided the very same blessings America has received in abundance, make it appear as though Jeremiah was tuned in to America and her covenant.

But Jeremiah was not finished commenting on this subject. In the Book of Jeremiah, Chapter 31, he defines the relationship between God and Ephraim as the "new covenant" (verse 31). He also points out that on an earlier occasion God made this covenant with Israel when He "took them by the hand to bring them out of Egypt," but that they had broken that covenant (verse 32). And finally, he states that the Lord would bring this covenant back and "put my law in their inward parts, and write it in their hearts; and [I] will be their God and they shall be my people" (verse 33).

In comparing this new covenant with what was clearly an ancient *national* covenant—even that covenant made with the children of Israel on their exodus from Egypt—implies that this new covenant is but another attempt at a *national* covenant. The fact that this new covenant must be "writ[ten] in their hearts" perhaps implies that these national covenant-makers would need to *feel* their responsibility under the covenant more than they would actually deduce the details in an academic sense. For, when the time came for Ephraim to enter America, they were already a "lost tribe." Their identity was lost—but their covenant was not. Their covenant was *written in their hearts* because of who they really were.

In addition, to say the Lord would place His "law in their inward parts, and write it in their hearts," implies that these covenant recipients would have a passionate and soulful conviction of God's law that would drive the infrastructure of their nation and their relationship with God. As we explore American historical evidence of the American Covenant, there will be no question as to the fulfillment—particularly the fulfillment of this portion—of Jeremiah's prophecy. He truly saw the American Covenant-makers. He knew they stemmed from Israel through Ephraim. And he knew theirs would be a divine mission, critical to the salvation of God's children.

★ ★ ★ ★

Having analyzed the scriptural references above, we openly acknowledge that we are not prophets with the authority to offer conclusive arguments as to what the Old Testament may or may not reveal about America. We acknowledge that, like everything else, there are other interpretations. However, where our interpretations especially gain traction is during our forthcoming analysis of American history. For American history proves to be the great corroborator.

As Pastor Armstrong noted, "It was Ephraim who was to become the company, or multitude, of nations...[But] these promises never were fulfilled in them, in times of Bible history. If these promises ever have been fulfilled, we must look for their fulfillment between the close of Bible history and the present!"[10] We would agree with Armstrong that the Israelites "migrated from ancient Assyria northwest toward Europe...the specific key that unlocks these closed doors of prophecy is the definite knowledge of the true identity of the American and British nations."[11]

In the final analysis, we will suggest that the Founding Fathers—to include Washington, Adams, Madison, Jefferson, Franklin and thousands of others from those early American generations—were modern-day American Covenant-makers, not only through their words and deeds, but also by virtue of the authority of their birthright through Joseph/Ephraim. When Jeremiah prophesied of Ephraim's return to Zion (as reviewed above), he noted that the inspired call would come to "go up to Zion unto the Lord our God." He also noted that the call would come from "the watchmen upon the mount of Ephraim" (Jeremiah 31:6). Might these inspired Founders be the watchmen? Perhaps we should pay closer attention to the messages they left us.

It is interesting to observe that many of the American founders share personal preferences and attributes with Joseph/ Ephraim—a love of justice, freedom, and independence (and a willingness to rebel against tyranny in order to preserve these gifts). As the ancient scriptural account in 1 Kings 12 details, it was Ephraim who led a violent and successful revolt on behalf of the Northern Kingdom against Judah and the Southern Kingdom. And what was the motivation behind this revolution? *Unfair and unauthorized taxes* levied by the Southern Kingdom.

Beginning Down the Historical Trail

The history that corroborates the Scripture is that of the American experience. But before entering that magnificent era, we should briefly mention what historical evidence exists of an Israelite migration to western Europe and Britain. For, if such a thing occurred, we should expect to at least find remnants of it. Admittedly, delving into this particular history is difficult, for these migrations purportedly began thousands of years ago and were characterized by cultural and genetic assimilations. Furthermore, while books have been written on this subject, the scope of *this* study—of America and scripture— does not include a comprehensive review of all that is known on the western European connection. Notwithstanding, we will introduce some important ideas.

Language is one of the most enduring characteristics of a people. So we will start there. In his book, *Hebrew and English: Some Likenesses Psychic and Linguistic,* the renowned linguist, Dr. J. Courtney James concluded that "the similarities between the English language, which has come in great part from the Celtic and Germanic languages, and Hebrew, are more than structural." For the similarities represent harmony in both "etymology and in the thought processes involved in verbalizing ideas."[12] Another prominent scholar and linguist Dr. Edward Odlum, conclusively agreed. In his book, *God's Covenant Man: British Israel*, Dr. Odlum stated the following:

> Much has been said and written in relation to the foundation of the English language....I wish to say that as a result of long years of careful work and comparison, I am safe in saying that the construction of the Hebrew, the old British and the English of the King James Translation of the Bible are more similar than any other known language is to either the present or old British construction. The order of words to express a simple statement, the very spirit and genius of the thoughts, nature and sentiment, the strength and directness, conciseness and lofty ideality, and the predominating religious feelings permeating the whole manifest aims and temper of the people, are common to the Hebrew, ancient British, Welsh and English languages, and mark them in a class apart from all other systems of human speech.[13]

Dr. James' and Dr. Odlum's supporting evidence for their claims are too exhaustive for this study. Though, as one of many parts of their evidence, both have published long and quite startling lists of English words that are almost identical to the Hebrew. William Tyndale, a valiant sixteenth century linguist and believer who gave his life for the cause of translating the Bible into English (and thus influenced the King James translation of the Bible), declared that "The English tongue agreeth with the Hebrew a thousand times more than with the Latin."[14]

Other scholars have noted the interesting construct of words like "England" and "Anglo-Saxon." The word "England" is derived from the word "Angle-land"—the Angles being a Germanic tribe that migrated to the British Isles during the fifth and sixth centuries B.C. *Angle* is a Hebrew word meaning "Bull" or "Ox." These animals are the biblical symbol for Joseph, as in "Let the blessings come upon the head of Joseph...

His glory is like the firstlings of his bullock" (Deuteronomy 33:16-17). Other examples of the same are also very present in the biblical account.[15]

"Saxon" also has a fascinating proposed origin. Some speculate that it has its origins in the name "Isaac." Dropping the "I" from Isaac (vowels are not used in Hebrew spelling), leaves us with "Saac." God told Abraham: "In Isaac shall thy seed be called" (Genesis 21:12; see also Romans 9:7 and Hebrews 11:18). The Israelites are called "the house of Isaac" (Amos 7:16). If our theory is correct, the Anglo-Saxons were derived from this same biblical house—they are "Isaac's sons." Or, in the Hebrew, they are "Saac's sons"—hence the name "Saxons."[16]

Similarly, we might also consider the word "British." Bible scholars and linguists explain how the Hebrew word for "covenant" is *Berith*. "In the original Hebrew language vowels were never given in the spelling. So, omitting the vowel 'e' from berith, but retaining the 'i' in its anglicized form to preserve the 'y' sound, we have the anglicized Hebrew word for covenant: *brith*....The Hebrews, however, never pronounced their 'h's'.... Incidentally, this ancient Hebrew trait is also a modern British trait....The Hebrew word for 'covenant' [therefore] would be pronounced, in its anglicized form, as *brit*." Finally, the Hebrew word for "man" is "ish," which means "of or belonging to." Put them together and the translation is quite incredible. "British" in its Hebrew form literally means *Covenant Man* or *Covenant People*. It should also be noted that the Hebrew "ain" means land; "Britain," therefore, is translated *Land of the Covenant*.[17]

The connections continue. The flag of Great Britain is called the "Union Jack," to be interpreted as "Union of Jacob." The British coat of arms includes images of a lion and a unicorn.[18] The lion is the ancient symbol of Judah (see Genesis 49:9). The unicorn clearly represents Joseph/Ephraim. We shall complete the previously cited Old Testament scripture: "Let the blessings come upon the head of Joseph...His glory is like the firstlings of his bullock, and his horns are like the horns of unicorns: with them he shall push the people together to the ends of the earth; and they are the ten thousands of Ephraim" (Deuteronomy 33:16-17). Finally, the crown worn by the ancient kings of Ireland consisted of *twelve* points! And the British crown is adorned with *twelve* jewels.[19] Is this mere coincidence?

Other compelling historical interpretations worthy of consideration revolve around the Tribe of Dan, which would have traveled northwest with Ephraim. "Dan shall be a serpent by the way," declared Jacob-Israel in his blessing (Genesis 49:17). This has also been translated "Dan shall be a serpent's trail," indicating that Dan would leave markers behind as he migrated. True to the suggestion, wherever the Danites went in the scriptural record, they renamed the land/region after their father, Dan (see Joshua 19:47; Judges 18 12, 27-29). Moses' version of the Danite blessing declares, "Dan is a lion's whelp; he shall leap from Basham,"(Deuteronomy 33:22), which is a northern district in Palestine. Bold historians find connections between Danites and northern European traditions, which they claim suggest Dan migrated there.

As Dan was fond of renaming lands along his trail, it is interesting to note the many names pegged today in regions in and near northern Europe: the Danube, Don, Daneister, Daneiper, Denmark, and others. (It should be noted that, since the Hebrew language uses no written vowels, "Dan" is spelled Dn, making it possible for Israelite predecessors in Europe to have substituted any vowel between D-n). The ancient seal of Denmark includes an animal which represents the land of Denmark—it is described as "A lion's whelp with a serpent's tail."[20]

Other British traditions tell of the prophet Jeremiah, who spoke so often of Joseph/Ephraim. Based on several traditions—none of which are conclusive—Jeremiah visited the land of the north (Britain) and brought what is called the "lia-fail," or "the stone of destiny." Many believe this is the same sacred stone—called the Stone of Scone—that was built into the coronation chair of Great Britain. A sign near the stone and chair once read: "Jacob's pillar-stone" (see Genesis 28:18).[21]

A more stunning British tradition teaches that Jesus Christ Himself, while in his youth, before beginning his ministry, visited the British Isles. These traditions are prevalent in southwest England. One historian listed over twenty locations in the region (to include Cornwall, Somerset and Gloucestershire) where these traditions are celebrated. Some surmise that Christ had come to visit family members who had migrated in earlier days to the isles.[22] Even today, William Blake's *Jerusalem*, is a celebrated British anthem. The lyrics are impressive:

> *And did those feet in ancient time,*
> *walk upon England's mountains green?*
> *And was the holy lamb of God,*
> *On England's pleasant pastures seen?*

Such traditions that support British-Israelitism go much deeper than we can discuss here. The evidence includes written records, ancient folklore, artifacts (to include grave-markers), and even DNA. This can all be studied and vetted out in scholarly works written by respected modern historians and geneticists. Such works include Dr. David Goldstein's, *Jacob's Legacy: A Genetic View of Jewish History;* genealogist Donald Yates', *When Scotland Was Jewish: DNA Evidence, Archeology, Analysis of Migrations, and Public and Family Records;* geneticist A.E. Mourant's, *The Genetics of the Jews;* historian Jon Entine's, *Abraham's Children: Race, Identity, and the DNA of the Chosen People;* and many others.[23]

Beyond just Britain, scientific and historical data regarding the final destiny of Joseph/Ephraim and the lost tribes often indicate that these ancient wanderers landed in places as diverse as Africa, India, Afghanistan, Pakistan, the Caucuses, China, Japan, and the ancient indigenous nations of North America.[24]

The Scientific and archeological evidence pertaining to the lost and grand ancient civilizations of North America (which is still pouring in today) is quite stunning. Connections between North American Indians and the Israelites include physical artifacts and architecture, shared customs, and even shared DNA.[25] These connections, of course, are highly relevant in the context of the covenant. Might God have led other children of Joseph to this same promised land in earlier eras? As we shall see in Part II of this book, many of America's prominent explorers and settlers, upon witnessing these ancient societies upon the land, believed it was so. Indeed, they often called their indigenous neighbors *lost Israelites*.

If Joseph/Ephraim and the covenant blessings are imbedded in these many regions, the implication for a full and final gathering of Israel, and for a fullness of gospel truth to be spread throughout the world, is quite powerful. Perhaps the Lord has, in His own way, been preparing the world for a final perpetuation of His Gospel by placing His chosen families in regions throughout the world, that they might lead the Christian march to salvation in God's due time. For the Lord said to Israel: "Thou shalt spread abroad to the west, and to the east, and to the north, and to the south: and in thee and in thy seed shall all the families of the earth be blessed" (Genesis 28: 4, 14). Some have spoken of the *believing blood of Israel*. "I am the good shepherd, and know my sheep," stated the Christ, "and am known of mine....My sheep hear my voice, and I know them, and they follow me" (John 10:14, 26-27).

In the end, we have here—in addition to the scriptural suggestions—historical evidence that Joseph/Ephraim would be saved to build a covenant nation unto God: a nation to serve as His base of operations in the last days. One powerful indicator in this history has to do with witnesses who served to bridge the gap between biblical and modern times. Flavius Josephus, the first century Romano-Jewish historian, wrote of ancient Israel in his acclaimed work, *Antiquities of the Jews.* Josephus stands unique as our first recorded commentator about ancient Israel after the lost tribes wander off the pages of the Bible. Writing several hundreds of years later, Josephus concurs with our interpretation, stating, "There are but two tribes [Judah and Benjamin] in Asia and Europe subject to the Romans, while the Ten Tribes are beyond the Euphrates till now, and are an immense multitude, and not to be estimated by numbers." [26]

Another important link between the Bible and modern history is the Talmud—the Jewish book of laws and histories originating from the first several centuries A.D. This sacred book declares the following: "Like as the day grows dark, and then grows light, so also after darkness is fallen upon the Ten Tribes, God will ultimately shine light upon them." The commentary continues: "The Ten Tribes shall not return again, for it is written: 'And he cast them into *another land* like this day.'" [27]

It is our contention that both scripture and history fulfill these ancient utterances from witnesses who were closer to the ancient scene than others of recorded history. Indeed, Joseph/Ephraim was led out to become a multitude of people. They were led to the *north country*, to the coastline, to the *isles* of the sea. They were carried *over the wall* of water to *another land*. That land is America.

Modern-day Evidence of the Fulfillment

Could this all be one huge coincidence? Is it just chance that Israel—Joseph/Ephraim—was foreordained to inherit an unknown land, separate from his brother-tribes, even a land of *liberty, protection,* and *prosperity,* destined to be even more blessed than Jacob's progenitors? Is it just chance that the Scriptures then leave a biblical trail of this family—a trail that indicates their northwesterly migration, which leads them directly to the British Isles? Is it mere chance that this family was told that its new land would exist by a *well,* upon an *isle,* that they would be *planted* to a *coastline*? Is it simply dumb luck that so much history and tradition of the British Isles connect in wondrous ways to ancient Israel and to Joseph/Ephraim? And what are the chances that, once this migration occurred, Great Britain "magically" turned into the most powerful nation on the earth—powerful enough to protect the sacred family line. Due to its small size and easy accessibility for foreign aggressors (it is surrounded by water), Britain has been an easy target for thousands of years. Yet, all who have tried could not conquer it. Roman invasions lasted years, the Spanish Armada took a stab, the French under Napoleon gave it a go, and Germany attempted to subdue it two distinct times during the two World Wars. Yet Britain (translated, *Land of the Covenant*) would not fall. She had a mission under God to preserve and support the covenant-makers.

Declared Sir Winston Churchill: "I have a feeling sometimes that some Guiding Hand has interfered. I have a feeling that we have a Guardian because we have a great Cause, and we shall have that Guardian so long as we serve that Cause. And what a Cause it is." Dr. H.A Wilson, the Bishop of Chelmsford, England agreed: "If ever a great nation was on the point of supreme and final disaster, and yet saved and reinstated, it was ourselves...It does not require an exceptional religious mind to detect in all this the hand of God. It has been a miracle...We have been saved for a purpose."[28] The Methodist minister, and English barrister, Richard Reader Harris took it a step further. Believing that the Bible suggests that the ancient Israelites had indeed landed in Britain and brought the covenant with them, Harris wrote the following: "If this be true, it adds tremendously to our responsibilities, and opens before us in a way that no human tongue can describe, spiritual possibilities, temporal possibilities, national possibilities, and universal possibilities."[29]

Even if we can accept all this as luck, chance, or coincidence, what can we say when this family was preordained to cross *over the wall* to a land of *everlasting hills*, ringing with the greatest abundance of *liberty*, *protection*, and *prosperity*? And what can we say when we find that British colonists did in fact fulfill this divine mandate? For they *did* cross the waters into this most blessed land of *everlasting hills*. Then, what can we say when, upon their arrival, they identified themselves as "Israel" and incessantly invoked the same Israelite covenant upon the land? (That they identified themselves as Israel will be well-documented in forthcoming chapters.) Then the kicker: what are the chances that, after all of this, the land-colony of America settled by the British happens to become the *only* land in world history proven to have been even more blessed than ancient Israel? (Remember, Jacob-Israel promised that Joseph's land would be greater than his own.) Indeed, in *all* of history, America is the ultimate example of *liberty*, *protection*, and *prosperity* under God Almighty. It has saved Christianity and therefore it has preserved mankind's ability to seek and find salvation. Such divine power—to include its scriptural and historical framework—should not be sidelined, belittled, or ignored.

In the final analysis of these Old Testament promises, and with the advantage of historical hindsight, it is difficult to argue with Pastor Armstrong:

> God did cause the birthright nations—and them *only* —to become *suddenly* the recipients of such national wealth, greatness and power as no nation or empire ever before had acquired! Together they—the British and Americans, descendants of only one tribe, Joseph—came into possession of more than two-thirds—almost three-fourths—of all the cultivated resources and wealth of the whole world. It sounds incredible!... The most amazing fact of all history is this sudden skyrocketing from virtual obscurity of two nations to the most fabulous wealth and economic power ever possessed by any people. Britain became Great Britain—a gigantic, stupendously wealthy commonwealth of nations—the United States, the greatest nation of history.[30]

All of this represents the covenant fruits that the Almighty delivered to His children. We turn again to the words of Christ, as He addressed the ancient people of the Old World who were in the midst of casting him off:

> "[T]he Kingdom of God shall be taken from you, and given to a *nation* bringing forth the fruits thereof."

(Matthew 21:43)

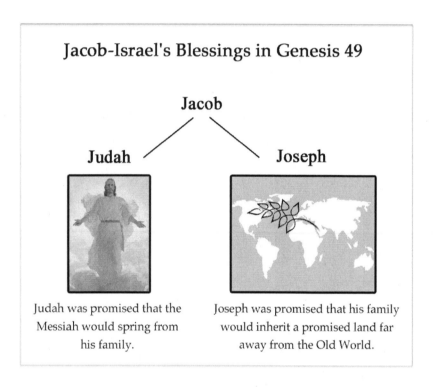

Jacob-Israel's Blessings in Genesis 49

Jacob

Judah

Joseph

Judah was promised that the Messiah would spring from his family.

Joseph was promised that his family would inherit a promised land far away from the Old World.

"We the People" of the Covenant

Of all the fruits bearing forth the witness of who Americans really were and are under God, nothing compares to their own modern history. They knew that their mission was divine and they knew their nation was given to them by God through the covenant. They were able to invoke the covenant because they, collectively and individually, had, as the prophet declared, *God's law and covenant in their inward parts, written in their hearts* (see Jeremiah 31:33). A preeminent example of one who possessed such innate conviction was George Washington. He declared the following in his first inaugural address as the first president of the United States. His message not only reflects his own understanding of the American Covenant, but that of those who came before him in discovering, settling, and founding the new nation.

> [I]t would be peculiarly improper to omit in this first official Act, my fervent supplications to that Almighty Being who rules over the Universe, who presides in the Councils of Nations, and whose providential aids can supply every human defect, that his benediction may consecrate to the liberties and happiness of the people of the United States.

Washington then warns:

> We ought to be no less persuaded that the smiles of Heaven can never be expected on a nation that disregards the eternal rules of order and right, which Heaven itself has ordained.

And finally, he concludes:

> Having thus imparted to you my sentiments…I shall take my present leave; but not without resorting once more to the benign parent of the human race, in humble supplication that since has been pleased to favour the American people…for the security of their Union, and the advancement of their happiness; so his divine blessing may be equally conspicuous in the enlarged views, the temperate consultations, and the wise measures on which the success of this Government must depend. [31]

Can there be any doubt that Washington possessed an understanding of the American Covenant and of his associated obligations to the people and to God? As he accepted the presidency, it seems as though he felt the weight of his responsibility within the context of that relationship.

Moments before this address, Washington was sworn in as the first president of the United States. This "swearing in" ceremony makes the inaugural address even more significant, as it truly portrays our first president in his role as American Covenant-maker. For example, consider the words of the oath of office, which are found in Article II, Section I of the Constitution of the United States: "I do solemnly swear that I will faithfully execute the office of the President of the United States, and will to the best of my ability, preserve, protect, and defend the Constitution of the United States."

The profundity of that promise is revealed as we examine the true nature of the Constitution as national scripture. The Constitution (as will be detailed later) does nothing less than prescribe the formula for securing those American Covenant blessings of *liberty, protection,* and *prosperity.* It is but the modern political version of the ancient promise to Joseph found in Genesis 49. In swearing to uphold the Constitution, each president is committing himself and the nation to God and the American Covenant. Surely, these are covenant-making words; and just as sacred covenants are written in sacred scripture, so this national covenant is written in our national scripture.

In reflecting upon this singular event of our nation's first inaugural ceremony, we should not underestimate the manner in which this presidential oath or covenant is administered. The recipient raises his right arm to the square, placing his other hand upon the Bible, and repeats the words of the covenant. To reflect how seriously this covenant is made, if the words are not said precisely as revealed in the Constitution, it will at times be re-done until correct—even to this day. In the presidential inauguration ceremony of 2009, there was question as to whether the president-elect repeated every word of the covenant correctly. And so, the chief justice was invited to the White House after the ceremony to repeat it again, just to be sure.[32]

In that first inauguration, Washington added two seemingly spontaneous actions to the ceremony, which suggest he had a spiritual understanding of what he was doing (i.e.

entering into). Upon completing his recital of the oath, Washington declared: "So help me God," then "bowed down reverently" and kissed the Bible.[33] Almost every president since followed this precedent.[34] It is an outward expression to demonstrate to whom the covenant was made. Fittingly, this first oath of office ushered in a new form of constitutional government, which many referred to (and still do) as the *federal* government; and the root word for *federal*—the Latin *foedus*—directly translates into the English word "covenant." Furthermore, the oath was taken in the nation's first capital city, New York, in a building called Federal Hall, or as we might interpret it, *Covenant Hall*. [35]

Perhaps the only thing that would convince us further of Washington's acknowledgment, on his inauguration day, that he was entering into the American Covenant with God would be if he had said so. Indeed, how splendid it would be if he had, on that historic and sacred day, broadcast the message that he was entering into an extended version of that perpetual covenant derived from Abraham and ancient Israel. Perhaps he did. There is a powerful piece of evidence from the inauguration ceremony that perhaps represents the most underreported sacred event in American history. As Washington took his oath, with his right arm raised to the square (in symbolic gesture of covenant-

making), he placed his left hand upon a page of an opened Bible. Historians assert that Washington's hand was placed on a randomly opened page within the Holy Bible. If it was random, then it was also amazingly coincidental. For, in a gesture almost too astonishing to believe, Washington placed his hand precisely on the pages that included Jacob's American Covenant promise to Joseph in

Washington's Inauguration, by Allyn Cox
Courtesy of the Architect of the Capitol.

Genesis 49, complete with its description of his posterity crossing "over the wall" to a new land of "everlasting hills," ringing with *liberty, protection,* and *prosperity.*[36] It was as if Washington knew those verses about Joseph's seed were about him and the nation he would lead.

The reason historians have long commented on the randomness of the page selected by Washington has to do with the seemingly insignificant choice of verses on the page. After all, its meaning in reference to America only becomes clear after careful assemblage of other reference points to create a meaningful interpretation of Jacob's blessing to Joseph. Clearly something of eternal significance was revealed and comprehended on that historic day.

But Washington was certainly not alone in his role as American Covenant-maker. To be sure, every American from coast to coast and border to border is a participant in the covenant. Even though it was given to Ephraim to lead the administration of this early covenant, it would eventually be given to the entire citizenry of the United States to participate in its blessings and obligations. Naturally, some understand it and/or live it better than others; but nevertheless, all have their place, regardless of race or religion. As a modern Christian leader noted: "Men and women of all denominations have helped settle this land—Catholics and Protestants, Jews and Greeks, Muslims and Hindus…those who helped establish this great country believed in and worshipped God."[37] These were and are all American Covenant-makers. Every American carries within them a light that will lead to God. Every American has the freedom to choose to follow that light, in keeping the commandments and serving God as best they know how, or to flee the light, in acting against their conscience. Just as the law of gravity assures us that a pebble will fall if we drop it, the law of God assures us that our nation will fall if we fail to keep His covenant. The laws of God are immutable.

Not insignificantly, thousands of Americans take an almost identical oath to that of the president every year, raising their arms to the square and repeating the constitutional promise, as they are sworn in to positions of trust. As one who has participated in such an event on two occasions (once for the Central Intelligence Agency and once for the Department of Homeland Security), I can testify to the power and solemnity in which this oath is received. Furthermore, every year thousands more stand with their arms to the square and take a similar oath, as they are sworn in as citizens of the United States. They covenant to "support and defend the Constitution" and "to bear true faith and allegiance to the same;" and they publically promise to "bear arms on behalf of the United States when required by law." As one who has witnessed this solemn assembly, with its participants wiping tears from their eyes, I can attest to its spiritual power, as particularly manifested by the concluding phrase of the oath—"so help me God."[38] More touching are the countless others that have made the ultimate sacrifice, supporting the covenant through the shedding of their own blood.

Moreover, Americans far and wide make and renew this national covenant every time they take a stand on those God-inspired principles of the Constitution, every time they sacrifice for the good of others, every time they reflect upon our national motto —"In God we trust." Americans declare their participation in the covenant every time they plead to God through song to "stand beside her and guide her through the night with the light from above" (from *God Bless America*), or when they intone the words, "Long may our land be bright with freedom's holy light, protect us by thy might, Great God, our King" (from *My Country 'Tis of Thee*). And finally, Americans certainly covenant with God and country every time they put their hands over their hearts and "pledge allegiance" to "one nation under God." It is through making these sacramental gestures of our national covenant that *We the people of the United States* truly become *We the people of the American Covenant*.

Many prophets throughout the ages have recorded their visions and revelations, which oft times pertain to the people they lead and the issues of their day. There are a few events and experiences that carry so much profundity in relation to God's plan that the prophets have seen them in prophetic vision and have recorded them in scripture. Examples include the coming of the Messiah. Yet another, as we have seen throughout this chapter, is the American Covenant!

But more than just adding enormous credibility to the entire concept of the American Covenant, this study of ancient scripture and modern history will lead us to the powerful conclusion that modern-day citizens of the United States have fulfilled ancient prophecies—they have become the American Covenant-makers. Consequently, the story of the American Covenant—including the promised blessings and obligations given through Abraham to Ephraim and on to George Washington and others—becomes *our* story. And as the torch has now been passed to us, if we adhere to the covenant as did our forefathers, the privilege will be ours as Americans to continue assisting God in His holy work by living up to our obligations under the covenant. Thus, *liberty, protection,* and *prosperity* will abound; a fullness of freedom to make choices will thrive; and God's children everywhere will then have unfettered access to Him and the salvation only He can bring—all according to His omniscient plan.

ENDNOTES

[1] See Herbert W. Armstrong, *The United States and Britain in Prophecy* (New York: Everest House, 1980), 87-89.

[2] Armstrong, *The United States and Britain in Prophecy,* 162.

[3] Leslie Pearson Rees, *Ye Have Been Hid: Finding the Lost Tribes of Israel* (New York: Digital Legend Press, 2011), 13.

[4] Armstrong, *The United States and Britain in Prophecy,* 57.

[5] Prominent scholars who have promoted this theory (often called British-Israelism or American Israelism) include the following: the Canadian geologist and Bible scholar Edward Faraday Odlum, M.A., B.Sc., F.R.F.S. (1850–1935); Roger Rusk the brother of US secretary of state Dean Rusk, Hebrew scholar and professor in physics for 28 years at the University of Tennessee; British General Sir Walter Walker KCB, CBE, DSO & bar (1912–2001); William Ferguson Massey, Prime Minister of New Zealand 1912–1925; Patience Strong (1907–1990), English Poetess; John Fisher, 1st Baron Fisher (1841–1920), GCB, OM, GCVO, Admiral of the Fleet; C. A. L. Totten, professor of Military Tactics at Yale University (1889–1892); John Cox Gawler (1830–1882), Keeper of the Monarch's Crown Jewels; John Bracken, PC (1883–1969), 11th Premier of Manitoba (1922–1943) and leader of the Progressive Conservative Party of Canada (1942–1948); Thomas Bavin KCMG (1874–1941), 24th Premier of New South Wales; Robert Randolph Bruce, Lieutenant Governor of British Columbia (1926–1931), Arthur Cherep-Spiridovich (1858—1926); Sir Standish G. Crauford, Brigadier-General, Bart., C.B., C.M.G., C.I.E., D.S.O, author of *Our Celtic Heritage* (1867); David Davidson, Esq., C.E., M.C., F.R.S.A., (1844–1956), famous British structural engineer; Sir Errol Manners K.B.E (1883–1953), distinguished Royal Navy admiral; Lt.-Col. J.A.McQueen, D.S.O., M.C. Military Intelligence; Joseph Cockfield Dimsdale PC, KCVO, Bt, Lord Mayor of London (1901–1902); William Henry Fasken, Brigadier-General, author of *Israel's Racial Origin and Migrations* (1934); James Bernard Nicklin, (b. 1881); inventor and author of *Testimony in Stone* (1961), Sir George Grey, KCB (1812–1898), Governor-General of New Zealand; Reader Harris, K.C. (1847–1909), barrister and King's Counsel; George Jowett (1891–1969), world-class gymnast, author of The Drama of the Lost Disciples (1961); Oliver Lodge FRS (1851–1940), prominent British physicist; Rev. Lawrence Graeme Allan Roberts (born 1844), Commander of the Royal Navy, author of *British History Traced From Egypt And Palestine* (1927); Herbert Aldersmith, F.R.C.S M.B. LSA (1847–1918), renowned English physician, Adam Rutherford, F.R.A.S., F.R.G.S.; founder of the Institute for Pyramidology and E. Raymond Capt; Professor Charles Piazzi Smyth, Astronomer Royal for Scotland, Fellow of the Royal Astronomical Society, and Fellow of the Royal Societies of London and Edinburgh, Dr. George Moore, Member of the Royal College of Physicians, John Pym Yeatman, Esq., Fellow of the Royal Historical Society, C.O. Groom Napier, geologist and Fellow of the Royal Statistical Society, Dr. Herbert Aldersmith, Fellow of the Royal College of Surgeons; Charles Marston, Fellow of the Society of Antiquaries of London (who funded major archaeological excavations across Palestine between 1929-1938). This list quoted from http://enwikipedia.org/wiki/British_Israelism.

Prominent religious leaders who have promoted this theory, and published work in support of it, belong to various churches, to include the Anglican Church, the Methodist Church, the Wesleyan Methodist Church, Baptist congregations, to include the Calvary Baptist Church, Disciples of Christ church, the Church of Jesus Christ of Latter-day Saints, Pentecostal congregations, Catholic congregations, Christian Scientist church, and many others. For a detailed list of these leaders and their publications, see the subsection titled "Support" at http://enwikipedia.org/wiki/British_Israelism.

[6] Vern Swanson, *Dynasty of the Holy Grail* (Springville: Cedar Fort, 2006), 8.

[7] See 2 Kings 17; See also Steven D. Greene, *The Tribe of Ephraim* (Springville: Horizon Publishers, 2007), xiii.

[8] See *Apocrypha*, 2 Esdras 13:39-47, full text available at www.sacred-texts.com.

[9] George Reynolds, *Are We of Israel* (Salt Lake: Geo. Cannon and Sons, 1895), 27-28.

[10] Armstrong, *The United States and Britain in Prophecy*, 55.

[11] Armstrong, *The United States and Britain in Prophecy*, 8.

[12] Rees, *Ye Have Been Hid: Finding the Lost Tribes of Israel*, 256.

[13] Rees, *Ye Have Been Hid: Finding the Lost Tribes of Israel*, 260.

[14] David Daniell, *William Tyndale, A Biogrpahy*, 229.

[15] Swanson, *Dynasty of the Holy Grail*, 139; Rees, *Ye Have Been Hid: Finding the Lost Tribes of Israel*, 135; Edward Odlum, *God's Covenant Man: British Israel* (London: Robert Banks and Sons, 1916), 74.

[16] Armstrong, *The United States and Britain in Prophecy*, 120.

[17] Armstrong, *The United States and Britain in Prophecy*, 120; Rees, *Ye Have Been Hid*, 145; Vaughn Hansen, *Whence They Came: Israel, Britain, and the Restoration* (Springville: Cedar Fort, 1993), 30. Other publications concerning the English language connection to the Hebrew include the following: James Cowles Pritchard, *Eastern Origin of the Celtic Nations* (1857); Henry Rowlands (1655–1723), *Mona Antiqua Restaurata: An Archaeological Discourse on the Antiquities, Natural and Historical, of the Isle of Anglesey, the Ancient Seat of the British Druids* (1723); Charles Edwards in 1676 entitled *Hebraismorum Cambro-Britannicorum specimen*; Charles Vallancey, *An Essay on the Antiquity of the Irish Language* (1772); John Rhys, *The Welsh People* (with D. B. Jones, 1900). For more information, see "Hebrew-English Language Connection," available at http://en.wikipedia.org/wiki/British_Israelism.

[18] Rees, *Ye Have Been Hid*, 145.

[19] Armstrong, 126; Vaughn Hansen, *Whence They Came?*, 74.

[20] Rees, *Ye Have Been Hid*, 140-142; Armstrong, 121-124. See also John Cox Gawler, *Dan: The Pioneer of Israel*; Edward Hine, *The British Nation Identified with Lost Israel*.

[21] Rees, *Ye Have Been Hid*, 155; Armstrong, 124-126. See also Ellen M. Rogers, *The Coronation Stone and England's Interest in It* (Revised 1928); Wallace Connon, *Stone of Destiny (1950)*.

[22] Hansen, *Whence Came They?*, 92-93; Swanson, *Dynasty of the Holy Grail*, 38-47.

[23] See also J.H. Allen, *Judah's Scepter and Joseph's Birthright*; E. Raymond Capt, *King Solomon's Temple: A Study of its Symbolism* and *Jacob's Pillar: A Biblical Historical Study*; Steven M. Collins, *The Lost Ten Tribes of Israel, Found*; and Yair Davidy, *Lost Israelite Identity* and *Hebrew Ancestry of Celtic Races*.

[24] One of the most fascinating *Lost Tribe* traditions is found within the ancient and obscure Lemba nation, which exists today in various parts of southern Africa. The Lemba believe they are of Israelite descent. Apart from the oral tradition of their ancient genetics, they also share many Hebrew-like beliefs and rituals, to include monotheism (they claim to worship the God of Israel), the practice of circumcision, Hebrew-like burial rituals, animal sacrifices, the following of lunar cycles, and strict dietary laws akin to Jewish kushrat. During the mid-nineties, geneticists thought to test the Lemba claims through DNA experiments. To the shock of many, including the geneticists (but not to the Lemba), there was clearly Semitic-type blood running through the veins of the Lemba. For details, see Dr. David Goldstein, *Jacob's Legacy: A Genetic View of Jewish History* (New Haven: Yale University Press, 2008), 46-59.

[25] According to Dr. Roger Kennedy, former director of the Smithsonian's American History Museum, "Few realize that some of the oldest, largest, and most complex structures of ancient archaeology were built of earth, clay, and stone right here in America, in the Ohio and Mississippi valleys. From 6,000 years ago until quite recently, North America was home to some of the most highly advanced and well organized civilizations in the world—complete with cities, roads, and commerce." See Roger Kennedy, *Hidden Cities—The Discovery and Loss of Ancient North American Civilization*. Free Press, 1994.

In the highly acclaimed, award-winning, documentary, *The Lost Civilizations of North America*, more than a dozen highly accredited scholars in the fields of archaeology, anthropology, history, and genetics explore connections between these ancient American civilizations and ancient Israel and its surrounding areas. For example, it is shown how the ancient Hopewell Mound Builders of America likely used geometry and mathematics in their architecture that coincide precisely with the architecture of ancient Egypt. Furthermore, scholars discuss findings of peculiar artifacts that include an ancient form of Hebrew writing. A complete rendition of the Ten Commandments was also discovered among the artifacts of these ancient Native Americans.

Geneticists have also made it clear that there exists DNA correlations between Native American populations and Semitic populations. While most DNA among Native Americans has been connected to Asia, new DNA evidence indicates that Haplogroup X is also found in abundance among North American indigenous populations. Haplogroup X, according to geneticists, is derived from the "hills of Galilee" and also from other Jewish and European populations in and around Israel. Anthropology professor Deborah Bolnick, of the University of Texas-Austin, published a 2008 report in the *Journal of Physical Anthropology*. In it, she documents how she and her team identified Haplogroup X in the bones of the ancient American Hopewell Mound Builders. See Beth Alison Shook, et al, "Using Ancient mtDNA to Reconstruct the Population History of Northeastern North America," *American Journal of Physical Anthropology*, Vol. 137:14-29, 2008; Virginia Morell, "Genes May Link Ancient Eurasians, Native Americans, *Science*, Vol. 280, Issue 5363, 1998; David Glenn Smith, "Distribution of mtDNA Haplogroup X Among Native North Americans," *American Journal of Physical Anthropology* 110:272 (1999); Ripan S. Malhi and David Glenn Smith, "Brief Communication: Haplogroup X Confirmed Among in Prehistoric North America, *American Journal of Physical Anthropology* 119:84-86 (2002); Jason A. Eshleman and Ripan Malhi, "Mitochondrial DNA Studies of Native Americans: Conceptions and Misconceptions of the Population Prehistory of the Americas," *Evolutionary Anthropology* 12:7-18 (2003); Jeanette Fedar, "Differences in mtDNA Haplogroup Distribution Among Three Jewish Populations After Susceptibility to T2DM Complications," *BMC Genomics*, Vol.9:198, April 2008; Doran Behar, "Counting the Founders: the Matrilineal Genetic Ancestry of the Jewish Diaspora, *PLOS ONE*, Vol. 3(4):1-16 (2008).

[26] See Jon Entine, *Abraham's Children: Race, Identity, and the DNA of the Chosen People* (New York: Grand Central Publishing, 2007), 131-132.

[27] Jon Entine, *Abraham's Children*, 132.

[28] Vaughn Hansen, *Whence Came They?*, 126-127.

[29] Richard Reader Harris, *The Lost Tribes of Israel*, Preface.

[30] Armstrong, 159-160.

[31] George Washington's First Inaugural Address, April 30, 1789, as quoted in William J. Bennett, *The Spirit of America* (New York: Touchstone, 1997), 381-382.

[32] See "Obama Retakes Oath of Office After Flub," available at http://www.msnbc.msn.com/id/28780417/

[33] Description by Washington Irving, as quoted in William J. Bennett, *The Spirit of America* (New York: Simon and Schuster, 1997), 381.

[34] "Inaugural History," PBS Online News Hour (data online): available from www.pbs.org/newshour/inauguration/history.html.

[35] Bruce Feiler, *America's Prophet* (New York: Harper Collins, 2009), 28, 78.

[36] That Washington had his Bible opened to Genesis 49 during his swearing-in ceremony is documented in H. Paul Jeffers, *The Freemasons in America* (New York: Kensington Publishing Corp., 2006), 28; Bruce Feiler, *America's Prophet* (New York: HarperCollins, 2009), 78; Internet searches will also clearly confirm this fact of history.

[37] Gordon B. Hinckley, *Standing for Something* (New York: Random House, Inc, 2000), xxiii.

[38] The Naturalization Oath of Allegiance can be found at www.cavanaughlegal.com/us-citizenship-naturalization/citizenship-ceremony.

CHAPTER 3

THE COVENANT RULES

Righteousness exalteth a nation:
but sin is a reproach to any people

—Proverbs 14:34

Before Washington could receive God's blessings during the Battle of Long Island, he knew that his people must demonstrate righteousness. This is why he called them to repent and turn to the Almighty (a pattern he maintained throughout his national career, as we shall see later in this book). If America is a covenant land, then we must see ourselves as participants in this covenant. As such, we must understand the rules of the covenant—we must understand the blessings and obligations associated with it.

As discussed in the previous chapter, many ancient prophets called to and warned Joseph/Ephraim well after Joseph/Ephraim had walked out of the recorded biblical text. Indeed, the Bible does not record any instance in which the Lost Tribes actually gained access to the words of Ezekiel, Hosea, Isaiah, Jeremiah, and the others. So, in the absence of any biblical proof—or even of any known possibility—that the

Lost Tribes would or could gain access to these words, who then were the prophets calling to and warning? For whom did the prophets record their instructions pertaining to the covenant? Perhaps they were reaching out to *us*. Perhaps they were calling *us* to the covenant. Perhaps we should listen more intently to their message.

To those who possess a promised land, the Lord has declared, "Now therefore hearken, O Israel, unto the statutes and unto the judgments, which I teach you...that ye may live, and go in and possess the land which the Lord God of your fathers giveth you" (Deuteronomy 4:1). It should be noted that when Moses gave this command, he was speaking not only to Judah, but to Joseph and the other tribes—for they had not as-of-yet divided. It should also be noted that Moses was very aware of the fact that Joseph's people would one day inherit *another* promised land. For Moses himself repeated the same blessing to Joseph/Ephraim that Jacob-Israel had bestowed upon that choice family. Indeed, Moses prophesied of Joseph's future land—he called it "his [Joseph's] land"—wherein resided "the lasting hills," and where *liberty*, *protection*, and *prosperity* would reign (see Deuteronomy 33: 13-17). To be sure, the statutes and judgments upon the promised land would—in addition to Canaan—apply to America.

> *And it shall come to pass, if thou shalt hearken diligently unto the voice of the Lord thy God, to observe and to do all his commandments which I have commanded thee this day, that the Lord thy God will set thee on high above all the nations of the earth.*

> *(Deuteronomy 28:1)*

> *If then their uncircumcised hearts be humbled...Then will I remember my covenant with Jacob, and also my covenant with Isaac, and also my covenant with Abraham will I remember; and I will remember the land.*

> *(Leviticus 26:41-42)*

Some commentators enjoy pointing out their opinion that the Old Testament statutes to the ancient nation cannot apply to us today. They point out how many aspects of the Law of Moses are rigid and even oppressive (e.g. animal sacrifices, excessive corporal punishment, etc.). If we reject these strenuous statutes for ourselves today, then how can we make any claim on any other of those laws and commandments for the nation? Upon considering this issue, we must remember that the Law of Moses was issued to the Children of Israel long after the principal commandments and promises surrounding the land were given. The national covenant rules were issued to Abraham, Isaac, Jacob, and Joseph long before we see the more strict law. Indeed, Jacob-Israel bestowed the promise of America upon Joseph long before the Law of Moses was implemented. Is it not possible that the Law of Moses was given specifically to the generations of Israelites in their post-Egyptian slavery era? Is it not possible that their condition (perhaps their extreme disobedience) required tougher laws? Did Christ Himself not fulfill the law of Moses, giving us a higher law by which to live today (Matthew 5:17-18)?

We should not believe God is so static that he cannot deal with His children and with His nations on a case by case basis in ways that best serve them and His cause. Too many (mostly secularists) pretend God is a static Parent and, as parts of the Law of Moses seem unconstitutional, they want to cast out all biblical commands to the nation. They want to cast out the Bible. In truth, the rules of our covenant represent a conglomeration of both the sacred Scripture and of our national scripture, which includes the Declaration of Independence and the Constitution. God gave us *all* these laws and promises. As we see (in coming chapters) how the Founders applied the Bible to the nation they built, we will see how God worked through them to restore the covenant. It is American history, and the presence of the covenant in this history, that lead us to conclude that the national covenant, as defined by scripture, is fully applicable to us today.

It is clear in the biblical account what is expected for those who possess a promised land. The blessings and obligations are laid out, as is God's purpose for bestowing the covenant in the first place. As Americans possess a promised land—and one which was perhaps foreordained in the Bible itself—Americans *must* pay attention to the rules.

Blessings of the American Covenant

If God gives blessings in furtherance of His ultimate purposes in bringing to pass the salvation of His children, then it follows that the three prominent American Covenant blessings of *liberty*, *protection*, and *prosperity* were given for this same eternal end.

For example, just as the ancient Israelites relied upon their national covenant to receive the blessings of *liberty* (as they did in overcoming Egyptian slavery), that they might work out their salvation freely, so did modern Americans. As will be seen in the coming chapters, the Founding Fathers indeed relied on the same covenant in both word and deed as they discovered, settled, and developed their new land. Like the Israelites, they too invoked God and covenant on a regular basis, and were thus blessed with the freedom they sought. As both groups strove toward righteousness, they were inspired from on high to conceive precious documents, laws, and institutions that would establish and protect their *liberty*.

The same can be said for the covenant blessing of *protection*. Just as the ancient Israelites relied upon their national covenant with the Lord to prevent enemies (like the Philistines) from threatening their national laws and institutions of freedom, the American Covenant-makers in modern times have done likewise. Even in its days of youth and inexperience, the fledgling American nation found victory (often times in miraculous ways) against mightier foes because God fought its battles, per the promises of the covenant. History is clear that it was America's reliance on God and the American Covenant—a reliance reflected in national prayers, national religious acts, and other national efforts at worthiness —that enabled her to defeat the British threat to the New World in the eighteenth century, the Confederate/human slavery threat to the new nation in the nineteenth century, the fascist and communist threat to the world in the twentieth century, and the terrorist threat to mankind in the twenty-first century. Notably, all of these foes of America, like those foes of the Israelites, were and are led by God's adversary. Their intention was oppression and exploitation. They thus presented (and continue to present) a grave threat to liberty and, by extension, to man's opportunity for spiritual growth. In both the ancient and modern cases, the national covenant invites God to wield the sword of truth and justice. And thus we see the American Covenant blessing of *protection* fulfilled.

As far as the national covenant's promise of *prosperity* is concerned, the same applies. The Lord has proven that He does offer national wealth as part of His national covenants, as far as it serves His ultimate designs. Just as the Lord blessed the Israelites with temporal sustenance and a land filled with natural resources, so He did with the United States of America. The wealth provided to the nation (in the aggregate, as these are *national* blessings, not *individual* blessings, per se) positively affects God's plan in multiple ways. We will outline some of these ways below. As we do so, we would do well to remember that this particular blessing must be received with warning, for it can lead to pride and destruction (as the chronology of Israel and its leaders teaches). Also, as we recognize how national wealth can be imperative to God's plan, we might also consider that one of the tactics of the adversary's assault on God's people is to impoverish them. An oppressive financial burden might inhibit their ability to worship God and might prohibit the spreading of the gospel.

First, private wealth in the United States generates significant government revenues, which in turn pay for the many institutions—including military, law enforcement, and diplomatic entities—necessary to protect God's children both at home and abroad from the constant threats to their freedom. We see how this covenant blessing works in conjunction with the covenant blessing of *protection*.

Second, wealth in America frees up time for good men and women to work on projects that keep our nation strong, virtuous, and free under God. For example, if the Founding Fathers had to scavenge for food, who would have written the Declaration of Independence or the Constitution? The positive impact of those documents on the world has been incalculable.

Third, American wealth has encouraged the invention, development, and/or the massive distribution of priceless technologies. Consider the wonders of radio, television, air transportation, and the Internet—to name a few. Consider how much faster and stronger Christ's church and message have spread across the world because of such technologies.

And fourth, the wealth generated in America directly and positively affects contributions to churches and synagogues across the nation, which affects the ability of the citizenry to remain true to their individual covenants. (It is worth noting here that the paying of tithes was commanded by God, even unto the ancient Israelites, as recorded in Deuteronomy 14:22 and Malachi 3:8-10.) This is without mentioning the proportion of emergency, welfare, and missionary funds America distributes across the globe, as compared to other nations. And so, the general blessed state of the U.S. economy, provided under the American Covenant, thus forwards God's work in significant ways. It is, after all, financial success that contributes to the spreading of constitutional and Judeo-Christian principles throughout the world.

These American Covenant blessings of *liberty, protection,* and *prosperity* benefit us as a nation, as families, and as individuals in ways too numerous to list, thus making America the hope and example of all nations. But of all the benefits we as Americans receive as heirs of the national covenant, the most important and eternally significant benefit is the ability and privilege given to us to utilize these blessings of the covenant in supporting and enhancing God's gift of liberty. And thus we assist the Lord in furthering His work and glory on earth.

Obligations of the American Covenant

And so, the question that remains is as follows: What are we, as a nation, required to do under this covenant to retain its lofty blessings?

The first national obligation is to keep the commandments. As the nation is comprised of many theologies and many religious institutions, there must be a common set of obligations. We might look back to the various obligations of previous national covenants for clues to what ours may be. The people of the American Covenant can certainly be expected to at least live the basic tenants of the Ten Commandments, to include recognizing and worshiping God, avoiding idolatry, honoring parents, not killing, not committing adultery, not stealing, not lying, etc. Religions the world over may disagree on doctrine, but almost all of them maintain the basic moral codes of these basic commandments. Such codes are so basic that they even provide the foundation for most laws that govern most lands. In a symbolic gesture of this fact, there are several engravings of Moses and the Ten Commandments throughout the U.S. Supreme Court building.[1] They represent a minimum standard which does not require membership in, or endorsement of, any particular religion. Though nobody should ever have morality forced upon them (lest God's law of liberty be violated) there is no excuse for the violation of these basic commandments. The

Lord has, after all, made His position on this matter clear within the context of the national covenant. He made it clear with the recipients of ancient Israel's national covenant: for "righteousness exalteth a nation: but sin is a reproach to any people" (Proverbs 14:34).

Moses with the Ten Commandments, by Rembrandt, 1659

The people of the national covenant must indeed be obedient to the commandments given by the God of the covenant in order to continue to receive the promised blessings and to carry out the divine mandate. It should be enough to accept this principle without question, based alone on the Scriptures. But there are actually very practical and comprehensible applications of this principle in terms of the covenant. For example, if the people are not willing to adhere to a certain basic moral behavior and to certain basic commandments, how can the Lord trust that this people will be willing to do anything in forwarding His work under the covenant? The commandments, and the people's reaction to them, thus become a preliminary indicator for the Lord to determine if the nation is willing and ready—to determine if the covenant blessings and purposes will be placed into the people's hands.

Furthermore, the work under the covenant may require that certain actions be performed by the nation in furtherance of God's cause. (We will see examples of these specific required national actions in the chapters that follow.) But in order for this to occur, the people must be privy to God's inspiration so as to receive and carry out His divine instruction. And in order for the people to be worthy of this inspiration, they must be obedient to His commandments. God needs a people who can receive and comprehend His designs, which underlines the necessity for the covenant people to obey the commandments and thereby be privy to that inspiration. And so again, per the covenant, if America is not willing to obey the commandments, God has neither reason nor obligation to bestow the covenant blessings.

The importance of the people's general obedience under the covenant especially applies to a republic, like the United States. Under a republic, the policymakers and administrators, who possess the power of government to be a force for good, are directed and influenced by the people. As such, the *people* hold the power and influence, and *their* worthiness and light—or conversely, *their* wickedness and darkness—flows upwards to those in power. Therefore, when the people in aggregate are living the commandments, God can direct the leaders and thereby have confidence that His designs for the nation will be accomplished.

The need for the covenant nation to obey the commandments, then, is paramount. And American history proves it. As we will see, only general righteousness brought the covenant blessings and fulfilled the covenant purposes.

The second obligation we have as a nation under this covenant is to serve God. There is a noteworthy aspect of this particular obligation. As we serve the God of the land by preserving and promoting the inspired institutions that promote liberty and personal agency, blessings will flow from God in more than one way. First, as we act to fulfill this national duty, God recognizes our efforts in obedience and thus blesses us with the covenant blessings—blessings that often come about through miraculous measures.

And second, the very act of seeking and applying those covenant blessings that support liberty is in some ways a self-fulfilling blessing. In other words, the very thing God requires us to do, if we do it, will *naturally* provide the covenant blessings that support freedom. As we, for example, work to elect leaders that respect the First Amendment, we can expect that, as a natural consequence, our First Amendment rights—which include the covenant blessings of *liberty*—will be preserved. The Lord is obviously deliberate and purpose-driven when deciding which obligations will fulfill His covenants. Though God will allow us to sacrifice greatly in our efforts to comply with the national covenant obligations, this is not to say we are ever alone in fulfilling them. For with the adversary ever on the attack, our efforts alone to secure the covenant blessings will never be enough (much like our efforts to secure individual salvation). But as long as we are striving toward this goal, the Lord will back our efforts and always provide the full measure of the promised blessings after we have done all we can do. When it comes to His covenants, there is certainly truth to the adage, *"God helps those who help themselves."*

And finally, by applying the first national obligation—to keep the commandments—the nation will more easily fulfill the second. For, an obedient nation is sufficiently sanctified, and will, therefore, have the light, knowledge, and divine assistance it needs to appropriately "serve" God.

As we manifest our commitment to keeping God's commandments and serving Him, He will more easily lead our efforts. Only then will the world have the assurance that the vision set forth by our founding documents will continue to be realized. Only then will the world know that the nation will continue producing leaders that understand America's divine role and will carry out this vision—leaders like George Washington, who recognized that America, under the "smiles of Heaven," had created a "sacred fire of liberty."[2] Or leaders like Abraham Lincoln, who understood that it was America's divine calling to establish, "under God...a new birth of freedom."[3] Or John F. Kennedy, who declared to the world, and issued caution to the tyrant, that "the rights of man come...from the hand of God," and that America "will pay any price [and] bear any burden...for the success of liberty."[4] Or leaders like Ronald Reagan, who declared that "America as a place in the divine scheme of things...was set apart as a promised land" intended for "people who had a special love of freedom," and that "we were preordained to carry [this] torch of freedom to the world."[5]

As the nation commits to keeping His commandments and serving Him, it must be ever mindful of a general requirement underlying both these obligations, and that is to publicly and regularly invoke God and the covenant. Specifically, the United States government must do what it has done since its founding, by officially issuing, in the name of the people, public recognitions, proclamations, acts, and prayers— all unto God. Examples of these include the Pledge of Allegiance taken "under God," national days of prayer, the issuance of the national motto: "In God We Trust," and other like-minded actions. These national actions represent tokens and symbols of the American Covenant. Their overall effect is to encourage—though never compel—the people to keep the commandments and serve God. In other words, they remind and influence the people to turn to the Lord and fulfill the obligations of the American Covenant, making them worthy to receive the covenant blessings and worthy to participate in God's work. Furthermore, these national invocations in and of themselves represent a powerful offering to God, which will result in added blessings from Him. Altogether then, these national actions performed for God bring an added measure of the covenant blessings, and thus propel God's work to higher places. Such has been the covenant pattern throughout American history.

The modern-day critic will, of course, balk at the suggestion that government involve itself in such spiritual encouragement, interpreting the great American principle of "separation of church and state" as being in conflict with such ideals. However, the ultimate conclusion of this study fully supports, and even promotes, the principle of "separation of church and state." For this constitutional principle protects our liberty unto spiritual growth from the threat of a meddling and potentially tyrannical government. Indeed, it prevents the government from favoring, rejecting, or in any way influencing any particular religious denomination. It keeps the government's hand out of our personal religious preferences, allowing God—not imperfect men—to influence the personal religious upbringing of His children.

What the critic does not understand (and what this book will hereafter show) is that there is a *great* difference between "separation of church and state" and "separation of God and state." The former allows us to pursue our personal religious goals unmolested unto progression, while the later does the exact opposite. For, the latter leaves us without a source of protection, without a guardian and deliverer of our longed-for and indispensable liberties. More than anybody, it is God who desires all to be free to choose any religion or no religion. So why would we not want Him involved in our affairs? Why would we, as a nation, not invoke His name and covenant as much as possible? As ancient Israel painfully learned, the only way to guarantee the blessings of the national covenant—even the cherished gift of freedom—is to invite God in and allow Him room to wield the sword of truth and justice. To put it simply and concisely (but in a phrase that for the secularist is too ironic to grasp), *we are indeed for "separation of church and state"—under God.* The Founding Fathers understood this, as their history clearly reveals. But somewhere along the line, many Americans have forgotten it.

Let us, therefore, redouble our efforts to live the covenant obligations. For, as we succeed in so doing, the national blessings of *liberty, protection,* and *prosperity* will flow in greater measure. If we fail, however, we will suffer the tragic loss of these great American blessings under our great American Covenant. After all, if we don't prove ourselves worthy of these blessings and/or if we refuse to use these blessings for the purposes they were given, why would God continue to give them at all? Such a warning is especially powerful when pondering the fate of earlier nations, such as ancient Israel, who possessed the national covenant, but who at times failed to adhere to the prophetic warnings concerning it, and were thus at times "forsaken" and swept off the land (Jeremiah 4:29). The United States of America is certainly no more indispensable to God's plan than was ancient Israel. It follows, then, that even though the Lord is utilizing the United States in these days for His purposes, if we as Americans fail Him we will lose our place in His plan, as He turns to another source to carry out His purposes. But what a tragedy it would be for this nation and its citizenry to squander this divine privilege, blessing, and responsibility!

Carefully etched into the Great Seal of the United States of America, front and center, just above the eagle's head, there is what appears to be a clear and distinct Star of David—a sure sign of Israel. Just as this sign is hiding in plain-sight within our own principal symbol, so is the rich history of America's connection with Israel also hiding in plain-sight—but longing to be heard. Good Americans have long *felt* this connection more than they could fully articulate it. *Why,* they ask, *do I love and support the nation-state of Israel? Why do I care so much?* The answer: *Because you are connected by blood and covenant.* Indeed it is nothing if not scriptural and divinely ordained that

America has allied itself with the modern nation-state of Israel. Speaking about a time beyond what the Bible records—*after* Joseph/Ephraim had walked out of the biblical text—Isaiah prophesied: "And he shall set up an ensign for the nations, and shall assemble the outcasts of Israel, and gather together the dispersed of Judah...The envy also of Ephraim shall depart, and the adversaries of Judah shall be cut off: Ephraim shall not envy Judah, and Judah shall not vex Ephraim (Isaiah 11:13)." And here we are today—in the midst of this prophecy.

The Great Seal

But what will we do now? Will we live the covenant as Americans? Will we live in a way that allows God to bless us and the world with the covenant promises? It is the purpose of this book to encourage such righteousness in our nation—to encourage a national life worthy of the covenant. This encouragement will come most profoundly as we learn of our Founding Fathers and as we internalize their deep knowledge and conviction of the covenant.

We have thus far reviewed an interesting account with intricate connections to heaven and history. Admittedly, the skeptic may still justifiably conclude that the arguments made in these first chapters are a matter of theory and conjecture. As such, in the chapters that follow, we will dive into the historical account of our Founders. In doing so, we will expand the examination, develop the doctrine, corroborate the concept, and perhaps even satisfy the skeptic. And through it all, we will detail one of the greatest historical sagas ever told of God and country.

ENDNOTES

[1] Newt Gingrich, *Rediscovering God in America* (Nashville: Integrity House, 2006), 87.

[2] From George Washington's First Inaugural Address, April 30, 1789, available at www.nationalcenter.org/washigtonfirstinaugual.

[3] Lincoln, as quoted in William J. Bennett, *America, the Last Great Hope, Volume II, From a World at War to the Triumph of Freedom* (Nashville, Thomas Nelson, 2007), 368.

[4] From John F. Kennedy's Inaugural Address, January 20, 1961, Washington D.C., available at www.jfklibrary.org.

[5] Ronald Reagan, as quoted in Paul Kengor, *God and Ronald Reagan* (New York: Regan Books, 2004), 95.

PART II

Living the American Covenant

Chapter 4

Divine Discovery

Our Lord unlocked my mind, sent me upon the sea, and gave me fire for the deed. Those who heard of my enterprise called it foolish, mocked me, and laughed. But who can doubt but that the Holy Ghost inspired me.

—Christopher Columbus

Tragedy struck God's earth that dreadful day that Christ's chief apostle Peter, even he who was given the "keys of the Kingdom" (Matthew 16:19), was nailed upside down on a cross, murdered in cold blood. According to tradition, this occurred during the Roman persecutions under Nero, around 65 AD, and it marked the beginning of severe Christian struggles against dark and evil forces. This event highlighted the wicked darkness in the world that sought to snuff out Christianity—a darkness that had steadily grown since the fateful day when the Messiah was rejected, scorned, and murdered by His own.

But the adversary did not only attack the church. Evil also attacked a fundamental foundation of (and prerequisite for) the church: man's ability to worship according to the dictates of conscience. The Devil had once again employed his age-old stratagem of striking God's children where he could best hinder spiritual growth—he struck at their liberty. The Devil's success in this wicked endeavor is reflected in the fact that during this rather dark era (what historians have called the Dark Ages) virtually all governments took a page from Satan's war plan and wickedly oppressed, controlled, and/or limited their subjects. Thus, they often kept the people from God and truth. Satan's influence over governments and men had caused such a withdrawal of light and inspiration that he not only drove out much of the church, but also drove out the possibility for God to establish a national covenant among His children. The adversary certainly knew the power of a national covenant in God's plan, and so he fought to subdue it.

This dark era of world history was by no means Satan's first or last attempt to attack man's liberty, but it was certainly one of his most successful ones. As such, the Lord would not stand idly by. For He had promised that he would restore Israel and her covenant. Naturally, if the Lord was to commence any kind of gospel enlargement, He would first have to restore a fullness of freedom whereupon that gospel might flourish. He would need to counter Satan's attack by establishing a national covenant. This new national covenant would require a new land, far from the poisonous environment of the Old World. This new land was foreordained to be America.

With so much riding on America, its discovery and settlement would be no casual undertaking. As discussed earlier, the Scriptures suggest this discovery and settlement would come about in a divine way. God would raise up a choice people and bring them "over the wall" to America, the land of their inheritance, where, under the American Covenant, *liberty*, *protection*, and *prosperity* would together support and enhance the fullness of freedom necessary for mankind to progress and find access to the saving principles of the gospel. But is there anything in the historical annals of America that support such scriptural claims? Did the discoverers and settlers of this land say or do anything that would corroborate this proposed scriptural and prophetic narrative? The answer to these questions is, most definitely, *yes*! And the next two chapters will prove it. We will see how the historical record is clear that these discoverers and settlers of America truly arrived under God and covenant, settled their land under God and covenant, and strived to live under God and covenant. And this they did that God's work and glory might thrive. Through their words and deeds, we will see that the covenant they were working under was, indeed, this ancient national covenant—The American Covenant.

The Raw Land

Being that America is a choice land, it is very fitting that even a cursory review of its raw, physical state—even the land itself before any modern-day heirs would arrive and develop it—demonstrates its inspired and preordained place under the covenant. For example, the happy void of any obvious or credible oppressive force already on the American continent would enable God to influence and manipulate righteous political systems for His purposes, thus encouraging the reign of *liberty*. Furthermore, its abundant natural resources (from precious metals, to fertile ground, to rivers, to harbors, etc.) would allow for *prosperity* to flourish among its future inhabitants. And finally, its deep physical isolation, created by super-sized oceans on either side, would provide built-in *protection* against foreign evil-doers. In short—and not coincidently—the raw land itself would offer the beginnings of the three gospel-necessary blessings of the American Covenant: *liberty, prosperity,* and *protection*. This special land had certainly been set aside and reserved for a special purpose.

The Renaissance

We scripturally established in the previous chapter how the Lord would bring to pass the discovery and settlement of the land America. After having selected and led His chosen ones to European lands, He would then lead them, in His due time, to the New World. But before they could attain the New World, two questions would need answering. First, how would the chosen discoverers journey the great distance from apostate Europe to the Promised Land? And second, how would the Lord identify and prepare these chosen, would-be American settlers and covenant-makers from among the European masses? God would provide answers and solutions to these questions and concerns through the inspired era of the European Renaissance.

It was during the fourteenth and fifteenth centuries that the dark clouds of oppression and stagnation began to part ever so slightly. The Lord began to open the heavens just enough to inspire a flourishing in the arts, sciences, and literature. Beautiful cathedrals were built, world famous artwork was created, advancements in medicine came forth, and printing by movable type was developed. People began to see outside the oppressive box that was the Dark Ages. It was a time of rebirth known today as the Renaissance. Among the many enlightened happenings of the time, certain developments stand in the forefront as accomplishing the purposes of God.

One such development was the discovery of the compass. Though actually invented by the Chinese in around 1000 AD, it was rediscovered and further developed by the Europeans during the Renaissance period. Its usage launched both maritime trade and exploration to unprecedented levels.[1] The horizon began to extend a little further and the New World approached the brink of discovery.

While the compass would serve as a tool of deliverance to the New World, God would still need a way to develop a chosen people who would serve as the "delivered." He, in large part, fulfilled this requirement through the inspired invention of the Gutenberg printing press in 1455. With the new and massive availability of literature, thanks to this brilliant development of the Renaissance, millions began to read the Bible and ask questions for the first time.* They began to seek out personal witnesses of God and establish relationships with Him. This led them to the realization of the true spiritual state of the world—that obstructions to God's Gospel had, in fact, been put in place. As these enlightened ones grew in both numbers and in their spiritual understanding, it would only be a matter of time before God had enough of He needed to begin the discovery and settlement of His new land and covenant.

Incidentally, as this spiritual growth of the would-be American Covenant-makers was born from the fruit of the Gutenberg press, it becomes more significant that out of more than 130,000,000 items in the U.S. Library of Congress' collection, one of the only two items on permanent display in the Library's Great Hall is a Gutenberg Bible (the other item is also a Bible).[2]

One person in particular who was inspired by the proliferation of the Bible, and who in turn inspired the would-be American-covenant-makers, was a German monk named Martin Luther. Luther longed for a purer Christianity, and so on October 31, 1517 he nailed to the door of the Wittenberg Church his Ninety-five Theses, which exposed and challenged certain false principles espoused by the dominating religious forces of the day. The religious movement known as the Reformation had been born, as had a hero in the eyes of Christian disciples.[3]

---

* In the 1430's Johann Gansfleisch zum Gutenberg developed a technique for mechanical printing. His invention arrived in a world starving for mental stimulation. Within fifty years of his first press, over twelve million books had been printed in over one thousand shops. See Warren Chappell, *A Short History of the Printed Word* (New York: Alfred A. Knopf, 1970), 84.

But Luther was not alone in his mission, as others would also help truth seekers discover some light in the darkness. This they did at great risk, knowing their actions would upset the authoritarian and oppressive religious order of the day. There was, for example, John Wycliffe, who produced the first English translation of the Bible in 1455, which ultimately inspired Luther's progression.[4] Another was the martyr William Tyndale, whose own translation of the Bible in 1526 had a direct influence

Martin Luther

both on the King James Version of the Bible and, sadly, on his

William Tyndale

own state-sponsored execution order for heresy in 1536. (The masses were, tragically, prohibited by the authorities from having the audacity to seek direct access to the Bible. Tyndale paid for this oppressive policy with his life.) Before his life was taken, Tyndale publicly justified his translation to his critics saying, "I will cause a boy that driveth the plough shall know more of the scripture than thou dost."[5] The list of persecuted reformers would continue on from John Zwingli, who convinced Zurich, Switzerland, that the Bible, not creeds and ceremony, was the only true religious standard, to John Calvin, who did the same in Geneva. And then there was John Knox, who helped spread these inspired ideas to the rest of Europe.

We should thank our Heavenly Father for the mass printing of the Bible and for the reformers who encouraged its distribution. The fruits of these efforts inspired a reformed religious thought which, consequently, produced purer generations of Christians—even hundreds upon thousands of open-minded, God-fearing men and women, brave enough to ask questions and seek truth. It was, after all, from among these truth-seekers, inspired by the newly available Bible, that God would choose the first American Covenant-makers, leading them to the New World for the purposes of Heaven: to establish a new people who would bring back old and true elements of Christ's Gospel.

Christopher Columbus

With the developments and progress surrounding both compass and printing press in Renaissance Europe, the Lord

had set the stage for a major movement toward the discovery and settlement of the Promised Land.

Armed with the necessary tools and spirituality provided to him through the inspired era of the Renaissance, the chosen Columbus was prepared to be the instrument in God's hand who would find that New World which had been

Christopher Columbus

divinely set apart for God's chosen people. And he was prepared to be the servant who would make known this discovery to Europe, even that land containing the remnants of scattered Israel. With the news of this great discovery, these modern-day Israelites could then follow God's promptings and settle America, claim their blessings of the promised American Covenant, and thus serve God in enlarging Christianity. Of such was the significance of Columbus and his discovery.

The following historical analysis of Columbus' life and writings serve as proof of his profoundly divine role in God's plan. We will see that Columbus, in his capacity as American Covenant-maker, did knowingly covenant with God in discovering the Promised Land. Furthermore, he even seemed to be blessed with an understanding of what great spiritual blessings his discovery would bring to the world.

101

★ ★ ★ ★

Born near Genoa, Italy, in the midst of the Renaissance, Columbus, from his earliest days, seemed connected with God and recognized heaven's influence in his life. Columbus wrote:

> When I was a young boy, I went to sea to sail and I continue to do it today....I have found our Lord very well disposed towards my desire, and I have from him the spirit of intelligence for carrying it out. He has bestowed the marine arts upon me in abundance and that which is necessary to me from astrology, geometry, and drawing spheres and situating upon them the towns, the rivers, mountains, islands and ports, each in its proper place.[6]

Columbus eventually married the daughter of the governor of a small Portuguese island in the western-most parts of the known Atlantic. Columbus and his wife moved to this island where Columbus became acquainted with maps and map-making. These maps excited him into a divine conviction of the existence of an untapped western route to the Indies.[7] He would solicit support from various governments for his proposed exploration of this possible route (ultimately convincing Spain to finance the enterprise), by emphasizing the economic benefits of more rapid and efficient trade, particularly the spice trade with the Indies. However, as the following historical references suggest, Columbus knew his desired mission meant more than this; he knew God had a wiser and more profound purpose for his western exploration.

This more profound purpose was perhaps revealed to Columbus through his consistent study of the Bible, which was made available to him through the above-referenced developments of the inspired Renaissance. According to one renowned Columbus scholar, he "was a careful student of the Bible."

> He studied it systematically together with the opinions of learned scholars and commentators who

were held in the highest regard in his day. The focus of the discoverer's interest was the prophesied latter-day enlargement of the Christian Church which would take place through the discovery and evangelization of all the world's nations and tribes, with the consequent renewal and enrichment of Christendom.[8]

Columbus perhaps sensed the advent of this renewal. And he would stop at nothing to facilitate its coming.

But his vision ran deeper than his desire and intention to simply enlarge and enrich Christendom. As one scholar pointed out, "[Columbus] wished to discover the Indies to get enough money to rebuild the temple [at Jerusalem]," so that God's people might "go back to the temple to the Holy of Holies."[9] In her 2006 article, "Columbus's Goal: Jerusalem," Stanford scholar Carol Delaney laments the fact that, even today, too many intellectuals—blinded by preconceived notions—fail to see that "[Columbus'] ultimate goal, the purpose behind the enterprise, was Jerusalem!" She concludes that Columbus firmly believed that "what he accomplished was not so much a 'discovery' but a revelation—an important step in uncovering God's plan."[10] Delaney's colleague, Leonard Sweet, adds that Columbus' voyage was not a commercial venture as much as it was a "spiritual quest" and a "medium of redemption."[11]

The evidence of Columbus' inspired vision is clear and convincing. As he stated in his personal diary (from his initial 1492 voyage), he planned to take any monetary gain from his discovery and direct it to the "Holy Sepulchre."[12] Some ten years later, his life still dedicated to the development and further exploration of the New World, he maintained this vision. Columbus declared, "This enterprise was undertaken with the purpose of expending what was invested in aiding the holy temple and the holy Church."[13] Furthermore, Columbus firmly believed, and testified, that Spain's financing of his voyage was a fulfillment of a certain prophecy. According to the Abbot Joachin, "Jerusalem and Mount Zion [were] to be rebuilt by the hand of a Christian" from Spain. Columbus recited this prophecy and declared that he was that very Christian.[14] At one point during his voyage, one of his ships ran into serious trouble. And the record implies that, in that moment of doubt, the only thing that really concerned Columbus was whether his possible failure might hurt his ability to help rebuild Jerusalem and her temple.[15] Up until the day before his death, Columbus was still working on setting up a fund for the purpose of liberating and rebuilding Jerusalem.[16]

Columbus' vision of a rebuilt Jerusalem is one of many indicators that he held a special place in his heart for the Jewish people. In light of the generally negative feelings towards Jews in Columbus' day, particularly in Spain, Columbus' feelings of attachment to them is remarkable. He often spoke of his admiration for the Hebrew nation and his desire to be one with them. Perhaps this had to do with Columbus' inspired notion (if only a feeling) about who he really was. Columbus' son wrote about his father, stating, "[His] progenitors were of the Royal Blood of Jerusalem."[17] Historians are divided over Columbus' genetic connection to Israel and the Jews. But it is believed that the Columbus family (*Colon family* in Spanish) belonged to the Colons of Catalonia, who were part of the old Catalan-Aragonese confederation. It is well established that the Colons owned much property in Barcelona's *Call Judio*—English translation: *The Jewish Quarter*.[18] Perhaps this connection partly explains his affinity for the Hebrew nation.

Born in Western Europe, could Columbus have been a descendent of the Lost Tribes? Might he have felt the promptings leading him "over the wall" of water to the promised land he and his people were to inherit? Might his deep study of the Scriptures be responsible for this knowledge? It is possible that Columbus understood the deeper meaning of the ancient prophecy, directed at post-biblical Israel: "And he shall set up an ensign for the nations, and shall assemble the outcasts of Israel, and gather together the dispersed of Judah...The envy also of Ephraim shall depart, and the adversaries of Judah shall be cut off: Ephraim shall not envy Judah, and Judah shall not vex Ephraim (Isaiah 11:13)." Was Columbus' deep affection for Judah a partial fulfillment of this prophecy? Did he perhaps understand that he was connected to them through blood and covenant?

How else might we explain how Columbus believed his westward journey would somehow restore the Jewish nation and its temple? Furthermore, how else might we explain how Columbus' discovery *did in fact* accomplish just that? For his discovery led Ephraim to America, where a nation dedicated to the God of Jacob was established. That very nation would later be first in line to support and uphold the nation-state of Israel once God brought His chosen Judah home and helped them establish their Zion/Israel in 1948. Indeed, Columbus began a chain of events that resulted in the fulfillment of his own profound desire and prophecy.

Is all this just one huge coincidence? Furthermore, is it just a coincidence that in the very *month* Columbus received orders to sail out for his pending discovery, the Jews were exiled from Spain? Columbus, quite presciently, felt inclined to include the following in his personal journal: "In the same month in which their Majesties issued the edict that all Jews should be driven out of the kingdom and its territories, they gave me the order to undertake with sufficient men my expedition of discovery to the Indies."[19] The Devil pulled in one direction. God immediately pulled back in the other; and He did so in the person of Christopher Columbus. *Columbus knew it.*

★ ★ ★ ★

With knowledge of Columbus' deep conviction of gospel principles, and with an understanding of his belief that these principles were related to his western exploration, we are now prepared to understand the richness of his story. We are now prepared to comprehend profound aspects of his western exploration that would otherwise fall through the cracks of secularized history.

And so, as the story goes, Columbus secured three ships for his journey, the *Nina*, *Pinta*, and *Santa Maria*, all of which embarked on August 2, 1492. As could be expected, considering the nature of this particular voyage, the crew was apprehensive and restless from the beginning. As the weeks passed without success, and with rations diminished to threatening levels, murmurings of mutiny began resounding through the decks of the ships. Eventually the captains of the other vessels informed Columbus that the men could no longer be restrained. Columbus asked for three days. Though there is no record of what Columbus did next, one might assume he dedicated himself to much prayer. There is at least one indication that perhaps some spiritual confirmation was received. For on the night he spoke to his captains, Columbus wrote in his journal that the root meaning of his own name was *Christo-feren*, or "Christ-bearer."[20] The discoverer was so overcome by this self-recognition, that he even changed his official signature to represent this new title.[21]

Before the three days had expired, signs of land appeared, and on October 12, 1492, the ships landed on the shore of a Caribbean island. With Natives watching in awe, Columbus disembarked triumphantly, then, with tears streaming down his face, gave thanks to the Almighty, in Whose honor he named the land San Salvador ("Holy Savior").[22]

Landing of Columbus, by John Vanderlyn. Courtesy of the Architect of the Capitol.

That Columbus would praise God for this discovery was only natural; for he knew it was the power of God that made his discovery possible. He was not shy about expressing this fact. For example, on a particularly difficult occasion during one of his New World explorations, Columbus received a revelation, which he himself later described in the following words:

> Exhausted, I fell asleep, groaning. I heard a very compassionate voice, saying: "O fool and slow to believe and to serve thy God, the God of all!...Thou criest for help, doubting. Answer, who has afflicted thee so greatly and so often, God or the world?...Not one jot of His word fails; all that He promises, He performs with interest; is this the manner of men? I have said that which thy creator has done for thee and does for all men. Now in part He shows thee the reward for the anguish and danger which thou hast endured in the service of others." I heard all of this as if I were in a trance, but I had no answer to give to words so true, but could only weep for my errors. He, whoever he was, who spoke to me, ended saying: "Fear not; have trust; all these tribulations are written upon marble and are not without cause."[23]

Further proof of Columbus' understanding of the covenant nature of his journey is represented in the events surrounding his return voyage to Spain. Knowing that the news of the great discovery would begin a chain of events leading to a renewal of Christianity, the adversary seemed intent on doing all possible to deny Columbus' return. The storms against them raged so violently that the crew believed they would not make it. The adversary certainly knew that if Columbus and his crew were to perish, news of the discovery would perish with them.

Columbus responded by leading his crew in much prayer. This, of course, was not unusual for Columbus. He was known for holding regular church services on deck.[24] However, this particular set of prayers was perhaps more pronounced than the others. As days passed with no reprieve from the storm, the crew decided to make an offering to God. They promised that if their lives were spared, they would make a pilgrimage to a chapel back home and hold a special meeting and worship service. Lots were drawn on at least three occasions in the midst of the storm to determine who would lead the pilgrimage. All three times it fell on Columbus himself. The crew believed it a sign from God (the odds against Columbus picking the winner all three times were 60,880 to 1). When the ship finally arrived off the shores of Portugal, with hardly a single sail having remained intact, the crew knew who it was that had brought them safely to harbor. The covenant blessing of *protection* was already in force.[25]

But perhaps the greatest proof of Columbus' knowledge of God's hand in these historic events is found in his personal witness, as written by his own hand: "Our Lord unlocked my mind, sent me upon the sea, and gave me fire for the deed. Those who heard of my enterprise called it foolish, mocked me, and laughed. But who can doubt but that the Holy Ghost inspired me?"[26]

In a similar spirit, Columbus wrote the following to the king and queen of Spain concerning his discovery of America. The following is recorded in a little-known collection of Columbus' writings, known as his *Libro de las profecias*, or his *Book of Prophecies*:

> With a hand that could be felt, the Lord opened my mind to the fact that it would be possible to sail from here to the Indies, and He opened my will to desire to accomplish the project. This was the fire that burned within me when I came to visit Your Highnesses. All who found out about my project denounced it with laughter and ridiculed me....Only Your Majesties had faith and perseverance. Who can doubt that this fire was not merely mine, but also of the Holy Spirit who encouraged me with a radiance of marvelous illumination from his sacred Holy

Scriptures, by a most clear and powerful testimony from the forty-four books of the Old Testament, from the four Gospels, from the twenty-three Epistles of the blessed Apostles—urging me to press forward? Continually, without a moment's hesitation, The Scriptures urge me to press forward with great haste.

I spent six years here at your royal court, disputing the case with so many people of great authority, learned in all the arts. Finally they concluded that it was in vain, and they lost interest. In spite of that, [the voyage West] later came to pass as Jesus Christ our Savior had predicted and as He had previously announced through the mouths of His holy prophets.[27]

It is astonishing that Columbus proposed, in this letter, that biblical passages reflected the sacred work God had accomplished through him. In support of his claim that the Lord "predicted" his discovery through His prophets, Columbus included within his *Book of Prophecies* a number of biblical references. Among these references are certain noteworthy prophecies: Isaiah 14:1-2, Isaiah 66:19 and John 10:16.[28]

Isaiah 14:1-2 reads: "For the Lord will have mercy on Jacob, and will yet choose Israel, and set them in their own land: and the strangers shall be joined with them, and they shall cleave to the house of Jacob. And the people shall take them…and the house of Israel shall possess them in the land of the Lord." This scripture ties into Columbus' discovery in that it appears to make reference to the promises of the American Covenant, as detailed in Chapter 2 of this book. For it references heaven's gift of a new land given to the descendants of Jacob and Israel, which gift would be a blessing also to other groups of God's children who would join Israel.

Isaiah 66:19 similarly prophesies the following: "And I will set a sign among them…to the islands afar off, to them that have not heard my fame, neither have seen my glory; and they shall declare my glory among the Gentiles."

John 10:16 reads: "And other sheep I have, which are not of this fold: them also I must bring, and they shall hear my voice; and there shall be one fold and one shepherd." What connection is to be made between this scripture and Columbus' discovery? Columbus' arrival meant that a renewed advent of Christ to the Native American inhabitants was on the horizon, as his discovery would pave the way for Ephraim to enter the Americas and eventually provide them the principles of Christianity.

Amazingly, Columbus' scriptural references, which he clearly implied were related to his voyage and discovery, have direct connections to America's place in the enlargement and renewal of Christianity. Again, one is compelled to consider how much revealed knowledge Columbus really possessed concerning the significance of what he had accomplished.

In light of the above, it seems likely that, at some point, Columbus truly understood that his discovery of the New World meant a renewed opportunity for the Lord to restore His national covenant and offer the world the blessings of His Gospel. This might explain the following words he wrote to his friend Amerigo Vespucci: "I feel persuaded, by the many and wonderful manifestations of Divine Providence, that I am the chosen instrument of God in bringing to pass a great event— no less than the conversion of millions who are now existing in the darkness..."[29] He would similarly inform the king and queen of Spain that, with his discovery now completed, "[t]he gospel must now be proclaimed to so many lands in such a short time."[30] Perhaps Columbus was familiar with the ancient prophecy for modern-day Israel. Calling to the Lost Tribes, the Lord declared: "I am a father to Israel, and Ephraim is my firstborn. Hear the word of the Lord, O ye nations, and declare it *in the isles* afar off" (Jeremiah 31:9-10).

Columbus was especially desirous and anxious for this spiritual endeavor concerning the New World to develop sooner rather than later. For he voiced his opinion often that the end of times was fast approaching, and that his mission in the New World was key to preparing the way for the Second Coming of Christ.[31]

The very first sentence Columbus placed in his sacred *Book of Prophecies* perhaps sums it up best: "Here begins the book, or handbook, of sources, statements, opinions and prophecies on the subject of the recovery of God's Holy City and Mount Zion, and on the discovery and evangelization of the isles of the Indies and of all other peoples and nations."[32]

In a symbolic gesture of Columbus' divine missionary intentions and profound understanding about his voyages, he insisted on erecting a large cross upon every island he landed upon.[33] Considering what his discovery would eventually mean in a land without knowledge of the Christ, his symbolic gesture was profound.

Columbus heard the call of the covenant and bravely adhered. And the world took one giant step closer to the glorious renewal of Judeo-Christian principles—even principles of salvation. Columbus' dying words were: "In mansus tuas, Domine, commendo spiritum meum" (into thy hands Lord I commend my spirit).[34]

In addition to the historical evidences above, there exists another account, though anecdotal in nature, worth mentioning regarding Columbus' discovery of America and its connection to the expansion of Christianity. In his work entitled *The Life and Voyages of Christopher Columbus*, the renowned American historian and author, Washington Irving, spends much time discussing the spiritual inspiration of Columbus, and how he seemed to be "selected by Heaven as an agent" in carrying out his western explorations.[35] Irving then recounts a report he discovered—while poring over documents in Spain—which describes an event that allegedly occurred during Columbus' exploration of the Caribbean. According to the report, one member of Columbus' crew, an archer, while hunting for wild game on the island known today as Cuba, encountered three strange looking men. These men "were of as fair complexions as Europeans" and were wearing long "white tunics reaching to their knees." The strangers were described as being "so like a friar of the order of St. Mary of Mercy." The three were interacting with a tribe of Natives. Frightened at the scene, the archer ran back to the ship and told his commander what he had witnessed. Columbus then sent at least two separate expeditions to search for the three men, but to no avail.[36]

Irving then apologizes for including the account in his book, as no corroborating evidence existed that such light skinned people wearing such clothing resided in the New World at the time of the discovery and exploration. Though Irving concluded that the story was most likely born of error, he did feel so inclined to include it in his book. Perhaps Irving's find and publication of the archer's story was divinely inspired. If God was working to pave the way for Columbus, it stands to reason that He had divine help. Perhaps angelic personages had been sent to prepare the Natives for the grand discovery?

Another event that seems to be a shadow of angelic assistance is recorded by the historian/settler/missionary, Bartolome De Las Casas, who was a personal friend of Columbus.* During the crucial moments at sea, as described

---

* De Las Casas, also known as "Apostle to the Indies" expressed his belief that the Native Americans were of the Lost Tribes of Israel. One of the first explorers and settlers in the New World, De Las Casas believed he had discovered an ancient dialect being utilized by the Natives. He called it "corrupt Hebrew." His affinity for the Natives moved him to seek for their protection against the brutality forced upon them by European settlers. See Jon Entine, *Abraham's Children*, 144.

above, when Columbus agreed, on threat of mutiny, to find

land within three days or turn around, he would spend time fretting and watching for signs of land late into the night. On the final night, Columbus and one of his crew members spotted a small light due west, shining from the direction they were traveling. According to De Las Casas, Columbus said the light "was like a small wax candle being raised and lowered." Columbus believed it was a

Bartolome De Las Casas   heavenly sign (perhaps someone holding a candle, awaiting them?), and it gave him encouragement to press forward at a more rapid pace. Shortly thereafter, a cliff was spotted in the moonlight; the Americas had been discovered.[37]

N otwithstanding the greatness of Columbus' work under God, there has been a growing sentiment in the world to degrade him and his accomplishments. His detractors regularly offer up two criticisms. First, the allegation that Columbus forced the Natives into an oppressive socio-political state; and second, the allegation that Columbus really did not discover anything, as people were already inhabiting the land upon his arrival.

Admittedly, Columbus did support a policy of forced servitude upon certain segments of the Native American population, and at times even commanded violent death raids upon them. Before the critics condemn him all at once, however, certain contextual explanations should be noted. For one thing, though Columbus came in peace, and initially thought he had secured peace with the Natives, there were many violent Native uprisings against him and his crew, which resulted in bloodshed on both sides.[38] While this does not justify the tragedies that fell upon the Native Americans at the hands of the discoverers, it at least explains the fear and paranoia which led to Columbus' controversial actions. Furthermore, Columbus did, at one point, come to recognize the immoral conditions being forced upon the Natives. He argued that the Natives should be converted to Christ "by love and friendship rather than force."[39] Additionally, in a letter dated from 1496 to the king and queen of Spain, he wrote: "Procure for the Indians, that are coming under our rule, the same protections as those we have been speaking of [in Spain]...I want them to have the same protection like I have as if they were my own flesh."[40] Columbus wrote a similar plea the following year, but his letters did little to alter the terrifying fate that was to fall upon the Natives.

There is no question that Columbus made mistakes in his dealings with the Natives, making him susceptible to a vast array of criticism and scrutiny. But Columbus surely recognized these failings better than any critic and openly confessed, "I am a most unworthy sinner, but I have cried out to the Lord for grace and mercy, and they have covered me completely."[41] Fortunately for us all, perfection is not a requirement to be an instrument in the hands of God.

The second prominent critique of Columbus—that too much credit is given him, as America had already been "discovered" centuries before him—is reflected in cries from around the nation demanding that Columbus be downgraded in our history books and educational curriculum. I remember walking on a college campus one Columbus Day and witnessing a group of students and Native American protestors wearing T-shirts with an image of a Native American (Indian) Chief, complete with headdress, along with the words "Columbus Who?" printed on them. Only without the insight into Columbus and his work, as laid out above, could one choose to behave this way toward Columbus.

Nobody is trying to make the ridiculous argument that Columbus discovered the land first, for Native Americans had indeed already discovered it. Surely, their own ancient histories of discoveries and settlements are important. Furthermore, Columbus was not even the first post-ancient explorer to touch down on the New World.* But these arguments are irrelevant to Columbus' greatness. For in spite of the fact that Columbus was not the first to discover the land (as it *had* indeed already been found many times before), he was the one who, in the last days, did it under the hand of God and through the inspiration of the Spirit. He was also the one who, under this same inspiration, publicized his discovery at the right time and to the right people, thus commencing the great migration of those chosen ones who would come to the New World.

And who were these chosen ones that would settle the New World? They were, for the most part, the European descendants of Joseph, even the Ephraimites, whose responsibility it would be to establish a national covenant in America, and then, building upon this covenant, usher in a renewal and expansion of Christianity. It was to be a covenant land that would bless Judah, help restore ancient Israel, and spread God's truth and salvation. This is what Columbus set out to do. This is what Columbus ultimately ended up doing. Perhaps the simple beauty of his accomplishment has become so obvious to some that it is taken for granted, forgotten, or even scoffed at. Though modern-day critics may never fully comprehend what his discovery really meant to the world, Christians should suggest that Columbus be celebrated and honored as an inspired man and a key American Covenant-maker.

---

* It is recorded that hundreds of years before Columbus discovered America, explorers from Scandinavia and other parts of the world visited its shores, but they did not publicize their voyage as inspired of God and did not share their discovery in a way to inspire any mass migration. See Greene, *The Tribe of Ephraim*, 127-128.

Amerigo Vespucci

Columbus was not alone in his role as inspired explorer. One who would share his spotlight was the Italian explorer, Amerigo Vespucci. Vespucci was born in Florence, Italy, in 1454 to a prominent and respected family. His early education converted him into one of the rare scholars of his day, particularly in math and science. Weightier, perhaps, was his religious upbringing, which instilled in him, according to one historian, a "profound sense of dependence upon the protection of God."[42]

By 1492, when Columbus made his discovery, Vespucci was residing in Spain attending to family business. He became so enthusiastic about the discovery that he developed a long lasting friendship with

Amerigo Vespucci

Columbus. While he revered what Columbus had done, he was not shy about respectfully disagreeing with Columbus on one point: Vespucci believed that the new land was not an extension of the Eastern continents, as Columbus taught, but that it was an independent continent. He wanted to prove it and told Columbus: "I am strongly moved to tempt the ocean myself."[43]

By 1497, Vespucci had convinced the king of Spain to sponsor his voyage in order to "assist in the discovery." Shortly thereafter, Vespucci landed on the American mainland. With his skills using the astrolobe and quadrant, Vespucci was able to confirm that this land was in fact a completely separate continent, even a "New World."[44]

But what real significance does such a discovery bear on the development of the American Covenant? America and her covenant were developed out of a sense of new hope, new life, and an independent culture, completely cut off from the Old World. Without Vespucci's find, those chosen Ephraimites might not have viewed their new land in such a light, and might not have ventured out on their many journeys in the first place. They might not have known or felt that America was in fact a "new world," even a land far from the reach of oppressive rulers, where new ideas could be explored and any question could be asked. And so we should thank Vespucci for his courageous discovery.

Vespucci, like Columbus, indicated an understanding of covenant principles with God and strived to adhere to what he considered his calling. In a letter to a friend, Vespucci explained the dangerous, even life-threatening, storms that had plagued his small fleet throughout its initial voyage. He then stated that "during these tempests of sea and sky, so numerous and violent, the Most High was pleased to display before us a continent, new lands, and an unknown world....To Him be honor, glory, and thanksgiving."[45]

After his return home, the king appointed Vespucci to train every Spanish naval captain. By carrying out this particular mandate, Vespucci did much for the then future exploration and settlement of the newly discovered continent. It was during this time that the "New World," as Vespucci regularly described it, would begin to take on his first name, as scholars began referring to it as the "Land of Amerigo" (or Land of Americus). The name stuck and later evolved into *America*.[46]

ENDNOTES

1 "The Compass," available from www.neo-tech.com/businessmen/part5.html.

2 Newt Gingrich, *Rediscovering God in America* (Nashville: Integrity House, 2006), 96-97.

3 See Henry Eyster Jacobs, *Martin Luther: The Hero of the Reformation, 1483-1546* (New York and London: G.P. Putnam's Sons, Knickerbocker Press, 1973).

4 See W.R. Cooper, ed. *The Wycliffe New Testament* (London: The British Library, 2002), v.

5 See John Foxe, *Book of Martyrs*, 1877, as cited in David Daniell, *The Bible in English: It's History and Influence* (New Haven, Conn.: Yale University Press, 2003), 142; Alister McGrath, *In the Beginning: The Story of the King James Bible and How it Changed a Nation, a Language, and a Culture* (New York: Doubleday, 2001), 33.

6 Pauline Moffat Watts, "Prophecy and Discovery: On Spiritual Origins of Christopher Columbus' Enterprise to the Indies," *American Historical Review* (Feb.1985): 95; alternate translation of the same offered by Jacob Wasserman, *Columbus, Don Quixote of the Seas*, translated by Delno C. West, and August Kling (Gainesville, FL: 1991), as quoted in Greene, *The Tribe of Ephraim*, 117.

7 Pauline Moffatt Watts, "Prophecy and Discovery: On Spiritual Origins Christopher Columbus' Enterprise of the Indies," *American Historical Review* (Feb. 1985), 95; Ferdinand Columbus, *The Life of Admiral Christopher Columbus*.

8 Delano West and August Kling, in their introduction to Christopher Columbus, *Libro de las profecias*, trans. Delano C. West and August Kling (Gainesville: University of Florida Press, 1991), 3.

9 Hugh Nibley, *Temple and Cosmos* (Salt Lake City: Deseret Book Company, 1992), 31.

10 Carol Delaney (2006), "Columbus's Ultimate Goal: Jerusalem." *Comparative Studies in Society and History*,48, pp. 261, 287.

11 Leonard Sweet, "Christopher Columbus and the Millennial Vision of the New World, *The Catholic Historical Review* 72, 3 (1986), p.383.

12 Delaney, 261.

13 Delaney, 266.

14 Ferdinand Columbus, *The Life of Admiral Christopher Columbus by His Son Ferdinand Columbus* (New Brunswick: Rutgers University Press, 1959), 8; Chris and Ted Stewart, *Seven Miracles That Saved America*, 43- 44; Delaney, 266.

15 Delaney, 275.

16 Delaney, 266.

[17] David Hatcher Childress, *The Lost Cities of North and Central America* (Kempton: Adventures Unlimited Press, 1998), 414; See also Francesco Tarducci, *The Life of Christopher Columbus*, Volume 12 (H.F. Brownson Publishing, 1891), 2.

[18] Jon Entine, *Abraham's Children: Race, Identity, and the DNA of the Chosen People* (New York: Grand Central Publishing, 2007), 179.

[19] Columbus, as quoted in Entine, 178.

[20] Peter Marshal, *The Light and the Glory* (New Jersey: Fleming H. Revell Co.: 1940), 39.

[21] Delaney, 263.

[22] Columbus (Ferdinand), 59.

[23] Columbus, as quoted in De Lamar Jensen, "Columbus and the Hand of God," *Ensign*, October 1992, 6-13.

[24] Delaney, 262.

[25] These events surrounding Columbus' first return to Europe are more particularly described in Marshall and Manuel, *The Light and the Glory*, 49-53.

[26] Columbus, as quoted in Jacob Wasserman, *Columbus, Don Quixote of the Seas*, translated by Delno C. West, and August Kling (Gainesville, FL: 1991); and as quoted in Greene, *The Tribe of Ephraim*, 117.

[27] Quoted in *Book of Prophecies*, translated by Delno C. West and August Kling (Gainesville: 1991); Also quoted in Greene, *Tribe of Ephraim*, 116-117.

[28] Delaney, 270-2; Pauline Watts, 95-96.

[29] Lester Edwards, *The Life and Voyages of Vespucci* (New York: New Amsterdam Books, 1903), 79.

[30] Christopher Columbus, as quoted in Steven Waldman, *Founding Faith: Providence, Politics and the Birth of Religious Freedom in America* (New York: Random House, 2008), 4.

[31] Delaney, 261, 263, 268-9.

[32] As quoted in Delaney, 268.

[33] Peter Marshal and David Manuel, *The Light and the Glory* (Grand Rapids: Revell, 2009), 45.

[34] Columbus (Ferdinand), 284.

[35] Delaney, 274.

[36] Washington Irving, *The Life and Voyages of Christopher Columbus*, Vol. 6 (New York: Peter Fenelon Collier, 1897), 329-332.

[37] Marshall and Manuel, *The Light and the Glory*, 42.

[38] Marshall and Manuel, *The Light and the Glory*, 62.

[39] Christopher Columbus, as quoted in Steven Waldman, *Founding Faith: Providence, Politics and the Birth of Religious Freedom in America* (New York: Random House, 2008), 4.

[40] Christopher Columbus, *Letters to King Ferdinand and Queen Isabel 1496 Raccolta Collection* (Roma: Raccolta di Documenti e Studi Publicati dalla R. Commissione Colombiana, pel Quarto Cenetenario dalla Scoperta dell' America, 1894), 270.

[41] Christopher Columbus, as quoted in *God Bless America: Prayers & Reflections For Our Country* (Grand Rapids: Zondervan, 1999), 111.

[42] Edward Lester, *The Life and Voyages of Americus Vespucius* (New York: New Amsterdam Book Company, 1903), 62.

[43] Frederick J Pohl, *Amerigo Vespucci, Pilot Major* (New York: Columbia University Press, 1944), 83.

[44] Amerigo Vespucci, Trans. By George Taylor Northrup, *Mundus Novus* (New Jersey : Princeton University Press, 1916), 2; Lester 75-79.

[45] Amerigo Vespucci, *Mundus Novus*, translated by George Tyler Northrup (New Jersey: Princeton University Press, 1916), 17.

[46] German Arciniegas, *Amerigo and the New World* (New York: Alfred Knopf, 1955), 296.

CHAPTER 5

SACRED SETTLEMENT

*Now as the people of God in old time were called
out of Babylon civil, the place of their bodily
bondage, and were to come to Jerusalem, and there
to build the Lord's temple…so are the people of
God now to go out of Babylon spiritual to
Jerusalem (America)…and to build themselves as
lively stones into a spiritual house, or temple, for
the Lord to dwell in….for we are the sons and
daughters of Abraham by faith.*

—Pilgrim Leader, John Robinson

With the discovery accomplished, the next phase in God's
plan for America could commence: the settlement of the
Promised Land by his chosen ones of the covenant. But did
these early American settlers (these likely descendants of
Ephraim) say or do anything that would lead us to believe they
understood this covenant? Did they comprehend that they
were settling the land under an ancient promise that connected

back to ancient Israel? Are the bold and profound scriptural theories presented in Part I of this book corroborated by the history of these chosen American colonizers? The answer to these questions is most definitely *affirmative*.

Comprehending the Covenant

According to one historian, "Particularly noteworthy was the ever-present religiously oriented sense of mission which guided people of all ranks to the New World early during the period between 1607-1820....A favoring Providence was seen as directing the destiny of His 'chosen people' in the abundant wilderness called America."[1] The renowned nineteenth century French historian Alexis de Tocqueville would describe this exodus to America as "the scattering of the seed of a great people which God with His own hands is planting on a predestined shore."[2]

These founding generations of Americans even referred to their land as the "New Israel,"[3] as if they understood the prophecies surrounding Joseph of old and his son Ephraim.[4] The idea that their new land was connected to Israel is also reflected in the fact that they consistently named their towns and cities after biblical locales—Bethel, Bethlehem, New Canaan. More than one thousand of their towns were thus named. They also regularly named their children after prominent Hebrews mentioned in the first five books of the Bible.[5]

These early Americans understood and worked to keep the American Covenant. They understood early on that if they were to receive *liberty, protection,* and *prosperity,* it would only be through obeying God and adhering to this national covenant. For example, in 1620 the Pilgrims' pastor, John Robinson, after leading his people in fasting and prayer, sent them off to America with profound instructions for living the covenant. "We are daily to renew our repentance with our God," stated Robinson, "especially for our sins known...[For] sin being taken away by earnest repentance and pardon thereof from the Lord...great shall be [your] security and peace."[6]

Upon landing in America in 1620, after a treacherous journey at sea, the Bible-carrying Pilgrims aboard the *Mayflower*, according to their leader William Bradford, "fell upon their knees and blessed the God of Heaven who had brought them over the vast and furious ocean."[7] Upon their arrival, Bradford exhorted them, "Come, let us declare the word of God in Zion."[8]

The Pilgrims' connection to the covenant is further developed as we witness their continued actions toward God.

William Bradford

Bradford stated that just when they thought they would perish in the wilderness, "they cried unto the Lord, and he heard their voice."[9] Bradford described how his people's intensified relationship with God took on a covenant nature: "So," stated Bradford, "they committed themselves to the will of God and resolved to proceed."[10] And, notwithstanding severe hardships, blessings were poured out upon them. For example, upon their arrival in the Promised Land, the Pilgrims had little to eat. A search party went ashore and miraculously found a large cache of Indian corn that had been placed in a large iron pot and left abandoned.[11] Like manna from heaven, this miracle saved them.

Similar miracles came in the form of unlikely alliances formed with the local Native American population. One Native American, Samoset, showed up unexpectedly one spring day to the Pilgrims. To the astonishment of the Pilgrims, Samoset spoke clear English, came in peace, and offered much welcomed advice to the Europeans. If that miracle was not

*Interview with Samoset with
the Pilgrims
(book engraving 1853)*

startling enough, imagine the Pilgrim's doubly surprised reaction when another Native American arrived in their camp. His name was Squanto. Not only did Squanto also speak English, but he stayed with the Pilgrims during their first year in the wilderness and taught them how to plant corn, hunt, and fish. This "special instrument sent of God," as Bradford described him, literally saved their lives. [12]

And then there was the Indian Chief, Massasoit, who commanded his braves to resist the temptation to show violent resistance to the European settlers, and instead helped and supported them. According to one historian, "Massasoit was a remarkable example of God's providential care for the Pilgrims. He was probably the only chief on the northeast coast of America who would have welcomed the Europeans as friends." [13]

Even in the Pilgrims' first written charter, which may be modern America's earliest form of a written constitution, the national covenant is made clear. Consider the following introductory words of this document, known as the Mayflower Compact of 1620:

> In the name of God, Amen...Having undertaken for the glory of God, and Advancement of the Christian faith...a Voyage to plant the first colony...do by these Presents, solemnly and mutually in the Presence of God and of one another, covenant and combine ourselves together into a civil Body Politick for our better Ordering and Preservation, and Furtherance of the Ends aforesaid. [14]

A similar comprehension of the American Covenant was expressed by a second group of migrants known as the

Puritans, who also settled in New England—not far from the Pilgrims' Plymouth Plantation—and established the Massachusetts Bay Company. In the spring of 1630, John Winthrop, the newly elected governor of the Bay Company, offered one of the most famous speeches ever given concerning the American Promised Land. This speech, given as the Puritans were in route to America, has been deemed by scholars the "Urtext of American literature;"[15] and for the purposes of this study, it could also be deemed one the most significant American Covenant texts as well. In explaining to his fellow

John Winthrop

American Covenant-makers how they had "taken out a Commission" under the Lord in crossing the great waters to the Promised Land, Winthrop declared: "Thus stands the cause between God and us, we are entered into Covenant with him for this work...Now if the Lord shall please to hear us, and bring us peace to the place we desire, then hath he verified this Covenant and sealed our Commission."[16]

Landing of the Puritans in America, by Antonio Gisbert

Winthrop reminded his early American migrants and covenant-makers what happened to ancient Israel when they failed to live their end of their national covenant: "it lost [them] the Kingdom." And that his people would not fall into the same tragic state, he implored them to live the covenant correctly, lest the Lord "make us know the price of the breach of such a Covenant."[17]

Winthrop then famously prophesied that God "shall make us a praise and glory,"

> that men shall say of succeeding plantations: the Lord make it like that of New England for we must consider we shall be as a City upon a Hill, the eyes of all people are upon us; so that if we shall deal falsely with our God in this work we have undertaken and so cause Him to withdraw his present help from us, we shall be made a story and a byword through the world.[18]

Winthrop then detailed the covenant obligations. He explained that his people must, under their covenant, "delight in each other, make each others' Conditions our own, rejoice together, mourn together, labor, and suffer together, always having before our eyes our Commission and Community in the work...."[19] As one Puritan wrote of his early American countrymen, "they joined together in a holy Covenant with the Lord and with one another, promising by the Lord's assistance to walk together...and to cleave to the Lord."[20]

Winthrop went on to list the promised blessings of the covenant. Fittingly, the promised blessings he revealed to his people were identical to those blessings promised by Jacob to Joseph, as detailed in the Old Testament scriptures cited earlier —even the blessings of *liberty*, *protection*, and *prosperity*. Indeed, the blessings, according to Winthrop, for living this covenant included God's "wisdom, power, goodness and truth," along with the promise that the "God of Israel is among us, when ten of us shall be able to resist a thousand of our enemies." And finally, Winthrop reminded his people that by "obeying

126

[God's] voice and cleaving to him" they secure "our life, and our prosperity."[21]

Winthrop's colleague in the cause, Pastor John Cotton, also weighed in on the power and importance of the covenant. Using 2 Samuel as the basis for his sermon, he applied Old Testament principles to his American Puritans. Quoting the Bible, Pastor Cotton declared: "Moreover I will appoint a place for my people Israel, and will plant them, that they may dwell in a place of their own, and move no more; neither shall the children of wickedness afflict them any more, as before time." Cotton went on to explain that such would be their covenant blessing if they "with a public spirit" lived in righteousness, "that they do not degenerate as the Israelites did." Only then would the covenant take force and only then, as Cotton concluded, would the Puritans "prosper and flourish....[For] when He promiseth peace and safety, what enemies shall be able to make the promise of God of none effect?"[22]

And yet further evidence that the Puritans knew their national covenant was somehow an extension of the ancient covenants with Israel, is found in the fact that they named their principal city Salem, which name is a root of the word Jerusalem, and which name translated from Hebrew means "peace," even that prominent fruit of the national covenant. Their self-proclaimed connection to Israel continued into later Puritan generations, which oft referred to their founder Winthrop as *Nehemias Americanus*, thus comparing him to the ancient Israelite leader Nehemiah. The Bible records that Nehemiah led his people out of Babylon back into the Promised Land, rebuilt the walls of Jerusalem, and inspired his people to return to their national covenant.[23]

The American Covenant perhaps reached a climax among the Puritans when Winthrop's good friend and colleague, Thomas Hooker, had a most inspired revelation. Hooker thought to take these national covenant principles and apply them to a more democratic system of government. Hooker was concerned that a theocracy, however well intended, could stifle the liberty necessary for true progression. Declared Hooker: "There must of necessity be a mutual engagement, each of the other, by their free consent, before by any rule of God they have any right or power, or can exercise either, each towards the other." Hooker felt so strongly about it that, after gaining the blessing of Winthrop, he left the Bay Colony and established his own colony under the *Fundamental Orders of Connecticut*.[24] The first type and model of a free and democratic government under God in America had been set. And though it was far from what the Lord would need as a political foundation for bringing full liberty unto salvation, America had, under its covenant, taken one step closer.

In the spirit of Hooker, William Penn would also strive to create a covenant land ringing with religious tolerance. Having suffered severe religious persecution in

William Penn

the Old World, Penn migrated to America in 1682 to establish a land of liberty. He called his American enterprise a "Holy Experiment." He established the city of Philadelphia, "the City of Brotherly Love," and welcomed the religious dissidents who had suffered in the Old World. Persecuted Christians flocked to Penn's city in droves—Mennonites, Amish, Anabaptists, German Lutherans, Irish Catholics, and many others. Penn's open heart allowed him to easily seek friendships with Native populations. With Israel on his mind, Penn believed he saw something familiar in certain Native groups. In 1683, Penn wrote, "I am ready to believe them of the Jewish race, I mean of the stock of the Ten Tribes. They agree in rites; they reckon by moons; they offer their first fruits;[and] they have a kind of Feast of Tabernacles." While mixing with the Natives, Penn said he sometimes felt as if he were residing in the Jewish Quarter in London.[25]

The covenant connections and principles which the settlers had so firmly planted in the land, eventually reached that chosen American generation, which God would raise up to first declare and achieve independence from Britain and then to build His American nation as we know it today. Though the early settlers struggled on and off to live their covenant, they persevered enough to keep it alive for those chosen ones. As late as 1676, the leaders of the new land were still fighting hard to remind their countrymen to renew their covenant. One such leader, Peter Folger, was especially concerned about the national covenant. Folger insisted that his people must "turn to God," then added poetically: "Let us then search what is the sin that God doth punish for; And when found out, cast it away, and ever it abhor." Folger's name stands out as one covenant-maker who served as a bridge to that chosen revolutionary generation of Americans; for his grandson was none other than Benjamin Franklin.[26] And just what miracles and progress Franklin's generation witnessed under the American Covenant, even that covenant which their forbearers delivered to them, will be detailed in later chapters.

The American Covenant legacy of these early settlers would continue even beyond Franklin and his revolutionary generation. On December 22, 1820, during the bicentennial celebration of the founding of the Mayflower Compact, renowned statesman Daniel Webster gave a speech in which he famously invoked the covenant. He emphasized the covenant's promised blessings, even "those principles of civil and religious liberty," which he concluded had only come to America through the early settlers' great sacrifice and endurance. He then exhorted his fellow Americans "to transmit the great inheritance unimpaired" that all in the future might enjoy these same blessings.[27] And finally, he acknowledged that this national covenant was part and parcel of the Christian Gospel. Webster concluded:

> Finally, let us not forget the religious character of our origin. Our fathers were brought hither by their high veneration for the Christian religion. They journeyed by its light, and labored in its hope. They sought to incorporate its principles with the elements of their society, and to diffuse its influence through all their institutions, civil, political, or literary. Let us cherish these sentiments, and extend this influence still more widely; in the full conviction, that this is the happiest society which partakes in the highest degree of the mild and peaceful spirit of Christianity.[28]

John Adams later said of the speech that "if there be any American who can read it without tears, I am not that American. It ought to be read at the end of every year, forever and forever."[29]

In spite of these wonderful connections between history, heaven, and the American Covenant, many might find it ironic to credit these early American settlers for helping to develop the promised land of liberty. For their religious heritage, particularly their Puritan heritage, is often recognized as being intolerant and even cruel toward dissenting viewpoints—something not conducive to the covenant purposes of offering religious freedom unto eternal salvation. And though they felt they needed strict codes in order to maintain unity, and thus strength, in confronting the challenges of cultivating a wild and dangerous land, no amount of reasoning can easily justify the banishments, beatings, and even executions carried out at times against congregants for not agreeing with and/or obeying their church leaders.[30] Though there is plenty of evidence that the

Lord was attempting to counter this evil culture, even early on,* there is no question that the adversary was using and influencing these extreme elements in early America to counter God's gospel plan for America. Fortunately for us all—and as we will see through the continuing story of the American Covenant—the Lord would eradicate these wicked cultural and political elements from the land in furtherance of His gospel purposes.

Notwithstanding the early presence of such wickedness, we must recognize that at this point of migration and settlement, the American Covenant was merely in its embryonic state in the New World. Therefore, a degree of tolerance must be offered to these early American Covenant-makers. After all, and in spite of their imperfections, they had in fact entered into the covenant with God, which set the spiritual precedent for America. Thanks to this spiritual precedent, as the nation developed and formed its Constitution (thus ridding itself of much of the wicked intolerance), it made sure to keep the national covenant intact. And this would allow God to bless the government with what it needed to ensure the safety of personal liberty and thus the safety of the gospel. In reflecting upon these early American societies, we must take care not to throw the proverbial baby out with the bath water.

Historian Steven Waldman, one of the fiercest modern-day critics of the cruelty and intolerance of these earliest Americans, even conceded—after launching into a detailed analysis of the wickedness described above—that "[c]ountless

---

* During this period of early settlement in the seventeenth century, certain inspired colonies, such as the one established by the aforementioned Puritan, Thomas Hooker, attempted a more liberal society. Pennsylvania and New York at times employed (though not always successfully) a policy of religious freedom. During this early period, Rhode Island, under the inspired guidance of Roger Williams, and Maryland, under the inspired guidance of Lord Baltimore, also fought the adversary's attack on America by enforcing religious tolerance. See Steven Waldman, *Founding Faith: Politics, Providence and the Birth of Religious Freedom in America* (New York: Random House, 2008), 14-16.

settlers created families, grew communities, and survived against great odds in large part because of their faith in Jesus Christ."

> These stories do not generally make the history books because they deal with the mundane, and awesome, power of God in people's lives. It's quite possible none of us would be here today if their religious beliefs and practices hadn't enabled...[them] to persevere against gruesome odds. They were not for the most part hypocrites or sadists. In most cases, they tried to create a world that would bring them closer to God, following his commandments as best they knew how. [31]

A Deeper Understanding

It is impressive enough that these early settlers understood the national covenant that had brought them to the New World. But did their knowledge extend into deeper realms? Did they know that what they were working on was something that transcended a national covenant and entered into something infinitely more powerful—even God's enlargement and renewal of His *church* covenant among His children? If the Lord had revealed such things to them, it would certainly make sense. For if these early settlers believed and taught their posterity that such an enlargement and renewal of Christianity was possible, and possibly on the horizon in America, then later generations would be open to that enlargement and renewal as it developed and arrived.

Though it is impossible to fully comprehend what deeper understanding these settlers possessed, the historical record implies that they did have something of a more profound gospel understanding. And though this study is focused on America's national covenant, it would be incomplete without analyzing what they knew concerning their divine role in building upon this national covenant.

One of the earliest expressions of this deeper comprehension came from the aforementioned Pastor John Robinson who, in speaking to the Pilgrims just before they set sail for the New World, encouraged these brave Christian settlers to seek out further light and knowledge in their new land, as greater gospel progress was yet to come:

> Here also he put us in mind of our church covenant, at least that part of it whereby we promise and covenant with God and one another to receive whatsoever light or truth shall be made known to us from His written Word...For saith he, it is not possible the Christian world should come so lately out of so thick anti-Christian darkness, and that perfection of knowledge break forth at once.[32]

Robinson provided a similarly powerful allusion to their divine role in God's work when he stated:

> Now as the people of God in old time were called out of Babylon civil, the place of their bodily bondage, and were to come to Jerusalem, and there to build the Lord's temple...so are the people of God now to go out of Babylon spiritual to Jerusalem (America)...and to build themselves as lively stones into a spiritual house, or temple, for the Lord to dwell in....for we are the sons and daughters of Abraham by faith.[33]

Robinson's message would not be lost on his most prominent congregant, and leader of the Pilgrim migration, William Bradford, who also knew why his people were called to America. Bradford recognized long before what Satan had done to the Old World. "...[W]hat wars and oppositions ever since [the gospel was brought to the earth], Satan hath raised, maintained and continued against the saints," explained Bradford. Bradford went on to explain that Satan did this so as to prevent the "truth [from] prevail[ing] and the churches of God [from] revert[ing] to their ancient purity and recover[ing] their primitive order, liberty and beauty."[34] Bradford recognized the adversary's success in days past and, like his brethren, had his mind oriented toward renewing and enlarging the gospel of Christ.

Pilgrims Going to Church (1867) by George Henry Boughton

The Pilgrims at Plymouth were not the only ones to receive this deeper comprehension; for their Puritan neighbors in Salem also knew something more profound concerning their own divine mission under the covenant. Winthrop, for example, was very clear on why he had led the migration to, and the settlement of, the Promised Land. He explained that he did so "to carry the gospel into those parts of the world... [away from] all other Churches of Europe [which] are brought to desolation...and who knows but that God hath provided this place [America] to be a refuge for many whom he means to save out of general calamity."[35] He may not have known all the detailed plans of God, but Winthrop no doubt recognized what darkness had pervaded the earth, and he seemed focused on a renewal and enlargement of truth. He knew why he was there. "I have assurance that my charge is of the Lord," he declared, "and that he hath called me to this work."[36]

Another early American Puritan of New England, who shared this vision, was the minister Jonathan Edwards. A major participant in developing a God-centered nation during early eighteenth century America, Edwards declared: "God presently goes about doing some great thing in order to make way for the introduction of the church's modern-day glory—which is to have its first seat in, and is to rise from [this] new world."[37]

Edwards' colleague, Judge Samuel Sewall,* took it a step further. He declared that America was to be the host-nation of the "New Jerusalem."[38] He believed God had revealed this to him. He stated that his New England colony was but a preface to the future millennial city. This, according to Sewall, is why the New England settlers had named the colony Salem.[39] He believed the actual New Jerusalem would be built somewhere on the new continent, perhaps south of the Puritan colony.[40] Sewall also pled with his brethren to include the Native Americans in their plans to build the spiritual America. The Natives were, according to Sewall, "Israelites unawares" who deserved a place in building the New Jerusalem and the kingdom of God on earth.[41]

Samuel Sewell

The historian Perry William summed it up succinctly:

> Winthrop and his colleagues believed...that their errand was not a mere scouting expedition: it was an essential maneuver in the drama of Christendom. The Bay Company was not a battered remnant of suffering Separatists thrown upon a rocky shore; it was an organized task force of Christians, executing a flank attack on the corruptions of Christendom. These Puritans did not flee to America; they went in

---

* Samuel Sewall's inspired nature was revealed when he stood before his congregation and humbly confessed before man and God that the Salem Witch Trials, which he had participated in, were an abomination and that he and his brethren had been wrong to pursue this course of action. See Richard Francis, *Judge Sewall's Apology*, xiii.

order to work out that complete reformation which
was not yet accomplished in England and Europe.[42]

Let us not take for granted the divine purpose and
calling felt by these Pilgrim and Puritan American Covenant-
makers. They were more correct in their vision than even they
could have possibly known at the time. For they had not only
been establishing the spiritually infused political foundations
that would set the nation on its proper course, but they also
brought to America a culture, mission, and appetite for further
gospel truth. They believed this "complete reformation" would
occur in America. And they knew they were to help initiate it.
But only at that then future date, when this reformation would
at last take hold in America, would the fullness of what they
had done come to light. Only then do we begin to see what
they so clearly and prophetically felt.

The enlargement of Christianity would indeed
continue, as true disciples stood upon the backs of their
American ancestors. For example, by 1628 the great Puritan
migration to America was well under way, which would, over
the following sixteen years, see the arrival to America of over
20,000 Puritans.[43] As one author put it, this placed into
America an overwhelming influx of "people who had entered
into a deep covenant relationship with God, through the
person of His Son, Jesus Christ."[44] These chosen ones who rode
this later wave of the great migration had just as clear a vision
of what they were doing as their predecessors had. As one
second generation American Puritan, John Higginson, so
prophetically explained:

> It hath been deservedly esteemed one of the great
> and wonderful works of God in this last age, that the
> Lord stirred up the spirits of so many thousands of
> his servants...to transport themselves...into a desert
> land in America...in the way of seeking first the
> kingdom of God...for the purpose of "a fuller and
> better reformation of the Church of God, than it hath
> yet appeared in the world."[45]

Again, their vision could not have been truer. Earlier in this chapter we saw how the settlers' ideas regarding the national covenant had set the appropriate national covenant foundations. But more than that, we now see how these early settlers' deeper gospel understanding also planted in America an awareness of greater things to come. These early settlers, after all, were the remnants of scattered Israel, and as such possessed that *believing blood*. American historians have commented on this unique religious characteristic in early America, often referring to these early Americans as "seekers" who broke with the authoritative religious structures of the Old Word and sought things like "personal revelation" and "witnesses of the Spirit."[46] That these early settlers possessed such *believing blood*—passing it on from generation to generation—was no accident. For it was their children—also infused with this blood and culture—who would become conspicuous actors in building the church. Indeed, they would carry and offer the covenant to us today, allowing *all* who believe to come unto the covenant—to come unto salvation. "If you belong to Christ, then you are Abraham's offspring, heirs according to the promise" (Galatians 3:29).

Pulitzer Prize-winning historian Gordon Wood attributes much of this liberal and democratic approach to religion as stemming from the revolutionary spirit that pervaded America, particularly after it won its independence from Great Britain. He argued that for the first time on a very large scale, people took "responsibility for their salvation like never before." This, according to Wood, created in America an increase in "visions, dreams [and] prophesyings."[47] And so, the American Covenant is connected to the renewal of Christianity in a powerful way—for it was this covenant that ultimately provided liberty and democracy, which in turn created the spirit and environment that facilitated the opening of hearts and minds to eternal truths. In short, the American Covenant helped activate the *believing blood* of Israel.

Edward Johnson, a first generation American Puritan and contemporary of Winthrop, opened his book *Wonder Working Providences of Sion's Saviour in New England*, with the following declaration: "Then judge, all you, (whom the Lord hath given a discerning spirit), whether these poor New England people be not forerunners of Christ's army, and the marvelous providences which you shall now hear, be not the very finger of God."[48]

Dark Stirrings

In spite of the spiritually glorious sentiments connected with this American discovery and settlement, there was also evil lurking therein. The adversary certainly understood the powerful tool America and her covenant would be in God's great war against evil and oppression. As such, Satan would deploy his armies early on in an effort to preempt and stomp out the American Covenant before it became operational in the advancement of righteousness.

The results of these evil tactics would find themselves represented in at least two obvious attacks on America and her purposes under God. First, and as already mentioned above, certain American settlements, colonies, and states would allow their local governments to influence, support, and even sponsor specific religious denominations, while at the same time discriminate against others. In some instances these state-run religions would go so far as to apply corporal punishment, banishment, and even executions upon those who refused to adhere to certain religious obligations such as church attendance and other subjective religious standards.[49] Second, the importation and practice of slavery would introduce to America not only the absolute oppression of a race, but also a sense of justified intolerance of any given set of minorities—racial or religious. Native Americans represented one group that often found itself victims of this cruelty. So pervasive were such wicked sentiments, that they found themselves codified and legislated in the land.

These two cancers in America were planted early and, if left unchecked, would grow and stifle the covenant and its fruits of salvation. They represented Satan's plan as set forth from the beginning of time. It was his *modus operandi*. It was that same old ploy: control and limit man's liberty to thwart his spiritual growth.

America's ability to conquer these attacks would only be as good as its ability to live the American Covenant; for if the people adhered to the covenant successfully, the Lord would provide America with the tools necessary to defeat Satan, thus securing a fullness of liberty. As the story of the American Covenant continues to develop in the chapters ahead, we will see how this eternal struggle over liberty and salvation plays out in the hands of God, as He leads His American Covenant-makers through heaven-backed wars and through inspired constitutions until America sufficiently rejects wickedness and congeals into that nation God designed it to be.

Conclusion

Throughout the past two chapters we have seen how the historical record corroborates what the scriptural-based theory (put forth in Part I of this book) proposed. That is, we have achieved validation of the notion that God indeed set up a modern-day American Covenant and inspired its recognition in the hearts and minds of the chosen discoverers and settlers of the chosen land. These first explorers, voyagers, immigrants, and settlers were an integral part of the American Covenant, as would be the millions that would follow them. It was through obedience and adherence to God (as displayed by Columbus, Vespucci, Pilgrims, Puritans, and the generations they would breed), that God would provide the *liberty*, *protection*, and *prosperity* promised through the Covenant, just as we saw prophesied in the previous chapters by father Jacob to the heirs of Joseph (Genesis 49:22-26).

To be sure, in these last two chapters of the covenant story, we have witnessed the partial fulfillment of the promised *protection*, as given to Columbus, Vespucci, and others as they successfully braved vast and unknown waters and forged through vast and unknown lands. We have seen the partial fulfillment of the promised *liberty*, as given to the Pilgrims, Puritans, and other settlers who, at last, could worship God according to the dictates of their consciences. And we know of the fulfillment of the promised *prosperity* that these early Americans would eventually create for the future heirs of the covenant.*

Though the covenant and its ultimate gospel fruits would not fully manifest themselves in the early settlements of America, we have certainly seen how the early settlers did understand the covenant and did foresee greater things to come. They were forerunners, called to set the precedent and spirit in the land, so that later generations might take this precedent and spirit and improve upon it, all in preparation for God's work and glory.

The story of these settlers has been all but lost to Americans today. But if we forget their story, we will forget the covenant. Just as their story has been hiding in plain sight, longing to be told, so have two monuments to them also been hiding in plain sight, longing to be recognized. As we internalize these symbols, inspired of God, we will better live our covenant in the land.

---

* In spite of great hardships, we know that by the mid 1750's, America had grown to maintain the highest per capita wealth in the world. See Joseph J. Ellis, *Patriots, Brotherhood of the American Revolution*, (lectures recorded by Recorded Books, Inc, and Barnes and Noble Publishing, 2004), Study Guide, 10. And America has since only grown stronger and stronger until eventually becoming, as it is today, the world's superpower.

One of these monuments resides off the beaten path in Plymouth, Massachusetts. It is an eighty-one-foot-tall granite sculpture dedicated in 1889. It is entitled, *The National Monument to the Forefathers* and it is a tribute to, and a reminder of, the covenant.

Configured in an octagonal shape, the Monument contains several pedestals upon which stand several figures and depictions. Upon its tallest, most centralized, and principal pedestal stands the heroic figure of "Faith" with her right hand pointing toward heaven and her left hand clutching the Bible. Upon the other pedestals are seated figures emblematical of the principles upon which the Pilgrims founded their land: Freedom, Morality, Law and Education. Under "Freedom"

National Monument to the Forefathers

stand "Tyranny" and "Peace;" under "Morality" stand "Prophet" and "Evangelist;" under "Law" stand "Justice" and "Mercy;" and under "Education" are "Youth" and "Wisdom." On the face of the pedestals, beneath these figures, are marble reliefs representing scenes from Pilgrim history. Under "Freedom" is "Landing;" under "Morality" is "Embarcation;" under "Law" is "Treaty;" and under "Education" is "Compact."

The Monument includes four large panels with powerful verbiage. The front panel is inscribed as follows: "National Monument to the Forefathers. Erected by a grateful people in remembrance of their labors, sacrifices and sufferings for the cause of civil and religious liberty." The right and left panels contain the names of those who came over on the *Mayflower*. The rear panel contains a quote from the Pilgrim leader, William Bradford:

*Thus out of small beginnings greater things have
been produced by His hand that made all things of
nothing and gives being to all things that are; and
as one small candle may light a thousand, so the
light here kindled hath shone unto many, yea in
some sort to our whole nation; let the glorious
name of Jehovah have all praise.*

The other covenant monument is comprised of the oversized oil-on-canvas paintings that decorate the interior of the great rotunda of the U.S. Capitol Building. These paintings outline the very American Covenant story we have witnessed in these last two chapters. Within this impressive display are three paintings placed in chronological order, which express three deeply symbolic events pertaining to the covenant. First, the painting *The Landing of Columbus* depicts the miraculous arrival on the shores of the Promised Land. Second, the painting *The Embarkation of the Pilgrims* depicts the chosen Ephraimites observing a day of fasting and prayer on the decks of a ship preparing to lead them *over the wall* to America. Depicted in the work is a rainbow, which "symbolizes hope and divine protection" [50]—even those hallmarks of the American Covenant. Finally, the painting *The Baptism of Pocahontas* depicts a Native American girl who, after the long night of gospel apostasy, at last finds access to spiritual light, reminding us of those sacred principles soon to be delivered to the world as a result of this divine discovery and sacred settlement.

Embarkation of the Pilgrims, by Robert W. Weir.
Courtesy of the Architect of the Capitol.

ENDNOTES

[1] R. Mathisen, *The Role of Religion in American Life* (Washington D.C.: University Press of America, 1982), 1.

[2] William J. Bennett, *The Spirit of America* (New York: Touchstone, 1997), 365-366.

[3] William J. Bennett, *The Spirit of America*, 366.

[4] See chapter 2 of this book: *The Covenant-Makers.*

[5] Entine, *Abraham's Children*, 143.

[6] John Robinson, as quoted in Marshall and Manuel, pp. 145, 148.

[7] William Bradford, as quoted in Jon Meacham, *American Gospel: God, the Founding Fathers, and the Making of a Nation* (New York: Random House, 2006), 38.

8 Entine, *Abraham's Children*, 143.

9 Meacham, *American Gospel: God, the Founding Fathers, and the Making of a Nation*, 38.

10 Meacham, *American Gospel: God, the Founding Fathers, and the Making of a Nation*, 39.

11 Marshall and Manuel, 157.

12 Marshall and Manuel, 164-169.

13 Marshall and Manuel, 168.

14 "The Mayflower Compact, 1620," quoted in *Let Freedom Ring, The Words That Shaped Our America* (New York: Sterling Publishing Co., Inc, 2001), 11.

15 Matthew S. Holland, *Bonds of Affection* (Washington D.C.: Georgetown University Press, 2007), 1.

16 H. Sheldon Smith et al, *American Christianity, An Historical Interpretation with Representative Documents*, Vol.1: 1607-1820 (New York: Charles Scribner's Sons, 1960), 102; Also quoted in Holland, 273-4.

17 Winthrop, as quoted in Matthew S. Holland, *Bonds of Affection* (Washington D.C.: Georgetown University Press, 2007), 273-274.

18 John Winthrop, "A Model of Christian Charity," *Winthrop Papers, 1498-1649*, Vol. 2 (Boston: The Massachusetts Historical Society), 282-95.

19 Winthrop, as quoted in Holland, 274.

20 Edward Johnson, as quoted in Marshall and Manuel, 204.

21 Holland, 274-275.

22 John Cotton, as quoted in Marshall and Manuel, 197.

23 Marshall and Manuel, 207-8.

24 Marshall and Manuel, 251-2.

25 Entine, *Abraham's Children*, 144; see also http://www.pbs.org/godinamerica/people/william-penn.html.

26 Marshall and Manuel, 279.

27 Daniel Webster, as quoted in Toby Mac and Michael Tait, *Under God* (Minneapolis: Bethany House, 2004), 144.

28 Verna M. Hall, *The Christian History of the Constitution of the United States of America* (San Francisco: Foundation for American Christian Education, 1975), 248.

29 John Adams, as quoted in Mac and Tait, 144.

30 For a full account of the abuses inflicted upon dissenters, see Steven Waldman, *Founding Faith: Politics, Providence and the Birth of Religious Freedom in America* (New York: Random House, 2008), 6-13.

31 Steven Waldman, *Founding Faith: Politics, Providence and the Birth of Religious Freedom in America* (New York: Random House, 2008), 17.

[32] Timothy L. Hall, *Separating Church and State* (Chicago: University of Illinois Press, 1998), 184.

[33] John Robinson, as quoted in Marshall and Manuel, 142-3.

[34] William Bradford, as quoted in Marshall and Manuel, 139.

[35] John Winthrop, as quoted in Marshall and Manuel, 195.

[36] Marshall and Manuel, 196.

[37] Edwards, quoted in Cleon Skousen, *The Majesty of God's Law* (Salt Lake City: Ensign Publishing, 1996), 19.

[38] Richard Francis, *Judge Sewall's Apology* (New York: Harper Collins Publishers, 2005), 37, 201.

[39] Richard Francis, *Judge Sewall's Apology*, 201.

[40] Richard Francis, *Judge Sewall's Apology*, 355.

[41] Richard Francis, *Judge Sewall's Apology*, 37, 201.

[42] Marshall and Manuel, 196.

[43] Marshall and Manuel, 185.

[44] Marshall and Manuel, 186.

[45] John Higginson, as quoted in Marshall and Manuel, 21.

[46] Author Terryl Givens quotes several historians who made these claims, to include Ronald Walker, Timothy Smith and Dan Vogel, in his book, *By the Hand of Mormon* (Oxford: Oxford University Press, 2002), 230.

[47] Gordon S. Wood, "Evangelical America and Early Mormonism," *New York History* 61 (October 1980): 364, 367, and 361.

[48] Edward Johnson, as quoted in Marshall and Manuel, 199.

[49] Jon Meacham, *American Gospel: God, the Founding Fathers, and the Making of a Nation* (New York: Random House, 2006), 43; and Steven Waldman, 5.

[50] Newt Gingrich, *Rediscovering God in America*, 79.

CHAPTER 6

A HEAVEN-SENT REVOLUTION

*We have it in our power to begin
the world over again. A situation,
similar to the present, hath not
happened since the days of Noah
until now.*

—Thomas Paine, 1776

With the discovery and settlement of America complete, the Lord would elevate His choice land to the next level by making it completely free and independent from the Old World proprietors, whose Old World influence in America continued to threaten the liberty required for a fullness of Christianity and a global opportunity at personal salvation. The Lord would call for a clean political slate in America that He might more effectively influence the making of a new government to serve as His base of operations. Unfortunately, such a new and independent system would only come through a bloody revolution. So God would inspire His new American settlers to turn to their American Covenant, that He might pour upon them the covenant blessings of *liberty, protection,* and *prosperity*

147

—those blessings required to ultimately secure independence against all odds. Indeed, the American Revolution represents one of the clearest examples of the American Covenant in action. Through it we can see how, as the Founders worked to live according to their obligations, the Lord continued providing the covenant blessings that ultimately created an independent nation whose hallmark would be an abundance of liberty unto a fullness of salvation.

The next wave of chapters will reveal how America worked under God and this national covenant in achieving, through the Revolution, such freedom unto gospel salvation. The historical account will corroborate the scriptural suggestions detailed earlier. We will see that God was wholly behind the American Revolution, and that He backed His actions by the American Covenant. All together, the following narrative will not only further prove the reality and power of this national covenant, but will show how this covenant clearly advanced the work and glory of God.

Washington Crossing the Delaware, 1851 by Emanuel Leutze.
The Metropolitan Museum of Art.

Recall from Chapter 2 that it was promised to Joseph's seed, by Jacob, that their "bow [would] ab[i]de in strength, and the arms of [their] hands [would be] made strong by the hands of the mighty God of Jacob" (Genesis 49:24). As descendants of Joseph, American revolutionaries were the beneficiaries of such prophetic blessings. But why would God deem it necessary to bless the revolutionaries with these most powerful national blessings? Why would God want America to win? In other words, how *exactly* did the American Revolution help to accomplish God's purposes? It is only in answering these questions that we might fully comprehend *why* God so powerfully intervened in America and its war for independence. We will now open up the discussion by reviewing three eternally enduring reasons God brought about the American Revolution.

1. A Needed Separation from Britain

The most obvious gospel purpose of the American Revolution can be explained through reviewing the socio-political developments that were occurring at the time of America's beginning. After the discovery of America, a series of conflicts ensued among the European powers over who would control the new continent. Great Britain emerged victorious as the principal proprietor of the most developed parts of North America. Though the British government initially respected and supported the early American colonists, its political structure would not support God's purposes for America. Britain's power structure consisted of a parliament and a monarchy, which meant that while it practiced a form of representative democracy, such representation was limited, as the king still controlled many aspects of government. For

DON'T TREAD ON ME

One of the first military banners carried by the Continental Army. It is often referred to as the Gadsden Flag, named after the American general Christopher Gadsden. Its symbolism can be traced back to the publications of Benjamin Franklin.

the Americans, who had no representation in parliament, the king's power seemed even more overbearing. Furthermore, the king controlled a state religion, which was capable of making things difficult for new and non-traditional religious thought.[1] Religious freedom, as it was during Colonial America, was not where it needed to be.

Britain's monarchical system (however partially democratic it might have been) placed a disproportionate amount of power in the hands of a few. Accordingly, under such a system, Satan would need only influence the hearts of these few to successfully implement wicked politics against the Lord's work. Indeed, a monarchical system is simply not a great tool for producing the religious freedom God desires for His children. A democratic-republic, however, would counter such dangers, as Satan—instead of only having to influence a few—would have to influence a large majority. As such, Britain had to be routed out by the Almighty's American faithful so that democracy's protection could be ushered into America and that the Lord's kingdom and fullness of salvation might safely follow.

The revolutionaries recognized this unsafe political environment stemming from Britain, which explains their oft quoted revolutionary refrains, to include "No taxation without representation," "Don't tread on me," and "All men are created equal." However, they did not (for the most part) fully comprehend that the break with Britain was really all about creating *religious freedom* in America in preparation for God's work. In fact, they did not even necessarily comprehend or emphasize the notion that they were fighting for religious freedom *at all*. After all, most of the colonials worshiped God as they desired without major obstruction from the British.

Furthermore, America would never have justified its revolution on religious persecution from Britain because America was not overwhelmingly concerned with this issue at the time. To be sure, the American colonial system allowed its own home grown religious sects (such as those in New England) to dominate certain colonial and local governments, which often led to persecution of minority religious sects. Such practices occurred independent of any British meddling and continued long after independence from Britain was secured.

Finally, the Declaration of Independence, which lists the many American grievances against the British, thereby justifying the Revolution, does not even hint at religious intolerance or religious persecution by the British as one of America's justifications for independence. As will be shown later, the principal justifications had more to do with political rights and property rights than with religious rights. Political and property rights were, of course, important ideals. They would enhance freedom in America; and freedom, in whatever form, helps bridge the gap between man and his Maker. However, it was religious freedom, specifically and above all else, that God needed in America; and the general American desire for more religious freedom at that time was simply not strong enough alone to justify war for the colonists. But the religious freedom problem needed fixing nonetheless. Indeed, things were not good in America for minority sects like Jews, Catholics, Mennonites, certain Baptist congregations, and others. Though religionists in the majority felt alright at the time, unless things improved for *all* religions, *nobody* would be safe. The ability for mankind to *fully* reach Deity would not be safe.

In short, without being able to witness what horrible things the adversary could do in America through a monarchical system to harm God's plan for saving His children —as the Lord did not permit this scenario to fully play out—the revolutionaries would have found it difficult to emphasize a threat of British religious persecution. They would have found it difficult to see God's ultimate designs for the Revolution. However, just because the revolutionaries did not see the end from the beginning does not mean that God could not inspire them to work on His behalf for His ultimate purposes. It was enough that they knew they were on God's errand and that this errand included a separation from British rule and a new form of independence and liberty. As we will see, God would ensure that this foundation, born of Revolution, would end in a form of religious freedom unprecedented in the world.

2. A Needed Expansion of Religious Freedom at Home

Another reason the Lord would have inspired the Revolution was to secure greater religious freedom for a renewal and expansion of His Gospel, not only from monarchical threats, but also from American-based, domestic threats. As recently noted, in addition to monarchical threats to freedom, colonial America was also plagued by religious intolerance stemming from its own American-based religions, which had taken too much control over colonial governments and thus made it difficult for minority religions. Even with the British gone, an enlargement of the gospel still might have found obstructions under such an American environment. Fortunately, as we will see in the forthcoming chapters, the Revolution not only pushed back a foreign monarchy, but also initiated a process that would shore up religious protections at home against domestic religious persecution. This occurred in part because the Revolution made it difficult for Americans, on a moral level, to fight to the death to eradicate Great Britain's domineering influence over America, while at the same time tolerate its own domestic-based persecution over religious minorities. Consequently, through the experience of the Revolution, a new era of religious tolerance and liberation of thought had been born in the Promised Land.

We recognize this new and positive influence through statements born out of the Revolution, such as the following declaration made by Thomas Jefferson in 1777, at the height of the Revolution: "Almighty God hath created the mind free... All attempts to influence it by temporal punishments or burthens...are a departure from the plan of the Holy Author of our religion...all men shall be free to profess and by argument to maintain, their opinions in matters of religion." Jefferson made this statement in support of "A Bill for Establishing Religious Freedom in Virginia." But as the issue of increased religious freedom was still only budding and congealing as a byproduct of the Revolution, it would remain but a bill until 1786, some three years after the war, when it at last became state law.[2] But it was the Revolution which stirred men's hearts toward that kind of liberty-bearing legislation.

Beyond legislation, the flame of liberty produced by the Revolution also manifested itself in Americans' personal religious endeavors. It caused them to feel free enough, perhaps for the first time, to seek God outside of the sometimes rigid Old World frameworks. According to Pulitzer Prize-winning American historian, Gordon Wood, the Revolution allowed Americans, for first time on a very large scale, to take "responsibility for their salvation like never before." This, according to Wood, created in America an increase in "visions, dreams [and] prophesyings."[3]

Not only did this revolutionary fever cause Americans to produce state legislation and feel free enough to look for God outside of rigid frameworks, but it also inspired them to apply this new feeling of freedom to their new nationally-binding government. When they at last developed the Constitution, they naturally included protections that would defend minorities and minority religions.

In short, though the Revolution's initial purpose was to push back a foreign threat, it also shook up oppressive establishments at home, thus creating the political foundations of religious freedom. The Founders did not enter the

Revolution to generate such a shake-up at home (their target was most certainly foreign political oppressors, not domestic religious oppressors). But we can be assured that the Lord knew the end from the beginning, and inspired His founding American generation accordingly.

3. A Needed Influence for the World

Another reason the Lord would have inspired the American Revolution has to do with how positively the nations of the earth responded to it. The dark ages following the death of Christ and his apostles had dimmed the lights on inspired governments throughout the world. At the time of the Revolution, even the most "advanced" and supposedly "enlightened" governments in the world—to include England, France, and their European cousins—were dominated by corrupt and oppressive monarchies and aristocracies. But the American Revolution would challenge all this; for it was the American Revolution that provided the world with an opportunity to see, witness, and feel the powerful flame of liberty produced by that spirit generated through righteous revolutions. This American example and influence would ultimately awaken would-be revolutionaries in these oppressed lands near and far, thus providing them with the confidence to contract that infectious spirit of independence and successfully fight to be free from their own oppressive governmental regimes.

It was this world-wide awakening stemming from America that would ultimately compel those chosen revolutionaries in the world, from South America to Europe and beyond, to bring liberty and personal agency—and by extension, the opportunity to access gospel truths—to God's children everywhere. But without the spark and flame of an American Revolution, liberty's fire might not have extended the world over in preparation for God's work in these areas.

One example of a national movement commencing under the influence of this American spark and flame was the French Revolution which began in 1789, on the heels of the American Revolution. This French movement brought the masses to the realization of their self-worth in relation to something greater than kings and queens, thus instilling in them a sense of their God-given rights. Inspired by the recent American Revolution, French revolutionaries adopted the American spirit and spread it to all the people of Europe longing to be free.*

Within two decades of the American Revolution, the world saw democratic uprisings, revolutions, and constitutional reforms in places like Sweden, Poland, Belgium, the Dutch Provinces, Naples, Russia, Spain, and Portugal.[4] It was a miracle. As one historian observed, "As late as 1860, the United States occupied a singular position in the world. The democratic spirit of the American Revolution had inspired European reformers for eighty-five years, and the impulse was not yet extinguished."[5] These movements, inspired by America, marked the beginning of the end of European totalitarian and monarchical powers, and thus set the stage for democracy, religious tolerance, and thus an enlargement of the gospel on earth.

It was not just in Europe. Within approximately eighty years from the time America declared its independence in 1776, over eighteen countries in the Western Hemisphere alone, also drawing on the American example, had fought and gained their independence from their respective monarchical oppressors.[6] And this, of course, led to even more open

---

* It should be noted that some of these revolutions, including the French Revolution, had initially ended tragically with thousands executed by revolutionaries turned tyrants. But even in these tragedies, the political situations eventually stabilized under constitutional principles of civil and religious freedom, thus achieving the inspired result in the end.

governments and societies which would eventually accept, protect, and help proliferate Christianity.

The American Revolution has even influenced modern-day movements in both China (students at Tiananmen Square) and in the nations of the Former Soviet Union, whose people, struggling to be free of Communism, would incessantly quote Thomas Jefferson and other American revolutionaries. They found in these American patriots their inspiration for freedom.[7]

Furthermore, the newly-born free nations stemming from these revolutionary movements would oft times emulate the U.S. Constitution in drafting and forming their new governments. This also clues us in on where their inspiration for independence and civil and religious liberty truly was derived. But again, had America remained revolution-less, such an infectious spirit which brought so much good to the world might never have been born and spread. The political barriers to religious freedom might not have fallen so swiftly in the world.

Also, it has been suggested that the American revolutionary spirit of independence inspired—beyond encouraging religious freedom on a *political* level—a feeling of *personal* and *spiritual* liberation in the hearts of Americans. This allowed many to feel confident and inspired to seek God outside what many considered to be restrictive religious frameworks. This openness and freedom allowed such individuals in America to find and accept a greater understanding of the gospel. That being the case, the same can be said for other nations of the world, whose own revolutions similarly created open, enlightened, and searching spirits among their citizenry. This eventually led many to gospel light, once that gospel light was made available to them. And so, more than just removing political barriers to religious freedom, these revolutions also removed personal barriers to God's truths. As these spiritual feelings sprung from revolutions, and as these revolutions sprung from that first revolution, even the

American Revolution, we see why God brought on the American Revolution in the first place.

With such divinely inspired blessings riding on the wings of the American Revolution, it is no wonder that even the earliest of the Founding Fathers—without the luxury of historical hindsight, but with the light of God's inspiration—could articulate the magnificent blessings their successful revolution would offer to the world. Though the Founders could not fully comprehend how their revolution would inspire other revolutions, thus facilitating the delivery of the gospel to the world, they knew enough to catch glimpses of the eternal plan. For example, the American sage, Benjamin Franklin, declared:

> Tyranny is so generally established in the rest of the world that the prospect of an asylum in America for those who love liberty gives general joy, and our cause is esteemed the cause of all mankind….It is a common observation here that our cause is the cause of all mankind, and that we are fighting for their liberty in defending our own.[8]

Furthermore, in a 1776 letter published by the *New England Chronicle*, signed simply by "A Freeman," the following was declared to all America: "[W]e expect soon to break off all kind of connection with Britain, and form into a Grand Republic of the American United Colonies, which will, *by the blessing of heaven, soon work out our salvation….*"

> Never was a cause more important or glorious than that which you are engaged in; not only your wives, your children, and distant posterity, but humanity at large, the world of mankind, are interested in it; for if tyranny should prevail in this great country, we may expect liberty will expire throughout the world. Therefore, more human *glory and happiness* may depend upon your exertions than ever yet depended upon any of the sons of men.[9]

And it was this same spirit that inspired the founder Thomas Paine to eloquently and prophetically proclaim the following in his 1776 work, *Common Sense* (which, very fittingly, was responsible for much revolutionary spirit in colonial America): "We have it in our power to begin *the world* over again. A situation, similar to the present, hath not happened since the days of Noah until now."[10]

And finally, Abraham Lincoln, who admittedly had in his day a greater historical perspective than his predecessors (he served some eighty years after the revolutionary Founding Fathers), but who was nonetheless inspired, declared the following about what American independence had meant for the world:

> It was not the mere matter of separation of the colonies from the motherland, but that sentiment in the Declaration of Independence which gave liberty not alone to the people of this country, but hope to all the world, for all future time. It was that which gave promise that in due time the weights would be lifted from the shoulders of all men, and that all should have an equal chance. This is the sentiment embodied in the Declaration of Independence.[11]

It is no wonder that Lincoln called the United States the "last best hope on earth."[12]

Such commentaries by such inspired founders as Franklin, the "Freeman," Paine, and Lincoln lend credibility to the idea that the Revolution truly was bigger than just America. The Revolution's influence would eventually be so far-reaching in the world that even those early Americans on the battlefields, quite amazingly, felt the magnitude of their actions. The fact that history has vindicated their predictions should cause us to pause and reflect upon the truly inspired nature of our founding generations.

But regardless of what they knew or did not know, the Lord understood these world-wide gospel benefits that would be born of the American Revolution.

Conclusion

The Revolution was clearly a powerful movement brought to America by Heaven. Not only does the Spirit of God testify of this truth, but the eternal fruits of the Revolution reveal why the Lord would inspire and guide it through to its victorious end. Whether we are discussing the needed break with Britain's dangerous system of government, or the needed spark for religious freedom at home, or the needed proliferation of the spirit of freedom abroad, the purposes of the American Revolution all lead to the same eternal and inspired end. In every case, it is about freedom and liberty trumping various forms of tyranny and oppression, so that God's children might seek salvation under a fullness of liberty and that the gospel of Jesus Christ might flourish at home and abroad. This explains why the Lord intervened in the American Revolution utilizing one of His most powerful tools —a covenant.

While the revolutionaries could not fully understand these purposes, even though they sometimes caught glimpses, God knew what He was doing. Like Lincoln said of the Civil War, so it can be said of the Revolutionary War: "[T]he Almighty has his own purposes."[13] As long as God was on their side, the revolutionaries did not need a full explanation. It was enough that they knew they were fighting for liberty under God, and that victory would come only to the extent that they adhered to their covenant. This, as we shall see, they most definitely understood.

★ ★ ★ ★

While the logic presented above lends ample credibility to the notion that the American Revolution is inseparably connected to God's plan for America, the details concerning exactly *how* God worked through the American Covenant in blessing the American revolutionary cause are less known. As such, the next several chapters will utilize the historical record to expound not only on *why*, but *how*, the Lord executed the miracle that was the American Revolution and War for Independence. As we explore this fascinating era of American history, we will identify the fingerprints of God everywhere. Along the way, we will corroborate the scriptural and gospel-based claims put forth in this book regarding God's hand and covenant in America and her revolution. And in the end, we will have no doubt of the power and reality of this covenant and its grand purposes under Heaven.

ENDNOTES

[1] William J. Bennett, *America, The Last Best Hope* (Nashville, Nelson Current, 2006), 40.

[2] Thomas Jefferson, 1777, as quoted in Newt Gingrich (Nashville: Integrity House, 2006), 45.

[3] Gordon S. Wood, "Evangelical America and Early Mormonism," *New York History* 61 (October 1980): 364, 367, and 361.

[4] Richard Bushman, "1830: Pivotal Year in the Fulness of Times," *Ensign.* September 1978, 9.

5 Richard Bushman, "1830: Pivotal Year in the Fulness of Times," *Ensign*. September 1978, 9.

6 For a complete list of these nations and the dates of their independence see Kenneth W. Thompson, *The U.S. Constitution and the Constitutions of Latin America* (New York: University Press of America, 1991), 87-94.

7 Stephen Ambrose, *To America, Personal Reflections of an Historian* (New York: Simon and Schuster, 2002), 7.

8 Benjamin Franklin, as quoted in Walter Isaacson, *Benjamin Franklin, An American* Life (New York: Simon and Schuster, 2003), 339.

9 McCullough, *1776*, 63, emphasis added.

10 From Thomas Paine's *Common Sense*, as quoted in John Ferling, *Adams vs. Jefferson, The Tumultuous Election of 1800* (New York: Oxford University Press, 2004), 25, emphasis added. The full text of Paine's *Common Sense* is available at www.earlyamerica.com/earlyamerica/milestone/commonsense/text.html.

11 Abraham Lincoln, as quoted in Gordon Leidner, *Lincoln on God and Country* (Shippensburg: White Mane Books, 2000), 44.

12 Lincoln, as quoted in Bushman, "1830: Pivotal Year in the Fulness of Tmes," *Ensign*. September 1978, 9.

13 Leidner, *Lincoln on God and Country*, 113.

CHAPTER 7

THE SPIRIT OF INDEPENDENCE

*Glorious it is for the Americans to be called by
Providence to this post of honor....it is a miracle in
human affairs...the greatest revolution the world
ever saw.*

—Benjamin Franklin

In the previous chapter we asserted that the American
Revolution holds a preeminent place in the plan of the
Almighty. We will now corroborate this powerful assertion
through exploring the details within the historical account. In
so doing, we will witness powerful and heavenly
manifestations, both on and off the battlefields of war; we
will see tokens and signs of the gospel, which are
astonishingly laced throughout the Revolution's history; and
we will identify the American Covenant, which was always at
the core of this heavenly movement and is thus reflected in
God's actions toward the American revolutionaries and, in
turn, is reflected in the revolutionaries' actions toward God.

Ultimately, we will see that it was through this covenant that America received the blessings of *liberty*, *protection*, and *prosperity*, even those blessings necessary to defeat its enemies and eventually create the environment where Christ's Gospel could flourish.

We will begin our analysis of this historical narrative by discussing God's spiritual and physical interventions into revolutionary America. While the next chapter will focus on God's miraculous and *physical* interventions on the battlefields of the American War for Independence, it is the purpose of this chapter to reveal how His powerful and *spiritual* influence touched the hearts and souls of the Founders, and thus called them, directed them, and upheld them in the cause of revolution. Patriots both past and present have referred to this spiritual influence as the *The Spirit of Independence* or *The Spirit of '76*. As the Founders listened and adhered to this Spirit, they were fulfilling their end of the covenant, thus allowing God to bless their righteous cause.

Though the presence of this revolutionary American spirit, and the nomenclature we have assigned it, are well known, the actual details concerning how it was delivered and received during this historic time are perhaps less known. As such, in an effort to further prove God's hand in America and thus further validate His national covenant with America, we will attempt here to make such details known by exploring and developing five evidentiary concepts found within the historical record. These concepts show how the Lord hurled His power and influence, even this *Spirit of Independence*, down upon colonial America. They are, in no particular order, 1) The Spiritual Preparation of George Washington; 2) The Otherwise Inexplicable Decision of the Revolutionaries; 3) The Testimonials of the Rebels; 4) The Great Awakening; and 5) The Conversion of the Founders.

The Spiritual Preparation of George Washington

It seems clear that the unseen hand of the Lord intervened early and often in the life of Washington, thus preparing him for the preeminent role he would play in the creation of America and the establishment of the national covenant.

Washington was born in Westmorland County, Virginia, in 1732. Washington's forbearers first immigrated to America in 1658, in large part to be free of the Old World's religious persecution[1]—an appropriate heritage for Washington. Though precious little is known about his childhood, we do know that his father, Augustine, was a relatively successful planter, businessman, and civil servant, and that his mother, Mary Bell,

Portrait [of Washington] in the Uniform of British Colonial Colonel, by Charles Wilson Peale, 1772

was both attentive and strict with her children. Both were devout parents to George and instilled in him the important values that would serve him later in his divine calling. Such values included strict obedience, deep humility, and an enduring love of God.

One of the few stories we know from his childhood demonstrates the parental teaching of such obedience and humility. When George was four-years-old, he decided to surprise his mother one morning by bringing her a bunch of her award-winning peonies from the family garden. As young George warmly and enthusiastically presented his offering, he was met by a stern reproach and a vigorous paddling. Such tough love may seem inappropriate for a four-year-old, but his father explained to him that the peonies were intended to stay where they were. The deeper lesson, as Augustine lovingly taught, is that every action made, even if

165

done with good intention, is accompanied by consequences. Young George had to learn to develop the foresight to see such consequences and act responsibly.[2]

Another story told of young Washington was when his father helped him plant cabbage seeds in a pattern that spelled out the name G-E-O-R-G-E. When the cabbage grew out enough to make visible the boy's name, he was astonished. According to one source, upon seeing the boy's reaction, Washington's father pointed to the cabbage and then told him, "This is a great thing, an important thing, a vital thing…I want you to understand, my son, that I am introducing you to your *true* Father, the source and sustenance of all life."[3]

In addition to such lessons, Augustine taught George the more profound meaning of life based in obedience, humility, and love of God. "The Ten Commandments," he would repeatedly tell his children, "cover the major issues of life; there is nothing that equals them…in application to our general problems."[4] Furthermore, young George was instructed to write, repeat, and apply several maxims, one of which stated, "Labour to keep alive in your breast that little spark of celestial fire called conscience."[5]

These lessons would be invaluable to Washington when confronted with the great challenge that was the American Revolution and nation building. One might even draw direct correlations between these childhood lessons and Washington's poised and wise decisions on the battlefield, as will be seen throughout the following chapters. We will see these attributes reflected, for example, in his constant submission to the Congress during the conflict, his impressive concession of power back to the people at war's end, and most importantly, his ever-enduring appeals to, reliance upon, and constant recognition of the Almighty's hand in the affairs of America.

Though his upbringing helped form the exceptional man he would become, his youth was spent largely in the usual pursuits of the Virginia gentry: riding, fishing, hunting, planting, and dancing. He eventually made a prosperous career for himself as a land surveyor, spending much time exploring the uncharted territories in the western parts of Virginia. At the age of twenty-one, due in part to his exceptional knowledge of these uncharted lands, Washington became a major in the Virginia militia, which would serve under the British during the American land claim battles known as the French and Indian War. Though he fought and led courageously—making a name for himself within Virginia —his short military career was less than successful, as he lost most of his engagements with the French, including his embarrassing surrender of the British Fort Necessity. After not receiving the promotion he desired, Washington abandoned the military for what he thought would be forever.

With his military service completed at age twenty-seven, he returned to private life, married the wealthy widow Martha Custis, and eventually inherited, and developed, the plantation known as Mount Vernon. Apart from his responsibilities of running a successful plantation operation, Washington was active in church and community affairs. He also served in the Virginia House of Burgesses, but consistently maintained a low profile, introducing no legislation and making few speeches. He would maintain this same quiet demeanor as a Virginia delegate to the Continental Congress in 1774, when the whispers of revolution were evolving into a solidified voice. Though he expressed disdain for British tyranny, he failed to make any speeches or earn any appointment to a congressional committee.[6]

As such, it may have come as a surprise to some when —at the Second Continental Congress in June 1775—the delegate from Massachusetts, John Adams, perhaps the loudest and most influential voice for American independence, nominated Washington to be commander-in-chief of the Continental Army.[7] And perhaps more surprising was the ease with which his nomination was accepted by the Congress. After all, though Washington's appointment would bring much needed support from the southern states (particularly the powerhouse that was Virginia), and though he had indeed been a military man at one time in his life, critics would have had good reason to balk at the decision.

First, with so little formal education, which ended for him at age fifteen, Washington's academic training paled in comparison to the many highly-educated and accomplished delegates that surrounded him, namely, Thomas Jefferson, John Adams, Richard Henry Lee, Benjamin Rush, James Wilson, and many others. Second, Washington had been retired from any military service for *fifteen* years. As the Pulitzer Prize-winning scholar David McCullough pointed out, "he was by no means an experienced commander. He had never led an army in battle, never commanded anything larger than a regiment. And never had he directed a siege."[8] In fact, the only military experience he possessed, as already noted, had yielded less than impressive results.

Washington himself recognized his inadequacies before Congress. In his acceptance speech, he stated:

> I am truly sensible of the high honor done to me in this appointment, yet I feel great distress from a consciousness that my abilities and military experience may not be equal to the extensive and important trust....I beg it may be remembered by every gentlemen in the room that I this day declare with utmost sincerity, I do not think myself equal to the command I [am] honored with.[9]

And it wasn't as though the Congress had no other choices for their commander-in-chief. On the contrary, there were several whose military experience far surpassed that of Washington. For example, Washington's original second-in–command, Charles Lee, had traveled the world fighting as a British officer and had even served as a military advisor to the King of Poland; he was most definitely "a professional soldier."[10] Another long standing professional soldier was Horatio Gates, who at one point during the war almost managed to oust Washington as commander. Gates was many years older than Washington and displayed far greater familiarity with military affairs. Having served at length as a British officer, he possessed without question "greater professional experience than Washington." And still there were others such as Thomas Conway and Thomas Mifflin, both of which, as military executives and chief administrators, had more military experience than Washington (which may explain why they both would aspire underhandedly to unseat Washington as commander).[11] Even the famous and highly competent John Hancock, who presided over Congress, desired the position and thought it might be his.[12]

Yet reason seemed overshadowed by something bigger than any of the delegates could fully comprehend. It was perhaps only in the wisdom and influence of the Lord that Washington could have been so readily selected. Adams, as will be shown later, was unarguably a spiritually connected man, which lends further credibility to the idea that his supporting and propping up of the General was perhaps wholly inspired. It seems as though Washington agreed with this sentiment when, as the newly appointed commander, he wrote to his wife that "far from seeking this appointment, I have used every endeavor in my power to avoid it, not only from my unwillingness to part with you and the family, but from a consciousness of its being a trust too great for my capacity....it has been a kind of destiny that has thrown me upon this service...."[13]

Perhaps it was "destiny," or better said, *divine intervention*, which prompted and encouraged Adams and Congress to select Washington. The Lord needed someone who was sufficiently humble and obedient—someone worthy to responsibly manage the vast power that was to be handed to America's first commander-in chief. Incidentally, Charles Lee and Horatio Gates would—like thousands of others—betray and/or cower from the American cause by war's end, seeking the selfish above all else.* Washington, on the other hand, would stay faithful, always respecting his position as servant to the people, always conceding power to Congress (consistently acknowledging Congress as the rightful representatives of the people), and always seeking the guidance of God. Even his harshest critics agreed that "he could not be bribed, corrupted, or compromised."[14]

Indeed, Washington was the Lord's choice. His humility and obedience compelled him to look so often to God, which in turn allowed God to influence and direct the affairs of His people. Such qualities in Washington are what ultimately built this nation and its covenant. As Washington exhibited humility and submissiveness to God, he made himself and the nation compliant with the covenant obligations, thus calling down the needed covenant blessings. It is no wonder he would be the chosen American revolutionary head.

Notwithstanding the above analysis of Washington's divine ascension to power, prominent historian Joseph Ellis would reject the idea that God had anything to do with it,

---

* Lee was captured by the British in 1776, and then almost immediately volunteered information to the British command on how to defeat the struggling Continental Army. See David McCullough, *1776*, 266. Lee was later suspended by Congress for betraying Washington. See Willard Sterne Randall, *Alexander Hamilton, A Life* (New York: Harper Collins, 2003), 176.

In an effort to gain Washington's seat as commander, Gates became a "cunning egoist" who conspired against Washington when Washington most needed his generals' support. Then, perhaps worse, in 1780, Gates led a counter-attack in the South which resulted in his defeat at Camden. When defeat was imminent, Gates jumped on the "fastest horse he could find, [and] did not stop retreating until he was 160 miles from the battlefield." Plunged into deep disgrace, he was replaced by Nathaniel Greene and did not return to the army for two years. An investigation into his conduct was subsequently ordered. See Thomas Fleming, "Unlikely Victory," *What If? The World's Foremost Military Historians Imagine What Might Have Been* (New York: Penguin Putnam Inc, 1999), 173; See also "Horatio Gates," *Columbia Encyclopedia, Sixth Edition. 2001-2005*, available online at www.bartleby.com/65/ga/Gates.

arguing instead that John Adams' role in the affair was exaggerated and that Washington's place as commander was a logical, secular-minded, "forgone conclusion." As proof, Ellis offers up the valid point that perhaps Washington was the most obvious Virginian, and Virginia's support was a necessity. Ellis' other argument was that Washington's commanding physical appearance and his use of military fatigues in Congress swayed the judgment of the delegates in favor of him. That his physical attributes swayed the masses is one thing, but that they caused the delegates to appoint Washington is much less convincing, as it would require us to believe that the very intelligent and deliberate-minded congressional delegates could be taken by such physical trivialities.

But whatever reason one might give for why Washington was an obvious choice (even a foregone conclusion) is trumped by the main issue—his indisputable lack of military experience. Ellis himself admits, in the same language as McCullough, the military inadequacies of Washington, adding that the desperate General even turned to military textbooks to teach himself how to organize an army.[15] Could such a man, so lacking in a comprehensive knowledge of the task at hand, be deemed by the delegates to be an "obvious choice" or "forgone conclusion"? Only with God's influence penetrating the hearts of his fellow congressmen could such a notion be conceived.

The highly-educated, over-opinionated delegates of the Congress, who seemed to bicker and debate about anything and everything, were risking, as they put it, "our lives, our fortunes, and our sacred honor"* in this cause of independence. They were willingly and knowingly placing their lives, fortunes, and sacred honor in the hands of Washington. Yet there was little, if any, real debate surrounding his appointment when, as evidenced above, there was much to be debated. The truth is,

---

*As quoted from the Declaration of Independence

while Washington was not void of obvious qualities that lent themselves to positive judgments by purely secular minds, it was largely divine intervention that led to his rapid approval and ascension as commander of the Continental Army.

Beyond the events surrounding his inspired appointment by Congress, the evidence is clear that, from an even earlier time, a divine mantle accompanied Washington to

The battle of Monongahela

his national calling. One oft-told account, once found in American history textbooks (when it was still acceptable to speak of God in school) reflected this very sentiment. On July 9, 1755, in the battle of Monongahela, during the French and Indian War, a young Washington would miraculously survive an onslaught of enemy firepower that killed or wounded over half of the participants. With "death leveling my companions on every side of me," Washington would later explain, "by the miraculous care of Providence, that protected me beyond human expectations; I had four bullets through my coat, and two horses shot from under me, and yet escaped unhurt."[16] God's preserving hand was upon him. Washington's work had not yet been accomplished.

An epilogue to this story occurred some fifteen years later when a certain Indian chief named Grand Sachem, who had been at the battle of Monongahela, sat in a meeting with a group of Virginians, one of which was an older and more mature Washington. The meeting, which occurred in 1770, was recorded by Washington's adopted grandson, George Washington Parke Custis, in his 1827 work entitled "Recollections of Washington." During the meeting, the chief, recognizing Washington—still years before Washington would become famous—stood and said:

> I am a chief and ruler over many tribes. The hunting grounds of my people extend from the thunder of the Onigara and the Great Lakes to the far blue mountains. I have traveled the long and weary path of the wilderness road that I might once again look upon the young warrior [Washington] of the great battle. By the waters of the Monongahela, we met the soldiers of the King beyond the Seas, who came to drive from the land my French Brothers. They came into the forest with much beating of drums and many flags flying in the breeze. Like a blind wolf they walked into our trap, and the faces of these red-clad warriors turned pale at the sound of our war-whoop. It was a day when the white man's blood mixed with the streams and forests, and 'twas then I first beheld this Chief. [Points to Washington.] I called my young men and said: "Mark you tall and daring warrior! He is not of the red-coat tribe, he is of the Long-knives. He has an Indian's wisdom. His warriors fight as we do—himself alone is exposed to our fire. Quick! Let your aim be certain and he dies. Our muskets were leveled—muskets that, for all but him, knew not how to miss. I, who can bring the leaping squirrel from the top of the highest tree with a single shot, fired at this warrior more times than I have fingers. Our bullets killed his horse, knocked

the war bonnet from his head, pierced his clothes, but 'twas in vain; a Power mightier far than we shielded him from harm. He cannot be killed in battle. I am old and soon shall be gathered to the great council fire of the Land of the Shades, but ere I go, there is something bids me speak in the voice of prophecy. Listen! Give ear to my words ye that are gathered here. The Great Spirit protects that man and guides his footsteps through the trails of life. He will become the chief of many nations, and when the sun is setting on the remaining few of my people and the game has departed from our forests and streams, a people yet unborn will hail him as the founder of a mighty empire. I have spoken.

Washington reportedly responded after a long pause:

Our destinies are shaped by a mighty Power, and we can but strive to be worthy of what the Great Spirit holds in store for us. If I must needs have such lot in life as our Red Brother presages, then I pray that the Great Spirit give unto me those qualities of fortitude, courage, and wisdom possessed by our Red Brother. I, the friend of the Indian, have spoken.[17]

The prophetic nature of this dialogue is emphasized by the fact that it occurred some five years before Washington was called to lead the Continental Army.

Also prophesying about a young Washington, years before he would become a household name, was the Reverend Samuel Davies, who proclaimed: "I cannot but hope Providence has hitherto preserved in so signal a Manner for some important Service to his Country."[18] In a similar spirit, Washington's mother, upon her deathbed, reportedly told her son, "Go, George, fulfill the high destinies which Heaven appears to have intended for you."[19]

That Washington had been prepared by God for his calling under the covenant is evident enough. But the most convincing evidence will be detailed in later chapters, as we see the General in action under God. We will see him powerfully represented in his role as the revolutionary leader of the covenant, as he turns so often to both the Almighty and to the principles of that sacred text which detail America's covenant obligations. As Washington himself explained, "It is impossible to rightly govern the world without God and the Bible."[20] It is no wonder historians have called Washington the "Moses of the New World" and portrayed "the war [for Independence] as another exodus from Egypt."[21] Washington is surely worthy of this honor and distinction. There is a reason that the very spiritually and politically involved Abigail Adams (John Adams' wife) described Washington using the following words: "Mark his majestic fabric. He's a temple sacred from his birth and built by hands divine."[22]

Before entering the following chapters, which will corroborate these powerful descriptions of Washington, we will first address certain false, exaggerated, or misunderstood claims about him which have recently taken aim at his life and legacy. First, in a 2004 best-selling biography, Washington is accused of being overly self-absorbed and ambitious—the "most ambitious" of all the congressional delegates. Ironically, according to the critic, this deep pride manifests itself in Washington's seemingly humble demeanor, actions, and words, as viewed from Washington's aforementioned letters and communications to those supporting him. As proof of such a claim, the critic points out that Washington displayed the same self-doubt and reticence in response to all three of his great promotions: as commander of the army, as chairman of the Constitutional Convention, and as president of the United States. Apparently, nobody could *really* be that humble. "After all, Washington had been talked about as the leading candidate [for commander] for several weeks [before his appointment] and did nothing to discourage such talk, and had been wearing his uniform" in posturing for the position. Therefore, concludes the critic, Washington must have "fabricated" his humble acceptance of authority in an effort to hide his selfish motivation—hence, his obvious "pattern of postured reticence" in response to the honors given him.[23]

While not denying that, like any great leader, Washington possessed the necessary ambition to accomplish his goals, this critique hurled upon him must overcome the following questions: Would not a pattern of humility be more easily attributed to one's *actual* humility than to a "fabrication"? Does one's failure to actively discourage his own promotion by others really constitute an act of pride and ambition? Do we really know Washington's true motive for dressing in his old military fatigues from time to time? Would the most ambitious, power-seeking delegate of Congress return his great power to the people as Washington did at war's end —though thousands of years of military tradition would have justified him keeping it—just to maintain his fabricated show of humility? Would he have returned to Mount Vernon after only two presidential terms, when no law at the time compelled it and when the people would have elected him for life? And how do we explain David McCullough's comment that by age twenty-seven, "if he [had] seemed at times flagrantly, unattractively ambitious, he had long since overcome that"?[24] Finally, how do we explain the opinions of Washington's close friends and peers who called him "amiable" and "modest," "void of austerity" and with "no hint of arrogance"?[25]

The second critique, also advanced by modern-day scholars, puts into question Washington's relationship with God. One award-winning author recently described Washington's personal religion as follows: "A lukewarm Episcopalian, he never took Communion, tended to talk about 'Providence' or 'Destiny' rather than God, and—was this a statement?—preferred to stand rather than kneel when praying."[26]

This author's suggestion—which is a popular one among secular-minded critics—is problematic on several levels. For example, if Washington was not overly active as an Episcopalian, this says nothing of his feelings toward God. Like Adams and Jefferson (as will be discussed), perhaps Washington's faith transcended any one particular denomination. One's level of participation in any given religious sect is not necessarily an indication of one's faith and devotion to God. Notwithstanding this rationale, however, several eyewitnesses testified that Washington *did*, in fact, take communion regularly.[27]

Furthermore, the notion that Washington was less than a true believer because he used a variety of titles for God (other than "God") is weak and misleading for at least two reasons. First, it is documented that Washington used the title "God" on more than one hundred occasions. (This is, of course, counting only those times when these public pronouncements were actually documented.) Second, it was customary for Anglicans in eighteenth-century Virginia to refrain from using the title of "God." As one historian pointed out, "The avoidance [of using the title "God"] was not out of unbelief, but from a reverence for the sacred names and a desire to keep them from being profaned."[28] And so Washington often used alternate titles for God, such as *Providence* and *Almighty*.

The argument that Washington's alleged weak religion is somehow represented by the notion that he refrained from kneeling when praying is equally problematic and misleading. For how many praying people kneel in public? Indeed, such a practice is generally confined to private moments, far from the eye of reporters and historians. Perhaps this critique was aimed at the idea that Washington stood during formal church religious devotionals, while others knelt. If such is the case, we should defer to Washington's adopted granddaughter, Nelly Custis, who explained that her grandfather did in fact stand, "as was the custom" for Virginia gentlemen at that time.[29]

Perhaps the most frustrating element concerning these many attempts to belittle Washington's religion is that these critics make their analysis and simply omit the rich and abundant historical evidence which disproves their arguments. That is, they ignore the evidence that clearly shows how important God was to Washington. We have already outlined many examples that show the Lord was Washington's absolute strength and inspiration. And there are many more examples. Indeed, there are at least 270 documented references in which Washington recognizes the activity and interest of God in his life and in the life of America.[30]

In addition to ignoring such references, critics also have a tendency to omit the testimonies of his family and friends who declared unequivocally that Washington was a profoundly religious man. His family remembered seeing him "upon his knees at a small table, with a candle and open Bible thereon."[31] His secretary, Tobias Lear, confirmed the regular occurrence of these religious devotionals.[32] Colonel B. Temple, an aide to Washington, stated that in the absence of a chaplain, Washington himself would read the Bible to his troops. Temple further noted that, on more than one occasion, he walked into Washington's quarters and "found him on his knees at his devotions." Another of Washington's aides commented that "whenever the General could be spared from camp, on the Sabbath, he never failed riding out to some neighboring church, to join those who were publicly worshipping the Great Creator."[33] And these testimonies only scratch the surface of Washington's deep relationship with God and covenant, as we will see in the forthcoming chapters.

Indeed, Washington was *deeply* religious. He was also very private about his personal testimony, thus making himself vulnerable to critics who want so badly for him to be a purely secular character. Using the weak arguments discussed above, these critics often suggest that Washington was a Deist—one who believes in a God, but also believes that this God is not actively involved or interested in the affairs of man. However, based on the facts thus far presented concerning Washington and his relationship with God, any attempts to cast doubt on his personal religion, or to classify him as a Deist, seem futile— and by the end of the next few chapters will seem absolutely absurd.

The third and final popular critique of Washington relates to the unfortunate and very real fact that he participated in the evil practice of slavery. Though born into this culture, which taught him of slavery's benign normalcy, Washington struggled with it internally, particularly during the war years. On several occasions, Washington recognized the great immoral irony of his American generation: that it would enslave others while pursuing independence for itself. In an effort to resolve his internal struggle, Washington would endorse plans to emancipate slavery by war's end, but support for such schemes would be unattainable due to—in Washington's words—the "selfish passion" which reigned in the South.[34] By 1779, Washington himself had decided to sell his own slaves in exchange for hired labor (which made sense to him on an economic level as well), but later realized he could not, as most of his slaves belonged to his wife's family. Furthermore, selling his slaves would have resulted in the reprehensible separation of his slave families, which on a moral level he refused to permit—even when such refusal brought a decline in profits and transformed Mount Vernon into a "retirement home and child-care center for many of his slave residents."[35]

Unfortunately, Washington's own weakness perhaps barred him from the simple act of freeing the slaves he could (over one hundred of the Mount Vernon slaves belonged exclusively to him). Such an act of mercy would have partially solved his moral dilemma. In his defense, however, Washington was one of the precious few of the founding generation that did free his slaves upon his death. Not only did he free them but, as instructed in his Last Will and Testament, each was to be provided for and educated through a trust fund he established "to help them in their freedom." Washington's trust fund "continued to support his former slaves and their descendants well into the nineteenth century."[36]

Other evidence of Washington's more high-minded feelings regarding blacks in America includes his unusual willingness to work side by side with them, his constant instructions to his foremen to treat them well and not overwork them, and his acceptance of their enlistment into his Continental Army (up to fifteen percent of the Continental regulars were black).[37] We gain further insight on the issue through a letter Washington wrote to the black slave and poet, Phyllis Wheatley, in which he thanked her for her kind words, graciously praised her prose, and invited her to visit him at his headquarters.[38] We also witness his softened heart toward African Americans through a note in his will, in which he describes an "attachment" to his personal man-servant Billy Lee, whose "faithful service" to Washington earned him his freedom, along with his own annuity and free room and board for the rest of his life.[39]

Finally, in the years just following the creation of the United States, and with the South already threatening secession over the slave question, Washington's own thoughts, influenced by his understanding of America and her covenant with God, were nothing less than prophetic: "I clearly foresee," he declared, "that nothing but the rooting out of slavery can perpetuate the existence of our union." According to his attorney general, Edmund Randolph, if a civil war over the issue ensued, Washington—though a proud Southerner—"had made up his mind to move and be of the northern."[40]

Admittedly, these actions and sentiments towards his slaves, and blacks in general, seem inconsequential and petty within a twenty-first century viewpoint. However, in light of the times in which he lived, Washington certainly rose higher than could be expected from a Southern plantation owner.

But regardless of what one gleans from any of the above insights into his complexities and controversies, Washington's preeminent place in history is anchored to something far more significant, even his principal role in creating one nation under God for the eternal purposes of God. The biographical sketches offered above certainly demonstrate the Lord's influence in his early preparation and character. And this spiritual influence would only continue to grow in Washington, as the *Spirit of Independence* drove him to understand and regularly invoke the principles of the American Covenant. The following pages and chapters will continue to detail this history, allowing all to judge for themselves this man and the cause that he and his fellow Americans gave themselves to.

The Otherwise Inexplicable Decision of the Revolutionaries

The textbook reasons for why the American colonists went to war against Britain are simply not strong enough or compelling enough alone to explain the passion, dedication, and sacrifice displayed in revolutionary America. This is not to say that these textbook reasons do not justify a decision to enter the war; on the contrary, even the most rudimentary explanations for why the colonists went forward with their rebellion justify their actions. However, upon considering the full historical landscape in which the American colonists lived, their decision to proceed with the Revolutionary War, and thus endure what they did, compels even the patriots among us to ask, *Why did they do it? How did they think it was worth it in their time and space?* We shall see that there were overwhelming reasons *not* to fight for independence, which explains the perhaps surprising fact that only about one third of the colonial American population remained consistently in favor of the war.[41] So what kept this one-third focused and determined at any cost? What rounded out their reasoning and justification, giving them that extra push to endure unspeakable pains to separate themselves from Britain? It was the *Spirit of Independence*, even that divine, unseen hand that influenced, inspired, and supported this chosen American minority.

Without the variable of this divine power and influence, the equation for why the American colonists did what they did simply does not add up. With it, however, it all makes perfect sense. As we now discuss the full scope of how the colonists ended up in full-blown rebellion and revolution, we will see this *Spirit of Independence* manifest itself, thus offering further proof of God's hand in America and validating, once again, our covenant with Him.

In an attempt to prove this unconventional argument, let us first consider some key historical facts surrounding the decision to declare independence from, and commence war with, Great Britain. It is through analyzing this ultimate decision to go to war that we see how the *Spirit of Independence* must have played a key role. The events leading to this decision grew out of a series of political events beginning in 1763. Prior to 1763, the British refrained from over-engaging in the affairs of her American subjects, thus sustaining relative peace between the two nations. The following events, however, changed that relationship forever:

1763: *The Proclamation*: After pushing back the French, as a result of the French and Indian War, King George feels obliged to secure his American interests by reigning in all his American subjects, prohibiting their migration west of the Allegheny Mountains. This move is seen by many as an attempt to virtually confiscate much of the westward land claims held by some of the colonists, now to be used by the British to repay the debt for the recent war with the French.

1765:   *The Stamp Act*: The British impose a light tax on all paper goods (everything from stamps and legal documents to playing cards) for the purpose of offsetting some of the costs incurred by Britain to provide for the physical and economic security of the colonists. In response, some colonists form the secret organization, Sons of Liberty, which persecutes those agents responsible for enforcing the Stamp Act, forcing them to resign or face destruction to their persons and/or property.

1767:   *The Townshend Act*: After repealing the very controversial Stamp Act (after major protest and pressure from the colonists), Britain imposes a new set of indirect taxes on commodities as diverse as glass, paint, and tea.

1768:   Britain sends soldiers to enforce its royal acts.

1770:   *The Boston Massacre*: A handful of British soldiers open fire on a group of sixty American colonists who are physically harassing them. Five colonists are killed. The soldiers are ironically defended by the great American revolutionary, John Adams, who argues successfully that the soldiers acted in self-defense. They were acquitted in an American court.

1773:   *The British Tea Act:* After the Townshend Act is repealed (again, after much American protest), the British determine to maintain a standing tax on one commodity: tea.

1773:   *Boston Tea Party*: In response to the tea tax, colonial rebels, dressed as Mohawk Indians, board British vessels docked in Boston harbor and dump 23,000 pounds of tea into the waters below.

1774:   *The British Coercive Acts:* In response to the "Boston Tea Party," Britain enacts and enforces a policy which virtually takes over Boston and closes its ports.

1775: *Lexington and Concord*: In an effort to make preparations to counter the Coercive Acts, some colonists begin stockpiling arms in towns outside of Boston. British forces confront Massachusetts militiamen guarding their small strongholds and weapons caches in the towns of Lexington and Concord. (It was on this occasion that Paul Revere made his famous ride alerting the "Minutemen" that the "Redcoats" were coming). The armed conflict that ensued went down in history as "the shot heard round the world," and opened the curtains to the American War for Independence.

We will pause at this point in our chronology to examine *why* the Americans decided to push back at every effort Britain made to assert her influence, even when such rebellious action meant armed conflict with the world's leading superpower. The short answer, and the one taught to us in school textbooks, can be summed up through a series of speeches and writings by people like John Adams, Thomas Jefferson, Thomas Paine, and Patrick Henry. These men authored or recited the famous phrases that incited the *Spirit of Independence*: phrases such as "No taxation without representation," "Unite or die," "Don't tread on me," "All men are created equal," "Give me liberty or give me death," "natural rights," and the novel, even radical, argument for their day, that there is "no natural or religious reason [for] the distinction of men into kings and subjects."[42]

Without a doubt, the colonists were feeling the heavy hand of a monarchical system. They were being taxed without even indirect consent (no representation), their local laws were scrutinized by the king and abolished and adjusted from time to time, and they were forced to house and care for the British soldiers within the borders of America. But did these offenses, in and of themselves, really warrant a rebellion which would cause an unprecedented amount of blood to fall upon American soil? Perhaps so. Perhaps the revolutionaries were correct to fear they were headed down a road of oppression. Americans were certainly justified to fight for their inherent right of self-governance.

However, the American cause was not the popular campaign we might have imagined. To be sure, its critics, especially those from America, had reason to believe the revolutionaries were overreacting—that they were being paranoid. According to the great American revolutionary leader, John Adams, and as confirmed by a modern-day Pulitzer Prize-winning historian of the American Revolution, over fifty percent of Americans—perhaps as many as sixty-five percent—at various times during the Revolution, believed the American sacrifice for independence was *not* worth it.[43] (These percentages fluctuated month to month depending on how America was doing in the war.) Why would so many Americans oppose war with Britain? Because of the following unromantic facts that have been void from so many of our historical textbooks.

First, King George was not the crazy, power-hungry, inflexible tyrant—unwilling to make any concessions—that many interpretations of the American Revolution have painted him to be. Evidence suggests he was very modest for a king, close to his many young children (he had fifteen children) and faithful to his wife (which says a lot for one living in the adulterous royal culture that he did).[44] Most importantly, he was not unsympathetic to the complaints of the colonists. As noted above, he did repeal many of his taxes and policies in response to the protests of the Americans.[45] His goal was not to have unhappy American subjects. Just after the war had ended, the king expressed the following to the first American ambassador to Britain: "I wish you, sir, to believe, and that it be understood in America, that I have done nothing in the late contest but what I thought myself indispensably bound to do by the duty which I owed my people."[46] Perhaps extended patience by the colonists, along with more peaceful protests and dialogue with the Crown, would have borne fruit. Instead, the colonists turned to destruction and violence early on, mostly through groups like the Sons of Liberty, which—though again, was justified—promptly forced the British hand.

Second, the taxes that were laid on the Americans did not even exceed five percent of their individual incomes—and even less if the colonists refrained from consuming taxable commodities (the British levied a sales tax, not an income tax). Based on revolutionary rhetoric, modern Americans should have long ago overthrown their own government, which today demands upwards of twenty percent to forty percent of its citizens' income (and this modern tax is not only a sales tax, as it was for the colonists, but also a direct tax on actual *income*). Furthermore, was five percent (or less) too much to ask for the protection and infrastructure provided to the colonists? Similarly, was it too much to ask the colonists to provide for the wellbeing of the British soldiers who had protected them against foreign aggression? After all, not many years had passed since the king had repelled France's efforts to overtake their continent.

Third, apart from the British offenses listed above, additional complaints, as expressed in the Declaration of Independence, are vague and largely unsupported. Accusatory statements against the king, such as "he has excited domestic insurrections among us," "he has plundered our seas," "[he has] destroyed the lives of our people" and "[he has] declared us out of his protection and wag[es] war against us," seemed exaggerated to many critics of colonial America, who rightfully asked, *What proof do you have of this*? Indeed, few specific examples are given in the Declaration to support these claims.

Of course, these critics of colonial America would readily admit to the British "offenses," such as the levying of taxes, the Boston Massacre, the Coercive Acts (Siege of Boston harbor), and the attack on Lexington and Concord. But they could also make compelling arguments as to why these British actions could be seen as reasonable, defensive, and reactionary to colonial aggression. Again, the taxes were being levied mostly in order to pay for services rendered to the colonists. Furthermore, the British soldiers in the Boston Massacre were defended by John Adams and acquitted in a colonial court from any wrongdoing, as they were acting in self-defense against colonial rioting. Even Benjamin Franklin expressed understanding of British frustrations at colonial aggression, such as the Boston Tea Party, which he called an "an act of violent injustice on our part."[47] And finally, when the British sent soldiers to the scene of what they reasonably viewed as an insurrection, and when they learned that the colonists were stockpiling weapons against them in nearby towns, they were only acting reasonably to attack these colonial strongholds at Lexington and Concord.

Indeed, many of the colonial complaints were not unlike the one-sided, political, partisan rhetoric we hear daily, that only sounds fully justified when key facts are withheld. That spewing such propaganda was Jefferson's intent (to at least some degree) when drafting this section of the Declaration of Independence can be seen in an earlier draft of the Declaration, in which he goes so far as to accuse King George himself for the evil practice of the slave trade in America—though slavery existed in the New World hundreds of years before King George's birth. (The reason it was rejected by the delegates was that it was offensive to Southern slave owners who quite liked the practice in America.)[48]

The point is this: without detracting from the very inspired and true principles of freedom laced throughout the Declaration, and notwithstanding the very legitimate complaints such as lack of political representation, there is reason to believe the revolutionaries painted a gloomier picture than the truth. With the situation perhaps not as bad as we have imagined, we can see why so many Americans were opposed to war with Britain. Such reasoning to oppose this war is even more emphasized when considering the fourth and final argument many made against the need for revolution.

Fourth, as early as the 1750's, it was British policies and protections provided to the colonists that had caused America to possess the *highest per capita wealth in the world.*[49] Indeed, things were good in America, in that jobs and opportunities flourished. It was, after all, British America that welcomed an illegitimate child to its shores, who as a young man would arrive alone from a foreign land and shortly thereafter become the successful attorney and statesmen called Alexander Hamilton. It was British America that provided the system whereby a teenage runaway could arrive at Philadelphia without a penny in his pocket and become the wealthy, world-renowned inventor, businessman and statesman called Benjamin Franklin. And the success stories go on and on. Did such great and beneficial political and economic infrastructure offered by the British not overshadow any other complaint held by the colonists? Did it not justifiably warrant the relatively light taxes and other obligations placed on them?

King George certainly thought it did and understandably marveled at how the colonists could bite the hand that had fed them. He wondered out loud to his parliament how the Americans could forget that "to be a subject of Great Britain, with all its consequences, is to be the freest member of any civil society in the known world." And though the king claimed to be "anxious to prevent... the effusion of blood" and would "receive the misled [revolutionaries] with tenderness and mercy," he expressed his duty to not let America go:

> The object is too important, the spirit of the British nation too high, the resources with which God hath blessed her too numerous, to give up so many colonies which she has planted with great industry, nursed with great tenderness, encouraged with many commercial advantages, and protected and defended at much expense and treasure.[50]

The king was making the very compelling argument that the American cause of independence was not a war of necessity for the colonists, but of choice. And, as witnessed by the many Americans (usually the vast majority) who thought war with Britain was foolish, the king's message was not ill-received. The American delegate to the Continental Congress, Edward Rutledge, declared that the "sensible part of the house opposed the motion" for independence, then dramatically added, "No reason could be assigned for pressing into the measure [of declaring independence], but the reason of every madman."[51] Yet, by some miracle it seemed, there still existed throughout the colonies a group of men and women, consisting of roughly one-third of America's populace, who *never* wavered and were willing to sacrifice all for independence. And what's more, and further miraculous, these few, these chosen, found themselves at the proverbial helm of the American political ship.

Notwithstanding the powerful words of liberty and true principles of good government proclaimed by these revolutionary few, the questions still lingered then, as they do today: *Why* sacrifice all when things were pretty good at home? Though admittedly there were problems, how intolerable could they have been when prosperity abounded and America was among the freest of any society in the world at that time? Were members of the Continental Congress (who got America into the war) hungry, impoverished, suffering? To the contrary, there was very little these colonial elites did without. Were they being forced into a religion or limited in their ability to worship freely? In actuality, they participated in various religious denominations and, for the most part, enjoyed religious freedom. Then *why* throw themselves and the rest of America into a war of choice (not necessity) that would last eight years and result in the second most costly war—second only to the Civil War—in terms of casualties proportionate to population in all of American history? In today's numbers, the Revolutionary War would be akin to losing three-million American lives.[52]

Even the Pulitzer Prize-winning historian, David McCullough, in apparent awe at America's decided course, reminds us that "the Americans of 1776 enjoyed a higher standard of living than any people in the world...How people with so much, living on their own land, would ever choose to rebel against the ruler God had put over them and thereby bring down such devastation on themselves was...incomprehensible."[53] Another Pulitzer Prize-winning historian, Joseph Ellis, expressed a similar sense of bewilderment, when, upon explaining how he understood why the faithful began the war (they indeed were justified), "I'll be darned if I know why [they] stayed" (the justification seemed unworthy of the sacrifice).[54]

But no historian, even searching high and low for historical evidences, can ever tell us *why* they did it. Only through God—the same which guided our Founders—can it fully be explained. It is this spiritual foundation, not secular knowledge alone, that allows us to understand the actions of the Founders. No secular-based historian can explain why the Founders did what they did any more than they can explain why Moses put everything on the line and did what he did, challenging the Pharaoh. In each case, God's chosen ones were acting on inspiration, having been raised up for that very purpose. And though admittedly the Founders were not prophets in the mold of Moses, they were perhaps the closest thing God had to prophets in that time. They were His American Covenant-makers, and their inspired actions, though not fully understood by the world in which they lived, laid the groundwork for God's work in modern times.

As explained in the previous chapter, America needed to be free from a monarchical system (however relatively benign some felt it was at the time), as it could have too easily come down upon Christianity and its renewal and enlargement. America also needed a rebirth of liberty at home in order to root out its own domestic-based religious intolerance against minorities. Though this was a byproduct of the Revolution, and not a colonial justification for war, it was nonetheless God's intention; for this would clear the way for God's Gospel to grow upon the earth. And finally, America needed to ignite the flame of righteous rebellions in the world, so that this freedom unto gospel salvation might spread to all mankind. The Revolution would provide all these prerequisites for mankind to fully enjoy personal liberty and, thus, to enjoy a full measure of Christ's Gospel. Had *all* these would-be fruits of independence been common knowledge among the colonists, any and all of their sacrifices pursuant to the Revolution would be more fully comprehended today. However, as these godly justifications were generally unknown to the colonists, we see why the Lord needed to send the influential power of the *Spirit of Independence*—that His will be done. And, notwithstanding the logical reasons not to fight—and despite severe consequences and sacrifices—the Founders felt this Spirit and obeyed.

We have only scratched the surface on the mountain of evidence proving the powerful existence of God's *Spirit of Independence*, which worked unceasingly upon the hearts and souls of those inspired Founders. While we have outlined the abundant reasons why the mere decision to go to war was, on a secular level, void of perfect sense—though perfectly understood on a spiritual level—we have yet to examine the unbearable sacrifices this decision required. We will now examine some of these specific sacrifices made by the American faithful. In doing so, we will further comprehend how only God could compel good and sane human beings to voluntarily endure what these revolutionary faithful endured, and we will better appreciate the divine power and significance of the *Spirit of Independence* He sent as part of the American Covenant.

So, as the story goes, to the astonishment of Europe and Americans loyal to the Crown, these chosen few rebels, these recipients of the *Spirit of Independence*, these American Covenant-makers, would sacrifice everything. Consider, for example, the concluding words of the Declaration of Independence: "And for the support of this Declaration...we pledge our Lives, Fortunes and Sacred Honor." And they fully understood the meaning of these words and the consequences that would come to them for signing their names should their cause fail. Thomas Jefferson would love to recount how, on the heels of the Declaration, Benjamin Harrison, the very fat delegate from Virginia, nervously joked with the thin delegate Elbridge Gerry, saying, "Gerry, when the hanging comes, I shall have the advantage; you'll kick in the air half an hour after it is all over with me!"[55]

By war's end, out of the fifty-six signers, nine had been killed, five had been captured and suffered great pains at hands of the British, twelve had seen their homes burned, looted, or otherwise destroyed, and others literally went bankrupt investing all they possessed into the cause. Thomas Nelson, Jr., for example, a one-time governor of Virginia, borrowed almost two-million dollars using his own property as collateral, and handed it over to the American war machine. In the end, he was unable to make good on his debt and lost all he possessed. At one point in the war, Nelson even directed the cannons to destroy his Yorktown home, which had been captured, and was being utilized by British forces.[56]

Another signer, Samuel Adams, repeatedly turned down handsome bribes from the British to cease and desist from spewing his revolutionary rhetoric, even though he and his family were oft times on the brink of poverty and badly needed the money. And though he was reminded that his rebellious attitude toward the British might just find him on the end of a hangman's rope, Adams simply replied: "I have long since made my peace with the King of Kings! No personal consideration shall induce me to abandon the righteous cause of my country."[57] It was his stalwart position under God that inspired him in the early days of the Revolution to organize much of the initial rebellious activity against the British in New

England, which led many to refer to him thereafter as the *Father of the Revolution*.

Then there was Robert Morris, known as the "financier of the American revolution," who personally raised war funds when the Congress was unable to act for itself. He was responsible for funding at least two of the most crucial events of the war. First was the 1776 campaign in which Washington crossed the Delaware and took Trenton and Princeton (America's first real victory that turned the tide of the war), and second was the

George Washington, Robert Morris, & Hyam Salomon Memorial in Chicago, IL

Battle of Yorktown, which secured American independence. This he did without the slightest guarantee of ever seeing a penny of it returned to his coffers.[58]*

And of course there were the greats—Adams, Jefferson, Franklin, and others of whom much will be said later in this book.

The signers were not the only ones compelled by the spirit to sacrifice everything. There was, after all, the equally amazing group of inexperienced soldiers, referred to by the

---

* Perhaps Morris' most important ally in his efforts to finance the war was the Jewish revolutionary named Haym Salomon. Salomon immigrated to America in 1775, precisely as the Revolution began, and he threw himself into the American cause immediately and whole-heartedly. First working as a spy for General Washington (for which the British tried to hang him), Salomon later helped Morris raise funds for the colonial army. Adding his significant personal savings to the cause, Salomon died a penniless man. Passing away in 1785, just on the heels of the Revolution, this Hebrew-American patriot disappeared from the scene as quickly and mysteriously as he had arrived upon it. He came to fulfill his divine mission. When finished, he departed. See http://en.wikipedia.org/wiki/Haym_Salomon

enemy as the "ramble in arms," but officially known as the Continental Army. As one prominent historian explained:

> It was the first American army and an army of everyone, men of every shape and size and makeup, different colors, different nationalities, different ways of talking, and all degrees of physical condition. Many were missing teeth or fingers, pitted by smallpox or scarred by past wars or the all-too-common hazards of life and toil in the eighteenth century. Some were not even men, but smooth-faced boys of fifteen or less.[59]

These were the unsung heroes that kept the Revolution alive. The British could conquer every major American city (which they did), but as long as these dedicated soldiers remained together and on the move, striking where they could at the inspired direction of their beloved General Washington, the British could never stomp them out. Thus lived on the *Spirit of Independence*! It was this endurance that convinced Washington that he did not need to win the war as much as he simply needed to *not lose* it. And at the end of the day, it was the perseverance of these citizen soldiers that wearied the British into surrendering their lost cause.

The *Spirit of Independence* was manifested in soldiers like Nathan Hale, who upon being captured by the British as the first American spy would say, while being led to his execution by hanging, "I regret I have but one life to give for my country."[60] It was further manifested in those like the twenty-five-year-old Boston bookstore keeper Henry Knox and the thirty-year-old Rhode Island Quaker and metal worker Nathaniel Greene. Both these men possessed military knowledge only to the extent of what they had read in books, and yet both would become Washington's most trusted and successful field commanders, enduring the entire eight years of war.[61]

What's more, these chosen soldiers would endure without the prospect of a GI Bill or an extended peacetime military career waiting for them upon their return. In fact, they would often sacrifice all without even the prospect of food, blankets, shoes, or even payment! The only guarantee they really had was that death or serious casualty would threaten them at every turn. Naturally, many deserted the group. But that a sufficient number for eventual triumph would endure is something beyond the reach of mortal comprehension. It was a miracle.

But of all those who displayed this incomprehensible dedication to the cause, none could top him who they say embodied the revolutionary generation—George Washington. His indomitable spirit can most readily be seen during what would perhaps be the most crucial period of the war. It was mid-November 1776, and Washington and his men had recently seen their first real battle with the British on and around Long Island, New York. America failed miserably in this battle. It was an absolute disaster. As the world's superpower landed on the beaches of New York and attacked, all the Americans could do was turn around and run for their lives. And, as detailed in the Prologue, they only managed this escape through divine intervention. Nathanial Greene called it "the dark part of the night," Thomas Paine called it "the times that try men's souls," and over sixteen-thousand of the approximately twenty-thousand American troops that began with Washington at New York called it "quits," mostly by way of blatant desertion.[62]

And there stood the humiliated Washington in the middle of it all, leading the retreat out of New York, southward through New Jersey and Pennsylvania. All Washington had was his remaining, and meager, band of three thousand men— scarcely fifteen percent of what he possessed just weeks prior. And most of those were due to be honorably discharged in less than fourteen days. With well over thirty thousand British troops possibly on his trail, it was no wonder he blurted out, while stroking his throat, "my neck does not feel as though it was made for a halter."[63] Washington commented about his feelings at this time, saying that "if I were to wish the bitterest curse to an enemy on this side of the grave, I should put him in my stead with my feelings....In confidence I tell you that I never was in such an unhappy, divided state since I was born."[64]

Just when things could not possibly get worse, they did. During the retreat southward, Washington received word that the colonial governments, after learning of the New York debacle, had lost interest in pursuing war and were refusing to send backup troops. According to the dispatch, his would-be brothers in arms were "divided and lethargic, slumbering under the shade of peace and in the full enjoyment of the sweets of commerce."[65] As pointed out earlier, why fight a hopeless fight when things were, after all, pretty good at home?

Also during the retreat, the already heart-broken Washington mistakenly opened a letter from one of his trusted officers and friends (the letter was intended for another officer) in which he blamed and criticized Washington for the military failure.[66] Even members of Congress, in whom he had trusted and depended upon for direction, had themselves blamed Washington and began fleeing Philadelphia for fear of being captured. [67] A few congressmen even betrayed the cause, offering their services to the enemy.[68] As one-time patriots began switching over to the British side by the thousands, the enemy was well aware of America's hopeless state. "The fact is" reported one British captain in the field, "their army is broken all to pieces, and the spirit of their leaders and their abettors is all broken....I think one may venture to pronounce that it is well nigh over with them."[69] He was correct. By all accounts the war was over. America had lost.

Again, there stood Washington in the midst of the turmoil—all alone. For a moment all he could think about was how to escape, where to hide. Should they flee to the mountains of Augusta County, West Virginia? Or should they attempt to cross the Allegheny Mountains?[70] There was, however, an alternative solution that, at the moment, seemed too good to be true. Britain had offered a "free and general pardon" to all American rebels, including a guarantee of the "preservation of their property, the restoration of their commerce, and the security of their most valuable rights," if they would but denounce the rebellion and swear a simple oath of "peaceable obedience" to the king, as they had done so often before the conflict.[71] Furthermore, if Washington and the leaders in the Congress would swear to the same, the British even promised to capitulate and concede to them what they had asked for before the conflict, even to be "treated as a separate country within the framework of the empire" with "control over their own legislation and taxes."[72] In response to this offer, thousands more would immediately betray the American cause, lining up to take their oaths.[73]

The voice of reason spoke loud and clear to Washington and his men. *George, officers, enlisted men: Stop the madness! Accept the pardon! Go back to your plantations and farms. Go back to your families. Go back to the comforts of being the wealthiest nation per capita in the world. Go back to the pleasure of being counted amongst the freest people on earth. Britain's generous offer provides you with what you have asked for. Give the proposal a chance. Everyone else seems to see this and has surrendered. Nobody will blame you. It is over! Give it up!*

And yet, inexplicably, Washington and his inadequate band of patriots would not give it up. The General would excuse his betrayers, as he often would, saying that "we must bear up against them, and make the best of mankind as they are, since we cannot have them as we wish."[74] Then, as if total madness had set in, he would prepare for a counterattack at Trenton and Princeton, New Jersey. The *Spirit of Independence* was clearly working on Washington in these crucial moments of decision. Only the power of divine impulse could compel such illogical perseverance.

By turning down the royal pardon and continuing the fight, Washington was sealing his fate if captured. And by all estimations at the time, he would most likely be captured. He had been given his chance, and Britain would not forgive him for rejecting it. As best-selling author and historian Stephen Ambrose pointed out, had Washington been captured, "[h]e would have been brought to London, tried, found guilty of treason, ordered executed, and then drawn and quartered."

> Do you know what that means? He would have had one arm tied to one horse, the other arm to another horse, one leg to yet another, and the other leg to a fourth. Then the four horses would have been simultaneously whipped and started off at a gallop, one going north, another south, another east and the fourth to the west. That is what Washington was risking to establish your freedom and mine.[75]

It was not only during this crucial moment that Washington would show such unimaginable dedication, even at the great risk of losing everything he held dear. To be sure, Washington would push every human limit, both physical and emotional, throughout the entirety of the conflict. He would, for example, regularly rally his men by dangerously, even insanely, riding out beyond the front lines, coming within one hundred yards of the enemy, while aids would rush out to grab the bridle of his horse, forcing him to safety.[76] At one point, while British ships made plans to extort the plantations lining the Potomac River for supplies, including Washington's dear Mount Vernon, Washington expressed to his caretaker that it would be "less painful...that they burnt my house and laid the plantation in ruins" than to comply with their demands for supplies.[77] What's more, Washington would make all these sacrifices while refusing any and all payment due to him for his service, even though his long absence was forcing him to neglect his business, thus pushing him further and deeper into debt.[78]

Furthermore, there is no convincing evidence to explain any alternative intention for his sacrifices. By all accounts, what Washington desired more than anything else was a private life at his beloved Mount Vernon. "By God," Washington would say, "I had rather be on my farm."[79] As General of the Continental Army, Chairman of the Constitutional Convention, and as President of the United States, Washington openly and continuously expressed his overriding reluctance to accept, and temptation to abandon, such callings due to his overwhelming desire to return to his neglected family, work, and peace at home.[80] But Mount Vernon was *always* his to return to, from the time before his appointments (he could have declined), to the British offer of general pardon (he could have accepted), and on through his entire service to his country after the war (he could have retired). Yet he denied himself, just as his faithful contemporaries denied themselves of their own "Mount Vernons," and instead risked death for the sake of God and country. Only a heavenly influence could compel the sane to so freely and willingly act in a manner so contrary to both logic and to such strong personal desires. They internalized the will of God and made it their own.

The Testimonials of the Rebels

If it is true that the Spirit of God was especially active in the minds and actions of the American revolutionaries, then certainly those present in revolutionary America would have had something to say about it. Shamefully, far too many modern-day historical accounts of the Revolution minimize or simply omit any references to God and His influence over the whole affair. However, minimizing or slighting the spiritual testimonials of those who participated in the Revolution is most certainly disingenuous. For the leaders and followers of revolutionary America spoke loud and spoke frequently about the hand of God in America's struggle for independence. And they were, after all, *there*, which makes them infinitely more qualified to opine on the issue than any modern critic.

The long list of Founders who declared God's presence and influence during the Revolution is far too exhaustive to detail here. However, their voices will be documented throughout this narrative in the pages and chapters ahead. As you, the reader, come across them, you will see the overwhelming evidence and truthfulness of God's *Spirit of Independence*.

But in order to offer, here and now, a representative sample of this deeper understanding that existed in revolutionary America, let us briefly consider the words of certain colonial Americans who testified of God's hand. The following sample of those who bore this testimony is composed mostly of lesser known colonial Americans who do not play as prominent a role in the historical narrative represented in this book and therefore will be overlooked in later chapters. However, their testimonies are no less important and certainly represent how far reaching the *Spirit* was. The samples below are also limited to comments made during the height of the Revolution—even in the years leading up to and during the war itself—as post-war statements related to God and America will be discussed later.

One powerful testimony came from the Reverend Abraham Keteltas who, in the middle of the conflict, declared: "It is the cause of Justice...and the cause of heaven and against hell—of the kind Parent of the universe against the prince of darkness, and the destroyer of the human race."[81] The

Patrick Henry

Connecticut minister Ebenezer Baldwin referenced the Lord and His Second Coming, prophesying that the Revolution was "preparing the way for this glorious event."[82]

The great statesman Patrick Henry declared, in his famous *Give Me liberty or Give Me Death* speech in 1775, that "[w]e shall not fight our battles alone. There is a just God who presides over the destinies of nations, and who will raise up friends and fight our battles for us."[83] And Elbridge Gerry, a signer of the Declaration of Independence, recognized as early as 1775 that when it came to the Revolution, "the hand of Heaven seems to have directed every occurrence."[84]

Others who understood God's power in the Revolution —and appeared to even understand the national covenant and from where this covenant originated—were the New England colonials of Marlborough. In 1773, they collectively proclaimed that they had "implore[d] the Ruler above the skies, that he would make bare his arm in defense of His Church and people, and let Israel go."[85] In a similar spirit, the leader of the men of Pepperrell, Massachusetts, wrote to his New England countrymen—who were then suffering the wrath of Britain—in order to offer assistance. "Let us all be of one heart," declared the 1774 letter, "and stand fast in the liberty wherewith Christ has made us free. And may He, in His infinite mercy, grant us deliverance out of all our troubles."[86]

Also in 1774, the prominent John Hancock—president of Congress and signer of the Declaration of Independence— reminded his countrymen that they should "humbly commit our righteous cause to the great Lord of the Universe…let us joyfully leave our concerns in the hands of Him who raises up and puts down empires and kingdoms."[87]

Similarly, in March 1776, Chaplain William Linn made what appears to be an astonishing connection between the war, the renewal of the gospel, and the Second Coming. Chaplain Linn, upon invoking the blessings of God in battle, prayed the following: "Above all, may the peaceful reign of King Jesus soon commence, when the earth shall be filled with the knowledge of the Lord."[88]

Others with apparent insight included the Third Connecticut Regiment, whose motto during the war was, "An Appeal to Heaven." Pennsylvania troops carried a flag with words that seemed thematic of God's eternal war with Satan and seemed to reflect the very purpose of the American Covenant: "Resistance to Tyrants Is Obedience to God."[89]

One participant at the First Continental Congress, William Livingston, prophesied the following in 1768:

> The finger of God points out a mighty empire....The land we possess is the gift of heaven to our fathers, and Divine Providence seems to have decreed it to our latest posterity....The day dawns in which the foundation of this mighty empire is to be laid, by the establishment of a regular American Constitution... before seven years roll over our heads, the first stone must be laid." This prophecy, which was published in the New York *Gazette* in April 1768, occurred exactly seven years before the first shots rang out at Lexington, Massachusetts.[90]

Apart from the Founders' obvious recognition of God's influence in the Revolution, there is further proof to hush the inevitable critic, who will claim that all of the above was mere rhetoric. Such proof appears when we realize that the Founders not only spoke of God's influence around them, but actually acted, as a nation, in order to live worthy of His blessings. In doing so, they grew to understand and live the American Covenant. Such action is represented in the many declarations put forth by the first representatives of the people of the United States, even the Continental Congress, to encourage righteous living among their countrymen. One of the earliest of such declarations was announced in 1774, even at the threshold of the Revolution. It was a national plea to Americans, asking them to refrain from "every species of extravagance and dissipation," and specifically pointed out the dangers to the nation of sinful behavior, to include gaming, cockfighting, and exhibition of shows.[91] As one historian put it, "the colonials believed that they needed to prove themselves worthy of God's help."[92]

This was just the beginning of such congressional calls to national repentance—or, in other words, calls to the covenant. A study done by historian Derek Davies concluded that during the American Revolution, the Continental Congress invoked God so many times that—perhaps in order to break the monotony—they felt compelled to begin officially referring to Him with various titles, to include Nature's God, Lord of Hosts, His Goodness, Providence, Creator of All, Greater Governor of the World, Supreme Judge of the Universe, Supreme Disposer of All Events, Jesus Christ, Holy Ghost, and others. Concluded Davies: "So powerful were the religious influences on the independence movement that it becomes possible to say that those in the Continental Congress who made the political decision to separate from Great Britain did so only because they fully believed... [it to be] their religious duty." [93]

Whether or not these founders and revolutionaries knew the more profound reasons God was on their side—that it was all about creating a political foundation of freedom for the expansion of true religion—does not really matter. For they knew what they needed to know: that they were fighting for a new and better system of government based in liberty, that God was behind them, and that they would only be successful as they recognized Him and adhered to His commandments.

The Great Awakening

One largely overlooked experience which touched almost all of colonial America, and which supports the claim that God's Spirit was influencing the revolutionary cause, was the Great Awakening—that tremendous wave of spirituality which inundated the country in the years leading up to the Revolution. Led in large part by the inspired preacher, George Whitefield—who preached over eighteen thousands sermons

George Whitefield

throughout colonial America between 1736 and 1770—the Great Awakening marked a return to God and, hence, a return to the covenant.

According to one historian,

Through the universal, simultaneous experience of the Great Awakening, Americans began to become aware of themselves as a nation. They began to see themselves as God saw them: as a people chosen by Him for a specific purpose...Now through the shared experience of coming together as a group to hear the gospel of Jesus Christ, Americans were rediscovering God's plan to join them together by His Spirit in the common cause of advancing His Kingdom. Furthermore, they were returning to another aspect of his plan—they were not to operate as lone individualists but in covenanted groups.[94]

One prominent American who lived during the Great Awakening and caught this vision was Ezra Stiles, president of Yale. As early as 1760, he taught that God "is now giving this land to us who in virtue of the ancient covenant are the Seed of Abraham." He further taught that Israel's past is America's history: "The Lord freed us from Egypt by a mighty hand, by an outstretched arm and awesome power, and by signs and portents. He brought us to this place and gave us this land, a land flowing with milk and honey."[95]

Not only did this recommitment to God help colonial Americans understand their national covenant, but naturally encouraged them to live this covenant through obedience to the commandments. As the Pulitzer Prize-winning American historian, Gordon Wood, commented:

In the eyes of the Whigs, the two or three years before the Declaration of Independence always appears to be the great period of the Revolution, the time of greatest denial and cohesion, when men ceased to extort and abuse one another, when families and communities seemed particularly united, when the courts were wonderfully free of that constant bickering over land and credit that had dominated their colonial life.[96]

According to historian Steven Waldman, the Great Awakening not only led people back to God and covenant, but consequently encouraged them to seek Him out more freely and openly, thus inspiring a desire and movement for more religious freedom in America.[97] We have already pointed out that God's purpose in the Revolution was to encourage such religious freedom. We have also pointed out that most colonists did not initially see religious freedom as the cause for the Revolution, and therefore they did not fully recognize or comprehend that God was planning an enhancement of religious freedom as the principal purpose of their revolutionary movement. However, the fact that the Great Awakening was stirring hearts to this inspired end is a witness to God's hand in directing this era of American history. God certainly knew what we can only see in hindsight—that with American victory in independence, religious freedom would emerge as a powerful byproduct and then serve as a foundation for God's work in modern times. That the Lord infused these sentiments in America through the Great Awakening is evidence of His hand in preparing America for what would be the ultimate purpose of the Revolution.

Considering how the Great Awakening played right into the American Covenant and God's gospel purposes for America, and considering that it occurred and climaxed precisely during those crucial years leading up to the Revolution, it is difficult to deny the hand of the Lord. He had inspired this movement in order to improve His revolutionary generation and thus prepare them to humbly implore Him and to adhere to His covenant with them. For only then might He, in return, bless them with the gifts of the covenant. Only then might His plan for America be fully realized. In all this, we surely see the *Spirit of Independence.*

The Conversion of the Founders

That the *Spirit of Independence* existed and played an indispensable role should now be clear. What has not been made clear, however, is *how* the conversions to the American cause, as influenced by this *Spirit*, took place. And so, in an effort to understand the miracle by which the *Spirit* converted its adherents, and to add further proof of the existence of this *Spirit*, we will now briefly explore how such inspiration took hold of the Founders.

As is the case with most spiritual experiences, the Founders' individual conversions to the American cause for independence seemed to vary as to time, place, and circumstance. For those like Adams and Jefferson (respectively the *Voice* and the *Pen* of independence), they seemed to be born with it, long awaiting the opportunity to shower the world with principles pertaining to God and His blessings of liberty. Others, like Washington, seemed to gain their powerful testimonies upon receiving a specific call to duty.

But the one common thread in almost all such conversions was, very fittingly, a connection to the Christian churches of the day. It was from the pulpits that independence was preached and where hearts were changed and convinced to support the Revolution. As a witness to these miraculous conversions, John Adams commented in 1775 that the ministers would "thunder and lighten every Sabbath" in the cause for American independence. Jefferson would likewise state that the passion for this independence grew out of a "pulpit oratory [that] ran like a shock of electricity through the whole colony."[98]

As one American scholar proposed: "No other institution in America was so responsible for inspiring and motivating the War for Independence as the Protestant churches—and the few thousand Jews and Catholics of the land along with them."[99] There is even one account of a

Virginia pastor, Peter Muhlenbery, who one Sunday morning in 1775 told his congregation in the middle of a sermon that the time had come to fight. He then threw off his robe to reveal his combat uniform. He forthrightly recruited three hundred men, and marched off to war that very day.[100] That the zeal for independence was bred and spread through the churches of America certainly adds validity to the notion that God was behind the great conversions to the cause.

The *Spirit of Independence* not only filled the churches, but also made its way into the state legislative houses, where the decisions relating to American independence and revolution were being hotly debated. If the few converts to the cause were to convince their colleagues to join them (especially in light of the many logical reasons not to) the Spirit would certainly need to be among these legislative bodies. And God did send it there in abundance. Patrick Henry was one chosen to disseminate this Spirit. One historical commentator noted— after analyzing his public life—that Henry "had grown to understand how God moved through him and how to yield to the Holy Spirit to say what God wanted him to say."[101] Not coincidentally, Henry dedicated himself to daily personal prayer and Sunday evening family nights dedicated to the Lord.[102] And it was his famous *Give Me Liberty or Give Me Death* speech of 1775—packed with references to God and His will for America—that was largely responsible for moving his fellow Virginians to join the cause of independence. According to one witness, as Henry spoke there appeared an "unearthly fire burning in his eyes...Men leaned forward in their seats with their heads strained forward, their faces pale and their eyes glaring like the speaker."[103] "To Arms! To Arms!" was the response of his countrymen. Both Washington and Jefferson were in attendance. Shortly thereafter, the Virginia legislature voted to support independence from Britain.[104]

Similar impressions and conversions took place among the delegates at the Continental Congress in the most crucial moments. One of the most prominent examples of this took place on July 1, 1776, as the delegates convened one last time to debate and vote on whether the Declaration of Independence should be signed and executed. The highly respected delegate John Dickinson stood and made one final plea, with plenty of reason on his side, to stop the madness of declaring independence. To go forward with the declaration, he warned, would be "to brave the storm in a skiff made of paper." Aware of his logic, the delegates sat in silence as Dickinson took his seat. John Adams, whose spiritual character was no doubt inspiring his actions, then stood and countered Dickinson. In so doing, Adams delivered what David McCullough called, "the greatest speech of [his] life."[105]

Strangely, little is known about the precise content of this improvised speech, as nobody recorded it. Yet it was called his greatest based on the reaction it produced. Jefferson stated that though the speech was neither "graceful nor elegant," Adams delivered it "with a power of thought and expression that moved us from our seats." Adams himself testified that he had been "'carried out in spirit' as enthusiastic preachers sometimes express themselves." So powerful was the speech that, upon finishing, he was—most unusually—asked to stand and give it again. He set the tone of the day and converts to the cause were made. Joseph Hewes of North Carolina, who up until this point had opposed independence, was one of many that were overcome. As Adams later recorded, Hewes "started suddenly upright, and lifting up both his hands to Heaven, as if he had been in a trance, cried out, 'It is done! And I will abide by it.'"[106] The following day, July 2, 1776, the delegates voted to declare independence. There is no doubt that the *Spirit of Independence* had been converting souls to the cause.

But what about those chosen few who, for whatever reason, might have been initially unfeeling to this "electricity" from the pulpits of the churches and from the legislative houses throughout the country? The Lord would certainly need them as well. He would have to recruit them. The epitome of such recruits was none other than America's First Citizen, Benjamin Franklin. His almost emotionless and scientific rationale would give him much pause at America's sudden cries for independence. Furthermore, his tendency towards Deism would require more work on the Lord's part. But as Franklin—with his uncanny skills in

Benjamin Franklin

everything from science to diplomacy—would further the cause in ways others could not, the Lord would most certainly prompt him off the sidelines.

To illustrate Franklin's significant conversion, consider his initial and very open opinion against American claims of overbearing British persecution, which implied to many that Franklin had taken a firm stance against the need for any talk of independence. As late as January 1775, he would comment that "the two countries really have no clashing interests," and that it was merely an issue that "reasonable people might settle in half an hour." [107] Even after the dreaded Stamp Act and the colonial outrage that followed—and though he was no proponent of the act—he would write to a friend that "A firm Loyalty to the Crown and faithful Adherence to the Government of this Nation…will always be the wisest course for you and I to take, whatever may be the madness of the [American] populace or their blind leaders." [108]

In addition to such comments, which clearly undermined the American cause, as a delegate to Congress in the spring of 1775, the usually opinionated Franklin remained silent and passionless, even after the British had sacked Boston in response to the colonists' Tea Party. (As pointed out earlier, Franklin had sided with Britain in expressing disgust at America's destruction of the tea in the first place.) [109] Such behavior was alarming to his fellow delegates. One observer reported to James Madison that the delegates "beg[a]n to entertain a great suspicion that Dr. Franklin came rather as a spy than as a friend, and that he means to discover our weak side and make his peace with the ministers."[110] Even after the Battle of Bunker Hill and the burning of Charleston, both in June 1775, Franklin still supported a policy of unification with Britain by signing the Olive Branch Petition (written by delegate John Dickinson—the same delegate who would refuse to ever sign the Declaration of Independence).[111]

Furthermore, and on a personal level, why should he desire to revolt over the very system that had permitted him to become one of the wealthiest men in America, and perhaps the most famous individual in the world? Indeed, by risking an unlikely revolution, which seemed doomed to failure, both his wealth and fame might be pulled out from under him. Or worse, his life might be taken by the hangman's noose.

In spite of all this, by the end of July (seemingly overnight) Franklin had become "one of the most ardent opponents of Britain in the Continental Congress." This he would remain even after the British accepted the basic terms of his Olive Branch Petition (this British offer was part of the same rejected by Washington, as outlined above). "He does not hesitate at our boldest measures," wrote John Adams, "but rather seems to think us too irresolute."[112]

Almost immediately, Franklin volunteered to replace the British-run postal service and serve as America's first postmaster general. He designed and oversaw construction of a secret system of underwater obstructions to prevent enemy naval invasions. And he rushed to the scene of war—a Boston recently seized by the British. He went there that he might consult the newly appointed commander-in-chief, General Washington, on everything from warfare and troop discipline to ration allocation.

At age seventy, he could have been expected to remain in Philadelphia and consult from the comforts of his home. Instead, he insisted, not merely on traveling to Boston, but on taking a life-threatening diplomatic journey to Canada (during which he almost died). Then he traveled to New York in a final (and unsuccessful) attempt at independence through diplomacy with the recently landed British invaders. After returning to Philadelphia and acting as editor of the Declaration of Independence, he most poignantly relocated to France (in yet another death-defying voyage), where he would spend the balance of the war seeking and, through masterful diplomacy, securing France's support—an act that was largely responsible for the American victory. Finally, he would lead negotiations with Britain in the treaty officially ending the war, wherein Britain recognized the United States "to be free, sovereign and independent."[113]

In an almost humorous understatement, a follow-up report to James Madison, shortly after Franklin's sudden and passionate conversion, included the reassurance that "[t]he suspicions against Dr. Franklin have died away...I believe he has now chosen his side and favors our cause."[114]

But what caused the sudden and almost overwhelming change in Franklin that not only led to the dramatic string of events mentioned above, but also cost him his relationship with his only living son, the British loyalist William (a relationship never to be recovered)? What prompted the change within, which he knew would place him squarely onto the death list of the British? Upon signing the Declaration of Independence he would declare, "We must indeed all hang together, or most assuredly we shall all hang separately."[115] While scholars theorize over his largely inexplicable change of heart, a gospel perspective perhaps fills in the missing pieces. Knowing what we do about what American independence meant to God's purposes, and knowing the indispensable role played by this elder American, can there be any doubt the Lord influenced his heart with His *Spirit*? Such an idea is even supported by Franklin himself who declared while serving in France: "Glorious it is for the Americans to be called by

Providence to this post of honor....it is a miracle in human affairs...the greatest revolution the world ever saw."[116]

The insightful Abigail Adams, herself devoutly dedicated to the Lord, saw or felt this spiritual conversion in Franklin. Upon meeting Franklin shortly after his public commitment to independence, she wrote to her husband, stating, "I thought I could read into his countenance the virtues of his heart; among which patriotism shone in its full luster, and with that is blended every virtue of a Christian: for a true patriot must be a religious man."[117]

Of course, critics will argue that his sudden change of mind came about by what was expected of him politically as an American delegate to Congress, and that God had nothing to do with it. Franklin was—so the theory goes—simply playing to the American crowd. As historian Gordon Wood pointed out, Franklin's actions for independence came about as a result of him having to "overcome suspicions that many of his countryman had of him." Wood further explains, as mentioned earlier, that "some thought his position in the 1760s and 1770s had been sufficiently ambiguous that he might not be a true patriot after all."[118]

However, there are problems with this interpretation. First, Franklin had just as many, if not more, friends and supporters in Britain and other European countries as he did in America. After all, he had spent over two decades in celebrity status (as scientist and philosopher) in Europe. Furthermore, he was void of any family ties that would sway his allegiance to America rather than Great Britain. His wife had already died, and his only surviving son was a British loyalist. In other words, he had just as many people to disappoint—just as much political pressure on him—whether he voted for or against independence. If the only reason he could find for supporting American independence was the pressure he felt from his American colleagues, then it would have made much more sense for him to shun what appeared to be an ill-conceived revolution and simply return to Europe with the celebrity status that would be awaiting him there.*

Second, if Franklin had been unconvinced of the wisdom behind revolution, but did not want to shun his country and hazard a trip back to Europe, there was a much easier solution for him. He could have simply voiced his support for independence then floated off into retirement, even casually consulting from the comforts of his home just to keep up the act. He was already in his seventies and suffering from chronic gout and kidney stones; nobody would have batted an eye.

Yet his actions, as outlined above, reflect an unnaturally passionate, even overactive, approach to the American cause. Indeed, Franklin's conversion and subsequent actions are overwhelmingly inconsistent with the allegation that he acted on pressures stemming from colonial political correctness, especially in light of the alternatives available to him. Even Wood, putting his own analysis into question, ultimately concedes to this fact, stating that "[Franklin] had everything to lose and seemingly nothing to gain by participating in a revolution."[119] Only in the context of the *Spirit of Independence* are Franklin's actions comprehensible.

Unfortunately, many scholars would rather have *no* explanation than give credit to God, and thus they attempt to secularize Franklin as much as possible. However, such scholars have to contend with the fact—as they do when attacking Washington's conversion—that Franklin himself explained on several occasions that his conversion to the cause was indeed based in divine intervention. Admittedly, critics may claim that the few quotes utilized above regarding what

---

* Though some contend that Franklin would not have returned to Great Britain because he had been snubbed by certain officials, it is important to remember that he was a celebrity in *all* of Western Europe, particularly in France, where he was adored by all and would have been more than welcome to return for good.

was said by and of Franklin during the actual conflict represented nothing but quintessential politicking—even the disingenuous act of invoking God's name only to stir an audience. However, a glimpse into his post-war life confirms that when Franklin declared during the war that he had been "called by Providence,"[120] he meant it.

Consider, for example, the following statement he made near the end of his life while reflecting upon the War for Independence and his conversion to it: "If I had ever before been an atheist, I should now have been convinced of the Being and government of a Deity...If it had not been...for the interposition of Providence, in which we had faith, we must have been ruined."[121] That he had felt this during and after the war is supported by his obvious change of focus from scientist and rational philosopher (pre-war) to servant of the Almighty (post-war). Whereas before the war he tended to find limited use for God and religion, his post-war activities included the following: penning defenses against early American secularist attacks on religion,[122] proposing that the nation utilize as its official seal a depiction of Moses freeing Israel by the power of God,[123] proposing to the Congress that it open sessions with prayer,[124] promoting the general need for religion and virtue in order to stabilize the Republic,[125] and, as his final project in this life, publicly invoking the Almighty and exerting much energy in an effort to eradicate the evil practice of slavery.[126]

Furthermore, it was this change of heart that led to his other inspired commentaries on God and on man's obligation to God. The following includes a sample of such statements made in the sunset of his life:

- "I have lived, Sir, a long time, and the longer I live, the more convincing proofs I see of this truth—that God governs in the affairs of men."[127]

- "Doing good to men is the only service of God in our power; and to imitate his beneficence is to glorify him." [128]

- "I believe in one God, Creator of the Universe. That he governs it by his Providence. That he ought to be worshipped. That the most acceptable service we render to him is doing good to his other children." [129]

Franklin died on April 17, 1790. Near his deathbed, he had placed a picture of the Day of Judgment.[130] As an expression of his hope for eternity, he had originally penned the following epitaph for his tombstone:

> The body of B. Franklin (Like the cover of an old book, its contents worn out, stripped of its lettering and gilding) Lies here, food for worms. But the work is not lost: for it will (as he believed) appear once more, In a new and more elegant edition, Revised and corrected by the Author. [131]

He had also expressed faith, particularly later in his life, that death and afterlife would be joyful. "If [God] loves me," he declared, "can I doubt that he will go on to take care of me, not only here but hereafter?"[132]

It was Franklin who prophetically declared that the Revolution would eventually be responsible for destroying tyranny the world over, and that "our cause is the cause of all mankind, and that we are fighting for their liberty in defending our own."[133] He was right. As detailed in the previous chapter, it was because of his and his colleagues' actions pursuant to the Revolution, and under the American Covenant, that there was a proliferation of freedom in America and throughout the world. This freedom would one day permit an enlargement of Christianity, which would help God's children to eternal life. If Franklin's godly works—to include his efforts to bring about liberty unto the salvation of mankind—are an indication of his faith, we may rest assured that he was accepted into the bosom of his God.

★ ★ ★ ★

It was indeed that *Spirit of Independence* which was ultimately responsible for commencing the chain of events leading to gospel enlargement and thus to salvation. Clearly, Franklin's conversion by this *Spirit* is like unto the conversions of thousands of others who, through their efforts and the grace of God, also helped offer the world such eternal blessings. The inspired Founders even officially recognized the importance of such conversions to the cause in what was entitled the Congressional Decree of 1781. In this national decree, "Almighty God" is officially and formally thanked specifically for "heightening the number and zeal of the friends of liberty."[134] In other words, they were thanking God for the *Spirit of Independence* which ultimately converted enough people to the cause to bring victory to the righteous.

It was a spiritual conversion inspired by God that was at the heart of the American Revolution. As John Adams—even he who was in the center of the entire revolutionary experience—explained: "What do we mean by the American Revolution? The war? That was no part of the Revolution; it was only an effect and consequence of it. The Revolution was in the minds of the people...a change in their *religious* sentiment."[135]

Conclusion

When reflecting upon the ultimate fruit of America's independence, which included a free government and a base of operations for the Lord in these modern days where His truths could be renewed and spread, the idea that God was behind it is a foregone conclusion. Too much was at stake, in terms of His ultimate work and glory, to leave to chance. America's fate was most certainly His design and foreordained plan. This chapter has offered corroborating evidence of this notion. Through analyzing Washington's preparation, the unlikely decision by the colonists to go to war, the testimonies of the revolutionaries themselves, the Great Awakening, and the powerful conversions of the Founders, it is clear that the compelling factor driving American freedom was the Spirit of God.

The evidence clearly suggests that the Founders were acting, enduring, and sacrificing under this powerful spirit. It was a spirit only God could provide. It was a spirit that many of them openly recognized. And for those who did not recognize it, it was a spirit that worked on them just the same. It was a spirit that provides (even for us today) the only fully convincing explanation for why these few and chosen Americans endured what they did to create an America under God. It was, in fact, the *Spirit of Independence*. And as the Founders adhered to it the nation became all the more worthy of the covenant blessings. And as these blessings flowed in greater measure, America received what it needed to become God's chosen land—even a land whose people would work to expand and enlarge the gospel and share it with the world.

ENDNOTES

1 Janice T. Connell, *The Spiritual Journey of George Washington* (New York: Hatherleigh Press, 2007), 3.

2 William H Wilbur, *The Making of George Washington* (DeLand: Patriotic Education, Inc, 1970), 47-50.

3 Quoting Mason Locke Weems, *A History of the Life, Death, Virtues and Exploits of George Washington* (Philadelphia: Lippencott, 1918). See also Novak and Novak, *Washington's God, op cited* Note 11, Chapter 1; see also Connell, 6.

4 Wilbur, 42.

5 Michael Novak and Jana Novak, *Washington's God* (New York, Basic Books, 2006), 8.

6 John Bowman, *The History of the American Presidency* (North Dighton: World Publication Group, Inc), 12-13.

7 David McCullough, *1776* (New York: Simon and Schuster, 2005), 43.

8 McCullough, *1776*, 49.

9 McCullough, *1776*, 49.

10 McCullough, *1776*, 51.

11 Joseph J. Ellis, *His Excellency* (New York: Alford A. Knopf, 2004), 80-81.

12 McCullough, *John Adams*, 28.

13 McCullough, *1776*, 49.

14 Ellis, *His Excellency*, 74.

15 Ellis, *His Excellency*, 71.

16 Ellis, *His Excellency*, 22-23; Michael D. Evans, *American Prophecies* (New York: Warner Faith, 2004), 42-43.

17 Robert Hieronimus, *Founding Fathers, Secret Societies* (Rochester, Destiny Books, 2006), 51-52.

18 Ellis, *His Excellency*, 23.

19 Steven Waldman, *Founding Faith* (New York: Random House, 2008), 57.

20 George Washington, as quoted in H.L. Richardson, "A Most Uncivil War," *California Political Review*, Jan/Feb 2006, Vol. 17, No. 1.

21 Lynn D. Wardle, "The Constitution as Covenant," *BYU Studies* 27, no. 3 (1987): 9.

22 Abigail Adams, borrowing the words of John Dryden to describe Washington, as quoted in Stephen Ambrose, *To America* (New York: Simon and Schuster, 2002), 10-11.

23 Ellis, *His Excellency* 70-71.

24 McCullough, *1776*, 45.

25 McCullough, *1776*, 42.

26 Ellis, *His Excellency*, 45.

[27] Some of the eye witness accounts of Washington having taken Communion came from General Robert Porterfield, family members of Rev. Timothy Johnes, and family members of Alexander Hamilton, refer to Marshall and Manuel, 461.

[28] Marshall and Manuel, 358.

[29] Nelly Custis, as quoted in Marshall and Manuel, 460.

[30] Marshall and Manuel, 357.

[31] Testimony of Washington's private religious devotionals, as documented by his adopted daughter Nelly can be found quoted in Novak and Novak, *Washington's God*, 136; and testimony of the same, as documented by his adopted son George and others can be found quoted in Connell, *The Spiritual Journey of George Washington*, 83, 95.

[32] Marshall and Manuel, 459-60.

[33] Marshall and Manuel, 457-459.

[34] Ellis, *His Excellency*, 162-163.

[35]Ellis, *His Excellency*, 164- 167.

[36] Bennett, *Spirit of America*, 359-360.

[37] McCullough, *1776*, 37; Ellis, *His Excellency*, 46; Joseph J. Ellis, *Patriots, Brotherhood of the American Revolution*, Lectures recorded by Recorded Books, Inc, and Barnes and Noble Publishing: 2004, Lecture 7, Track 6, 00:06 min.

[38] McCullough, 1776, 77; a more detailed account of the incident can be found in the audio version of *1776* produced by Simon and Schuster Audioworks, New York, New York (2005); details of the account are also found in Mac and Tait, *Under God*, 39-42.

[39] Ellis, *His Excellency*, 263.

[40] Bennett, *America, The Last Best Hope*, 147.

[41] Joseph J. Ellis, *Patriots, Brotherhood of the American Revolution*, Lectures recorded by Recorded Books, Inc, and Barnes and Noble Publishing: 2004, Lecture 7, 3:40 min; John Adams also documented these same basic ratios between those who supported the war and those who did not, as quoted in McCullough, *John Adams*, 78.

[42] Walter Isaacson, *Benjamin Franklin, An American Life* (New York: Simon and Schuster, 2003), 307.

[43] Joseph Ellis, *Patriots*, lecture 7, 3:40min; John Adams, as quoted in McCullough, *John Adams*, 78.

[44] McCullough, *John Adams*, 333.

[45] McCullough, *1776*, 5, 11-12.

[46] King George, as quoted in McCullough, *John Adams*, 336.

[47]Walter Isaacson, *Benjamin Franklin* (New York: Simon and Schuster, 2003), 275.

[48] David McCullough, *John Adams* (New York: Simon and Schuster, 2001), 131.

[49] Joseph J. Ellis, *Patriots, Brotherhood of the American Revolution*. Lectures recorded by Recorded Books, Inc, and Barnes and Noble Publishing: 2004. Study Guide, 10.

[50] McCullough, *1776*, 11.

[51] Edward Rutledge, as quoted in McCullough, *John Adams*, 118.

[52] David McCullough, "The Glorious Cause of America," *BYU Magazine*, Winter 2006, 48-49.

[53] McCullough, *1776*, 158.

[54] Joseph J. Ellis, *Patriots, Brotherhood of the American Revolution*, Lectures recorded by Recorded Books, Inc, and Barnes and Noble Publishing: 2004, Lecture 7, Tr.6, 2:00 min.

[55] Jon Meacham, *American Gospel* (New York: Random House, 2006), 76.

[56] Marshal Foster and Mary Elaine Swanson, *The American Covenant, The Untold Story* (Thousand Oaks: The Mayflower Institute, 1981), 118-119.

[57] Sam Adams, as quoted in Marshall and Manuel, 330.

[58] Marshal Foster and Mary Elaine Swanson, *The American Covenant, The Untold Story*, 119; see also Benjamin Lossing, *Signers of the Declaration* (New York: J.C. Derby Publisher, 1856).

[59] McCullough, *1776*, 34.

[60] Nathan Hale, as quoted in *Let Freedom Ring, The Words that Shaped Our America* (New York: Sterling Publishing Co., 2001), 34.

[61] McCullough, *1776*, 20-21, 58.

[62] McCullough, *1776*, 168, 247, 249, 251.

[63] McCullough, *1776*, 249.

[64] McCullough, *1776*, 227.

[65] McCullough, *1776*, 250.

[66] McCullough, *1776*, 254-255.

[67] McCullough, *1776*, 255-256.

[68] McCullough, *1776*, 270.

[69] McCullough, *1776*, 251.

[70] McCullough, *1776*, 249.

[71] McCullough, *1776*, 258.

[72] Isaacson, 318-319.

[73] McCullough, *1776*, 258.

[74] McCullough, *1776*, 256.

[75] Stephen Ambrose, *To America, Personal Reflections of an Historian* (New York: Simon and Schuster, 2002), 12.

[76] Ellis, *Patriots, Brotherhood of the American Revolution*, lecture series; McCullough, *1776*, 213. In an effort to rally his men, Washington placed himself in a dangerously advanced, forward-deployed, position at the Battles of Kips Bay, Trenton, Princeton, and Yorktown.

[77] Ellis, *His Excellency*, 74-75.

[78] McCullough, *1776*, 48.

[79] Bennett, *America*, 163.

[80] Ellis, *His Excellency*, 191.

[81] Abraham Keteltas (1777), as quoted in Steven Waldman, *Founding Faith: Providence, Politics, and the Birth of Religious Freedom in America* (New York: Random House, 2008), 41.

[82] Waldman, *Founding Faith*, 41.

[83] Waldman, *Founding Faith*, 42.

[84] Waldman, *Founding Faith*, 42.

[85] Marshall and Manuel, 324.

[86] Marshall and Manuel, 329.

[87] John Hancock, as quoted in Marshall and Manuel, 330.

[88] Waldman, 70.

[89] Waldman, 69.

[90] Marshall and Manuel, 331 and 323.

[91] Waldman, 43.

[92] Waldman, 43.

[93] Waldman, 43.

[94] Marshall and Manuel, 306-307.

[95] Bruce Feiler, *America's Prophet: Moses and the American Story* (New York: HarperCollins, 2009), 59-60.

[96] Gordon Wood, *The Creation of the American Republic: 1776-1787* (Chapel Hill: The University of North Carolina Press, 1969), 102; as quoted in W. Cleon Skousen, *The Five Thousand Year Leap Forward* (Washington D.C.: The National Center for Constitutional Studies, 1981), 52.

[97] See Waldman, 27-32.

[98] Jon Butler, *Awash a Sea of Faith: Christianizing the American People* (Cambridge: Harvard University Press, 1992), 201-202.

[99] Novak, *On Two Wings*, 34.

[100] Marshall and Manuel, 367.

[101] Mac and Tait, *Under God*, 158.

[102] Mac and Tait, *Under God*, 157.

[103] Report of Henry Speech by a Witness, "An Old Baptist Clergyman," reprinted in *Patrick Henry: Life Correspondence and Speeches*, Vol. 1, 267-268.

[104] Available at http://en.wikipedia.org/wiki/Patrick_Henry; and Mac and Tait, *Under God*, 157-159.

[105] McCullough, *John Adams*, 126-7.

[106] The details and background of this great speech of Adams, to include the quotes used in this book to describe it, can be found in McCullough, *John Adams*, 126-129.

[107] Isaacson, 285.

[108] Gordon S. Wood, *Revolutionary Characters* (New York: Penguin Press, 2006), 80.

[109] Walter Isaacson, *Benjamin Franklin* (New York: Simon and Schuster, 2003), 275.

[110] Isaacson, 292.

[111] Isaacson, 296.

[112] Isaacson, 298.

[113] Isaacson, 415.

[114] Isaacson, 298.

[115] Isaacson, 313.

[116] Isaacson, 339, 332.

[117] Isaacson, 304.

[118] Wood, *Revolutionary Characters*, 84.

[119] Wood, *Revolutionary Characters*, 70.

[120] Isaacson, 339.

[121] Isaacson, 467.

[122] Isaacson, 468.

[123] Waldman, *Founding Faith*, 107.

[124] William J. Bennett, *The Spirit of America* (New York: Simon and Schuster, 1997), 383-385.

[125] Isaacson, 468.

[126] Isaacson, 465.

[127] Benjamin Franklin, as quoted in Bennett, 385.

[128] Benjamin Franklin, as quoted in Bennett, 366.

[129] Benjamin Franklin, as quoted in Isaacson, 468.

[130] Isaacson, 469.

[131] Isaacson, 470.

[132] Waldman, 24.

[133] Benjamin Franklin, as quoted in Isaacson, 339.

[134] Novak, *On Two Wings*, 21.

[135] John Adams, as quoted in Dinesh D'Souza, "Created Equal: How Christianity Shaped the West," *Imprimis*, November 2008, Volume 37, Number 11, 4, emphasis added.

CHAPTER 8

MIRACLES AT WAR

[America has] without arms,
ammunition, discipline, revenue,
government or ally, with "staff
and sling" only, dared, "in the
name of the Lord of Hosts," to
engage a gigantic adversary.

—Continental Congress, 1779

Providence has heretofore
saved us in remarkable
manner and on this we must
principally rely.

—George Washington, 1777

Our discussion of the Revolutionary War has thus far been
focused on the divine inspiration that governed the individual
actions of those chosen American revolutionary leaders.
However, in spite of their greatness, these American colonists

were, in fact, a group of imperfect, under-prepared human beings challenging the world's superpower. As such, if they were to defeat Britain on the battlefields of war, they would have to rely on their covenant with the Lord, pleading often for further assistance from above. And in light of what gospel significance hung in the balance, such prayers would be answered time and time again. Particularly in crucial moments of the conflict, God would unveil His hand and deliver some of the greatest miracles recorded in battlefield history.

The Revolution's first armed conflict occurred in April 1775, near Boston, at Lexington and Concord, Massachusetts. In response to colonial resistance, and in an effort to arrest rebel leaders and seize stockpiled weapons, the British attacked America at these sleepy New England villages. These initial skirmishes would fittingly be called the "shot heard round the world." Beginning from this point in the Revolution's chronology, we will see how the colonists tried to remember God and keep His commandments. As they did, He would bless them with miracles to *protect* them, *prosper* them, and ultimately, provide them the *liberty* they sought—and this He did to advance His purposes for His children. These miracles at war were nothing less than the American Covenant in action.

Miracle at Boston

The events at Lexington and Concord were the result of a build-up of British forces in Boston, which came to America to quash the rebellion. Emboldened by Britain's aggressive movements, the faithful New Englanders, though largely unorganized, began preparing militias to fight back. By June 1775, these American militias had taken a stand against the British at Boston, but were attacked and driven further back and away from Boston at the Battle of Bunker Hill (a battle which actually took place mostly on neighboring Breed's

Hill). With the loss of this high ground, the American militias lost their only real tactical advantage over the enemy. As Britain's complete control of Boston and its harbor congealed, Washington had only barely received his congressional commission as commander-in-chief. By July 1775, Washington had arrived to meet his largely scattered and disoriented citizen-soldiers who were camped just outside of Boston, across the Charles River, near and around Cambridge. Notwithstanding his troops' weakened and unprepared state, Washington had come in eager anticipation to fight back, retake Boston, and end the British occupation of America.

Washington Taking Command of the American Army, published by Currier & Ives, 1876

Boston and its surrounding areas were indeed shaping up to be the location of the first large-scale battle of the war; for if the British did not attack first, Washington most certainly would. However, within hours of an intended attack (from one or both sides), the British picked up and left. This decision by the British to abandon Boston possibly saved the American cause. For had there been an armed conflict, Washington's Continental Army would most likely have been crushed. To be sure, the Americans had already lost their strategic advantage at Bunker and Breed's Hills. Furthermore, upon entering and studying Boston several days after the British evacuation, it became stunningly clear to Washington and his men that the British position there had been far too powerful for the Americans to overcome. This was in addition to numerous other disadvantages plaguing Washington's enfant army. In retrospect, it seems Washington's plan to attack the British in their Boston stronghold would have proved suicidal to America and her cause.

The British commander, General William Howe, knowing he had possessed such advantages while still controlling Boston, had himself already begun a full scale assault against the rebels. Shortly after calling for the attack, however, he called off the attack and pulled his troops completely out of Boston.

So *why* did the British decide to forsake their Boston stronghold, from whence they might have ended the conflict? The easy answer has to do with the suspicion that the British had always intended to leave Boston in order to instead launch an attack at New York. However, the details behind how the British evacuation actually played out leave little doubt that it was *the Lord* who made sure the British left, thus ensuring the survival of the Revolution. It is within the details of this story that we witness the first battlefield miracles of the war.

In an effort to explain how this miracle took effect, we return to the newly appointed Washington. For months after his arrival outside of Boston, he had been frantically preparing for his ill-conceived attack, while the British waited patiently to see if he dared walk into their trap. Washington had decided that the loss of Bunker and Breed's Hills required that he find another favorable position from whence to stage his assault. The location he chose was the unoccupied high ground south of Boston. This sought-after land was called Dorchester Heights, and was separated from Boston only by the harbor. Not only would Dorchester give Washington excellent battlefield position, but it would also, he hoped, compel the British, under threat of an imminent American attack, to launch a preemptive strike against the Americans at this new position. This would draw the British out of Boston and allow Washington to use his advantageous high ground to engage and defeat them in battle. Once this began, Washington planned on sending other troops across the water by boat, where they would attack the British stronghold at Boston and take the city back.[1]

Washington's long-shot plan clearly hung on his ability to gain the high ground at Dorchester. However, considering the close proximity of Dorchester to Boston, in clear sight of the ever-vigilant British eye, the American officers could only wonder how Washington could possibly move on such a position without causing an immediate and devastating British response. Furthermore, even if by some miracle he could take this high ground, American troops, having sensed the hopeless situation, were beginning to walk off the scene with the already scarce supply of weapons and powder, leaving Washington with fewer and fewer resources with which to man the proposed position.[2] Washington commented on his difficult situation, stating that, rather than commanding the army during this siege on Boston, he would have "retired to the backcountry and lived in a wigwam."[3]

So secure was General Howe of Washington's predicament that he confidently declared: "We are not under the least apprehension of an attack on this place from the rebels." Even upon considering the prospect that Washington might move on Dorchester, Howe remained unconcerned. For if Washington attempted something so foolish, Howe made it clear that, "We must go at it with our whole force."[4] The British could not afford to allow the Americans to gain the high ground, and Howe knew that if the Americans made an attempt for it, he would see it and immediately and powerfully prevent it. Washington understood this, which is why he had to configure some way to take the Heights in complete secrecy.

The necessity to work in secrecy had already been in the forefront of Washington's mind. Since he arrived outside of Boston, he knew his ability to conceal knowledge from the British would be paramount. He knew, for example, that if Howe, at any point, had learned how extensively disadvantaged the Americans were, he would have commanded a British attack immediately upon the Americans and ended the conflict. If the Americans survived, said Washington, it would only be because "the finger of Providence is in it, to blind the eyes of our enemies...from knowing the disadvantages we labor under."⁵ But if there was ever to be a *specific* moment during the Boston conflict when Washington would *especially* need this finger of Providence to blind his enemies, it would be upon his orders to advance on Dorchester.

A glimmer of hope entered in for the Americans when, after over two months and three-hundred miles of "rough forest roads, freezing lakes, blizzards, thaws, mountain wilderness, and repeated mishaps that would have broken lesser spirits several times over," Henry Knox, the twenty-five-year-old Boston bookseller turned American commander, had accomplished the impossible. He transported, by horse and sled, over 120,000 pounds of mortars and cannons from Fort Ticonderoga to an anxious Washington outside of Boston.⁶ Though Washington had sent Knox on this difficult errand, the probability of a positive outcome had never been great. But Knox had accomplished it. And the timing of his return with the desired cannons could not have been better, for Washington was on the eve of advancing on Dorchester.

Notwithstanding this miracle, however, Washington knew he was in immediate need of another. He still had to accomplish the impossible task of moving these guns and his troops to the heights of Dorchester without the British first discovering and then thwarting his designs. He needed Providence to blind the British eye. And it seems Washington believed God would in fact intervene in this venture. For, despite every reason to think it would not work, the General would faithfully (if not a bit naively) persevere with his plan.

At midnight on March 2, 1776, the Americans launched a series of cannon and mortar fire from their position outside of Boston upon the British inside of Boston. The British immediately returned the gesture. The exchange continued on and off through March 4, but did little damage. Washington's intention, after all, was not to destroy, but to cause a loud distraction while his men, armed with Knox's cannon, advanced on the unoccupied heights of Dorchester. This they attempted on the night of March 4. With some four thousand troops and hundreds of wagons carrying thousands of pounds of weaponry, taking this high ground in secret, and directly in front of the British position, seemed an impossible feat. Even with the distraction of cannon fire and the scattered hay bales stretching across the landscape, which had been placed there earlier for concealment, it seemed doubtful.

Then out of nowhere, heavenly cloud-cover dropped down to provide concealment for the Americans. As one witness to the event, Reverend William Gordon, observed, "A finer [night] for working could not have been taken out of the whole 365. It was hazy below [the Heights] so that our people could not be seen, though it was a bright moonlight night above on the hills." Even the Pulitzer Prize-winning historian David McCullough had to admit that it was "as if the hand of the Almighty were directing things."[7]

George Washington at Dorchester Heights, by Emanuel Gottlieb Leutze (1816-1868)

By the next morning, at least twenty cannon and thousands of troops were in position to make a move. When daylight appeared, the shock was overwhelming to the British. "My God," exclaimed General Howe, "these fellows have done more work in one night than I could make my army do in three nights." One British officer reported back to London: "This morning at day break we discovered two redoubts on the hills of Dorchester...They were all raised with an expedition equal to that of the genie belonging to Aladdin's wonderful lamp."[8]

231

Though shocked and less confident, Howe decided that his soldiers and his Boston stronghold were still enough to defeat Washington. Just as Washington had anticipated, Howe would prepare for a preemptive strike against the Americans. Howe ordered his men to ready themselves for the attack, which would commence on March 5. Washington had recently given similar orders to his own men to prepare for his pre-conceived amphibious assault on Boston. As the British troops pushed off into Boston Harbor in their advance toward the Americans, God once again intervened, in what one of Washington's officers called the "hurrycane."[9] As McCullough explains:

> What had been an abnormally warm, pleasant day had changed dramatically...By nightfall, a storm raged, with hail mixed with snow and sleet... windows were smashed, fences blew over. Two of the [British transports]...were blown ashore. The American lieutenant Isaac Bangs, who was among those freezing at their posts on the high ground of Dorchester, called it the worst storm 'that ever I was exposed to.' Clearly there would be no British assault that night.[10]

The British had been temporarily stopped. Howe was then forced to reconsider his options. Whereas before he was full of confidence that victory would be his, suddenly much had changed. With the Americans standing strong on Dorchester, and with the recent humbling blow caused by the great storm, Howe and his men were losing their will to fight. "I could promise myself little success," wrote Howe, "by attacking them under all the disadvantages I had to encounter; wherefore I judged it most advisable to prepare for the evacuation of the town."[11] And so they left.

As stated before, however, if there had been a battle at any point during the standoff (whether that battle commenced from the British side or from the under-experienced and over-zealous American side) it seems the colonists would have been defeated, perhaps even putting an end to the American cause.

After all—and notwithstanding the American's new position and the recent storm—the British maintained a superior stronghold. Upon entering Boston several days after the British evacuation, a stunned Washington determined it to be "amazingly strong. 20,000 men could not have carried it against one thousand…The town of Boston was almost impregnable, every avenue fortified."[12] Washington added that the British position had been "the strongest by nature on this Continent, and strengthened and fortified in the best manner and at an enormous expense."[13] Additionally (and this goes without saying), the British possessed far more professional and seasoned troops. The colonial troops were merely citizens and farmers who had not had adequate time to train. As McCullough points out, Washington had "insufficient arms and ammunition, insufficient shelter, sickness, inexperienced officers, lack of discipline, clothing and money."[14]

Washington's plan to send troops into Boston, then, would have ultimately been suicide for America. Washington "had been repeatedly saved," according to McCullough, "from his headlong determination to attack, and thus from almost certain catastrophe."[15] To make matters even worse, and unbeknownst to anyone at the time, an overwhelming British naval fleet was already on its way to support Howe.[16]

But God's actions (first, bringing Knox and his artillery just in time; second, delivering Washington to Dorchester Heights; and third, thrusting down the devastating storm on the advancing British) had influenced Howe to throw up his hands and retreat. It was a triple miracle too hot for the British to handle. In the wisdom of God, and through His power, the British withdrew and Washington's well-intended, but ill-conceived plan to move on Boston, would not be carried out. The Americans had been preserved, that they might further prepare and fight again another day. McCullough called it "The 'miracle' of Dorchester Heights."[17]

That the Lord had wrought a miracle was not lost on Washington, especially as he entered Boston and became awakened to the superior position Howe had possessed. Though Washington had had his own intentions for seizing and arming Dorchester (to instigate battle), it seems that he now realized why the Lord had delivered his men and artillery to Dorchester—to deter the British so as to *prevent* a battle America would have lost. Though Washington was initially disappointed that the storm had quashed his plan of attack, he now seemed to understand why it had happened. He began to accept the storm as God's protection for America. Washington confessed as much to his secretary, Joseph Reed, declaring that he did not ultimately "lament or repine at any act of Providence," for, "whatever is, is right."[18] Additionally, in a letter to his brother, Washington explained that he now realized that "much blood was saved and a very important blow...prevented." Washington called it a "remarkable interposition of Providence" and admitted that it was carried out by Heaven for a "wise purpose."[19]

Abigail Adams, who as a resident of a Boston suburb witnessed these events from afar, shared these same sentiments. Declared Abigail: "Surely it is the Lord's doings and it is marvelous in our eyes."[20] Others agreed that the Lord had been in Boston. More than just saving the Continental Army, it seems God's intervention had also served as an opportunity for Americans to feel the power of their national covenant.

Reflecting upon this first miracle of war, Americans would graciously remember that it was not long before that the First Continental Congress had passed its very first act—an official and heartfelt prayer to God, which included the words from Psalm 35: "Plead my cause, O Lord, with them that strive with me: fight against them that fight against me." John Adams would later comment that the prayer was one that "heaven had ordained" and that it brought tears to the eyes of the delegates. "It was," he said, "enough to melt a heart of stone."[21] Washington himself had participated in this prayer. Shortly thereafter, this prayer had been codified into a national covenant of sorts, when Congress officially called upon the nation to forsake sin and turn to the Lord for His blessings.[22]

By the time Washington had arrived outside the British occupied Boston in July 1775, the Congress had again covenanted with the Lord in its official Declaration of the Causes and Necessity of Taking Up Arms, which stated: "With a humble confidence in the mercies of the Supreme and impartial God and ruler of the universe, we most devoutly implore His divine goodness to protect us happily through this great conflict."[23] Days later, Congress backed this covenant with the announcement of a national day of prayer, which again called on Americans to "unfeignedly confess and deplore our many sins."[24] John Adams declared, during this month of national covenant awareness, that "[m]illions will be upon their knees at once before their great Creator, imploring His forgiveness and blessing; his smiles on American Councils and arms."[25]

In addition to actions of Congress, Washington himself put forth great efforts to secure the blessings of the American Covenant prior to the siege of Boston. He called for government-sponsored chaplains for his troops, instructed his soldiers to attend Sunday service "to implore the blessings of heaven upon the means used for our safety and defense," and encouraged his men to "shew their gratitude to Providence, for thus favouring the Cause of Freedom and America" that they might "deserve his future blessings."[26]

But perhaps most importantly, on March 6, 1776, almost immediately after having secured Dorchester Heights, and days before the British evacuation—indeed, right when the miraculous intervention would be needed—Washington issued the following General Order. It was a direct call to the covenant.

> Thursday...being set apart by...this Province as a day of fasting, prayer and humiliation, to 'implore the Lord and Giver of victory to pardon our manifold sins and wickedness, and that it would

please Him to bless the Continental army with His divine favor and protection,' all officers and soldiers are strictly enjoined to pay all due reverence, and attention on that day to the sacred duties of the Lord of hosts, for his mercies already received, and for those blessings, which our Holiness and Uprightness of life can alone encourage us to hope through his mercy to obtain.[27]

America had clearly called on God, and God had clearly answered. As such, the scene in the newly-liberated Boston could not have been more joyous for the American beneficiaries of this divine answer and intervention. With the British at last evacuated and with the Americans high in spirits, a triumphant Washington was preparing to leave the now safeguarded New Englanders. But first he would pause on the Sabbath to hear a sermon by the Reverend Abiel Leonard, who fittingly chose for his text, Exodus 14:25: "The Egyptians said, Let us flee from the face of Israel; for the Lord fighteth for them."[28] The colonists were indeed a branch of modern-day Israel, fully equipped with that same national covenant the reverend was now sermonizing over. Perhaps many of them remembered that, not long before the events at Boston, the preacher William Stearns had exhorted them, declaring, "[L]et America's valorous sons put on the harness, nor take it off till peace shall be to Israel."[29] They seemed to know the covenant was real and that it was now theirs. And they would rely upon it again in the very near future.

Miracle at Long Island

Nobody was naïve enough to believe the British evacuation of Boston meant an end to hostilities. In fact, as the British fleet headed southward down the eastern coastline, it became clear to everyone that Howe would begin preparations for a military strike against the commercial and cultural hub of America— New York City. New York would make an ideal headquarters for Howe, as it was crawling with loyalists in support of Britain. New York was also surrounded by rivers and harbors, making it an easy target for the world's most powerful navy. In anticipation, Washington immediately sent his forces to defend New York. By April 1776, the Continental Army had arrived in New York and began making its preparations for battle. And God, in turn, began making preparations for His next major miracle in behalf of the Americans.

For a full description of the Miracle at Long Island, refer back to the Prologue. The important facts are: 1. Just as he had done during the siege at Boston, Washington issues multiple orders and requests while in New York for his men to pray to God and adhere to the national covenant obligations—that is, to display their highest moral conduct; 2. The Almighty responds with a stunning miracle that allows the colonial army to escape and thus live to fight another day. The covenant had been activated once again. David McCullough sums up this miracle:

> But what a close call it had been. How readily it could have gone all wrong—had there been no northeast wind to hold the British fleet in check through the day the Battle of Long Island was fought, not to say the days immediately afterward. Or had the wind not turned southwest the night of August 29. Or had there been no fortuitous fog as a final safeguard when day broke....Incredibly, yet again—fate, luck, Providence, the hand of God, as would be said so often—intervened. [30]

Washington and his men kept their end of the covenant and God kept His. In His wisdom, Providence allowed Washington and his band of inexperienced men to engage the enemy at Long Island, thus acquiring the much needed taste of battle that would serve them in the future, while at the same time miraculously pulling them from the grips of destruction. The Revolution would live on!

Miracle at Trenton and Princeton

Though the Lord certainly worked His miracle at Long Island, Washington's situation in the aftermath remained bleak. The overwhelming defeat at New York had convinced some fifteen thousand American troops to immediately abandon the cause, leaving Washington with a meager three thousand men. And the only thing these faithful soldiers could do in that moment was run away as fast as possible from the thirty-thousand British troops on their tails. Thus began Washington's famous retreat southward through New Jersey and Pennsylvania.

Washington at the Battle of Princeton, engraver unknown, published by Louis Kurz, Chicago, 1911

Yet despite the overwhelming reason to lose all hope, Washington and his band of faithful would not. As discussed in the previous chapter, the *Spirit* was with them. Furthermore, they knew that God had not worked the aforementioned miracles only to have His soldiers quit. And so, Washington would again appeal to the covenant, which was perhaps made a bit easier considering Congress had codified the covenant at least twice between the events at New York and the southward retreat: first, through the Declaration of Independence, and second, through the declaration for a Day of Fasting and Repentance (December 11, 1776), whose purpose was to officially "implore of Almighty God the forgiveness of the many sins prevailing among all ranks, and to beg the countenance as assistance of his Providence in the prosecution of the present just and necessary war."[31]

Armed with this tried and true covenant, Washington would go forward with faith—not only in courageously leading a dangerous retreat, but in preparing a counter-strike at the British-held town of Trenton, New Jersey, located just east of the Delaware River. On Christmas night, 1776, Washington's men, whose retreat had led them down the west side of the Delaware River, would divide into three parties and cross at separate locations over the Delaware River, then attack the enemy at dawn. The operation got off to a bad start when Washington's party was the only one able to break through the ice and successfully land on the shores near Trenton. His main concern at the time was to land without alerting the enemy. Once again, the Lord would intervene by helping to make this mission stealth. McCullough stated, "as during the escape from Brooklyn, Washington's other daring river-crossing by night, a northeaster [wind/storm] was again, decisively, a blessing..." [32] The enemy could not see or hear them coming.

As Washington's party was the only one that made it across, thus diminishing greatly his expected resources, the element of surprise would be all the more essential. As such, the Lord's storm would remain healthy, thus covering the Americans (both the sound and sight of them) until the early morning attack. Washington's specific target was the fifteen-hundred professional Hessian soldiers (mercenaries hired by the British) guarding Trenton. The Hessians would certainly not expect an ailing citizen army on the run to attack them the day after Christmas, especially in such awful weather. Even if the Americans did attempt such a thing, the Hessians had every reason to believe that their defensive posts just outside the town would surely detect any such American advance. Unfortunately for the Hessians, nobody had informed them about the American Covenant.

At just after eight o'clock on the morning of December 26, 1776, Nathanial Greene led the charge into Trenton. The Lord's cover had worked, and He literally *had their backs*. "The storm continued with great violence," wrote Henry Knox, "but was in our backs, and consequently in the faces of the enemy."[33] The Hessians were completely caught off guard. Knox noted that "[t]he hurry, fright and confusion of the enemy was not unlike that which will be when the last trump will sound."[34]

After what resulted in a violent display of house to house fighting, which lasted about forty-five minutes, the Hessians laid down their weapons and surrendered. With over twenty Hessians killed and over ninety others wounded, the Americans stood victorious without a single death in battle and with only four wounded men. Knox concluded that "Providence seemed to have smiled upon every part of this enterprise."[35] Among the brave American soldiers standing proud at battle's end were several future greats: Alexander Hamilton (first U.S. Secretary of the Treasury), John Marshall (second U.S. Chief Justice of the Supreme Court), and James Monroe (fifth U.S. president).[36]

Hope for America had returned. However, on January 1, 1777, all enlistments would expire. The entirety of the Continental Army, at least what was left of it, would be free to go home. Washington knew this would cripple the Revolution, and so he gathered his troops. The drum roll began and the General asked all those willing to extend their tours to step forward. Not a soul budged. A depressed Washington turned his horse and began riding away. Then suddenly he stopped, returned to his men, and according to a credible witness, stated the following:

> My brave fellows, you have done all I asked you to do, and more than could be reasonably expected, but your country is at stake, your wives, your houses, and all that you hold dear. You have worn yourselves out with fatigues and hardships, but we know not how to spare you. If you will continue to stay one month longer, you will render that service to the cause of liberty, and to your country, which you can probably never do under any other circumstance. [37]

Needless to say, as the drums began to sound again, the men, this time, stepped forward. According to Nathanial Greene, "God Almighty inclined their hearts to listen to the proposal and they engaged anew."[38] Washington would capitalize on the spirit accompanying this renewal of covenant and attack the enemy forthwith, this time up the road from Trenton at another British stronghold—the town of Princeton, New Jersey.

The British, aware of such a possibility, employed one of their brightest field commanders, Lord Charles Cornwallis, to protect Princeton. Upon arriving at Princeton on January 1, 1777, an anxious Cornwallis left a portion of his troops to guard the town, and then led over five thousand troops down the ten mile road to Trenton to squash the rebellion once and for all. With the temperature above freezing, the muddy roads made it very difficult for the British to mobilize troops and cannons. Fatigued, Cornwallis' troops camped just outside of view from Washington, who was nestled in at Trenton. Cornwallis claimed he would "bag him" in the morning. But when the British arose and launched their attack at dawn, not one American soldier was to be found. As he did at Long Island, Washington had managed to fool the British by keeping a few soldiers behind to stoke the fires, giving the perception that they had camped down for the night, when in reality the Americans had mobilized.

But this time they were not on the retreat. In an almost insanely risky move, Washington, in the dead of night, led thousands of troops with horses, baggage, and cannons through obscure back roads that twisted right around Cornwallis' position. Though the Americans were traveling over the same muddy roads which had slowed Cornwallis only hours earlier, a providential drop in the temperature had frozen the roads, making it possible for the Americans to move their carriages and cannon rapidly.[39] By morning, when Cornwallis realized he had been duped, Washington was already hitting the British stronghold at Princeton. "I believe," declared Knox, "they [the British at Princeton] were as astonished as if an army had dropped perpendicularly upon them."[40] And why wouldn't they be astonished? With Cornwallis having just left in the direction of the American rebels, the prospect of Washington getting through him to Princeton would have been nothing short of miraculous. Yet it had happened.

The battle of Princeton was more violent and furious than that at Trenton. Sensing his troops' need of spirit and courage, Washington would lead the charge himself on horseback. This was something he would often do, much to the chagrin of his aides, who would run to his side and attempt to reign him back in to safety. "I shall never forget," wrote one young officer present, "what I felt...when I saw him brave all the dangers of the field and his important life hanging as it were by a single hair with a thousand deaths flying around him. Believe me, I thought not of myself."[41] As other troops entered in from strategic points around the town, the British surrendered.

The fall of Trenton and Princeton, though minor battles in and of themselves, had an enormous effect throughout the colonies. The author Mercy Warren, who personally witnessed the Revolution, wrote that Washington's victories created a "change instantaneously wrought in the minds of men." Warren continued, "[There are] no people on earth in whom a spirit of enthusiastic zeal is so readily kindled, and burns so remarkably, as among Americans."[42] This spirit, even the *Spirit of Independence,* was not only alive and well, but was at last proliferating throughout all of America. It would seem the Lord knew such a spirit was necessary for the years ahead. As such, He inspired the miraculous events surrounding the Trenton and Princeton experience.

McCullough concluded that even though it had only been weeks earlier that America was bogged down in "as dark a time as any in the history of the country...suddenly, miraculously it seemed, that had changed because of a small band of determined men and their leader."[43] Though McCullough was most likely, and rightly, referring to Washington as this leader, the true leader of the victories was He who sat in a higher realm. Washington himself understood and believed this. Days after his victory at Princeton, he declared: "Providence has heretofore saved us in remarkable manner and on this we must principally rely."[44] Convinced more than ever that his success on the battlefield was fully contingent on the binding power of America's national covenant with the Almighty, Washington would "principally rely" on it again and again.

Miracles of 1777: Saratoga and Valley Forge

As great as those initial victories had been, the war would require over five more years of heartache, pain, and bloodshed before the Americans would achieve their independence. Fully aware of what lay ahead, Washington would again turn to God. Not long after Trenton and Princeton, Washington declared to his men that he, the commander-in-chief, "has the full confidence that in another Appeal to Heaven (with the blessing of providence, which it becomes every officer and soldier humbly to supplicate), we shall prove successful."[45]

It would not take long for Washington to be proven correct once again. In the fall of 1777, just weeks after Washington's above-quoted invocation and "appeal to heaven," the national covenant would bless the American cause at the very significant Battle of Saratoga. In September 1777, British General John Burgoyne invaded the Mohawk Valley near the town of Saratoga where an American regiment was detached. After an unsuccessful attempt at the Americans, Burgoyne decided to wait for reinforcements before attempting a second strike. By all accounts, Burgoyne's principal weakness was his inability to mobilize due to the large amount of material goods he had selfishly seized for his personal gain, including the fine china he and his men refused to part with. Furthermore, while the British waited, they entertained themselves with their large entourage of prostitutes that Burgoyne permitted to follow along.[46] In the meantime, Washington repeatedly rebuked such behavior in his own men. He was issuing official pleas to the Almighty and demanding strict moral behavior of his soldiers. That the Americans were fighting under a covenant with the Lord, and that the British were not, is clearly reflected in their very different perspectives on moral behavior.

It was perhaps this difference that explains why the Americans were able to defeat Burgoyne and the British at Saratoga in October 1777. Washington understood that it was God and covenant that provided the victory. Upon learning of the triumph, he promptly ordered services of thanksgiving and stated, "Let every face brighten, and every heart expand with grateful joy and praise to the supreme disposer of all events, who has granted us this signal success."[47] This American victory was not only significant in that it demonstrated the power of adhering to the national covenant, but also in that it provided the proof required by would-be American allies that the American cause was winnable. As a direct result of Saratoga, both France and Spain began their indispensable support of the American Revolution.

Following this victory, Congress would reemphasize the true source of America's strength and success—its national covenant with God. On November 1, 1777, Congress once again officially invoked this covenant in its Thanksgiving Proclamation, in which Congress called on Americans to perform acts to "please God through merits of Jesus Christ" and to support "the means of religion, for the promotion and enlargement of that Kingdom, which consisteth 'in righteousness, peace and joy in the Holy Ghost.'" The proclamation further instructed Americans to "join the penitent confession of their manifold sins, whereby they had forfeited every favor, and their humble and earnest supplication that it may please God, through the merits of Jesus Christ, mercifully to forgive and blot them out of remembrance."[48]

This public invocation to Heaven could not have been timelier, for the Lord and His blessings would be needed almost immediately thereafter. Within weeks of Saratoga (and after earlier American defeats at the Battle of Brandywine Creek and then at the Battle of Germantown), Washington and his very spent colonial army were compelled to hunker down for the winter of 1777 in Valley Forge, near Philadelphia. Without proper supplies (some went without shoes or shirts) and without adequate food (some were forced to eat a soup of burnt leaves and dirt), the army's suffering was acute. Yet notwithstanding, Washington and some of his officers seemed to hint at something divine even in this situation. While the British grew fat and happy in New York and Philadelphia, Washington's men were forced to learn humility, resilience, and other needful lessons for eventual victory. Wrote Washington, "To see Men without Cloathes to cover their nakedness, without Blankets to lay on, without Shoes, by which their Marches might be traced by the Blood from their feet, is a mark of Patience and obedience which in my opinion can scarce be paralel'd."[49] One of Washington's most faithful commanders, Nathaniel Greene, would concur, adding that "we bear beatings very well...the more we are beat, the better we grow."[50]

Washington, who stayed close to his men in Valley Forge (when he certainly could have justified relocating to more comfortable quarters), would also experience the spiritual growth of such a humbling experience. Two legendary stories of Washington at Valley Forge, both of which are apocryphal, tell the tale. First is the well-known account of his mighty prayer. According to the story, a local resident and Quaker named Isaac Potts, whose religion had initially compelled him to stand against the Revolution, happened upon the spiritually powerful scene. The fullest account of what he saw was written by the Rev. Nathanial Snowden

(1770-1851) in his "Diary of Remembrances." Rev. Snowden, an ordained minister and graduate of Princeton, related the following experience:

> I was riding with him [Mr. Potts] in Montgomery County, Penn, near to the Valley Forge, where the army lay during the war of ye Revolution. Mr. Potts was a Senator in our State & a Whig. I told him I was agreeably surprised to find him a friend to his country, as the Quakers were mostly Tories. He said, "It was so and I was a rank Tory once, for I never believed that America c'd proceed against Great Britain whose fleets and armies covered the land and ocean, but something very extraordinary converted me to the Good Faith!"

> "What was that?," I inquired. "Do you see that woods, & that plain?" It was about a quarter of a mile off from the place we were riding, as it happened. "There," said he, "laid the army of Washington. It was a most distressing time of ye war, and all were for giving up the ship except for that great and good man. In that woods pointing to a point in view, I heard a plaintive sound as, of a man at prayer. I tied my horse to a sapling & went quietly into the woods & to my astonishment I saw the great George Washington on his knees alone, with his sword on one side and his cocked hat on the other. He was at Prayer to the God of the Armies, beseeching to interpose with his divine aid, as it was ye Crises, & the cause of the country, of humanity & of the world.

> Such a prayer I never heard from the lips of man. I left him alone praying. I went home & told my wife. I saw a sight and heard today what I never saw or heard before, and just related to her what I had seen & heard & observed. We never thought a man could be a soldier and a Christian, but if there is one in the world, it is Washington. She also was

astonished. We thought it was the cause of God, &
America could prevail.[51]

Critics—mostly secularists—have attempted to discredit
this story due to another account of a praying Washington at
Valley Forge. In this second
account, as printed in the
Aldine Press, Washington was
seen by one of his soldiers
praying in a barn, which
critics claim is a discrepancy
of the original story. Critics
therefore discredit any claim
that Washington was ever
seen praying at all in Valley
Forge. Of course, the more

The Prayer at Valley Forge, by H. Brueckner.
Courtesy of The Library of Congress.

reasonable explanation, perhaps beyond the reach of such
secularists, is that a God-fearing man like Washington prayed
many times at Valley Forge and therefore many accounts were
witnessed and recorded. One of Washington's generals at
Valley Forge, Robert Porterfield, told of how he once entered
Washington's private quarters to report an emergency.
Porterfield found Washington on his knees in prayer. He
reported the incident to Washington's aide, Alexander
Hamilton, who replied that "such was his constant habit."[52]

Furthermore, in light of the claims by close friends
and family members that Washington consistently
"maintained daily intercourse with Heaven by prayer," that
he "observed stated seasons of retirement for secret
devotion,"[53] and that he was constantly encouraging/
ordering his men to pray often (he was, after all, never
known to be a hypocrite), Potts' story becomes all the more
believable.

The second story has to do with the account of
Anthony Sherman, one of Washington's aides at Valley
Forge, who reportedly recalled the following experience,

later to be recorded and published by his friend, Wesley Bradshaw. The account appeared in an 1880 edition of the *National Tribune*:

> The darkest period we had I think, was when Washington, after several reverses, retreated to Valley Forge, where he resolved to pass the winter of 1777. Ah! I have often seen the tears coursing down our dear commander's careworn cheeks, as he would be conversing with a confidential officer about the condition of his poor soldiers. You have doubtless heard the story of Washington's going to the thicket to pray. Well, it was not only true, but he used often to pray in secret for aid and comfort from God. The interposition of whose Divine Providence brought us safely through the darkest days of tribulation.
>
> One day, I remember it well [in Valley Forge], the chilly winds whistled through the leafless trees, though the sky was cloudless and the sun shone brightly, [Washington] remained in his quarters nearly all afternoon alone. When he came out I noticed that his face was a shade paler than usual, and there seemed to be something on his mind of more than ordinary importance. Returning just after dusk, he dispatched an orderly to the quarters of the officer I mentioned who was presently in attendance. After a preliminary conversation of about half an hour, Washington, gazing upon his companion with that strange look of dignity which he alone could command, said to the latter:
>
> "I do not know whether it is owing to the anxiety of my mind, or what, but this afternoon, as I was sitting at this table engaged in preparing a dispatch, something seemed to disturb me. Looking up, I beheld standing opposite me a singularly beautiful female. So astonished was I, for I had given strict orders not to be disturbed,

that it was some moments before I found language to inquire the cause of her presence. A second, a third, and even a fourth time did I repeat my question, but received no answer from my mysterious visitor...By this time I felt strange sensations spreading through me. I would have risen but the riveted gaze of the being before me rendered volition impossible."

"Presently I heard a voice saying 'Son of the Republic, Look and Learn' while at the same time my visitor extended her arm eastwardly. I now beheld a heavy white vapor at some distance rising fold upon fold. This gradually dissipated, and I looked upon a strange scene. Before me laid spread out in one vast plain all the countries of the world—Europe, Asia, Africa and America.... 'Son of the Republic,' said the same mysterious voice as before, 'look and learn.' At that moment I beheld... [another] angel, standing or rather floating in mid-air, between Europe and America. Dipping water out of the ocean in the hollow of each hand he sprinkled some upon America....A second time the angel dipped water from the ocean, and sprinkled it as before..."

"A third time I heard the mysterious voice saying, 'Son of the Republic, look and learn.' I cast my eyes upon America and beheld villages and towns and cities springing up one after another until the whole land from the Atlantic to the Pacific was dotted with them. Again, I heard the mysterious voice say, 'Son of the Republic, the end of the century cometh, look and learn.' And the bright angel planted the standard upon them [in America] crying out, 'While the stars remain, and the heavens send down dew upon the earth, so long shall the Union last.'"[54]

If the account is true, it seems Washington sensed that Heaven was endowing him with knowledge that

America had most certainly been anointed for some great purpose, and that, in spite of his current difficulties, he should go forward with faith in God.*

Washington did just that. On December 18, 1777, Washington again asked his men "to observe a day of prayer and fasting, to give thanks to God for blessings already received, and to implore the continuing favor of Providence upon the American cause." After Washington read a sermon by one of his chaplains, which had been given to accompany and support the General's day of fast and prayer at Valley Forge, Washington wrote to thank him for "the force of reasoning that you have displayed." He then added that "it will ever be the wish of my heart to aid your pious endeavors to inculcate a due sense of the dependence we ought to place in that all wise and powerful Being on whom alone our success depends."[55]

Months later, Washington further instructed on the American Covenant in issuing the following General Orders:

> While we are zealously performing the duties of
> good Citizens and soldiers we certainly ought not to

---

* In yet another anecdotal account (this one reported by Time Magazine), while at Valley Forge, George Washington requested that Chaplain John Gano baptize him by immersion. "I have been investigating the Scripture," declared Washington, "and I believe immersion to be the baptism taught in the Word of God, and I demand it at your hands. I do not wish any parade made or the army called out, but simply a quiet demonstration of the ordinance." The ordinance was reportedly carried out in secret because Washington did not desire to make himself a member of Gano's congregation. Gano therefore had to break his church's policy by baptizing one who had no intention of joining the congregation. In 1889, Gano's grandchild and another relative swore in an affidavit that Gano's daughter had told them that the baptism had taken place. Historians have been unable to confirm or deny the veracity of the account. In Gano Chapel, at William Jewell College in Missouri, there is a painting of Gano baptizing Washington by immersion. See www.time.com/ time/magazine/article/0,9171,744297,00.html, and http://en.wikipedia.org/ wiki/John_Gano#Alleged_baptism_of_George_Washington, and http:// www.sluiceboxadventures.com/learn_history/JohnGano_02.htm

be inattentive to the higher duties of Religion. To the distinguished Character of Patriot, it should be our highest Glory to add the more distinguished Character of Christian. The signal Instances of providential Goodness which we have experienced and which have now almost crowned our labours with complete Success, demand from us in a peculiar manner the warmest returns of Gratitude and Piety to the Supreme Author of all Good.[56]

It was also during this time that Washington would again encourage his fellow countrymen to give thanks and credit to God, this time for France's decision to enter the war on America's side. "It having pleased the Almighty Ruler of the Universe propitiously to defend the cause of the United States," declared Washington, "by raising us up a powerful friend." This single act was, according to Washington, brought forth through God's "benign interposition."[57]

This was followed by yet another Washington reference to the importance of the American Covenant and America's obligation to it. On August 20, 1778, Washington wrote the following to one of his generals: "The Hand of Providence has been so conspicuous in all this [Revolutionary War], that he must be worse than an infidel that lacks faith, and more than wicked, that has not gratitude enough to acknowledge his obligations."[58]

Congress would also follow-up shortly thereafter with yet another reminder to Americans of their national covenant at this crucial point in the war. This time they appropriately connected America and her covenant with that ancient national covenant God had maintained with Israel. In a 1779 letter to the nation, Congress declared that America had "without arms, ammunition, discipline, revenue, government or ally, with 'staff and sling' only, dared, 'in the name of the Lord of Hosts,' to engage a gigantic adversary."[59] America was as disadvantaged against the British as David had been against Goliath. However, armed with a divine covenant, they could not lose.

Miracle at Yorktown

By 1781 the war had entered a stalemate of sorts, with the exception of the skirmishes in the South, brought on in large part by American guerilla-style attacks. In response, in January of 1781, General Lord Charles Cornwallis, commander of the British troops in the South, sent Colonel Tarleton to attack the American's under George Morgan at Cowpens, South Carolina. Tarleton's British forces were unexpectedly defeated. In response, on March 15, an embarrassed and aggravated Cornwallis moved on the American troops under Washington's southern commander, Nathanial Greene, at Guilford Court House in North Carolina. Though Greene was defeated there, he was not subdued, and forthwith decided to preserve his remaining troops by fleeing northward together with Morgan's troops. Still desirous to finish off Greene completely, Cornwallis would regroup and follow him northward. The chase was on.

In an attempt to cut off the fleeing Americans, Cornwallis ordered his soldiers to shed their heavy baggage, which helped them to rapidly gain ground. Cornwallis reached the Catawba River just hours after the Americans had crossed. Confident that victory would be his in the morning, Cornwallis decided to cross the river at dawn the following day. But during the night a storm flooded the river making a morning crossing impossible and allowing the Americans a head start.[60]

Cornwallis would again almost catch the Americans, first at the Yadkin River in North Carolina on February 3 and then at the Dan River, at the Virginia border, on February 13. In both cases, the Americans would safely cross just in time for a storm to flood the river, thus blocking a British attack. The British commander, Sir Henry Clinton, to whom Cornwallis answered, had to admit that God seemed to have intervened on America's behalf. Wrote Clinton, "...here the royal army was again stopped by a sudden rise of the waters, which had only just fallen [miraculously] to let the enemy over, who could not else have eluded Lord Cornwallis' grasp, so close was he upon their rear."[61]

After Cornwallis' failed chase left him in Virginia with nothing left to do, Clinton directed him to move his army, consisting of some 7,500 Redcoats, to secure the tobacco port at the peninsula of Yorktown, Virginia. From there, reasoned Clinton, Cornwallis' troops could be easily mobilized via the Chesapeake Bay by the superior British navy. As Cornwallis waited, Washington considered his options. Both sides immediately began plotting and scheming, believing that—with both armies on the verge of collapse—whoever dealt the next blow would secure ultimate victory. Times were tense.

Storming Redoubt No. 10 at Yorktown, by Eugene Louis Lami
Courtesy of Library of Virginia.

Washington, who at the time was directing the northern campaign, thought to launch an attack on the British in the north, believing an attack on Yorktown would be fruitless; for who could stop a Cornwallis retreat by sea? Perhaps he remembered that the Lord surely could. So, he changed his plans and went forward with faith, ordering his soldiers to begin congregating around the Yorktown peninsula in an attempt to box in Cornwallis. As the best-selling author and historian Thomas Fleming put it, "Instead, Washington marched south [to Yorktown] and a series of miracles occurred."[62]

The first of these miracles was witnessed as the British fleet out of New York set sail for Yorktown in order to rescue Cornwallis and his troops. However, the British fleet did not expect to run into a French fleet, which had barely arrived at the Chesapeake Bay, off the coast of Yorktown, in support of the American effort to trap Cornwallis. On September 5, 1781, the French ships turned on the incoming British and defeated them in what became known as the Battle of the Capes. The French fleet then proceeded to rejoin their American allies at Yorktown, while the British fleet was forced to return to New York to refit its ships, all the while leaving Cornwallis trapped and in an even more precarious situation. As William Bennett explained in his book, *America, The Last Best Hope*, between the years 1588–1941, the British "ruled the waves...with one important local exception...in the waters off Yorktown, Virginia, in 1781."[63] This one exception in over 350 years of British naval warfare history would directly contribute to the final battlefield victory that sealed American independence. This was no coincidence.

On October 10, having gathered many troops from around the country, Washington directed a young Alexander Hamilton to lead an eastward charge on Cornwallis' position on the Yorktown peninsula. Hamilton obeyed the orders and subsequently pushed the British right up against the Atlantic coast, and succeeded in capturing British fortifications along the way. This put the Americans in an ideal position.[64]

Even as he watched his men fall by the hundreds, a humiliated and panic-ridden Cornwallis was asking the same perplexing question that Washington (and every other man on the battlefield) was asking—*Where is that promised, superior British navy to rescue its soldiers?* The answer, as perplexing as the question, is the result of yet another divine intervention.

Having regrouped after their unlikely naval defeat at hands of the French, the British at last prepared once again to move out of New York to rescue the ailing Cornwallis. With plenty of time still to save Cornwallis' troops at Yorktown, the British fleet confidently made their preparations. Then the Lord stepped in once again. Fleming explains:

> In New York, a frantic Sir Henry Clinton proposed...
> a rescue plan that called for putting most of the army
> on navy ships and fighting their way into the

Chesapeake to join Cornwallis....On October 13, the fleet was supposed to sail—when a tremendous thunderstorm swept over New York harbor. Terrific gusts of wind snapped the anchor cable on one of the ships of the line, smashing her into another ship and damaging both of them....[The British] could not leave until the damage was repaired.[65]

By October 15, Washington and his French allies had begun launching a highly successful bombardment upon an ever-more trapped Cornwallis. As he had done before, and at great peril to his own life, Washington rallied his men by directing the attack from a forward deployed position, causing his aides, once again, to pull him back and away.[66]

Under severe fire, and with a tragic recognition that the British navy would not be coming to his rescue after all, Cornwallis immediately resorted to his desperate contingency plan—evacuate the Yorktown peninsula by ferrying his men northward over the York River and then march toward the British friendly New York. In a plan which resembled that of Washington's at Long Island years earlier, Cornwallis would attempt the crossing on October 16, by the cover of night. The only discrepancy of course was that when Washington attempted such an escape, he had been acting under a covenant with God. Unfortunately for Cornwallis, it was this single factor that would make all the difference. Fleming explains:

> About ten minutes [after midnight]...a tremendous storm broke over the river. Within five minutes, there was a full gale blowing, as violent, from the descriptions in various diaries, as the storm that had damaged the British fleet in New York. Shivering in the bitter wind, soaked to the skin, the exhausted soldiers and sailors returned to the Yorktown shore. Not until two A.M. did the wind moderate. It was much too late to get the rest of the army across the river. Glumly, Cornwallis ordered the guards and the light infantry to return.[67]

With no other option available, Cornwallis was forced to surrender to Washington on October 19, 1781. This final blow was enough to convince the British to terminate their war efforts (though the peace treaty signed at Paris—which officially ended the war—would not be realized until 1783). America was at last free.

As British soldiers approached the Americans to surrender Cornwallis' sword, the depressed British band began to play, very fittingly, the popular tune, "The World Turned Upside Down."[68] Indeed, the world was turning upside down, just as the Lord had planned it—all in preparation for the work he would accomplish through America.

Emphasizing the significance of the details of the Battle at Yorktown, as outlined above, Fleming offers the following insight:

> A Cornwallis getaway would have left the French and Americans frustrated and hopeless, facing a stalemated war they no longer had the money or will to fight. American independence—or a large chunk of it—might have been traded away in the peace conference. A Clinton invasion...would have triggered a stupendous naval and land battle that might well have ended in British victory—enabling them to impose the harshest imaginable peace on the exhausted Americans and shattered the French. Instead the Allies had landed the knockout blow.[69]

Though Fleming's above analysis is no doubt a sound one, Washington might take issue with one point from his conclusion. The "knockout blow" was first and foremost landed, not by the Allies, but by the Lord. "I take particular pleasure," Washington would explain in reference to his Yorktown victory, "in acknowledging that the interposing hand of Heaven, in various instances of our preparations for this operation, has been most conspicuous and remarkable."[70]

On October 20, 1781, only one day after Cornwallis surrendered, Washington directed yet another General Order to "recommend that the troops not on duty should universally attend with that seriousness of Deportment and gratitude of Heart which the recognition of such reiterated and astonishing interpositions of Providence demands of us."[71] Though the war was over, Washington would waste no time at all (not even one day) in encouraging compliance to that covenant which he had learned so convincingly to trust in and love. Somehow he knew that its power would be needed in the near future, even in the building-up of the newly independent nation.

Surrender of Cornwallis at Yorktown by John Trumball,
courtesy of the Architect of the Capitol.

Conclusion

Thus far in this book, we have seen many examples of the American Covenant in action. But there is perhaps no better representation of this covenant in action than the events surrounding the battles of the American Revolution. Consider again the prophecies, provided in Part I of this book, which speak of God and righteous war within the context of the American Covenant. There is that earliest recorded version of the American Covenant in the Book of Genesis, which states that Joseph and his posterity (American colonists) will thwart their enemies, even "the archers" that "shot at him and hated him;" and that he would defeat them, as his "bow abode in strength." And all of this was made possible through the strength provided "by the hands of the mighty God of Jacob" (see Gen. 49: 1, 22-26 and Chapter 2 of this book).

Have we not seen in this chapter the literal fulfillment of these promises and prophecies of the covenant? How many times did Congress, Washington, and others turn to the Lord, invoking the covenant, asking for national forgiveness, and pleading for national blessings? How often did these founding leaders invoke this covenant by pleading with the people to live worthy of its blessings? The Americans had indeed adhered to the covenant; and the blessings had, in turn, arrived in powerful measure.

Washington and his faithful Founders clearly did all that they could, and where they fell short, the Lord provided the balance of what was required. Who could say this was not the case at Boston, Long Island, Trenton, Princeton, Yorktown, and other major events during the Revolution? Such divine orchestration ensured American success, but also allowed the revolutionaries to work, toil, bleed, and sacrifice, thus producing an American example and legacy that others could follow. After all, it is often *sacrifice* that brings forth the blessings of heaven.

These blessings have been developed and carried on to the present. For, the Revolution's ultimate fruit to the world is enjoyed today. And what is this fruit? It is the expansion and development of freedom, even that freedom necessary to access, accept, and live the gospel of eternal salvation. Such is the significance of these miracles. Such is the significance of the covenant.

ENDNOTES

¹ Thomas Fleming, "Unlikely Victory," *What If? The World's Foremost Military Historians Imagine What Might Have Been*, James Cowley, ed (New York, Penguin Putnam Inc,1999), 162-163.

² McCullough, *1776*, 79.

³ McCullough, *1776*, 79.

⁴ McCullough, *1776*, 72.

⁵ McCullough, *1776*, 79.

⁶ McCullough, *1776*, 82.

⁷ McCullough, *1776*, 92.

⁸ McCullough, *1776*, 93.

⁹ Thomas Fleming, "Unlikely Victory," *What If? The World's Foremost Military Historians Imagine What Might have been* (New York, Penguin Putnam Inc, 1999),162-163.

¹⁰ McCullough, *1776*, 96.

¹¹ McCullough, *1776*, 97.

¹² McCullough, *1776*, 107; full quote available from *The Papers of George Washington: Revolutionaries War Series, Series 3*, 493-494, available at www.consource.org.

¹³ Letter from Washington to his brother John Augustine Washington, March 31, 1776, as quoted in *The Writings of George Washington, Volume 4, Electronic Text Center, University of Virginia*, available from http://etext.virginia.edu/toc/modeng/public/WasFi04.html.

¹⁴ McCullough, *1776*, 111.

¹⁵ McCullough, *1776*, 111.

¹⁶ Fleming, 163.

¹⁷ McCullough, *1776*, 111.

¹⁸ McCullough, *1776*, 110.

¹⁹ Letter from Washington to his brother John Augustine Washington, March 31, 1776, as quoted in *The Writings of George Washington, Volume 4, Electronic Text Center, University of Virginia*, available from http://etext.virginia.edu/toc/modeng/public/WasFi04.html; also quoted in part in McCullough, *1776*, 110.

²⁰ McCullough, *1776*, 105.

²¹ Novak, *On Two Wings*, 13-14 (prayer delivered on September 7, 1774).

[22] Waldman, *Founding Faith*, 43 (This congressional declaration was issued on October 20, 1774). Details of this congressional act were provided in Chapter 7 of this book, under the subheading *Testimonials of the Rebels*.

[23] Foster, *The American Covenant*, 33. (This congressional act was issued on July 6, 1775.)

[24] Waldman, *Founding Faith*, 70. (This congressional act was issued on July 20, 1775.)

[25] John Adams, as quoted in Waldman, *Founding Faith*, 108.

[26] Michael Novak and Jana Novak, *Washington's God* (New York: Basic Books, 2006), 65.

[27] General Orders from George Washington, March 6, 1776, as quoted in *The Writings of George Washington, Volume 4, Electronic Text Center, University of Virginia*, available from http://etext.virginia.edu/toc/modeng/public/WasFi04.html.

[28] McCullough, *1776*, 106.

[29] William Stearns, as quoted in Marshall and Manuel, 366-7.

[30] McCullough, "What the Fog Wrought," 199; McCullough, *1776*, 191.

[31] "Fast Day Proclamation of the Continental Congress, December 11, 1776," Worthington C. Ford, Gaillard Hunt, et al., eds., *The Journals of the Continental Congress, 1774-1789* (Washington, D.C.: Government Printing Office, 1904-37), vol. 6. p. 1022; also quoted in Novak, *On Two Wings*, 18.

[32] McCullough, *1776*, 275.

[33] McCullough, *1776*, 280.

[34] Henry Knox, as quoted in Marshall and Manuel, 400.

[35] Marshall and Manuel, 401.

[36] Bennett, *America, The Last Best Hope*, 89.

[37] Sergeant R———, "Battle of Princeton," *Pennsylvania Magazine of History and Biography*, vol. 20 (1896), 515-16.

[38] Nathanial Greene to Nicolas Cooke, Jan. 10, 1777, in *The Papers of General Nathanial Greene*, ed. Richard K. Showman and Dennis Conrad (Chapel Hill: University of North Carolina Press, 1980), vol.2, 4.

[39] Green, *The Tribe of Ephraim*, 151.

[40] McCullough, *1776*, 288.

[41] McCullough, *1776*, 289.

[42] McCullough, *1776*, 291.

[43] McCullough, *1776*, 291.

[44] George Washington (January 22, 1777), as quoted in Waldman, *Founding Faith*, 70.

[45] George Washington, "General Orders" September 1777, as quoted in Novak, *Washington's God*, 65-66.

[46] Larry Schweikart and Michael Allen, *A Patriot's History* (New York: Sentinel, 2004), 81-83.

[47] George Washington (October 18, 1777, in response to victory at Saratoga), as quoted in Waldman, *Founding Faith*, 69.

[48] Thanksgiving Proclamation November 1, 1777, as quoted in Waldman, *Founding Faith*, 71, 87.

[49] Ellis, *His Excellency*,112.

[50] Nathanial Greene, as quoted in Schweikart and Allen, *A Patriot's History*, 86.

[51] Quoted in "A Prayer at Valley Forge," *National Review*, December 5, 2005; variation of the story recorded by Bennett, *The Spirit of America*, 372-373.

[52] Marshall and Manuel, 457.

[53] Novak, *Washington's God*, 221.

[54] Wesley Bradshaw, *National Tribune* 4 (12) (December 1880), as quoted in Robert Hieronimus, *Founding Fathers, Secret Societies*, 49-50.

[55] Novak, *Washington's God*, 129-130.

[56] George Washington (May 2, 1778) as quoted in Novak, *Washington's God*, 90.

[57] Washington, as quoted in Ron Chernow, *George Washington: A Life* (New York: The Penguin Press, 2011); also available at cnsnews.com/news/article/new-documentary-examines-god-s-place-america-s-heritage-told-founding-fathers.

[58] George Washington (August 20, 1778), as quoted by Janice Connell, *The Spiritual Journey of George Washington* (New York: Hatherleigh Press, 2007), 96.

[59] Waldman, *Founding Faith*, 70.

[60] Foster and Swanson, *The American Covenant*, 161-162.

[61] Henry Clinton, as quoted in William Hosmer, "Remember Our Bicentennial—1781," Foundation for Christian Self-Government *Newsletter*, June 1981, 5; the account is also recorded in Foster and Swanson, *The American Covenant: The Untold Story*, 162; and is also recounted in Marshall and Manuel, 416-418.

[62] Thomas Fleming, "Unlikely Victory," *The World's Foremost Military Authorities Imagine What Might Have Been*, James Cowley, ed (New York, Penguin Putnam, Inc, 1999), 179.

[63] William J. Bennett, *America, The Last Best Hope* (Nashville, Nelson Current, 2006), 29, 101.

[64] Joseph J. Ellis, *Patriots, Brotherhood of the American Revolution*, Lectures recorded by Recorded Books, Inc, and Barnes and Noble Publishing: 2004, Lecture 7, Tr.6, 2:15 min; also recounted in Fleming, 180-1.

[65] Fleming, 180.

[66] Ellis, *Patriots, Brotherhood of the American Revolution*, Lecture 7, Tr.6, 2:15 min; also recounted in Fleming, 180-1.

[67] Fleming, 181.

[68] Marshall and Manuel, 420; Bennett, *America, The Last Best Hope*, 102.

[69] Fleming, 182.

[70] George Washington, as quoted in Foster and Swanson, 163.

[71] George Washington, as quoted in Novak, *Washington's God*, 66.

CHAPTER 9

SIGNS AND BLESSINGS IN WAR'S AFTERMATH

Glorious indeed has been our Contest: glorious, if we consider the Prize for which we have contended, and glorious in its Issue; but in the midst of our Joys, I hope we shall not forget that, to divine Providence is to be ascribed the Glory and the Praise....I consider it an indispensable duty to close this last solemn act of my Official life, by commending the Interests of our dearest Country to the protection of Almighty God, and those who have the superintendence of them, to his holy keeping.

—George Washington,
1783

It is clear from the previous chapters that God took a most active role during the Revolutionary War, as He repeatedly blessed the American cause through the national covenant. But the blessings certainly did not cease with the end of the conflict. For in the aftermath of war, we see further proof of the Lord's influence over America. This chapter documents some of these evidences at war's end, which lend further credibility to the divinity of America's purposes and to the reality of her covenant.

Deeper Connections to the Covenant

The narrative of the Revolution detailed in the past few chapters, culminating at the battle of Yorktown, includes an obvious reflection of the colonists understanding of the covenant relationship between God and America. But at war's end, as the dust finally settled, and as the stories of God's miracles were shared throughout the colonies, Americans began to see how powerful this covenant really was. Many even began to recognize the deeper meaning of what this covenant ultimately promised to all mankind. Such revelatory knowledge amongst the colonists would serve the new nation as it worked to form a righteous government under God. For that reason, this knowledge is counted as one of the great blessings in the aftermath of war.

One example of this greater comprehension of the covenant is witnessed through the words of the Massachusetts minister, David Tappan, who told his congregants that God had brought victory to America for one purpose—"that His [God's] own name might be exalted, that His own great designs...extending the Kingdom of His Son, may be carried into effect."[1]

Other declarations concerning the gospel purposes of America and the Revolution were made by one of the most prominent Christian leaders of the day, Timothy Dwight, who would serve as the president of Yale College. Some years after the Revolution, Dwight prophesied over the meaning of the newly independent America, declaring:

God brought His little flock hither and placed it in the wilderness, for the great purpose of establishing permanently the Church of Christ in these vast regions of idolatry and sin, and commencing here the glorious work of salvation. This great continent is soon to be filled with the praise and piety of the Millennium. But here is the seed, from which this last harvest is to spring.[2]

Amazingly, Dwight correctly and prophetically recognized that "the seed" of a now free and independent America would usher in an enlargement of Christ's church.

On an earlier occasion, in the midst of the Revolution, Dwight made it clear that such "independence and happiness [was] fixed upon the most lasting foundations, and that the Kingdom of the Redeemer... [would be] durably established on the ruins of the Kingdom of Satan."[3]

Timothy Dwight

Furthermore, as one historian pointed out, Dwight knew that the way for America to ensure the advent of this grand restoration was through the "reestablishment of the covenant relationship that their forbears had entered into with God and with one another." It was, after all, Dwight who declared in 1777, just as the Revolution was commencing, that "Nothing obstructs the deliverance of America but the crimes of its inhabitants."[4] Dwight confirmed the general recognition in colonial America that success and independence was contingent on living the American Covenant. Now, at war's end, he had seen this covenant largely fulfilled and was now sharing his vision of what this covenant would soon offer the world.

That these inspired Americans presaged the enlargement of the gospel as being the ultimate fruit of the Revolution should not be taken for granted. They were prophetic in their day. What's more, the shared vision of these ministers in post-war America was not the exception but the norm. As one historian explained, "With few exceptions, it seemed to the ministers of America that the Light, which had been brought [to America] by the first Christ-bearers, had at last [with independence now gained] been joined by the glory of his Kingdom come—or soon coming."[5]

Such powerful sentiments regarding God's purposes for the Revolution, particularly as expressed in post-war colonial America, did not stop with religious leaders, but was also expressed by political leaders. One such leader was Samuel Adams, the *Father of the Revolution*. His extraordinary vision of the Revolution's divine purpose prompted him to state that—with independence at last secured—it was now time for America to bring in "the holy and happy period when the kingdom of our Lord and Savior Jesus Christ may be everywhere established, and the people willingly bow to the scepter of Him who is the Prince of Peace."[6] Adams' amazingly accurate statement that the Revolution would usher in a period of gospel enhancement is perhaps corroborated by an earlier prophetic idea he put forth in 1776: "[T]he hand of heaven appears to have led us on to be perhaps humble instruments and means in the great providential dispensation which is completing."[7] There is no doubt that Adams saw the emerging power of America as becoming a key factor in this, God's final dispensation.

Another revolutionary leader whose understanding seemed to increase in the wake of war was none other than George Washington. Though we know he clearly witnessed, testified of, and believed in the existence of the American Covenant, one wonders how deep his knowledge extended. Did he see or feel at least something of the greater gospel purposes behind that covenant, even as he reflected upon the miraculous

American cause through which he said he could so clearly "trace the finger of Providence"?[8] The evidence suggests that he did. Particularly in the years after the war—after having ample time to reflect over its ultimate meaning—it appears he received further light and knowledge.

Washington stated his belief that God works "for wise purposes not discoverable by finite minds."[9] As Washington knew God had directed the Revolution, he no doubt considered that God quite possibly had His own profound purposes for the Revolution. Without attempting to put his finger directly on the greater purpose, Washington most certainly seemed to have an inspired inkling into what God had in mind. In 1789, while penning a draft of his first presidential inaugural address, Washington wrote the following:

> Can it be imagined...that this continent was not created and reserved so long undiscovered as a Theatre, for those glorious displays of divine Munificence, the salutary consequences of which will flow to another Hemisphere & extend through the interminable series of the ages? Should not our souls exult in the prospect? Though I shall not survive to perceive with these bodily senses, but a small portion of the blessed effects which our Revolution will occasion in the rest of the world; yet I enjoy the progress of human society & happiness in anticipation. I rejoice in the belief that *intellectual light will spring up in the dark corners of the earth.*[10]

Through gospel lenses, it is difficult not to see such comments as prophetic allusions to what would happen to Christianity post-war. Though the critic might balk at such a suggestion, there is further reason to consider the possibility. According to Washington scholars Michael and Jana Novak, Washington believed that this *intellectual light* was something born out of what the General himself called "the pure and benign light of Revelation."[11] It is possible he saw glimmers of a religious enlargement forming as a consequence of his Revolution.

Washington first made reference to this *light of Revelation* in what he believed would be his final circular address to Congress. In 1783, on the heels of victory, and with retirement now on his mind, Washington wrote this circular because, as he stated in the address, "I think it a duty incumbent on me to make this my last official communication; to congratulate you on the glorious events which Heaven has been pleased to produce in our favor." But offering congratulations on victory under God was just the beginning. There was another reason he felt so compelled to make this final address. For he said he felt obligated "to offer my sentiments respecting some important subjects." The first (and perhaps most powerful) subject he shared had something to do with the spiritual nature of America. Washington declared in this address to Congress that the freed Americans were now "to be considered as the Actors on a most conspicuous Theatre, which seemed to be particularly designed by Providence, for the display of human greatness and felicity." He went on to explain that as part of this divine American movement, "Heaven has crowned all [America's] other blessings" with every gift the new nation would need to fill the measure of its creation, and that "above all" these gifts there is one which has a "meliorating influence on Mankind... [which increases] the blessings of society." This gift he described as "the pure and benign light of Revelation."[12]

Furthermore, upon declaring that this light of America would soon "spring up in the dark corners of the earth," he implied that it would do so thanks in large part to an increase in "freedom of enquiry" (or what we might call personal or religious freedom). This he knew America would be offering through influence and example to the world.[13]

Though admittedly we can only speculate on what Washington meant by his above statements, it is clear that he knew God was behind America and that God had very significant blessings—even blessings associated with "light" and "revelation"—to offer the world through America. In Washington's words we perhaps see a deeper understanding of the American Covenant and what it would ultimately offer mankind in due time.

A few years before his death, Washington would again speak of the greater purpose of the American cause:

> If it can be esteemed a happiness to live in an age of great and interesting events, we of the present age are very highly favored. The rapidity of national revolutions appear less astonishing, than their magnitude. In what they will terminate, is known only to the great ruler of events; and confiding in his wisdom and goodness, we may safely trust the issue to him, without perplexing ourselves to seek for that, which is beyond human ken; only taking care to perform the parts assigned to us, in a way that reason and our own consciences approve of.[14]

That God had some great design planned as the crowning event of the American Revolution made too much sense for Washington to ignore. How else could he explain the endless stream of miracles he had witnessed throughout the cause? Why else would the Lord be so intricately involved? Indeed, something grand was on the horizon.

Even though Washington did not seem to know all the specifics, he did reveal an additional impression that sheds some light upon his personal testimony. Shortly after independence had been secured, Washington felt inclined to explain what had compelled him to fight in the first place. He stated that "[t]he establishment of Civil and *Religious Liberty* was the motive that induced me to the field of battle."[15]

From a gospel perspective, Washington's ultimate explanation for the Revolution seems entirely appropriate. We know that God inspired the Revolution and secured victory for America in order to create religious freedom for Christianity to take root and grow stronger than ever. However, this was not obvious during Washington's day. In fact, to list *religious liberty* as the principal motive for war could scarcely have been comprehended at the time. To be sure, when the colonists were planning and justifying their revolution, they created a document in which they declared their independence and in which they included a lengthy, perhaps even exaggerated, list of grievances against Britain (we reviewed these grievances in Chapter 7, and saw how they were based in political philosophies such as "no taxation without representation"). This document, of course, is the Declaration of Independence. Though the Founders attempted to publically blame the king for everything they could think of and place the accusations in the Declaration (at one point Jefferson even made the absurd suggestion to officially blame him for slavery),[16] nowhere amongst the many complaints against Britain found in the document will one find a grievance related to religious intolerance or religious freedom. This fact alone leads us to question why Washington would have placed religious liberty at the forefront of his motives. Perhaps he did know more than he let on. Perhaps he was speaking almost prophetically when he said what he did. As Washington was one of several Founders to make such conclusions (as we will see in later chapters), we will pause briefly here to explain how naming religious freedom as the *principal* motive for the Revolution in Washington's day would have required some inspired insight.

Admittedly, one might argue that Washington was simply referring to the fact that Great Britain maintained a state religion (the Church of England), which did cause some problems for certain religious minorities. Therefore, his statements about fighting for religious liberty should be obvious and expected. However, Great Britain did not pose an obvious and large-scale threat to religious liberty and, in fact, mostly respected religious freedom. This is evidenced by the many different denominations that were permitted to exist and thrive in America. The Founders themselves belonged to these different denominations and enjoyed their ability to worship freely therein. Had they not been able to worship freely, then complaints of religious persecution against the Crown would have been prominently listed in the Declaration of Independence—not completely ignored, as was the case. Furthermore, Washington himself, along with many other Founders, was an active member of Britain's state church, even the Church of England.[17] Again, any religious intolerance from Britain was mostly directed at certain minority religions and therefore did not conjure up enough outrage at the time to justify war.

This is not to say that Britain, and its interest in government-backed religious establishment, was benign. On the contrary, the British-American tie had to be severed for the purposes of God. British rule would have given the adversary a tool that could have easily been manipulated to stomp out any enlightenment, renewal, or growth related to Christ's Gospel. With so much power in the hands of a few—as was characteristic of the monarchy—the adversary would have had little trouble influencing the British elites to choose evil and obstruct God's work in modern times. Unless and until freedom existed for *all* religionists seeking salvation, nobody would be safe from Satan's ultimate desire to crush Christianity. But the colonists could not have easily perceived this in their day. Therefore, they would not have been able to easily articulate—at least with human understanding—why religious freedom was a valid justification to fight the British.

Furthermore, churches established in colonial America by the colonists themselves were just as guilty, if not *more* guilty, as the Church of England in their unjust practices toward certain religious minorities. For example, to the great peril of Quakers and Baptists, New England boasted of a state-established and state-sponsored religion—the Puritan religion, later known as the Congregational Church. This America-born church took care to acquire public monies for its support, while denying such monies to other religions. Furthermore, the religious establishment in New England made sure that minority religions were barred from enjoying a fullness of religious freedom. Baptist ministers in New England, for example, were not authorized to conduct marriages, were harassed, and were restricted on where they could preach. And these practices continued well after independence from Britain was gained.[18]

The point is this: as a whole, the colonists did not care that much about the fact that minority religions suffered some persecution. And if religious intolerance over minority sects was not significant enough to solve at home during peacetime, why would it, all of a sudden, be so significant as to warrant war with Britain, the world's superpower? The lack of any significant concern or interest regarding an increase in religious liberty at this point in American history rejects the suggestion that the colonists were willing to go to war over the issue.

But if the revolutionaries were not intentionally fighting specifically for an increase of religious liberty, how do we account for the fact that greater religious liberty was a primary fruit of the Revolution? The answer is simple. As the Americans gained independence and realized that the British could no longer threaten freedoms in America, only then was it brought into sharp focus that Americans were themselves allowing such persecution domestically. Only then did the plight of religious minorities begin to be more openly recognized and corrected. As one religious history scholar noted, the Revolution made it "difficult for patriots to attack the evils of the Anglican establishment, then turn around and defend the maintenance of an official state church [in America]."[19] Thanks in part to this new perspective, even a new spirit of freedom and a new emphasis on religious liberty, born out of the Revolution, the colonists would more readily apply protections for all religions when they at last created the Constitution. But this new perspective—though it was an intentional blessing from God, who sees the end from the beginning—was, for the revolutionaries, mostly an unintended consequence.

That Washington saw early on that the Revolution was about the creation of such religious freedom is perhaps evidence of his truly inspired calling. For, based on the arguments presented above, it seems that only by inspiration could one, in Washington's day, point to religious freedom as *the* focal point of the Revolution. Perhaps God's abundant Spirit, which called him to the Revolution and sustained him in war, also dropped revelatory hints about God's ultimate plan. Perhaps such spiritual glimpses encouraged the General to go forward with increasing faith.

Washington's comments about religious freedom being the principal reason for war become even more closely related to God and covenant when we consider that in the same address, just prior to making this statement, Washington first reminds his audience how important it is to "acknowledge publicly our infinite obligations to the Supreme Ruler of the Universe for rescuing our country from the brink of destruction; I cannot fail at this time to ascribe all the honor of our late successes to the same glorious Being." Then, immediately *after* his religious liberty declaration, and upon concluding his address, Washington again shows his understanding of the national covenant by stating that "it now remains to be my earnest wish and prayer, that the Citizens of the United States would make a wise and virtuous use of the blessings, placed before them."[20]

Washington continued to manifest this deeper understanding when he declared in 1790 that the purpose of America was to provide the means by which the religious minority (and he was specifically talking to and about religious minorities) might "sit in safety under his own vine and fig tree, and there shall be none to make him afraid. May the father of all mercies scatter light and not darkness in our paths, and make us all in our several vocations useful here, and in his own due time and way everlastingly happy."[21] Washington was proud that he had, under God's direction, helped create a country abounding with religious freedom, which he said was "unrivalled by any civilized nation of earth." Washington declared that the "bosom of America is open to receive, the oppressed and persecuted of all Nations and Religions, whom we shall welcome to a participation of all our rights and privileges."[22] Washington truly seemed to understand something about how the American Covenant had created, through the Revolution, a special foundation upon which God could safely bring His work and His glory.

The general comprehension of the American Covenant extended even further in post-war colonial America. In addition to understanding the ultimate purposes of the covenant, the revolutionaries at war's end also seemed to gain a deeper understanding about where this powerful covenant had its roots and origin. Many began to understand that the American cause represented a second chance for Israel, even the chance for a new covenant people to work out the purposes of God on earth.

It is a fact, as noted several times throughout this book, that this inspired connection with ancient Israel had repeatedly been made since the earliest colonists landed upon the New World. But at war's end, after having witnessed so much of the fulfillment of this ancient covenant with modern-day Israel, this connection became even more powerful. Many leaders, including congressmen, urged Congress to place the English language aside and make Hebrew the official national language. Though the idea never took hold, many universities did make Hebrew a required course.[23]

The revolutionary and President of Yale University, Ezra Stiles, taught that the ancient covenant of Israel was in fact fulfilled in his America. In 1783, the year America officially gained its independence, he gave a speech entitled, "The United States Elevated to Glory and Honor." In it, he interpreted a prophecy and commandment given by Moses to the Children of Israel. These words of Moses, found in Deuteronomy 30, refer to a gathering of Israel. Stiles explained its connection to modern-day America.

Ezra Stiles

> God determined that a remnant should be saved... recovered and gathered...from the nations whither the Lord had scattered them in his fierce anger...and multiply them over their fathers—and rejoice over them for good, as he rejoiced over their fathers. Then the words of Moses...will be literally fulfilled; when this branch of the posterity of Abraham [Ephraim] shall be nationally collected, and become a very distinguished and glorious people under the Great Messiah, the Prince of Peace. He will then make them "high above all nations which he hath made in praise, and in name, and in honor," and they shall become "a holy people unto the Lord" their God.[24]

The Protestant minister George Duffield referred to the newly independent America as the "American Zion" and connected the ancient covenants to the modern ones, likening Washington of the American Covenant to the Prophet Joshua of the ancient covenant, and likening the foreigner king of France, who came to the rescue of the American Israelites, to Cyrus, the foreigner who did the same for the ancient Israelites.[25] Declared Duffield:

> With Israel of old, we take up our song: 'Blessed be the Lord, who gave us not as prey to their teeth. Blessed be the Lord, the snare is broken and we are

escaped'...Here also shall our Jesus go forth conquering and to conquer, and the heathen be given Him for an inheritance, and these uttermost parts for a possession. The pure and undefiled religion of our blessed Redeemer—here shall it reign in triumph over all opposition.[26]

Washington was also compared on many occasions to the Prophet Moses. Americans sermonized over the notion that the General "has been the same to us, as Moses was to the Children of Israel." One colonial orator declared that "Kind Heaven, pitying the servile condition of our American Israel, gave us a second Moses, who should (under God) be our future deliverer from the bondage and tyranny of haughty Britain." Upon Washington's death, he was eulogized throughout the country well over four hundred times by varying orators in varying locales. Stunningly, approximately two thirds of the orations directly connected Washington to Moses.[27] Best-selling author and journalist, Bruce Feiler, explains why the colonists made this comparison, calling the parallels between the two leaders "striking."

> Biblical Israel and God's New Israel were formed on the twin shoulders of liberation and law. In both cases, one man was present at both moments. Both men had the unusual combination of skills—leadership and humility, fortitude and diplomacy—that could serve them well in dramatic moments of confrontation as well as years of slowly building a people. Beloved founders, both could have clung to power but resisted the temptation to turn their nations into monarchies. Reticent speakers, both left behind some of the most quoted words ever spoken.[28]

As further witness of this deeper comprehension that existed among the post-war colonists, we turn to the greats of the Revolution. Benjamin Franklin, for example, proposed that the new American nation should use as its official seal a depiction of Moses freeing Israel from its Egyptian oppressors through the power of God, represented by "Rays from the Pillar of Fire in the

Clouds." Thomas Jefferson proposed that the seal depict the Children of Israel being led in the wilderness "by a cloud by day and a pillar of fire by night."[29] In his second inaugural address as president of the United States, Jefferson further connected America's covenant to that of ancient Israel by declaring that in order to ensure the covenant blessings of *prosperity*, he would need "the favor of that Being in whose hands we are, who led our forefathers, as Israel of old..."[30]

And consider this post-war declaration made by Washington:

> May the same wonder-working Deity, who long since delivered the Hebrews from their Egyptian oppressors, planted them in a promised land, whose providential agency has lately been conspicuous in establishing these United States as an independent nation, still continue to water them with the dews of Heaven and make the inhabitants of every denomination participate in the temporal and spiritual blessings of that people whose God is Jehovah.[31]

A gospel perspective informs us of a deep connection between America and Israel; indeed, America represents a second chance for Israel, even a New Israel—a New Jerusalem. It represents a second chance for God to accomplish His work by virtue of a national covenant. We have already seen how the early settlers and revolutionaries grasped this idea. In post-war America, this idea flourished further. Through the miraculous wartime events detailed earlier—from Boston to Yorktown—the American Covenant, to include its more profound meanings in connection with Israel, had simply become obvious to the Founders at war's end. It had become obvious to the Founders not only because of what they had witnessed, but also—as author Steven Green points out in his book, *The Tribe of Ephraim*— because these Founders "carried that believing blood of Ephraim, cherishing liberty above safety...."[32]

This deeper comprehension of the covenant was indeed a great blessing to America, for it would serve to guide the newly independent colonies in their quest to build a united nation under God and covenant. Further, it was a witness to God of America's adherence to the covenant obligations, which guaranteed that the covenant blessings would continue to flow from heaven.

Washington's Ultimate Sign of the Covenant

In addition to the deeper comprehension of the covenant found in post-war America, there is more to the story. Indeed, there is one powerful event that occurred at war's end that not only emphasized the divine nature of the Revolution, but presented a sign of the American Covenant—a sign offered by that most prominent covenant-maker, General George Washington.

Though America had won its independence, its immediate stability and general happiness was in no way guaranteed. In fact, historical trends forecasted a gloomy immediate future. To be sure, throughout the history of the world, there has been an unfortunate pattern, which seems to dictate how national revolutions are supposed to end. The hero of the revolution, utilizing his victorious armed forces, along with his national popularity, propels himself into power and makes himself dictator over his people. Not only have we seen this pattern in ancient governments—like in ancient Rome—but also in more modern ones. In the mid-seventeenth century, for example, Oliver Cromwell would lead a popular revolution over the British monarchy only to then purge parliament and rule as king himself. In the late eighteenth century, the French Revolution would also oust the king, only to replace him by other dictators such as Napoleon. The nineteenth century would see countries like Mexico win their popular independence over Spain, only to see military dictators like Santa Ana throw out the constitution and rule according to his personal dictates. In the early twentieth century, the Russian Revolution would result in a series of communist dictators as bad, or worse, than any of the earlier Russian monarchs that had been overthrown. Through the balance of the twentieth century, the world would see a series of the most brutal dictators emerge out of popular, national revolutions: Hitler in Germany, Mao in China, Castro in Cuba, and the list goes on and on.

The question for the American story was, *Would Washington fall in line with the rest of the world's revolutionary leaders?* The choice would be his alone to make. For, as early as December 27, 1776, Congress had voted to make Washington a virtual dictator over the armed forces (without the luxury of rapid communication technology, Congress had no choice but to give Washington all power).

Upon receiving word back in 1776 that Congress had given him such powers, he immediately responded, stating:

> Instead of thinking myself freed from all civil obligations by this mark of their confidence, I shall constantly bear in mind that as the sword was the last resort for the preservation of our liberties, so it ought to be the first thing laid aside when those liberties are firmly established.[33]

By May 1782, this promise would be tested. With independence already "firmly established," the American officers began stirring the hearts of their soldiers against Congress, who had not yet made the final payments due to the army. One of Washington's colonels, Lewis Nicola, wrote to Washington and expressed the general sentiments of his men. He offered Washington the opportunity to do that which had always been done by revolutionary heroes: lead a coup on Congress and make himself king of America. (Nicola told Washington that he could use a different title than "king" if he wanted, but in effect, that is what he would become.) After all, who could have stopped Washington? By the end of the war, as McCullough points out, his men would have "follow[ed him] through hell."[34] Taking Congress, therefore, would have been easy. Indeed, the only person who could have stopped Washington was Washington. And that is exactly what happened. It was yet another demonstration of the powerful spirit working upon the General.

Shocked and horrified by Nicola's offer, Washington was determined to make good on his word to Congress. As such, he responded to Nicola, shooting back this stinging reply:

> With a mixture of great surprise and astonishment I have read with attention the Sentiments you have submitted to my perusal. Be assured Sir, no occurrence in the course of War, has given me more painful sensations than your information of there being such ideas existing in the Army as you have expressed, and I must view with abhorrence, and reprehend the severity. For the present, the communication of them will rest in my own bosom, unless some further agitation of the matter, shall make a disclosure necessary. I am much at loss to conceive what part of my conduct could have given encouragement to an address which to me seems big with the greatest mischiefs that can befall my Country. If I am not deceived in the knowledge of myself, you could not have found a person to whom your schemes are more disagreeable.[35]

So sure was Washington on the matter that he would express years later that God had intentionally barred him from having any children (it is believed he was impotent), so as to prevent any future temptations from them or his countrymen to create a monarchy of his name. "Divine Providence," he would write, "has not seen fit that my blood should be transmitted...by the sometimes seducing channel of immediate offspring." He would state thankfully that there was "no family to build in greatness upon my country's ruins."[36]

Though Washington's refusal to act on Nicola's request had restrained talks of a 1782 coup, within a year, and with things still unresolved with Congress, the officers again began scheming to turn the sword on Congress and take the country by force, even if Washington would not join them. This plot, which was being organized in early 1783 at the army camp in Newburgh, would go down in history as the Newburgh Conspiracy.

When Washington received word of the movement, he at once condemned it and traveled directly to the camp. On March 13, 1783, Washington called a meeting in a large building in the camp known as The Temple. Washington, in a passionate speech, pled with the men not to reverse all the good they had done. The soldiers were still visibly upset and apparently unmoved. Washington then prepared to read a letter from one congressman who expressed his desire to work out a peaceful negotiation with the army. Before reading the letter, Washington took out a pair of glasses, which he had only recently needed and acquired, then stated, "Gentlemen, you will permit me to put on my spectacles, for I have not only grown gray but almost blind in your service." Indeed, Washington, who had begun the conflict while in his early forties, had literally transformed before his soldiers' eyes, and was now tired and aging into his fifties. In that moment, the general recognition of his own personal sacrifice not only melted the anger in the room, but caused a complete change of heart. Many of those present wept openly.[37]

Washington finished his comments and left the officers to make their decision. They called off the coup. Word of the de-escalation arrived just in time to Congress, as it was preparing to declare a preemptive war on the military factions responsible. But thankfully, all would soon be forgiven as a peaceful settlement was at last agreed upon. Washington had once again proven to be the indispensable man.[38]

Thomas Jefferson would appropriately observe that "the moderation and virtue of [Washington] probably prevented the Revolution from being closed, as most others have been, by a subversion of that liberty it was intended to establish."[39] Even King George III, Washington's nemesis (and one who knew a thing or two about political power grabs) declared, upon hearing of Washington's intention to give back all power to

Congress, that he must be "the greatest man in the world."[40] And so he was. By Christmas 1783, Washington had retired from public life and began farming quietly at his beloved Mount Vernon.[41]

Though Washington's desire was to at last stay at home, within a few years of his retirement to Mount Vernon, James Madison began pleading with him to enter the public arena once again and head the Constitutional Convention, even that convention which would produce the United States Constitution. Though he attempted to persuade Madison to find somebody else, he knew he was needed. So he arrived at Philadelphia and successfully guided the process.

Then, and again due to no effort on his own part, Washington was elected unanimously as the nation's first president. Though no term limits had been specified at that point in the Constitution, and though he knew he could have remained as president for the duration of his life, Washington vowed to relinquish his position after one term. Unfortunately for him, the voters got to decide (not him), and they voted him in once more. He agreed, but made it clear that it would be his last. And it was.

As president, he would lead the United States down a steady course, always careful to govern under the limits given him by the divinely ordained Constitution. On one occasion, after acting wisely and constitutionally during two crucial moments (putting down the Whisky Rebellion in Pennsylvania, which he physically led, and signing the Jay Treaty, which averted another war with Britain), his political enemies foolishly and erroneously accused him of usurping power and acting like a monarch. Stunned and heart-broken, he emotionally declared, "By God, I had rather be on my farm than be made emperor of the world!"[42]

It was precisely this spirit of humility, derived from an understanding of America's relationship with God, which kept him in check and which made him great. Indeed, his greatness as president stemmed not so much from what he did, but from what he did *not* do. His powerful and divine restraint, even his ability to respect the constitutional harnesses placed upon him as president, had set the example and precedent for good governance.

When he at last was able to retire, his second term complete, he walked off the stage of John Adams' inaugural ceremony, and came face to face with the newly elected vice president, Thomas Jefferson, who was waiting for the former president to precede him through the exit gate. But Washington, in a sign of his recognition of the vice president's authority over his own (he was now a common citizen) insisted with "a firm gesture of command" that Jefferson go first.[43] He was surrendering power and inviting, by example, all his successors to do the same in their turn. Thus far, they all have.

In the end, Washington had indeed proven to be the exception to the rule of world history's revolutionary leaders. At least one revolution and its leader needed to set the example that other nations could follow in ushering in an inspired government in preparation for an enlargement of God's church. That this standard-bearer was Washington, a principal covenant-maker in the land divinely ordained from its conception, should be of no surprise.

Perhaps the crowning moment of the Revolution was when Washington laid his sword before Congress at the end of the great conflict with Britain, thus relinquishing all his power. As he did so, he could not help but invoke the American Covenant one last time, declaring to Congress the following on December 23, 1783:

> Glorious indeed has been our Contest: glorious, if we consider the Prize for which we have contended, and glorious in its Issue; but in the midst of our Joys, I hope we shall not forget that, to divine Providence is to be ascribed the Glory and the Praise....I consider it an indispensable duty to close this last solemn act of

my Official life, by commending the Interests of our dearest Country to the protection of Almighty God, and those who have the superintendence of them, to his holy keeping.[44]

Speaking to all Americans in this same spirit and near this same time, Washington declared:

If in the execution of an arduous Office I have been so happy as to discharge my duty to the Public with fidelity and success, and to obtain the good opinion of my fellow Soldiers and fellow Citizens; I attribute all the glory to that Supreme Being, who hath caused the several parts, which have been employed in the production of the wonderful Events we now contemplate, to harmonize in the most perfect manner, and who was able by the humblest instruments as well as by the most powerful means to establish and secure the liberty and happiness of these United States.[45]

So important was the covenant to Washington that he would, before leaving his post, once again impress upon his countrymen the importance of keeping the commandments.

I now make it my earnest prayer, that God would have you, and the State over which you preside, in his holy protection, and that he would incline the hearts of the Citizens to cultivate a spirit of subordination and obedience to Government, to entertain a brotherly affection and love for one another, for their fellow citizens of the United States at large, and particularly for their brethren who have served in the Field, and finally, that he would most graciously be pleased to dispose us all, to do Justice, to love mercy, and to demean ourselves with that Charity, humility and pacific temper of mind, which were the Characteristiks of the Divine Author of our blessed Religion, and without an humble imitation of whose examples in these things, we can never hope to be a happy nation.[46]

284

General George Washington Resigning his Commission,
Courtesy of the Architect of the Capitol.

It was in this spirit that the greatest revolutionary war for independence, perhaps in the history of the world, was concluded. It was General Washington's ultimate gift to America. And it was a powerful sign of the national covenant under which the General had been appointed to work—a sign that would make the nation worthy of further covenant blessings from above.

In light of Washington's actions here, we should consider one piece of undervalued American artwork that captures this experience in a marvelous way. It is a thirty ton sculpture of the General completed in 1840, and it currently sits in the Smithsonian's National Museum of American History. Entitled simply, *George Washington*, it depicts the General cradling a sheathed sword upon his left forearm and open palm, extending it forward as if to be returning it. It is a symbol of the General's inspired decision to return all power to the people after the war. That this act was part of a national covenant is also, most astonishingly, represented. First, the statue is full of imagery representing ancient Greece (the first seat of democracy), which reflects the covenant blessing of freedom. Second, Washington is flanked on both sides by small statues—one of a Native American and one of Columbus (reminiscent of Ephraim arriving in the Promised Land under the covenant). Finally, in a most stunning symbol of the covenant, Washington is depicted sitting upon a grand throne with a robe draped over his right shoulder. While his left arm and hand are returning the sword, his right arm and hand are depicted being raised to the square, with his index finger pointing to heaven.

George Washington, by Horatio Greenough, on display at the National Museum of American History, Washington D.C.

ENDNOTES

1 David Tappan, as quoted in Marshall and Manuel, 427.

2 Timothy Dwight, as quoted in Marshall and Manuel, 427.

3 Marshall and Manuel, 428.

4 Marshal and Manuel, 428.

5 Marshal and Manuel, 427.

6 Waldman, 88.

7 Waldman, 42.

8 George Washington, as quoted in Bennett, *Spirit of America*, 365.

9 George Washington, as quoted in Novak, *Washington's God*, 130.

10 Novak, *Washington's God*, 192-193, emphasis added.

11 Novak, *Washington's God*, 115.

12 Washington, Circular of 1783 to John Hancock and Congress, as quoted in "The Papers of George Washington," available at http://gwpapers.virginia.edu/documents/constitution/index.html.

13 Novak, *Washington's God*, 193.

14 Novak, *Washington's God*, 128.

15 Novak, *Washington's God*, 111.

16 McCullough, *John Adams*, 131.

17 Novak, *Washington's God*, 8, 12.

18 Waldman, 52, 136, 173.

19 Waldman, 52.

20 George Washington, in "Letter to the Reformed German Congregation of New York," available at http://teachingamerican history.org/index.asp? document print=361; also quoted in Novak, *Washington's God*, 130.

21 Washington, in a letter to the Touro Synagogue in Newport, Rhode Island, August 17, 1790, as quoted in Waldman, *Founding Faith*, 164.

22 Waldman, 63.

23 Cleon Skousen, *The Majesty of God's Law*, 23.

24 Cleon Skousen, *The Majesty of God's Law*, 15-16.

25 George Duffield (1783), as quoted in Meacham, 80-81.

26 Duffield, as quoted in Marshall and Manuel, 426.

[27] Bruce Feiler, *America's Prophet, Moses and the American Story* (New York: HarperCollins, 2009), 102-103.

[28] Bruce Feiler, *America's Prophet, Moses and the American Story*, 104.

[29] Waldman, *Founding Faith*, 107.

[30] Jefferson, as quoted in Waldman, 82.

[31] Washington, as quoted in Novak, *Washington's God*, 125.

[32] Greene, 152.

[33] McCullough, *1776*, 286.

[34] McCullough, "The Glorious Cause of America," 47.

[35] Novak, *Washington's God*, 33.

[36] George Washington, as quoted in Gordon S. Wood, *Revolutionary Characters* (New York, Penguin Press, 2006), 51.

[37] Fleming, 183-185.

[38] Fleming, 185.

[39] Novak, *Washington's God*, 34.

[40] Ellis, *His Excellency*, 139.

[41] Joseph J. Ellis, *Patriots, Brotherhood of the American Revolution*, Lectures recorded by Recorded Books, Inc, and Barnes and Noble Publishing: 2004, lecture 7.

[42] Bennett, *America: The Last Best Hope*, Vol. 1, 163.

[43] Bennett, *America: The Last Best Hope*, Vol. 1, 165.

[44] George Washington, as quoted in Novak, *Washington's God*, 173, 211.

[45] Washington's address at Princeton, August 25, 1783, as quoted in Novak,*Washington's God*, 183.

[46] George Washington, "Circular Address to the States," June 8, 1783, as quoted in William J. Bennett, *The Spirit of America* (New York: Simon and Schuster, 1997), 378-380.

CHAPTER 10

THE DECLARATION OF
INDEPENDENCE AS COVENANT

*[Independence Day] ought to be
commemorated as the Day of Deliverance by
solemn acts of devotion to God Almighty.*

—John Adams

*And for the support of this Declaration, with
a firm reliance on the protection of Divine
Providence, we mutually pledge to each other
our Lives, our Fortunes and our sacred
Honor.*

—Thomas Jefferson

In the previous chapters, we have corroborated our claims regarding the American Covenant and validated the scriptures which support them, by showing how God truly intervened in the American Revolution both spiritually and physically. If we are to believe that God was the source of inspiration and power behind the Revolution, then should we not expect to discover His hand in the supporting documents of this movement? Furthermore, if the Founding Fathers were types and shadows of prophets, should we not expect them to have left us with types and shadows of scripture? We can answer affirmatively to both these questions and point to the Declaration of Independence to support this affirmation. The Declaration is a gift of God, a true representation of the covenant. In proving that the Declaration is part and parcel of the American Covenant, we will find yet another witness that the ancient prophecies of this covenant have been fulfilled, thus proving the reality of this covenant and the truthfulness of its divine purpose.

National Scripture

A principal reason for connecting the Declaration to the national covenant is that the document itself, like scripture,

Declaration of Independence

reads like a covenant with God. It recognizes the fight for American independence as the work of God. It also recognizes that America's success hangs on its citizens' willingness to obey Him. It is no wonder that Samuel Adams, upon signing the document, declared, "We have this day restored the Sovereign to whom men alone ought to be obedient. He reigns in heaven...from the rising to the setting of the sun, His kingdom come."[1] Whether he understood it or not, Adams' statement would prove prophetic, as the Declaration did, in many ways, usher in God's kingdom, even a renewal of His Gospel. And Sam Adams knew he was not alone in implying that the Declaration was scripture-like. Referring to the Declaration, Adams explained that "The people...recognize the resolution as though it were a decree promulgated from heaven."[2]

That the Declaration is tightly connected to God and covenant is evidenced by the fact that God is referenced in the Declaration at least four times and given the titles of *Lawgiver, Creator, Judge,* and *Providence.* The historian and author, Michael Novak, placed these references together, along with their accompanying text within the Declaration, to show how this language reads like a covenant-based prayer.

> Creator, who has endowed in us our inalienable rights, Maker of nature and nature's laws, undeceivable Judge of the rectitude of our intentions, we place our firm reliance upon the protection of divine Providence, which you have extended over our nation from its beginning.[3]

Furthermore, a careful read of the Declaration plainly reveals that, throughout its entirety, it is an invocation of the very blessings of the American Covenant—the blessings of *liberty, protection,* and *prosperity.* The document clearly states America's intention to "secure" for America the "inalienable rights" of "Life, Liberty, and the Pursuit of Happiness," thus invoking the blessings of *liberty.* The document further states that it is America's intention to create and maintain "Safety and Happiness," thus invoking the blessings of *protection.* It also puts forth an economic plan, which includes the power to independently regulate its own trade, its own taxes, and its own geographic expansion of its territories, thus invoking the blessings of *prosperity.* Furthermore, these blessings are recognized as being accessible to America only through "a firm reliance on the protection of Divine Providence." The Declaration is a true reflection of the American Covenant as put forth by the Old Testament prophecies of Jacob to Joseph.

In fact, the Declaration is a direct fulfillment of these prophecies. And, again, these blessings of the American Covenant, if received and applied, have the ultimate effect of developing and protecting God's gift of personal liberty to man—a gift that is necessary for man's eternal salvation.

Such a perspective is backed by one of our most inspired presidents, John Quincy Adams, who—as the child of one of our greatest revolutionaries—was a first hand witness of the American Revolution. Asked Adams, "Is it not that the Declaration of Independence first organized the social compact on the foundation of the Redeemer's mission upon the earth? That it laid the cornerstone of human government upon the first precepts of Christianity?"[4] Not only does Adams recognize the covenant (or "compact") nature of the document, but clearly connects its purposes to those of the gospel.

Another allusion to the Declaration's connections to God and the national covenant is witnessed—yet too often overlooked—by thousands of visitors and tourists of the United States National Archives in Washington D.C., which houses and displays the original Declaration. Upon entering the building, all one has to do is look on the floor to see an impressive bronze engraving of the Ten Commandments—the most famous example of God's covenant with a nation.[5] It is not a coincidence that such a display welcomes visitors as a preface to the Declaration of Independence.

Further proof of the Founders' intention and inspiration to create the Declaration as a covenant, with blessings contingent upon national worthiness, can be found through analyzing the historical background and context in which the Declaration was written and issued. Shortly after the Declaration was signed, America experienced severe hardships, including Washington's defeat at New York and the poor harvest of that year. Though the Declaration had clearly recognized God's supremacy and indispensable role in America, this was evidently not enough to secure the full

Signing of the Declaration of Independence, John Trunbull 1819.

Courtesy of the Architect if the Capitol.

blessings of Heaven. Perhaps America's obligation in this covenant with the Almighty needed to be better understood and applied. The Declaration, which was directed at Britain, would require an appendage of sorts, directed at America alone, that its citizens might better adhere to their covenant. It was in this spirit that the Congress, just months after signing the Declaration, issued a national decree for a Day of Fasting and Repentance to take place on December 11, 1776. This document stated the following:

> WHERAS, the war in which the United States is engaged with Great Britain, has not only been prolonged, but is likely to be carried to the greatest extremity; and whereas, it becomes all public bodies, as well as private persons, to reverence the Providence of God, and look up to him as the

supreme disposer of all events, and the arbiter of the fate of nations; therefore,

RESOLVED, that it be recommended to all the United States, as soon as possible, to appoint a day of solemn fasting and humiliation; to implore of Almighty God the forgiveness of the many sins prevailing among all ranks, and to beg the countenance as assistance of his Providence in the prosecution of the present just and necessary war.

The Congress do also, in the most earnest manner, recommend to all the members of the United States, and particularly the officers civil and military under them, the exercise of repentance and reformation; and further require of them the strict observance of the articles of war, and particularly, that part of the said articles, which forbids profane swearing, and all immorality, of which all such officers are desired to take notice.[6]

The fact that this document was issued by the same group of statesmen who had only recently issued the Declaration—and inasmuch as they issued it in support of that same cause of independence—it is difficult not to see how it functioned as an appendage to the Declaration. Like the Declaration itself, it was a powerful invocation of the national covenant. (And let us not forget the many other like-minded invocations of the covenant given by Congress throughout the conflict, as documented in earlier chapters.) Fortunately, in the end, America adhered to this covenant and thus received those blessings required both for military victory and for the laying down of a firm political foundation —all designed to accomplish God's work on earth for His children.

In sum, the Declaration was issued in God's name; it specifically spelled out the covenant blessings; it was tightly connected to the Founders' understanding of a covenant with God; and finally, through faithfulness to this document, and through general obedience to God, these covenant blessings of the Declaration were received in preparation for the enlargement of Christianity. All of this leaves us with a powerful witness. It is a witness that the Declaration was, in fact, part and parcel of the American Covenant. Add to that witness the many spiritual manifestations accompanying the revolutionaries, along with the many battlefield miracles that supported the cause of independence, and the Declaration's place as national scripture and covenant becomes overwhelmingly secure.

A Miraculous Confirmation

The scriptures teach us that from time to time the Lord offers His children signs from Heaven in order to convey messages to them. Sometimes the purpose of such a message is to convey disappointment and to inspire change. Such was the case with the early camp of Israel, for example, who suffered through rough times in the wilderness, so that they might remember the Lord. Other times the purpose of such a message is to convey approval or to confirm a promise or covenant. Such was the case with the sign of a rainbow given to the Prophet Noah as a confirmation of a covenant with God.

In the previous chapters, we have seen many examples of such miraculous and symbolic messages given to America. These included miracles performed on the battlefields of war, which are proof of God's covenant with America and His desire to make this covenant known. However, there is one sign having to do with America's covenant that has not yet been mentioned. This particular sign from God is a miraculous event that places a seal of approval on the American revolutionary cause and confirms the Declaration of Independence as a covenant with the Almighty. And, as the Declaration is but an appendage of the American Covenant, this final miracle of the Revolution only confirms once again

295

the validity of the American Covenant itself. However, in order to fully comprehend this sign as a divine stamp of approval on the Declaration and as evidence of the American Covenant itself, we must first understand something about the two most important actors in the creation of the Declaration. Fittingly, they are the same principal actors involved in the miracle. They are John Adams and Thomas Jefferson. And so, before providing the details of this miracle, we will first briefly discuss these two men and their connection with the Declaration, God, and the covenant.

John Adams: The Voice of Independence

John Adams was born into a good, religious, middle class family in Massachusetts. Adams had toyed with the idea of following the example of his father and joining the clergy, but instead became a successful attorney in and around Boston. Adams was married to his best friend, Abigail, and found himself, throughout his twenties and thirties, practicing law, farming his land, raising his children, and getting involved in local politics. In 1774, on the eve of turning forty, Adams was elected by his countrymen to represent them in Philadelphia at the Continental Congress, which had been designed as a national venue to discuss, among other things, the emerging conflict with Britain.

John Adams

Though Adams had arrived at Philadelphia as unassuming and as normal as any of the other delegates, he found himself rising to his feet and taking the floor of the congressional convention so powerfully and so often that he soon made a name for himself. His speeches in favor of independence from Britain would be recognized as some of the most persuasive and powerful in the history of Congress. They were even described as being spiritually moving.[7]* Adams was also responsible for influencing Congress to appoint Washington as commander-in-chief. When considering the divine and critical nature of Washington's role in the Revolution, such a call by Adams was not only inspirational, but perhaps prophetic. After nominating Washington, Adams predicted that the "appointment will have great effect in cementing and securing the union of these colonies." He further prophesied that Washington would become "one of the most important characters in the world."[8] So trusted and respected was Adams among his fellow delegates, that he was repeatedly chosen to sit on the most important committees. He was, according to David McCullough, "the leading committeeman of the Massachusetts delegation, perhaps indeed of the whole Congress."[9] "It was John Adams," according to McCullough, "more than anyone, who had made [independence] happen."[10] He would appropriately become known as the *Voice of Independence.*

In light of his influence in the spiritually charged cause of American independence, we can assume that much of what Adams accomplished was inspired by the Spirit and that he was a direct instrument in the hands of God. His personal religion—he was a devout Christian—makes such a claim easy to accept. Adams' regular scripture study, church attendance, and regular observance of the Sabbath (including

---

* According to one anecdotal account of events surrounding the signing of the Declaration of Independence, a mysterious man's voice was heard by several of the delegates above all the vitriolic debate of the Convention. The voice declared loudly, "God has given America to be free!" Unable to identify the source of the voice from within Independence Hall, several took it as a heavenly sign to forget themselves and finish the work of the Convention. Some believe that the voice heard was but a legendary interpretation of one of those famous and spiritually moving speeches by John Adams. Refer to Robert Hieronimus, *Founding Fathers, Secret Societies* (Rochester: Destiny Books, 1989).

a reluctance to travel on Sunday),[11] are evidence of his spiritual character. He said of Christianity that it is "the brightest of the glory and the express portrait of the character of the eternal, self-existent, independent, benevolent, all powerful, and all merciful creator, preserver, and father of the universe." Adams' personal religion was made complete by his dear companion, Abigail. He remembered the testimony she bore to him on the day they met: "Men and woman are here to serve God and humanity. We are made in the image of God, and must fulfill our promise or we are a blasphemy to God. An hour wasted is an hour's sin." Declared Adams, "She makes me so happy...her Christian beliefs make her ever a joy to know."[12]

Adams' deep faith sometimes caused him to seek for truth outside the traditional religious frameworks of his own denominational/religious upbringing. When in Philadelphia, he was known for attending as many different churches and church services as possible, presumably to seek out further gospel light. He was often disappointed at what he found. For example, he expressed sadness at the churches' over-emphasis in their art of the agony of his Savior on the cross.[13] Furthermore, the popular doctrine that it is by faith *alone* that man is saved, *regardless* of his deeds in this life, was, according to Adams, "detestable" and "hurtful." He believed that such doctrine would "discourage the practice of virtue." (It seems Adams preferred the teachings in the book of James: "But be ye doers of the word, and not hearers only, deceiving your own selves" [1:22]; "For as the body without the spirit is dead, so faith without works is dead also" [2:26].) He further expressed disdain for the notion that mankind is inherently punished for Adams' transgressions.[14]

Another doctrinal problem for Adams was the popular theological proposition that if one does not accept Christ in mortality, even if *never* given the opportunity to hear the name Jesus Christ or to hold a Bible in his or her hand, then such is consigned to hell for eternity. In a letter to Jefferson, Adams explained that nine-tenths of the world had not heard of Christ and would, according to that doctrine, thus suffer forever. Adams rhetorically asked why God would permit "innumerable millions to make them miserable forever." He explained that the only answer to that question given him by the clergy was "For his Own Glory," which for Adams was an unacceptable and sickening explanation. "Is he vain?," asked Adams, "Tickled with Adulation? Exulting and triumphing in his Power and Sweetness of his Vengeance? Pardon me, my Maker, for these Aweful Questions. My Answer to them is always ready: I believe no such Things."[15]

Adams' faith also led him to believe in an unpopular idea (even today) that God would punish His children to bring about their repentance and righteousness. During the Revolution, Adams asserted the following:

> It may be the will of heaven that America shall suffer calamities still more wasting and distresses yet more dreadful. If this is to be the case, it will have this good effect, at least: it will inspire us with many virtues which we have not, and correct many errors, follies and vices, which threaten to disturb, dishonor and destroy us....The furnace of affliction produces refinements in states, as well as individuals.[16]

Often frustrated with the many differing and contradicting biblical interpretations espoused by the many opposing theologies presented in his day, Adams ultimately decided to shun denominational nuances and return to the basics. He wrote to Jefferson: "The Ten Commandments and The Sermon on the Mount contain my Religion."[17]

Whether Adams' theological conclusions were correct or not, we see in him, a man in deep pursuit of God's teachings. God could utilize such a man. For, his constant spiritual quest allowed God to teach him the truth about the Revolution—that heaven had wrought it to restore liberty under the covenant. Indeed, Adams knew something of the divine purpose underlying the American cause. He declared,

"It is the will of heaven that the two countries [America and Great Britain] should be sundered forever."[18] Adding to his testimony that God was in the Revolution, Adams declared his belief that it was God that placed him at the forefront of the American cause. "By a train of Circumstances, which I could neither foresee nor prevent," declared Adams in October 1775, "I have been called by Providence to take a larger share in active Life, during the Course of these struggles, than is agreeable either to my Health, my Fortune or my Inclination."[19]

So strongly did he feel about his calling having come from God that, as president of the United States, he prayed for a similar mantle to fall upon his successors. Etched into the fireplace mantle of the State Dining Room in the White House is his prayer, which reads: "I pray to heaven to bestow the best of blessings on this house [referring to the White House] and all that hereafter inhabit it. May none but the honest and wise men ever rule under this roof."[20]

Furthermore, he seemed to understand what his and his successors' role in achieving an independent and secure America, under God, was ultimately all about: religious freedom. Years before the Revolution, Adams seemed to sense such purposes behind his country when he declared the following in an article on political philosophy: "Let the pulpit resound with the doctrine and sentiments of religious liberty... Let us see delineated before us the map of man. Let us hear the dignity of his nature, and the noble rank he holds among the works of God, and that God Almighty has promulgated from heaven, liberty, peace and good-will to man!"[21]

Whether or not Adams was implying or prophesying at this early date that America should or would be the guardian of religious freedom, he seemed sure about it in his twilight years. In 1815, Adams expressed to a friend in a private letter that religious freedom contributed "as much as any other cause" to the fight for independence. He even recognized this sentiment as having "aroused the attention...of the common people."[22] This was, of course, a very visionary, and thus risky, proposition (and perhaps explains why he only expressed it in a private letter); for, as discussed in previous chapters, religious freedom did not even make it on the long list of official reasons to go to war with Britain.[23] But Adams had been at the center of the storm, and by 1815 (some thirty years after the Revolution), when he made this statement, he had had plenty of time to ponder the Revolution's more eternal purposes. Adams was ultimately correct about what the Revolution was all about. For religious freedom was exactly what God intended to extract from the Revolution. Indeed, the Almighty knew that this would become the issue of greatest importance to His work on earth in the last days. Adams' prescient insight on the matter seems to manifest his truly inspired soul.

It might even be argued that Adams' foresight went even deeper. Perhaps he knew something of a forthcoming gospel renewal and revival; and perhaps this knowledge was reflected in his personally expressed belief that the very settlement of America represented "the opening of a grand Scene and Design of Providence, for the illumination of the ignorant...."[24] Adding to this sentiment, Adams declared, in the middle of the devastations of the Revolutionary War, that "through all the gloom I can see the rays of ravishing light and glory. I can see the end is worth more than all the means."[25] Perhaps he spoke prophetically. Despite his annoyance at what he perceived as false Christian philosophies prevailing in the world, he expressed hope that, through the Bible, America could "purify Christendom from the corruptions of Christianity."[26] Such was his hope for America under God's plan.

Whatever Adams understood by his vision of "the opening of a Grand Scene of Providence" or by the "rays of ravishing light and glory," is ultimately speculative. What is sure, however, is that Adams had a clear insight into the existence and power of the American Covenant. He believed, as implied in the previous chapters, that the American revolutionary movement was one that was to be supported by a covenant with God. In support of the many aforementioned national decrees, proclamations, circulars, etc, which invoked and re-invoked the American Covenant, Adams was always among those at the forefront to promote them. It was not uncommon for Adams to make comments like the following, which he made at the commencement of the war: "Millions will be upon their knees at once before their Great Creator, imploring His forgiveness and blessing; his smiles on American Councils and Arms."[27]

In an even more direct commentary concerning the covenant, Adams had this to say about the success of the Revolution: "I have seen all my life such selfishness and littleness even in New England. I sometimes tremble to think that, although we are engaged in the best cause that ever employed the human heart, yet the prospect of success is doubtful not for want of power or wisdom but of virtue." Adams further believed, as discussed above, that any defeat upon the Americans might be God's way to cleanse the nation of its "vicious and luxurious and effeminate appetites, passions and habits." He ultimately believed, as he declared to a friend, that the American colonists would only be victorious "if we fear God and repent our sins."[28]

Adams' wife and most trusted advisor, Abigail, served to support and augment her husband's belief in the covenant. Even during the earliest days of conflict, Abigail wrote to her husband:

> I feel no anxiety at the large armament designed against us. The remarkable interpositions of heaven in our favor cannot be too gratefully acknowledged. He who fed the Israelites in the wilderness, who clothes the lilies of the field and who feeds the young ravens when they cry, will not forsake a people engaged in so righteous a cause, *if we remember His loving kindness.*[29]

Adams' feelings toward the Declaration of Independence, which he had been so instrumental in developing, also reflect his belief that that document was—like the Revolution itself—deeply attached to God and His purposes. So powerful was this connection for Adams that he even suggested, almost immediately after the Declaration had been passed in Congress, that Independence Day "will be celebrated by succeeding generations as the great anniversary festival." He then instructed those succeeding generations that "[i]t ought to be commemorated as the Day of Deliverance by solemn acts of devotion to God Almighty."[30]* Adams' suggestion that Independence Day should be celebrated in reverence to God convinces us further that he understood that America and her blessings of liberty were given by a national covenant and required national observance.

His love and passion for the independence of mankind was also reflected in his deep hatred of slavery, which he called "an evil of colossal magnitude."[31] Though he would not see the eradication of this evil in his lifetime, he would help set his nation on the right path towards the acceptance and application of greater liberties—liberties which would one day reach the most oppressed people in America. For, without the complete eradication of slavery, the American Covenant would never be able to fill the measure of its creation. Adams would have agreed with his colleague and fellow signer of the Declaration, John Jay, who boldly declared in December 1776 that "we have the highest Reason to believe that the Almighty will not suffer Slavery and the gospel to go Hand in Hand. It cannot, it will not be."[32]

Upon analyzing Adams, there is little question as to his inspired role in founding America and establishing the

---

* In this same statement, Adams suggested that these solemn acts of devotion to God should include "Pomp and Parade, with Shows, Games, Sports, Guns, Bells, Bonfires and Illuminations from one End of the Continent to the other from this Time forward forever more." See Joseph Ellis, *First Family* (New York: Alfred A. Knopf, 2010), 53. As we celebrate the Fourth of July today in the fashion Adams so presciently foresaw, let us heed his counsel to direct these celebratory activities to God Almighty.

covenant. He did this most powerfully through creating and carrying out the Declaration of Independence for the purposes of God. We have seen evidence of his inspired calling in our analysis above. We have outlined his religious nature, his deep desire to seek and find God, his recognition that the cause of America was the cause of God, and his clear understanding that America's national covenant with the Almighty would bring both victory and the promise of greater blessings to come. And finally, we have witnessed his ability to take all of the above and masterfully apply it to the fight for independence, thus becoming one of the most important revolutionaries in American history. Why would this man, who was as closely involved in the making of the Declaration as any other, say and do the things he did unless he understood that this document represented a calling, a mission, even a covenant from God?

Though Adams would go on to serve as ambassador to France and Britain, as well as the first vice president and the second president of the United States, his role as the *Voice of Independence* would continue to represent his most lasting contribution to America and her national covenant with the Almighty. For it was Adams, more than all the others, who influenced the decision to declare independence.[33] Adams once stated that "I must study politics and war that my sons may have liberty to study mathematics and philosophy."[34] He could have just as easily said that he had studied politics and war so that later Christian generations might have the liberty to grow the church. The idea, after all, is the same. Adams and his colleagues had indeed laid the groundwork of liberty upon which Christ's Gospel might flourish.

Thomas Jefferson: The Pen of Independence

One of Adams' most important colleagues in the cause of America, and in the creation of the Declaration of Independence, was Thomas Jefferson. Early in his career, before entering politics, the highly educated Jefferson spent his time in Virginia as a planter, lawyer, husband, and father. As a member of the Virginia House of Burgesses, still in his early thirties, Jefferson was dispatched to represent his state at the Continental Congress. There, he was befriended by John Adams. It was Adams' influential voice that proposed that the young Jefferson, known for his eloquence in writing, be tasked with composing the Declaration. This proposal was backed by a congressional mandate that Adams and Benjamin Franklin

form a committee to help Jefferson in drafting the document.[35] If Adams was the "Voice" of independence, then Jefferson was the "Pen."

With such an important role in this American cause under God, we might assume that, like Adams, Jefferson also shared a connection with God as he worked under divine influence. Though this certainly was the case, Jefferson was much more private when it came to his personal religion. It is a fact that Jefferson called himself "a real Christian...a

Writing the Declaration of Independence, by Jean Leon Gerome. (Franklin, Adams, Jefferson)
Courtesy of The Library of Congress.

disciple of the doctrines of Jesus;"[36] and that he testified that "[t]here is only one God, and He is perfect, and to love God with all thy heart and thy neighbor as yourself is the sum of religion."[37] However, Jefferson also made it clear that his personal religion should not be speculated upon, for "it is known to my God and myself, alone."[38]

Many secularists point to Jefferson's criticism of religion as proof that he was no believer. However, serious study of the matter reveals that Jefferson's apparent criticisms of religion were ultimately a reflection of his belief that man had distorted primitive Christianity. Indeed, his criticisms were a reflection of his search for the original gospel light, not of a disdain for Christianity. Like Adams, he had serious misgivings about the direction of religious thought in America. Jefferson stated: "But a short time elapsed after the death of the great reformer of the Jewish religion, before his principles were departed from by those who professed to be his special servants, and perverted into an engine for enslaving mankind, and aggrandizing their oppressors in church and state." Jefferson specifically pointed out the Council of Nicaea as having been especially damaging. The council members' attempt to define God was, according to Jefferson, a "mere Abracadabra of the mountebanks calling themselves the priests of Jesus."[39]

His disdain did not end with early orthodox religious interpretations, but was also directed at what he perceived to be falsehoods invented and spread by subsequent Christian-based religious movements. Jefferson hated the popular religious idea that man is predestined for salvation or hell, regardless of his actions or beliefs. "Like Adams, Jefferson was most bothered by this philosophy because it undermined morality. Any religion that eliminated good behavior as the path to salvation merited no respect, and any God who picked the favored few without considering the lives they led was an imposter, in Jefferson's view." The man who invented such a doctrine, according to Jefferson, "was indeed an atheist... [who] worshiped a false God."[40]

Jefferson, one of the greatest scientific minds in his day, even weighed in on a religious debate raging today: evolution verses intelligent design. Balancing both the spiritual and scientific, Jefferson landed squarely on the side of intelligent design, giving credit for creation to "an eternal pre-existence of a creator, rather than in that of a self-existent Universe."[41]

With so much of what he perceived as religious falsehood pervading his world, however, Jefferson did not know exactly where to draw the line between fact and fiction. This confusion, understandably, caused him to question certain miracles wrought, as reported in the New Testament. He would ask himself, *Had the churches invented those too?* But in the end, his "clear love of Jesus,"[42] along with his deep desire to discover the doctrines of Christ, combine as powerful evidence that Jefferson was an inspired man of faith.

Jefferson's faith produced great hope—hope that God would bring further light and knowledge to the world. Stated Jefferson:

> The religion-builders have so distorted and deformed the doctrines of Jesus, so muffled them in mysticisms, fancies and falsehoods, have caricatured them into forms so monstrous and inconceivable as to shock reasonable thinkers.... Happy in the prospect of *a restoration of primitive Christianity*, I must leave to younger athletes to encounter and lop off the false branches which have been engrafted into it by mythologists of the middle and modern ages.[43]

Jefferson voiced his desire for a renewal of the gospel when making the following observation: "Had the doctrines of Jesus been preached always as pure as they came from his lips, the whole civilized world would now have been Christian."[44]

Jefferson's vision of the church's renewal was so sure in his own mind that, on another occasion, he confirmed it once again, stating: "The genuine and simple religion of Jesus will one day be restored; such as it was preached and practiced by Himself. Very soon after His death it became muffled up in mysteries, and has been ever since kept in concealment from the vulgar eye."[45] Jefferson further explained:

I hold the precepts of Jesus, as delivered by himself, to be the most pure, benevolent, and sublime which have ever been preached to man. I adhere to the principles of the first age; and consider all subsequent innovations as corruptions of this religion, having no foundation in what came from him...*if the freedom of religion, guaranteed to us by law in theory, can ever rise in practice* under the overbearing inquisition of public opinion, *truth will prevail* over fanaticism, and the genuine doctrines of Jesus, so long perverted by his pseudo-priests, *will again be restored to their original purity.* This reformation will advance with the other improvements of the human mind, but too late for me to witness.[46]

Amazing are the allusions to the American Covenant found within these words. For Jefferson clearly recognizes that Christ's Gospel would "again be restored to [its] original purity" once the then relatively new law of "freedom of religion" (i.e. the Constitution) advanced from "theory" and "r[o]se in practice." Per the stipulations of the covenant, Jefferson felt that a gospel enlargement was contingent on the success of America's divinely inspired governmental foundations.

It seems Jefferson knew that his role in establishing the laws of America would set the stage for the gospel renewal, which he sought. Not only did he clearly state that American law would usher in such religious outgrowth, but he also promoted the divine principles behind this inspired law like few others ever did. Indeed, he promoted the very political foundations that the Lord required for the enlargement of Christianity, namely civil and religious liberty. So powerful were his inclinations toward such moral liberty, that he openly rebuked himself as a slaveholder and declared, in his famous *Notes on the State of Virginia*, that slavery is "the most unremitting despotism on the one part, and degrading submissions on the other."[47] In reference to the slaves, Jefferson concluded, "Nothing is more certainly written in the book of fate than that these people are to be free." As early as

1769, Jefferson even supported a Virginia Bill to emancipate slavery.[48]

His belief in full liberty is further reflected in his authorship of the Virginia Statute for Religious Freedom. It was this law that paved the way for a righteous division between church and state. This division inspiringly barred the government from oppressing or otherwise interfering with man's right to worship God. One of the greatest lines Jefferson wrote into the statute was, "Truth is great and will prevail if left to herself."[49] This Statute, written in the midst of the Revolutionary War, shows how Jefferson, like Adams, was inspired and visionary in his belief that America's goal should be the protection and preservation of religious freedom. As pointed out in previous chapters, this was not seen as a major issue in revolutionary America.[50] In fact, America was not yet ripe for such truth to take hold, as evidenced by the fact that Jefferson's statute was initially shelved by the state legislature and not revisited until well after the war, when the country began catching up to Jefferson's vision. Only then would another inspired founder, James Madison, resurrect it and see it passed.[51] Jefferson's forward-looking and inspired vision of America surely emphasizes his spiritually connected nature. When his statute was finally implemented, it not only affected Virginia law, but also influenced the Constitution of the United States.

Even at the end of his life, Jefferson possessed the inspired and correct understanding about what America was ultimately all about. Weeks before his death, Jefferson had been asked to draft a message to be read at the Fourth of July festivities for the celebration at the nation's capital. Jefferson wrote of the importance to use the Fourth of July celebration to "forever refresh our recollection of these rights, and an undiminished devotion to them." One scholar asked rhetorically, "What rights was he referring to? The pursuit of happiness? No taxation without representation? In these weeks before his death, those were not the rights Jefferson was thinking of most." What he had on his mind was religious freedom![52] Again, the Declaration never specifically addresses religious freedom, as religious freedom was not initially given by the colonials as a primary reason for revolution. However, this is what it was ultimately designed, by God, to provide. This is what the inspired and forward-looking Jefferson saw as the take-home message of the Fourth of July: "the free right to the unbounded exercise of reason and freedom of opinion."[53]

So important was liberty to Jefferson that he would go to his grave believing that his contributions to such liberty summed up his most important work. Of his countless accomplishments and titles achieved in mortality, he ordered that only three be mentioned on his tombstone: his authorship of the Declaration of Independence, his authorship of the Virginia's Statute of Religious Freedom, and his founding of the University of Virginia. As explained above, the first two on the list were directly connected to the development of liberty. The third, his founding of a university, is also connected to liberty. As Jefferson stated: "If a nation expects to be ignorant and free...it expects what never was and never will be."[54] It is no coincidence that Jefferson's self-decided greatest accomplishments were in line with God's preparatory work to usher in an enlargement of His Gospel.

Beyond possessing a life-long, deep understanding of the importance of liberty in America, Jefferson seemed to also comprehend that the gifts of this liberty were connected to God and covenant. When entering the Jefferson Memorial in Washington D.C., one gets this sense upon reading his words engraved upon the memorial's panels: "Almighty God hath created the mind free...All attempts to influence it by temporal punishments or burthens...are a departure from the plan of the Holy Author of our religion...all men shall be free to profess and by argument to maintain, their opinions in matters of religion."[55] Engraved upon an adjacent panel are these similarly relevant words from Jefferson: "God who gave us life gave us liberty. Can the liberties of a nation be secure when we have removed a conviction that these liberties are the gift of God?"[56]

Also engraved within the memorial are Jefferson's words from the Declaration of Independence, complete with his reference to God as the Creator who endowed us with the inalienable rights of liberty. We would do well to further consider the deep roots connecting the Declaration, not only to the blessings of *liberty*, but also to those other American Covenant blessings of *protection* and *prosperity*. As explained above, the Declaration recognizes all three covenant blessings as being "supported" and "protected" by "Divine Providence." In light of the fact that Jefferson was the principal author of the Declaration, his role as American Covenant-maker becomes all the more convincing.

That Jefferson believed in the covenant is evidenced by more than the mere implications he made, as cited above, that since these blessings come from God we are obliged to Him for them. To be sure, he laid out America's covenant relationship with God in even clearer terms. In his first inaugural address, Jefferson reminded his fellow-Americans that we should be "acknowledging and adoring an overruling Providence, which by all its dispensations proves that it delights in the happiness of man here and his greater happiness in the hereafter."[57] He would again invoke the covenant when later telling the nation that America's peace and prosperity should be credited to the "smiles of Providence."[58] His belief that America was under covenant is further supported by his warning that if America does not work towards national worthiness, to include efforts toward repenting of its sin of slavery, then God would punish them. "For God is just," declared Jefferson, while commenting on the wickedness of slavery, "and his justice cannot sleep forever."[59]

Jefferson drew the connection between his nation and God's covenant even closer by alluding to the idea that the ancient national covenants with Israel, to include *prosperity*

311

under God, were connected to those covenants of America. During his second inaugural address, he declared, "I shall need, too, the favor of that Being in whose hands we are, who led our forefathers, as Israel of old, from their native land and planted them in a country flowing with all the necessaries and comforts of life."[60] Promoting a similar message, Jefferson proposed that the official seal of the United States include a depiction of the "Children of Israel in the wilderness led by a cloud by day and a pillar by night."[61]

Finally, in one of Jefferson's most powerful quotes, which is memorialized in a unique position within the Jefferson Memorial—it spreads elegantly around the interior of the dome—Jefferson again refers to the national covenant. He does so by offering the covenant imagery of "the altar of God" as it relates to the sacrifice required for America's true eternal purposes. His immortalized words are as follows: "I have sworn upon the altar of God, eternal hostility against every form of tyranny over the mind of man."[62] With this covenant imagery, Jefferson sums up the American Covenant; for he explains in powerful simplicity that there are evil forces that would thwart our freedom of religion (forces that find their root in the Evil One who has spilled his war in heaven upon us all today, as the Book of Revelation implies). But Jefferson also suggests here that God has offered us a covenant that we make upon His altar to ensure, through our actions and His blessings, that full liberty—even that most precious prerequisite of salvation—be secured on this earth. Jefferson was certainly an inspired man whose knowledge, foresight, and wisdom ran deep.

Upon analyzing Jefferson's life, we have observed his inspired nature by pointing out his spiritual roots firmly attached to Christ, his insights into the religious thoughts of the day, and his testimony that a gospel enlargement was forthcoming by way of American liberty. Most importantly, we have seen how, through this inspiration, Jefferson invoked America's national covenant with God by seeking out those most important national covenant blessings of *liberty, protection,* and *prosperity.* There is no doubt that Jefferson, like Adams, was a true American Covenant-maker who laid the foundation for personal liberty and gospel growth.

Also like Adams, Jefferson's career was long and distinguished. In addition to being a famous architect, scientist, and inventor, Jefferson served as a state legislature, governor of Virginia, ambassador to France, first secretary of state of the United States, second vice president of the United States, and third president of the United States. However—and again, just like Adams—none of these high positions overshadow his singular role as the author of the Declaration of Independence. He would fight tooth and nail for the rest of his life in defense of those godly principles of liberty, as laid out in the Declaration. His role as the *Pen of Independence* contributed as much or more to the American Covenant and to the purposes of God than any of his other vast accomplishments.

The Confirming Miracle

Through reviewing the inspired lives and accomplishments of the two most prominent actors in the birth of Independence, we are now prepared to delve into the details surrounding the miraculous event which confirms as divine the work these two men were jointly responsible for—the Declaration of Independence (and by extension, the American Covenant). For we have established not only that Adams and Jefferson were the force behind the Declaration, but also that they were perhaps more connected to God and covenant than any of their colleagues (Washington excepted). With this understanding, we can see the significance in God's decision to make them the principal players in the miraculous sign from Heaven.

The scene of this historic miracle opens at the sunset of Adams' and Jefferson's lives. These two old and fading revolutionaries had been through much together. As the best of

313

friends, they had served together during the Revolution (first in Congress, then on the committee to draft the Declaration of Independence, and then as ambassadors to France). However, upon returning home to an independent United States, they became the bitterest of enemies, disagreeing over the direction the new country should take. Their personal conflict culminated when they confronted each other in one of the most vitriolic, hate-filled and mud-slinging presidential elections in U.S. history. As political enemies, their close personal connection had been severed. Indeed, they would refuse to even speak to each other for years.

Both men, and their families, were heartbroken at this prospect, for they had been so very close. For example, when Jefferson had joined Adams as a fellow diplomat in France, the Adams family had invited Jefferson to live with them in their home. Adams, at one point, even conceded to Jefferson that Adams' son—John Quincy—"was as much your son as mine."[63] When the Adamses departed France to work in London, Jefferson confessed that he was "in the dumps" and that "my afternoons hang heavily on me." Then, after Adams fulfilled his diplomatic mission and returned home (leaving Jefferson in Europe), Jefferson declared that, without Adams on his side of the Atlantic, "I now feel widowed."[64] Such bonds, when broken years later, had produced deep sorrow indeed.

But now, as old and weary men, their differences did not seem so important. After what seemed like a lifetime of silence between them, the two fading revolutionaries began to rekindle their old friendship through a series of letters— Adams writing from his home and farm outside of Boston and Jefferson from his Virginia estate, Monticello. These two men had outlived almost every other Founding Father of the revolutionary era. Now, all they had was each other, and so they reminisced about the glory days, about politics, and about those sacred things most important to them.

One of these most sacred subjects they discussed was prompted by the death of Adams' best friend and truest confidante—his wife, Abigail. Adams' love and devotion to his wife, and their bond together (which endured so much, with Adams being absent from her for a total of ten years during the revolutionary period) has become legendary. Abigail was everything to Adams, as documented by the many letters he wrote to her in his absence. She was his truest love, his truest political ally, and his truest friend.[65] Adams once referred to their fifty-four years of marriage as a "love feast."[66] And she clearly felt the same way towards him. "When he is wounded, I bleed," she once told a friend.[67] Understandably, the old man Adams was inconsolable upon the death of his life-long partner. After leaving her deathbed in tears, he exclaimed, "I wish I could lie down beside her and die too."[68]

Jefferson, seeing an opportunity to express his feelings about eternal things, reminded Adams that hope was not lost and that God certainly had an eternal plan which would one day banish the pain forever. Jefferson, too, had lost his dear wife, Martha. And as an expression of hope in dealing with that death, Jefferson had the following epitaph engraved upon his wife's tombstone: "In the melancholy shades below, The flames of friends and lovers cease to glow, Yet mine shall sacred last; mine undecayed. Burn on through death and animate my shade."[69]

In an effort to transfer such hope to Adams and to reassure his old friend—and perhaps himself—that a glorious reunion with their wives was not far away, he wrote the following in one of those legendary communications:

> The public papers, my dear friend, announce the fatal event of which your letter of October 20 had given me ominous foreboding. Tried myself, in the school of affliction, by the loss of every form of connection which can rive the human heart, I know well, and feel what you have lost, what you have suffered, are suffering, and have yet to

endure....altho' mingling sincerely my tears with
yours, will I say a word more, where words are
vain, but that it is of some comfort to us both that
the term is not very distant at which we are to
deposit, in the same cerement, our sorrow and
suffering bodies, and to ascend in essence to an
ecstatic meeting with the friends we have loved
and lost and whom we shall still love and never
lose again. God bless you and support you under
your heavy affliction.[70]

"I have always loved Thomas Jefferson,"[71] the elderly Adams
would say of his old friend. No doubt this letter confirmed his
sentiments.

Adams returned his own feelings and thoughts of that
glorious eternity, which was rapidly approaching. His mind
still upon his recently deceased Abigail, Adams wrote the
following to Jefferson:

I know not how to prove, physically, that we shall
know each other in a future state; nor does
revelation as I can find give any positive assurance
of such felicity. My reasons for believing it, as I do
most undoubtedly, are that I cannot conceive such
a being as the human, merely to live and die on
this earth. If I did not believe in a future state, I
should believe in no God...And, if there be a
future state, why should the Almighty dissolve
forever the tender ties which unite us so
delightfully in this world...[72]

All this talk of life after death
certainly had these two old revolutionaries
thinking about the eternities. Quite possibly,
they were touching on truth. One year
before his death, Jefferson, in a seemingly
reflective moment, wrote about how
mortality is a proving ground for greater
things to come and how we, as mortals, can
and should prepare. Advising the son of a

Abigail Adams

316

friend, the weary Jefferson counseled: "Adore God. Reverence and cherish your parents. Love your neighbor as yourself, and your country more than yourself. Be just. Be true. Murmur not at the ways of Providence. So shall the life into which you have entered, be the portal to one of the eternal and ineffable bliss."[73]

Jefferson's own portal to the eternal bliss was opening up, even as he wrote these words.

Then the miracle: John Adams and Thomas Jefferson, virtually the last of the prominent surviving signers of the Declaration of Independence, died. Why was this so miraculous? Because their deaths —which occurred for reasons unrelated to each other, and which took effect at their respective homes some five states away from each other—happened on the same day, within hours of each other. What makes this event particularly miraculous was the date—July 4, 1826: the fiftieth anniversary of the Declaration of Independence.

John Adams

Two revolutionaries dying on the same day might be a curiosity. But two revolutionaries who were so connected with God and His national covenant, and two revolutionaries who were the most prominent in achieving independence—even the "Voice" and "Pen" of the Declaration of Independence—dying on the same day, of unrelated causes, is more than coincidence. And that this all happened on the fiftieth anniversary of the Declaration of

Thomas Jefferson

Independence only seals the entire event as a singular act of God, to seal and symbolize their joint sacrifice in His work.*

It was a sign to the world that the American Covenant, embodied in so many ways by the Declaration itself, was true, living, and divinely administered. This was a covenant sign, as real as Noah's rainbow. And though the Adams-Jefferson miracle has sadly become all but lost to current generations of Americans, it was fully comprehended by those early Americans who experienced it.

---

* There is additional reason to believe that this Adams-Jefferson experience was an intentional sign delivered by Heaven. It has to do with events surrounding their reunification. The person responsible for bringing them back together in their old age was the prominent revolutionary, and fellow signer of Declaration, Benjamin Rush. Rush was a dear friend to both Adams and Jefferson. He approached Adams in 1809 (when Adams and Jefferson were still not speaking to each other) and told him about a dream he had recently had. In the dream, Rush was blessed to see a history book of the future. The history book he read told of the tumultuous relationship between Adams and Jefferson. But it also told of a great

Benjamin Rush

reconciliation between the two patriots. It told of a series of letters they wrote to each other at the end of their lives. In the letters, they discussed (in the words of the dream's history book), "many precious aphorisms [truths], the result of observation, experience, and profound reflection." According to the book, "It is to be hoped the world will be favored with the sight of [the letters]." The book then stated: "These gentlemen sunk into the grave nearly at the same time, full of years and rich in the gratitude and praises of their country." Rush's dream prompted Adams to extend the olive branch to Jefferson through the first of many letters. But nobody could have predicted that what would follow would directly fulfill Rush's dream. It was inspired. It was prophetic. See David Barton, *Benjamin Rush, Signer of the Declaration of Independence* (Aledo: Wallbuilders, 1999), 198-200; Joseph Ellis, *Founding Brothers* (New York: Alfred Knopf, 201), 220.

Adams' son, John Quincy, wrote in his diary that the miraculous nature of Adams' and Jefferson's twin deaths was a "visible and palpable mark ...of Divine favor, for which I would humble myself in grateful and silent adoration before the Ruler of the Universe."[74] Not insignificantly, John Quincy Adams was the president of the United States when the miracle occurred, thus making his sentiments even more profound, as he was (by position) a living head of the American Covenant. Another leading statesman of the day was Daniel Webster, who, while eulogizing Adams weeks after his death, echoed John Quincy, declaring the Adams-Jefferson miracle to be "proof" from the Almighty "that our country, and its benefactors, are objects of His care."[75]

There is more to the miracle than the miracle itself. There is, perhaps, a deeper lesson to be learned by analyzing the death scene. The scene at the Adams home in Quincy, Massachusetts, was recalled by several eyewitnesses. Days before Adams' death, he was asked what message he might have to be read as a toast for Quincy's upcoming Fourth of July celebration. "I will give you," replied Adams, "Independence forever."[76] Then, on the day of his death, even in the final moments leading up to his death, a semi-conscious Adams shifted in his sleep, and in a voice strong enough for several witnesses present to understand, said, "Thomas Jefferson survives."[77] Adams then passed away; the time was approximately six-twenty in the evening. A few hours earlier, at approximately one o'clock in the afternoon, Thomas Jefferson had passed away at his Monticello estate.[78] There is only speculation as to why Adams would utter these words in reference to Jefferson as his dying refrain. However, it seems reasonable to suggest that perhaps Adams, in his final moment, saw the spirit of his old friend Jefferson, who—having only just passed away himself—had come to accompany Adams to the place God had prepared.

Daniel Webster might have approved of such an interpretation, for he declared that "on our fiftieth anniversary… while their own names were on all tongues, [Jefferson and Adams] took their flight together to the world of spirits."[79] John Quincy added that while "the mortal vestments" of his father and Jefferson were "sinking into the clod of the valley, their emancipated spirits were ascending to the bosom of their God!"[80]

In the moments leading up to this joyous spiritual reunion, a strange yet fitting weather pattern occurred. Hours before Adams' final departure, a violent thunderstorm struck —"The Artilleries of Heaven," as some later called it.[81] Then, almost at the moment of Adams' death, as witnesses recalled, there was a final crashing thunder, which seemed to stop the storm. The rain ceased and the sun, which had just begun to set, broke through. John Marston, who was an eyewitness of the event, explained that the sunlight began "bursting forth…with uncommon splendor at the moment of his exit…with a sky as beautiful and grand beyond description."[82]

At that splendid moment, we might imagine Adams and Jefferson taking "their flight together to the world of spirits." And as we imagine them entering the spiritual realm, we might consider again how these two kindred spirits had made it clear in mortality that they had sought gospel truth throughout their lives. We might further ponder the fact that the most important gospel truth they hoped for (as indicated in their final

Peacefield, home in which John Adams passed away

correspondences with each other) was an eternal reunion with their respective wives, who had gone before them in death.

This leads us to the powerful and vital point: Adams, Jefferson, and all their colleagues did what they did in life so that a foundation might exist whereby they, along with all mankind, might participate in the type of heavenly experience we hope Adams and Jefferson received in the world beyond. In the pages above, we have detailed how it was under God and covenant that these two Founding Fathers laid this foundation. The increase of religious freedom in America that they initiated with their Declaration of Independence, and later with the Constitution, had prepared the way so that God might accomplish His work. Under the American Covenant, they had established the foundation that would allow everyone the liberty necessary to access eternal life though the grace of God.

The Founding Fathers' mission was complete, and they were at last given leave to return to the Maker of their nation. The deaths of these last remaining Founding Fathers seem to represent a sort of symbolic passing of the torch. The next generation and their divine mission regarding the covenant and the enlargement of Christianity would now commence.

Before their deaths, Jefferson had written to Adams that it was his hope that they might meet again in heaven "with our ancient colleagues and receive with them the seal of approbation, 'Well done, good and faithful servants.'"[83] Certainly, as they stood together with their loved ones, both men knew that their much anticipated day had arrived. Regardless of how much they knew in mortality, upon their deaths, all was surely revealed to them. They would gain tremendous perspective on the eternal purpose of their Declaration of Independence and how it worked as a reflection of the American Covenant in furthering God's work. We, too, should internalize this perspective and live accordingly. After all, it was for this very purpose that God sent us the Adams-Jefferson miracle in the first place.

Conclusion

The Declaration truly reflects the national covenant, not only through the covenant principles found within the text of the document, but also through the endless invocations to Heaven, and the miraculous responses from Heaven, surrounding this document.

As we now conclude our discussion of the American Revolution, let us not forget to add to this equation the many other declarations, invocations, actions, inspirations, tokens, signs, and miracles we have detailed in the last several chapters. These, along with the spirit of the Declaration, provide proof of the existence of the American Covenant during the period of the Revolutionary War. Throughout these last chapters dealing with this war, we have certainly witnessed God's will for America and have seen His workings pertaining to this land and its covenant.

And in powerful fulfillment of Old Testament prophecies, we have seen in these last several chapters how the thoughts and actions of that chosen generation of Founders played directly into the covenant. With their miraculous understanding of the covenant, they were able to embrace it and use it in bringing to pass God's will. We have witnessed all this through their spiritual conversions and preparatory experiences relating to the American cause, through their testimonials of God's hand in the conflict, through their Declaration of Independence, through their inspired foresight into God's truest purposes for America, through their remarkable declarations connecting their land and covenant to ancient Israel, through their endless stream of both informal and official invocations to God, through their humble recognition that only through their national obedience would they be blessed with victory, and through their equally humble recognition of the many miracles performed by God—both on and off the battlefields of war—which they knew had secured their ultimate success.

With the exception of ancient Israel, this American story stands unique within the annals of world history. Few other people in history have been surrounded by such powerful prophecy and fulfillment of prophecy. But perhaps this should be expected. For, in many ways, this American story is but an extension of these earlier Old Testament accounts and covenants.[84] Such is the eternal nature and grand purpose behind the American Covenant.

Through the lens of history we can see clearly the importance of God's work in fulfilling this covenant, particularly through the American Revolution. As explained earlier, the Revolution brought three indispensable fruits in support of God's work and glory. First, it rid America of a dangerous monarchical regime which could have obstructed God's work in growing His Gospel; second, it showered America with a spirit of liberty, which would eventually inspire the creation of a new government espousing and protecting this liberty, and thus providing the political foundations for personal agency and increased gospel light and knowledge; and third, it made America an ensign to the world, inspiring other nations to join America in turning away tyranny and oppression in exchange for principles of liberty. As the salvation of God's children was in the balance, it is no wonder God backed this inspired era of history with the power of a national covenant.

This covenant is the lifeblood of America and a powerful support to the gospel. Our American problem is that we have largely forgotten the story of this covenant. However, as we grow to more fully recognize the divine within our history, we will feel compelled to more fully adhere to the covenant—as did our forefathers—by living righteously, serving Him, and thus securing the blessings of *liberty*, *protection*, and *prosperity*. Only then will such blessings be perpetuated in support of God's kingdom.

In a final historical account related to the Revolution, we see the powerful presence of God and covenant once more. With the knowledge we have gained through examining the Revolution's history from a gospel perspective, this account will now carry with it a much deeper significance. Shortly after the war, Charles Thompson, secretary of the Continental Congress, proposed an idea to Washington. He wanted the two of them to collaborate on writing their memoirs of the entire war experience. After all, Thompson had been present during all the congressional actions, while Washington could account for the battles. Between the two of them, they could tell the entire story. However, upon outlining the project, they realized how the results simply did not add up. For no combination of America's congressional actions and/or military maneuverings could explain the American victory. By all accounts, the British should have won. Because of this, they decided against the memoir. The renowned historian of the American Revolution, Thomas Fleming, explains the decision: "It would be too disillusioning if the American people discovered how often the Glorious Cause came close to disaster." Washington and Thompson ultimately decided that they did not need to bother recounting the entire experience. For, as Fleming concluded, they "jointly agreed that the real secret of America's final victory in the eight-year struggle could be summed up in two words: Divine Providence."[85]

ENDNOTES

[1] Sam Adams, as quoted in H.L Richardson, "A Most Uncivil War," *California Political Review*, January/February 2006, Vol. 17, No.1, 25.

2 Sam Adams, as quoted in Marshall and Manuel, 391.

3 This idea and prayer is inspired by Michael Novak, *On Two Wings*, 18.

4 John Quincy Adams, as quoted in Newt Gingrich, *Rediscovering God in America* (Nashville: Integrity House, 2006), 30.

5 Gingrich, *Rediscovering God in America*, 27.

6 "Fast Day Proclamation of the Continental Congress, December 11, 1776," Worthington C. Ford, Gaillard Hunt, et al., eds., *The Journals of the Continental Congress, 1774-1789* (Washington, D.C.: Government Printing Office, 1904-37), vol. 6, 1022; also quoted in Novak, *On Two Wings*, 18.

7 The details and background of Adams' speeches and influence over Congress can be found in McCullough, *John Adams*, 126-129; details on Adams' influence can also be read in Chapter 7 of this book, under the subheading, *The Conversion of the Founders.*

8 David McCullough, *1776* (New York: Simon and Schuster, 2005), 43.

9 McCullough, *John Adams*, 88-89.

10 McCullough, *John Adams*, 129.

11 McCullough, *John Adams*, 20, 41.

12 John C. McCollister, *God and the Oval Office* (Nashville: W Publishing Group, 2005), 11-12.

13 McCullough, *John Adams*, 84.

14 Waldman, 35.

15 Adams, as quoted in Waldman, 184.

16 Adams, as quoted in Marshall and Manuel, 391.

17 Adams, as quoted in Michael Winder, *Presidents and Prophets* (American Fork: Covenant Communications, 2007), 17.

18 Adams, as quoted in McCullough, *John Adams*, 130.

19 James Grant, *John Adams, Party of One* (New York: Farrar, Straus and Giroux, 2005), 157.

20 Gingrich, 114.

21 John Adams, as quoted in Michael Novak, *On Two Wings: Humble Faith and Common Sense at the American Founding* (San Francisco, Encounter Books, 2002), 78.

22 Waldman, 40.

23 Refer to Chapter 9 of this book, under the subheading *Deeper Connections to the Covenant.*

24 Adams, as quoted in Waldman, 37; full quote in Skousen, *The Five Thousand Year Leap*, 304.

25 John Adams, as quoted in Marshall and Manuel, 392.

26 John Adams, as quoted in Waldman, 35.

27 John Adams, as quoted in Waldman, 108.

28 Adams, as quoted in Waldman, *Founding Faith*, 70.

29 Abigail Adams, as quoted in Marshall and Manuel, 382 (emphasis added).

30 McCullough, *John Adams*, 130.

31 McCullough, *John Adams*, 134.

32 John Jay, as quoted in Mac and Tait, *Under God*, 287

33 We refer again McCullough's statement: "It was John Adams more than anyone who had made [independence] happen," as quoted in McCullough, *John Adams*, 129. Also, refer to the accounts of Adams' great power in influencing the decision to declare independence, as detailed in Chapter 7 of this book, under the subheading, *The Conversion of the Founders*.

34 Adams, as quoted in Mac and Tait, 303.

35 McCullough, *John Adams*, 119-120.

36 Waldman, 77.

37 McCollister, 20.

38 Jefferson, as quoted in Winder, 21.

39 Waldman, 73-74.

40 Waldman, 74.

41 Waldman, 83-84.

42 Waldman, 80.

43 *Letter to Timothy Pickering, Esq..* Monticello. February 27, 1821. Retrieved January 18, 2010. See Norman Cousins, ed. *"In God We Trust": The Religious Beliefs and Ideas of the American Founding Fathers* (New York: Harper & Brothers, 1958), 157, 162

44 Jefferson, as quoted in Waldman, 80.

45 Winder, 22.

46 Jefferson (from letter written in November 1820), as quoted in Cousins, *In God We Trust*, 156. Emphasis added.

47 McCullough, *John Adams*, 331.

48 Jefferson, as quoted in Gingrich, *Rediscovering God in America*, 46.

49 Waldman, 124-125.

50 Refer to Chapter 9 of this book, under the subheading *Deeper Connections to the Covenant*.

51 Waldman, 124-125.

52Waldman, 91.

53 Jefferson, as quoted in Waldman, 91.

54 Jefferson (letter to Colonel Charles Yancey, January 1816), as quoted in Paul L. Ford, ed. *The Writings of Thomas Jefferson,* Vol. 10, 4.

55 Jefferson Memorial quotes, as quoted in Gingrich, *Rediscovering God in America,* 45-46.

56 Gingrich, 46.

57 Waldman, 81.

58 Waldman, 82.

59 McCullough, *John Adams,* 331.

60 Jefferson, as quoted in Waldman, 82-83.

61 Waldman, 107.

62 Jefferson, as quoted in William J. Bennett, *America The Last Best Hope,* Vol. 2 (Nashville: Nelson Current, 2007), 219.

63 Joseph Ellis, *First Family* (New York: Alfred A. Knopf, 2010), 115.

64 Joseph Ellis, *First Family,* 121, 136.

65 The vast correspondence between John Adams and Abigail can be found in William J. Bennett, *The Spirit of America* (New York: Simon and Schuster, 1997), 105-107, 109-11, 112- 115, 134-138.

66 McCollister, *God in the Oval Office,* 12.

67 Abigail Adams, as quoted in Bennett, *Spirit of America,* 137.

68 Joseph Ellis, *First Family,* 244.

69 Callister, 430, n. 330; Jefferson borrowed these words from Homer's *Iliad.*

70 Letter from Jefferson to Adams, as quoted in Waldman, 186-187.

71 Adams, as quoted in Bennett, *America, the Last Best Hope,* Vol. 1, 219.

72 Adams, as quoted in Michael Winder, *Presidents and Prophets* (American Fork: Covenant Communications, 2007), 17.

73 Waldman, 186.

74 John Quincy Adams, as quoted in Richard Brookhiser, *What Would the Founders Do?* (New York: Basic Books, 2006), 6.

75 Daniel Webster, as quoted in McCullough, *John Adams,* 648.

76 McCullough, *John Adams,* 645.

77 McCullough, *John Adams,* 646.

78 McCullough, *John Adams,* 646.

[79] Webster, as quoted in Mac and Tait, 305.

[80] John Quincy Adams, as quoted in Mac and Tait, 306.

[81] McCullough, *John Adams*, 646.

[82] McCullough, *John Adams*, 647.

[83] Thomas Jefferson in a letter to John Adams, as quoted in Meacham, 232.

[84] See Part I of this book.

[85] Thomas Fleming, "Unlikely Victory," *What If? The World's Foremost Military Historians Imagine What Might Have Been* (New York, Penguin Putnam Inc, 1999), 186.

CHAPTER 11

THE CONSTITUTION: A HEAVENLY BANNER

It is impossible for the pious man not
to recognize in [the Constitution] a
finger of that Almighty Hand which
was so frequently extended to us in
the critical stages of the evolution.

—James Madison

Though the American War for Independence had ended, the greater war with evil continued to rage. It is true that with American independence, the adversary had lost some ground in his efforts to obstruct America's spiritual destiny. However, his evil designs to thwart freedom—and thus to snuff out the opportunity for eternal salvation—continued to march forward. As such, the Lord would deliver a most inspired document—one which would direct and guide the newly independent nation in its fight against the adversary. It would be a document that would uphold and support God's gift of liberty unto eternal salvation. These next two chapters will show that the Constitution of the United States was and is this document, and that it was and is inspired by the Almighty to serve as yet another building block of the American Covenant.

Why God Sent the Constitution

Satan's fight against mankind has largely been over liberty and salvation. For the dragon has always wanted the destruction of man (see Revelation 12) and he knows that keeping the commandments and nourishing a testimony of Christ lead to man's salvation. Those righteous choices, made through personal liberty, are what enable eternal life. In order to destroy man's opportunity at eternal life, then, the dragon must first destroy that precious liberty.

We cannot emphasize enough that Satan's target is man's liberty—his freedom to choose—and that the reason God sent the United States Constitution was to preserve this freedom. Indeed, the Constitution is a primary defense mechanism against Satan's plan of attack.

It should be noted that the Constitution, in its effort to counter-strike at the adversary, is fulfilling the exact goal and purpose of the American Covenant. It is, in fact, part of the American Covenant. The Constitution even sets out to achieve this heavenly goal the same way the American Covenant does. As we will see in the next chapter, the Constitution fulfills ancient prophecy by providing America with the same national covenant blessings promised by father Jacob to modern America through his son Joseph, and through his grandson Ephraim. Indeed, the Constitution does nothing less than provide the divine and foreordained precursor blessings to support man's quest for salvation—it specifically provides *liberty, protection,* and *prosperity.*

Of course, under the national covenant structure, these blessings leading to eternal life are activated upon worthiness. Some will be surprised to see, in the pages and chapters to follow, that this covenant relationship is acknowledged and configured in the Constitution itself.

It should also be noted that the Lord certainly had more than just America in mind when He influenced the creation of the U.S. Constitution. For not only would the Constitution facilitate the renewal and enlargement of Christ's Gospel in America (which would eventually reach the world), but the Constitution would be the template for the nations of the world, that they might have for themselves a government that could receive and protect this renewed gospel once it arrived. A seven-volume study produced by the University of Virginia details how this constitutional influence occurred. Its introduction muses at how we "pay so little attention to the historical relationship...of the U.S. Constitution and other constitutions in Asia, Africa, Europe, and Latin America."[1] This University of Virginia study predates the creation of the constitutions in the newly liberated nation-states of the Former Soviet Union and in Iraq. These budding countries also follow the pattern of the U.S. Constitution.

Many of these foreign constitutions have practically copied the U.S. Constitution's structure. This U.S. influence, more often than not, was a result of positive action by the U.S., such as diplomacy, economic incentive, and (when necessary) war. Today, these nations enjoy three branches of government, checks and balances, and balance of powers. They also enjoy unprecedented human rights protections such as religious freedom. Remember, the U.S. Constitution came first. The other governments of the world, most of which were bogged down by tyranny and oppression, watched and then followed in turn. And these foreign governments have found success in this constitutional endeavor.

Proof of this success is found in the fact that where constitutional principles abound throughout the world, so do the principles of the Christian faith. Indeed, the mechanism for eternal salvation has been secured and extended throughout the world by the United States and its covenant.

Having presented a broad-brush explanation for why God sent us the Constitution, we will now take a closer look at the world as it existed just prior to the creation of the Constitution, so that we might witness the eternal struggle over freedom and observe the power the Constitution would bring to secure it. Indeed, we will witness how the Constitution shattered the dark and apostate gloom that covered and threatened the earth.

It is true that after winning its independence, America seemed an unlikely victim of the adversary's assault on liberty. After all, the very blessed and inspired nation had just witnessed the heaven-sent chain of events which, through its national covenant with God, had brought victory along with other blessings. So blessed was America during these post-war days (yet prior to the Constitution) that Thomas Jefferson commented, even during this transitional time, on the greatness of America's "equality, liberty, laws, people & manners." He declared, "My God, how little my countrymen know what precious blessings they are in possession of, and which no other people on earth enjoy."[2] So then, could this great nation not have secured and preserved man's rights and liberties without a constitution? Each state, after all, possessed its own constitutional laws full of protections and rights. Was a national constitution really necessary? History has taught us that it was.

Consider, for example, the case of Michael Servetus, who in 1553 was burned at the stake in Geneva, Switzerland, for no other reason than his alternative and outspoken view of Christianity. The reason this execution stands out among the millions of equally unjust acts against free thought, is that it was ordered by none other than the great religious reformer,

Michael Servetus burning at the stake, 1553.

John Calvin.[3] Calvin, like other inspired reformers responsible for freeing people from the chains of intolerance, was now, ironically, acting as intolerant toward others as his Catholic oppressors had acted toward him and his people. Even Martin Luther insisted that his religious views be enforced by his government, stating in 1536 that "secular authority is held to reprimand blasphemy, false doctrines and heresy and to inflict corporal pain on those who support such."[4] The spine-chilling lesson is all too clear: If even the most inspired among us can be influenced to assist the adversary's plan to thwart religious freedom through violently enforcing religious intolerance, anybody can—even the inspired American Founders or their offspring. As such, a broad-reaching, national, God-given protection against such adversarial attacks against liberty would certainly be required before a fullness of religious truth could be enlarged, proliferated and made fully available. The U.S. Constitution provided precisely this type of protection.

To understand how important and timely the U.S. Constitution was in the grand plan of the Almighty, consider the adversary's assault on freedom in the world leading up to the creation of America. In 1401, for example, the king of England issued a national edict, which called for the immediate arrest and punishment of anyone who preached religious thought contrary to the king's religion. If anyone was found guilty of a second offense of the same, the decree called for immediate death by hanging.[5] Then, of course, there were the similarly violent and seemingly endless atrocities surrounding the Catholic Inquisition, which was responsible for the torture and death of tens of thousands of non-believers from Spain to Asia and from Central to South America.[6] So successful were Satan's efforts to deny full liberty in the Old World, that even the "faithful" members of the state church had to risk life and limb just to pick up a Bible and read it. Such was forbidden by the clergy, who desired to control "God's law."[7] Furthermore, a large portion of seventeenth-century Europe was scarred by the horrific Thirty Years War, a conflict which claimed hundreds of thousands of lives mostly over religious intolerance. Finally, by 1685, the king of France, in the same evil spirit, demanded that all those unwilling to accept French Catholicism were to be immediately exiled or put to death.[8] Sadly, these examples represent only a portion of the religious intolerance that permeated the world during this era.

It is no surprise, then, that the adversary would take this evil influence, derived from his long-lasting war against liberty, to the shores of America. The adversary certainly knew this was the land set apart and foreordained for God's work in the last days. Though America had gained footing against this evil plan through achieving independence from the Old World —which was often tainted by darkness—the adversary had still managed to maintain his presence in the Promised Land through introducing two practices that threatened to destroy the divine purposes of America. First was slavery, which codified all that the adversary stood for and which permitted a spirit in the land and among the people that could not long coexist with the righteous administration of the gospel. This evil and oppressive practice made it difficult for the Lord to bless America under its covenant (as the blessings were contingent upon national worthiness). The second evil practice that persisted in America, even after independence had been gained, was direct (and legal) religious intolerance and persecution. This grew out of the colonial American tradition of allowing state and local governments to favor and support the more popular religious sects, thus encouraging the persecution of the less popular, minority sects. Unless and until *all* religions were free to worship, then *all* religions would be threatened by oppression. Christ's Gospel would be threatened.

The Constitution of the United States would work to fight both of these evil influences in support of God's Gospel purposes for America. In the next several chapters we will discuss how the creation, development, and proper application of the Constitution, over many years, drove out these evil inhibitors of man's liberty, making America a worthy safe-haven for personal progression unto eternal salvation. The sin of slavery would eventually be eradicated through the invocation of the covenant (all Americans should study the words and actions of Abraham Lincoln, which clearly manifest his deep understanding and application of the covenant). While the scope of this study does not include the complexities of slavery and how God fashioned and molded the Constitution in order to redeem the failing covenant, the chapters that follow *will* focus on how the Constitution first provided the basic tools necessary to stomp out oppression and intolerance, as particularly related to religious freedom, in supporting religious freedom and thus paving the way for further gospel light and knowledge.

The story of this fight over the destiny of liberty upon American soil begins with the many religious "dissidents" from Europe who eventually made their way to the land of America, so that they might find a place to worship freely. Ironically, like Calvin, Luther, and others, even these did not always abandon the very spirit of intolerance they themselves had sought refuge from. As many American victims of religious intolerance soon learned, the European influence of intolerance and persecution hovered over the New World as well. Indeed, many of the colonists were forced to pay taxes for the state-managed religions, were forced to attend church services, and could legally be whipped for not knowing the religious doctrines. Many people in New England were even executed for their nontraditional beliefs.[9]

335

Even after America had miraculously secured its independence, no national protection from religious intolerance had been put in place. To be sure, the British evacuation of America did little to immediately usher in religious freedom. Though the war had inspired a refreshing sense of liberty in America—which would eventually inspire the nation to adopt a policy of greater religious freedom—the war was not fought directly for religious freedom, and therefore did not immediately produce such blessings. As detailed earlier, the colonists entered the War for Independence on principles of political rights and property rights—religious rights were mostly sidelined. In fact, among the many grievances against the Crown listed in the Declaration of Independence, issues related to religious freedom or religious intolerance were nowhere to be found. The colonists mostly enjoyed religious freedom under Britain. Many, including Washington, even chose to be members of the Church of England. This is not to say British rule was benign. For it did make things hard on minority religious thought (just not enough to justify the majority to go to war). Also, its monarchical system could too easily serve as a tool of oppression for the adversary against gospel enlargement and proliferation. Britain had to go. But, again, their evacuation of the Promised Land did not mean America was fully free from threatening influences that needed to be dealt with.

It should be understood that—like the British—the colonists themselves practiced religious intolerance against these minority religions. The colonists continued this persecution well after the British had packed up and left. Simply put, religious intolerance was not much of an issue for the colonists at the time. It is not why they fought. However, the Lord utilized the Revolution to send a new spirit of liberty that would, apart from freeing the nation from Britain, also open the national heart to enhanced religious freedom. Indeed, though the colonists did not generally articulate religious freedom as a justification for war, the Lord, who sees the end from the beginning, knew the crowning fruit of the conflict would be religious freedom. And so, He influenced events toward that inspired end. However, this inspired end would take additional time and revelation, even after independence had been gained.

Without religious freedom immediately at the forefront of the revolutionary mind, we can see how, even after independence had been won, many states still controlled aspects of religion—something which sadly led to further persecution of minority religions. For example, even during the height of the Revolution, some states maintained control over minority religious thought by requiring that certain preachers attain licenses in order to preach. Since minority sects, such as Baptists, were unable or unwilling to attain state licenses to preach, it was not unusual for them to be subjected to public whippings and floggings, even at the hands of local, American law enforcement. Between 1765 and 1778, for example, over forty-five Baptist ministers were jailed in Virginia alone for nothing more than preaching.[10]

Such injustices were not limited to the South. During this same period (even during and after the Revolution) religious minorities in New England suffered equally under laws and customs of religious oppression. Baptist preachers in Connecticut, for example, were not authorized to perform marriages, were faced with continuous harassment, and were barred from preaching in certain locations. Its members were also forced to pay taxes in support of the state sponsored religion.[11] In Massachusetts, members of the New Light Baptist Church were likewise forced to pay taxes to benefit the state church, which was the Congregational Church (the successor of the Puritan Church). This was done upon punishment of imprisonment or seizure of property. And these laws were enforced. The New Light Baptists even had to deal with a state law which required infant baptism—something this Baptist sect believed to be a false doctrine.[12] The endurance of this unrighteous power over religious minorities wielded by the

New England states is further witnessed by the fact that both Connecticut and Massachusetts persisted in maintaining a state-sponsored religion, even after the U.S. Constitution had been ratified.[13] In fact, the complaints and allegations made by these persecuted religious minorities continued into the eighteen hundreds.[14]

Sadly, these were not isolated incidents, but they reflected an element of American culture that persisted throughout the land and affected other religious minorities such as Quakers, Mennonites, Jews, and Catholics. Several members of the Continental Congress even wanted to prohibit Catholics from fighting in the Revolutionary War. Additionally, many colonies disallowed Catholics from holding public office. Only three colonies permitted Catholics to vote, all but one of the colonies banned Catholic schools, and at least one of the colonies would have priests arrested just for crossing its borders.[15]

Even as late as 1834, an angry anti-Catholic mob attacked and destroyed the Ursuline Convent near Boston. Harvard College Library, Widener Library

Such was the tragic state of affairs in America, even at that inspired time of the Revolution. During this crucial period in history, it became an American problem that required an American solution. Though independence had been gained, America had yet to fill the measure of its creation. As one scholar of American religious rights recently noted, "The birth of religious freedom [in America] was not inevitable."[16] A miraculous intervention would no doubt be required to root out this influence of the adversary.

This intervention was on its way. The stage had already been set. For, the victory over the British had at last rid the nation of a dangerous monarchical regime and had also given birth to a new sense of liberty in America. Both of these fruits of the Revolution would have a profound effect on furthering God's work. But in light of the above, while God's work in the war for American independence was a necessary step, it was nonetheless a preliminary one. Certain wicked elements, even the aforementioned oppressors of religious freedom, still roamed the countryside and held positions of public trust. But now with the war won, and the land free from European interference, the Lord had a clean slate with which He could finally influence a new formula of government, one that would effectively deal with these remaining wicked elements. As such, within a decade after independence was achieved, the Lord would initiate the next phase of His plan by providing the crowning element of the American Revolution. He would provide the Constitution of the United States—a critical building-block of the covenant.

In an effort to recognize God's hand in the Constitution, thus seeing it for what it is—an essential element of the American Covenant and a tool unto salvation—these next two chapters are dedicated to analyzing its creation and content.

James Madison and the Commencement of a Plan

Though we now know the Constitution was created to protect religious freedom—and thus God's church on the earth

—its creation (even right after America gained its independence) was by no means a foregone conclusion. Its blessings were not inevitably bound for the Promised Land. It would take God's influence to make this happen.

James Madison, by Thomas Sully
Courtesy of the Library of Congress.

At about the time the flogging and unjust imprisonment of preachers was occurring in America (not to mention the even greater religious violations abroad), the newly independent America was dealing with a slew of other problematic issues, which dominated the public's attention. Since independence had been officially recognized in 1783, the individual states had seen little reason to remain as "united" with each other as they had been during the war (and even during the war they struggled with unity). As such, the national treasury fell to almost nothing, making it impossible for the nation to pay its sizable debt to its European creditors; and having to default on the loans meant poor credit for the new nation—something it could not afford to have.

As the bickering states continued to act more like individual countries than a united nation, other negative externalities emerged. For example, the colonies could not agree on a unified tariff schedule, nor was there any person or group (like a *national* customs service) assigned to enforce such a tariff (even if it had existed). Foreign countries, therefore, brought their goods in for free, while the Americans were forced to pay tariffs on their own exports.

Furthermore, with the standing army having been all but abolished since the war, there was little national security beyond the uncoordinated, understaffed, and underpaid state militias. This was an alarming notion, considering that France and Spain were gaining territory in the South while Great Britain still remained in the North.[17] Highlighting the embarrassing fact that the U.S. had no national security was an incident in 1783, when an armed mob of ex-Continental soldiers came knocking on Congress' door, looking for the money the government owed them. The delegates, without any defense, were forced to flee for their lives. Some of the states even felt so threatened and insecure that they were entering into negotiations with foreign governments, and in some cases even favored a reunification policy with the British.[18]

The problem turned violent when several unscrupulous factions within the individual states assumed control over the local governments. (Again, there was no national system with the power to temper such corruption.) These events resulted in policies that burdened farmers and the working class. Unable to pay their mortgages and taxes, many rose up in mob violence and burned public buildings. The local governments stood by and watched, having inadequate resources to control the mobs. (Again, there was no national system with the power to help control the mobs.) One of the most famous of these uprisings is known today as Shay's Rebellion. The governments' inability to make good policy and control mob-rule emphasized the need for some drastic political changes. Though America was still a land of hope, and though it still boasted of the freedom and liberty inherited by its independence, things were heading down the wrong path.

Fortunately, one young and highly inspired statesman from Virginia watched in horror as this social, economic, and political powder-keg waited to explode. He understood better than anyone that the individual states were, by nature, incapable of dealing with these *national* social ills, and that the current structure of the national government (composed of the Continental Congress and its Articles of Confederation) was far too weak to be effective. After all, the Articles of Confederation required a super-majority vote in Congress for binding policy, which was rarely achieved. Even if consensus was achieved, the delegates' respective state governments would often disregard the national congressional acts and do as they pleased. For, there was no national entity to enforce the national policy. (This is similar to how the United Nations functions today.)[19]

But this young Virginian decided he would no longer stand idly by, watching his government fail to provide the protections and services necessary for the pursuit of happiness. Heaven had moved him. After all, how could the Lord set up his base of operations in such a messy and insecure environment? His name was James Madison, and he was beginning to devise a plan. Through divine guidance, he began formulating the blueprints for the United States Constitution.

Before examining his plan and how it was carried out, we must first understand something about Madison's background; for in it we find the underpinnings of God's design for him and America. Born in 1751, Madison—who was generally described throughout his life as shy, small, and frail —was raised in the typical fashion of the American upper-class, graduating with high marks from the College of New Jersey (now called Princeton). Before his 30th birthday, he was elected as a delegate to the Continental Congress, from whence he made his above-mentioned observations at very close range. He would go on to serve as both a state and a national congressman, secretary of state, and eventually he would serve as president of the United States. However, it was these initial and inspired stirrings within him, occurring shortly after the war had ended, that produced the greatest fruit of his public life—the Constitution.

History books state that Madison's passion for writing the Constitution's blueprints stemmed from the observations he made, as noted above: no national security, no national treasury, no unified tariff schedule, general disunity among the states, and so on. This is certainly a correct view. Through a gospel lens, we also see how such issues needed resolution in order to provide a secure political foundation prior to any comprehensive and meaningful gospel enlargement. However, the more specific and relevant goal of the Constitution, which God appeared to be working toward above all else pursuant to His plans for America, was to secure total religious freedom.

It is here where we see God's hand over the advent of the Constitution. We have already emphasized how the Revolution had (as God designed) begun changing hearts and opening up American minds to understand the importance of making religious liberty part of the new government. This was, of course, an essential reason that America eventually adopted policies supporting religious freedom. However, the movement toward full religious liberty still grew slowly, not having been a generally articulated justification, among the colonists, for independence or war. Furthermore, as seen above, the most pressing issues of the day were unrelated to religious freedom. Again, victims of religious persecution were still merely the minority sects, and could easily be overlooked. However, James Madison would not overlook them. In fact, James Madison was

James Madison

perhaps the greatest champion in American history of religious rights, particularly for the religious underdog. He would keep the spirit and importance of religious freedom alive, reminding his fellow Americans what they had learned and felt as a result of their recent Revolution.

The miracle of it all is that the one person most responsible for creating the Constitution was also the most passionate about religious freedom. This did not necessarily need to be the case, for there were many other prominent promoters of a national government who might have easily overlooked the religious issue, and marginalized it in the

Constitution. Again, we should note the scholarly consensus that "[t]he birth of religious freedom [in America] was not inevitable."[20] Madison's placement in history, therefore, was no coincidence. The Lord had prepared him early on and raised him up to be "the father" of the Constitution. He would carry the true spirit of the Revolution with him and not neglect the indispensable blessing of religious liberty. God had led the nation toward the path of religious freedom through the war He had presided over. And He made sure His servant Madison was front and center on the scene, in the aftermath of this war, to ensure the nation did not get distracted from this heaven-lit path toward full religious freedom.

Madison's sensitivity to religious liberty developed at an early age. By the time he was twenty, he had witnessed and became appalled at the aforementioned discrimination and persecution against the Baptists in his state of Virginia, even though he himself was a devout member of the Church of England. Madison's sensitivity would soon be anchored by intellectual and spiritual conviction upon studying under the president of the College of New Jersey, Reverend John Witherspoon (the same divinely-inspired Witherspoon mentioned earlier, who prophesied of the hand of God in the Revolutionary War).

Madison soaked up Witherspoon's ideas on the importance of religious freedom: "The magistrate ought to defend the rights of conscience," Witherspoon wrote, "and tolerate all their religious sentiments that are not injurious to their neighbor." After graduating under the tutelage of Witherspoon, Madison felt inclined to continue with him an extra year to study Hebrew and ponder the meaning of the Scriptures.[21] At this point in his life, he seriously considered entering the holy ministry, but in the end, and for inspired reasons, he chose politics.[22]

Upon returning to Virginia, Madison (at the age of twenty-five) participated in the state convention to write Virginia's Declaration of Rights, which, as he had desired, set in motion the eventual termination of the religious persecution over minority religions. While the original language called for religious "toleration," it was Madison who changed the language to include a broader protection of man's most precious and inherent right. He declared "that all men are equally entitled to the free exercise of religion, according to the dictates of conscience, unpunished, and unrestrained by the magistrate."[23] Fittingly, this work began in 1776, while America was in the middle of its war for independence.[24] And though it was not immediately applied as Madison desired, it would set a foundation that would one day influence future documents and policies of America by changing the standard of religious freedom from mere toleration to full-fledged liberty.[25]

Years later, in 1784, Madison would again work to protect freedom of religion by fighting against a proposal in Virginia that would allow the state government to raise taxes in benefit of those whom the state determined were "Christian" clergy. Madison feared this would allow the government to wield too much power over private religion, thus setting a precedent which the government could one day expand upon. He feared government could eventually begin dictating to the churches, defining religions, and (while perhaps helping some) hurting minority religions that the local and state governments deemed unworthy. In his plea against the measure, Madison inspiringly argued: "The Religion then of every man must be left to the conviction and conscience of every man; and it is the right of every man to exercise it as these may dictate." He further argued that "[i]f this [religious] freedom be abused, it is an offense against God, not against men. To God, therefore, not to man, must an account be rendered." Madison won the argument, and the bill was rejected.[26]

Madison's observation that religious intolerance is an "offense against God" is perhaps more accurate than he could have understood at the time. Indeed, in order for God's plan to unfold, and in order for the enterprise and prospect of a gospel enlargement to develop, God needed disciples willing to open their hearts and minds to the mysteries and commandments of His kingdom. As Madison had pointed out years earlier, "Religious bondage shackles and debilitates the mind, and unfits it for every noble enterprise, every expanded prospect."[27] Madison seemed to understand something of what God required, and he worked tirelessly to achieve it.

With this legislative victory under his belt, Madison felt encouraged to expand religious freedom even further. And so, in 1785—almost immediately after defeating the clergy tax—he pulled out an old 1779 bill-proposal originally put forth by his friend, Thomas Jefferson. It was the Virginia Statute for Religious Freedom. Whereas the recently defeated clergy tax proposal halted only one particular aspect of religious intolerance, this statute utilized the same basic principles, but made them permanent and thus applicable to any future threat to religious freedom. The statute declared, "Almighty God hath created the mind free, [and] all attempts to influence it by temporal punishments...are a departure from the plan of the holy author of our religion."[28] The statute goes on to say that "no man shall be...enforced, restrained, molested, or burthened in his body or goods, nor shall otherwise suffer on account of his religious opinions or belief, but that all men shall be free to profess...their opinions on matters of Religion, and that the same shall in no wise diminish, enlarge or affect their civil capacities."[29]

When Jefferson had originally proposed the statute in the middle of the Revolutionary War, his countrymen had not yet felt enough of the revolutionary "spirit of liberty" to adopt the policy, and so it was temporarily shelved. However, a few years after the war, once the nation was sufficiently prepared, Madison brought it back (Jefferson was serving the country overseas at the time) and ushered it into law.[30] A new standard for religious freedom had been set.

Madison was a born champion of religious freedom. It was an issue passionately near and dear to him. His unique contributions to the cause of religious freedom become even more pronounced and inspiring when considering the following commentary put forth by Judge John Noonan:

> James Madison was, so far as I know, the first statesman who, himself a believer, had enough empathy with the victims of persecution to loathe the idea of enforced religious conformity and to work to produce law that would forever end it. It is easy to be tolerant if you don't believe. To believe and to champion freedom—that is Madison's accomplishment.[31]

Such was the man Madison. And his passion for religious freedom would not be confined to the borders of Virginia. He knew and felt that more must be done to protect religious freedom on the national level as well. Indeed, he understood, perhaps more than anybody, that it was religious freedom that, as he declared, "promised a lustre to our country."[32] He also understood, perhaps more than anybody, that *national* legislation would ultimately be the key to stomping out abuses over such rights.

And so, without downplaying his equally impassioned desire to deal with the many other more immediate national ills plaguing early America, Madison took his solutions for religious intolerance to the national level. On one occasion, just before heading to the national congress to do just that, Madison assured one leader of a minority religious sect that he would achieve "the most satisfactory provisions for all essential rights, particularly the rights of Conscience in the fullest latitude."[33]

But bringing religious freedom to the national level would not be easy, especially in light of the fact that no solid national venue for such national policies even existed at the time. Yet undeterred by his daunting responsibility, Madison set out to create the national venue (even the national government) he would need in order to create protections for religious freedom, nationwide. At last, by 1787, he had convinced the bickering states to send delegates of the

Continental Congress one more time to a convention at Philadelphia. There, he would see if, by some miracle, their many national social problems could at last find resolution. These problems included disunity on taxes and tariffs, national debts, foreign threats, and (most importantly for the purposes of God, even though they were underrated at the time) injustices related to *religious freedom.* Mr. Madison had a plan, and he greatly desired to share it with his fellow delegates.

Madison's plan carried the name of the state from whence its author hailed: The Virginia Plan. It proposed the abolishment of the weak Articles of Confederation and the adoption of a new national (or federal) government. Within it was the skeleton of our familiar political structure, rife with the oft-referenced ideas like "checks and balances," "separation of powers," "natural rights," and "three branches of government." In it was the recipe for a new national government to fulfill that which is the only real responsibility of any good government: to identify social ills (like those listed above) plaguing the people and fix them. Yet, the final product included so much more than just these catch phrases. As we will see in the following chapter, Madison's proposal set the stage for one of the most inspired systems for protecting liberties that the world has ever known. So powerful were these protections, that Madison originally did not feel the need to even add the First Amendment (the religious freedom amendment) to the Constitution, though he eventually gave in and drafted it himself.[34]

When he finally did draft and propose the First Amendment, Madison was so forward-thinking that he even wanted to include more powerful constitutional language to ensure that all states would respect religious freedom.[35] He was concerned that the First Amendment would *only* apply to the federal government, leaving state governments free to continue their government-backed support for majority religions, which naturally would lead to the discrimination, even persecution, of minority religions. And so, Madison proposed that the Bill of Rights include an amendment that prohibited states from violating, specifically, "equal rights of conscience [religious freedom], or freedom of the press." According to Madison, this would have been "the most valuable amendment on the whole list."[36] Unfortunately, his more powerful language was rejected, thus causing some unnecessary pains in the future for some religious minority groups (like Catholics, Jews, Mormons, and others), who were forced to suffer under the rule of sometimes oppressive state governments.[37/38]

Clearly, Madison possessed inspired insight beyond his years, and his involvement in securing such significant freedoms have been far too underrated in the annals of history. Speaking of his work in creating American religious freedom, William Bennett commented that "perhaps it was Madison's... unwillingness to beat his own drum that has caused us to fail to appreciate his great achievement."[39] But whatever the reasons may be that we have forgotten many aspects of this inspired and underrated founder, we will attempt now to resurrect his memory, complete his story, and learn of his plan for religious freedom; for all this is integral to the American Covenant.

It should be noted that, notwithstanding his most prominent role in applying such great ideas to a national government in America, Madison was not working in a vacuum. In fact, many political philosophers, including some in Europe, had theorized over similar models, and much smaller governments in much earlier days had even attempted to apply some of them. Even in Colonial America, John Adams had implemented many of these political concepts in his writing of the Massachusetts Constitution, which (for the most part) is still intact today. Madison himself modestly stated, after being lauded as the writer of the Constitution, that it was actually "the work of many heads and many hands."[40] And many of these heads and hands belonged to those inspired delegates who accepted Madison's invitation to Independence Hall in Philadelphia and came to the *Glorious Convention*.

The Glorious Convention

As the delegates shuffled into Independence Hall during that hot Philadelphia summer of 1787, Madison was tense and uneasy. After all, he had *intentionally* failed to mention to them the real cause for calling the convention: to present his Virginia Plan—even to present a new national constitution. With the exception of his closest circle of friends, Madison was virtually the only one that had any idea that this meeting could become what would famously go down in history as the *Constitutional Convention*. Madison knew that if the delegates had understood his true intention, they may not have participated. For they had come to Philadelphia under the impression (and under strict instructions from their respective states) that they *may possibly* amend certain aspects of the Articles of Confederation. They had no idea that they would be asked to form an entirely new national system.

Understandably, when Madison's plan was proposed, the delegates, fearful of a strong central authority, immediately protested. Some even threatened to leave the Convention, and others actually made good on the threat. Had it not been for the fact that America's two most inspired and respected citizens, George Washington and Benjamin Franklin, sat in council with them, and vigorously promoted the plan, the entire Convention might have ended before it began. With such foresight, Madison had worked tirelessly in the preceding months to secure Washington's commitment to chair the Convention.

But even among those who were willing to discuss Madison's plan, the dissension and contention became almost unbearable, as the details of his plan were hammered out (the most contested detail being how state representation in the new national congress would be configured). If the delegates had only understood how significant this work would be, perhaps they would not have allowed, as Benjamin Franklin pointed out, the interference of "all their prejudices, their passions, their errors of opinion, their local interests, and their selfish views."[41] God's church and man's salvation, after all, were at stake. Perhaps it was Franklin himself who understood better than anyone else that something bigger than anything they could imagine was behind the Convention. It was the eighty-one-year-old Franklin who, after weeks of virtual stalemate in the Convention, humbly offered the

Benjamin Franklin

last and only solution. In one of the most powerful improvised speeches of all time, Franklin declared:

> The small progress we have made after 4 or five weeks close attendance & continual reasonings with each other –our different sentiments on almost every question, several of the last producing as many noes as ays, is methinks a melancholy proof of the imperfection of the Human Understanding. We indeed seem to *feel* our own want of political wisdom, since we have been running about in search of it. We have gone back to ancient history for models of Government, and examined the different forms of those Republics which, having been formed with the seeds of their own dissolution, now no longer exist. And we have viewed Modern states all around Europe, but find none of their Constitutions suitable to our circumstances.
>
> In this situation of this Assembly, groping as it were to find political truth, and scarce able to distinguish it when presented to us, how has it happened, Sir, that we have not hitherto once thought of *humbly applying to the Father of lights to illuminate our understandings?* In the beginning of the Contest with G. Britain, when we were sensible of danger, we had daily prayer in this room for the divine protection.—

Our prayers, Sir, were heard, and they were graciously answered. All of us who were engaged in the struggle must have observed frequent instances of a Superintending providence in our favor. To that kind Providence we owe this happy opportunity in consulting in peace on the means of establishing our future national felicity. *And have we now forgotten that powerful friend? Or do we imagine we no longer need his assistance? I have lived, Sir, a long time, and the longer I live, the more convincing proofs I see of this truth—that God governs in the affairs of men.* And if a sparrow cannot fall to the ground without his notice, is it probable that an empire can rise without his aid? We have been assured, Sir, in the sacred writings, that "except the Lord build the House, they labour in vain that build it." I firmly believe this; and I also believe that without his concurring aid we shall succeed in this political building no better than the builders of Babel: We shall be divided by our little partial local interests; our projects will be confounded, and we ourselves shall become a reproach and bye word down to future ages. And what is worse, *mankind* may hereafter from this unfortunate instance, despair of establishing Governments by Human Wisdom and leave it to chance, war and conquest.

I therefore beg leave to move—that henceforth prayers imploring the assistance of Heaven, and its blessings on our deliberations, be held in this Assembly.[42]

Washington, as we have previously demonstrated, certainly understood Franklin's sentiments as well as anyone at the Convention, and therefore would happily add his own endorsement to such counsel. Standing before the Convention, during a heated debate, Washington declared: "If to please the people, we offer what we ourselves disapprove, how can we afterward defend our work? Let us raise a standard to which the wise and honest can repair; *the event is in the hand of God!*"

Historian John Fiske commented that *"from that moment* the mood in which [the delegates] worked caught something from the glorious spirit of Washington."[43] Indeed, the testimony from such spiritually powerful men seemed to change the entire environment, as a spirit of brotherhood and compromise, at last, entered Independence Hall. The Lord had intervened once again.

The key players at the Convention certainly felt the Lord's hand over them. For example, New York delegate Alexander Hamilton, the soon-to-be first secretary of the Treasury and, outside of Madison, the strongest proponent for a national government, would declare that the "sacred rights" placed within the Constitution were "written, as with a sunbeam, in the whole volume of human nature, by the hand of Divinity itself, and can never be erased or obscured by mortal powers."[44] Hamilton further stated, "I sincerely esteem it a system, which without the finger of God, never could have been suggested and agreed upon by such a diversity of interest."[45]

Another very active delegate at the Convention, Charles Pinckney, said the following of the Constitution: "When the great work was done and published, I was struck with amazement. Nothing less than the superintending Hand of Providence, that so miraculously carried us through the war... could have brought it about so complete, upon the whole."[46]

Madison, who was obviously closest to the entire Convention and its development, and whose notes are the singular source of the Convention's inter-workings, would, in the same spirit, declare the following:

> It is impossible for the pious man not to recognize in it [the Constitution] a finger of that Almighty Hand which was so frequently extended to us in the critical stages of the evolution....No people ought to feel greater obligations to celebrate the goodness of the Great Disposer of events and the Destiny of Nations than the people of the United States....And to the

same Divine Author of every good and perfect gift we are indebted for all those privileges and advantages, religious as well as civil, which are so richly enjoyed in this favored land.[47]

The congressional invoker of prayer, Ben Franklin, referenced the miracle of the final product when, just before putting his name to the document, he stated that it "astonishes me, Sir, to find this system approaching so near to perfection as it does." He further added, referring to the image of the sun carved into the back of Washington's chair, how painters find it difficult to distinguish between a rising and setting sun. "I have," he declared, "often in the course of the session...looked at that behind the President without being able to tell whether it was rising or setting. But now at length I have the happiness to know that it is a rising and not a setting sun."[48] On another occasion, Franklin further revealed his deep spiritual feelings towards the Constitution, when he declared:

I have so much faith in the general government of the world by Providence, that I can hardly conceive a transaction [referring to the creation of the Constitution] of such momentous importance to the welfare of millions now existing, and to exist in the posterity of a great nation, should be suffered to pass without being in some degree influenced, guided, and governed by that omnipotent, omnipresent, and beneficial Ruler.[49]

Another witness at the Convention, Benjamin Rush, stated his belief that "the hand of God was employed in this work, [just] as...God had divided the Red Sea to give a passage to the children of Israel" or had delivered "the ten commandments on Mount Sinai!"[50] Rush's analogy was especially poignant considering that the very Constitution he was making reference to was a part of the American Covenant, which had its origins in ancient Israel.

Even the commoners of America sensed the deeper meaning of their new Constitution. "I am convinced [the

Constitution] is the Lord's doing, and it is marvelous in our eyes," said a Connecticut farmer, as quoted in his local paper soon after the Convention.[51] Other newspapers of the day captured a similar feeling, which swept the new nation. The *Massachusetts Sentinel* projected a hope of what the Constitution should mean to the country: "May the GREAT IDEA fill the mind of every member of this honourable body that Heaven on this auspicious occasion favours America...."[52]

ENDNOTES

[1] Kenneth W. Thompson, ed, *Constitutionalism: Founding and Future*, Volume I (Lanham, University Press of America, 1989), viii. The entire seven volume study is entitled The Miller Center Bicentennial Series on Constitutionalism, and is produced by the University of Virginia's Miller Center of Public Affairs. The volumes, published by the same publisher listed above, include the titles *The U.S. Constitution and the Constitutions of Asia, The U.S. Constitution and Constitutionalism in Africa, Constitutionalism and Human Rights: America, Poland and France,* and *The U.S. Constitution and the Constitutions of Latin America.*

[2] Thomas Jefferson (1786), as quoted in John Ferling, *Adams vs. Jefferson* (New York: Oxford University Press, 2004), 33.

[3] Perez Zagorin, *How the Idea Religious Toleration Came to the West* (Princeton: Princeton University Press, 2002), 93-99, 107.

[4] Henry Kamen, *L'Eveil de la Tolerance*, Jeanine Carlander, trans. (Paris: Hachette, 1967), 41.

[5] Bobrick Benson, *Wide as the Waters: The Story of the English Bible and the Revolution It Inspired* (New York: Simon and Schuster, 2001), 67; John Foxe, *Foxe's Book of Martyrs*, ed. W. Grinton Berry (Grand Rapids, Mich.: Baker Book House, 2000), 86-87.

[6] Paul Kengor, *God and Ronald Reagan* (New York: Regan Books, 2004), 147.

[7] Harry Emerson Fosdick, ed. *Great Voices of the Reformation: An Anthology* (New York: Random House, 1952), 41, 242.

[8] Philip P. Wiener, ed., *Dictionary of the History of Ideas* (New York: Scribner's, 1973), 4:112-113.

[9] Linda Monk, *The Words We Live By* (New York: Stonesong Press, 2000), 128.

[10] Michael Novak, *On Two Wings: Humble Faith and Common Sense at the American Founding* (San Francisco: Encounter Books, 2002), 52.

[11] Steven Waldman, *Founding Faith: Politics, Providence and the Birth of Religious Freedom in America* (New York: Random House, 2008), 173.

[12] Waldman, *Founding Faith*, 52-53.

[13] Waldman, *Founding Faith,*136, 173.

[14] Waldman, *Founding Faith*, 173-4.

[15] Waldman, *Founding Faith*, 49.

[16] Waldman, *Founding Faith*, xvi.

[17] John Ferling, *Adams vs Jefferson* (New York: Oxford University Press, 2004), 43.

[18] Milton Cummings and David Wise, *Democracy Under Pressure*, 9th edition (Belmont: Wadsworth Publishing, 2003), 38.

[19] Cummings and Wise, 38.

[20] Waldman, *Founding Faith*, xvi.

[21] Novak, *On Two Wings*, 52.

[22] John C. Mcollister, *God and the Oval Office* (Nashville: W Publishing Group, 2005), 24.

[23] Waldman, 114.

[24] Novak, *On Two Wings*, 53.

[25] Waldman, 114-115.

[26] Waldman, 119-123; McCollister, 25.

[27] Madison, as quoted in Waldman, 106.

[28] Waldman, 124-125; full transcript available at *Library of Virginia*, www.lva.virginia.gov/whatwedo/k12/bor/vsrftext.htm.

[29] As quoted from Virginia Statute for Religious Freedom, available at *Library of Virginia*, www.lva.virginia.gov/whatwedo/k12/bor/vsrftext.htm.

[30] Waldman,124.

[31] John Noonan, *The Lustre of Our Country: The American Experience of Religious Freedom*, University of California, Berkeley, CA.: 1998, 4.

[32] William Bennett, *America: The Last Best Hope*, Vol I (Nashville: Thomas Nelson, 2006), 130.

[33] Novak, *On Two Wings*, 53.

[34] Waldman, 138-9.

[35] Waldman, 155.

[36] Monk, 215; Helen Veit, et al., eds., *Creating the Bill of Rights*: *The Documentary Record from the First Federal Congress* (Baltimore: Johns Hopkins University Press, 1991), 13, 188.

[37] The issue of whether or not state governments should have been obligated to adhere to the First Amendment (or to the other Bill of Rights) is a complicated one. Though a full discussion of this issue falls outside the scope of this study, we will introduce part of the debate. The intent of those Founders who rejected Madison's more all-encompassing application of the First Amendment was actually very benign. They wanted the individual states to be able to utilize the government to promote, support, or even *establish* religion. What better way, after all, to ensure that God's role in the land remained strong? However, Madison had a finer point he wanted heard. His point had to do with religious underdogs. What guarantees would *they* have if the religious majority, with the power of the state government at its side, did not like them? We have already discussed what naturally happens when the state gets behind any one or a few denominations. Religious rights for the minority get trampled upon. It is human nature.

For example, consider the plight of the New Light Baptists, the Catholics, the Jews, the Mormons, and others. After the Constitution was already in effect, many members of these minority sects were—due to their beliefs—severely persecuted (or at best went unprotected) by their state governments. This persecution often ended in their houses of worship being destroyed and burnt to the ground and in their leaders being publically flogged, imprisoned, or murdered. There is no question that these groups longed for the First Amendment to be applied in the state governments under which they lived. The First Amendment, if applied to the states, would have disallowed state officials to infringe upon the free exercise of religion. Yet, because the First Ammendment was not guaranteed under state law, this cherished constitutional right was completely denied them. This is what Madison saw as the potential threat to religious liberties. This is why he originally sought to have parts of the First Amendment applied to the states.

In the end, Madison acquiesced to his colleagues and the states were able to choose their own religious destiny without the restraints of the First Amendment. They thought it would work. Perhaps the states would maintain power to assume authority in religious exercise while respecting the religious minority. Alas, it did not work that way.

Abraham Lincoln saw the problem in his day. He recognized how mob rule within state governments oppressed the minority—both racial and religious. He sought, "under God...a new birth of freedom" (from Gettysburg Address). He pointed out that "in giving freedom to the slave, we assure freedom to the free" (as quoted in Carwardine, *Lincoln: A Life of Purpose and Power*, 217.)

One result of the Civil War was the controversial Fourteenth Amendment. The amendment promised that "all persons" regardless of what state they lived in, or what that state had to say about their rights, were United States citizens. Therefore, all persons were entitled to the blessings of the Constitution, to include the First Amendment, regardless of whether or not the states approved of granting these civil rights. Though most people at the time viewed the Fourteenth Amendment as pertaining only to African Americans, it was written for "all persons"—a hopeful prospect for the religious underdog. Perhaps help was on the way. In the years and decades following the advent of the Fourteenth Amendment, the Courts began seeing it this way. They began applying the Fourteenth Amendment to "all persons" and they began recognizing that, per the Fourteenth, all persons in every state were heirs of most all the Bill of Rights, to include the First Amendment. Though originally the Fourteenth was not applied in this way, is it not possible that God had His own purposes in this—to restore religious rights to all? If so, perhaps Madison was indeed inspired for his initial position on the matter.

Though the Fourteenth Amendment was largely ignored for decades, it laid the groundwork for what would become known as the Civil Rights Act of 1964—even that law which forced states (by federal punishment if necessary) to recognize the civil rights of *both* racial and religious underdogs. It should be noted here that if the states had not acted so recklessly with minority rights (both racial and religious), then the Fourteenth Amendment and the Civil Rights Act would not have been needed. But, as it turned out, wicked state policies forced the federal government's hand.

In some ways, this option represents the lesser of two evils. For, these legal addendums have brought unintended consequences to all believers. For example, they have permitted federal courts to weigh in on religious issues—and their decisions (while in earlier days had been appropriate) have recently been despicable. For example, they have recently made rulings that ban prayer in school or demand that religious depictions be torn from public or government buildings. This is exactly why the Founders desired that the states be free from the restrictions of the First Amendment. However, the problem here has more to do with the federal courts' (not to mention the state courts') misinterpretation of the First Amendment than the actual involvement of the federal government itself. The courts continue to misinterpret the First Amendment's use of the word "religion"—as in, the government's restriction to "establish *religion*." The Founders clearly understood that "religion" meant a particular denomination or system of belief—*that* was the thing not to be comingled with government. The courts today seem to believe that "religion" means anything up to and including God Himself. This allows them to push God out of every aspect of government. But they are wrong. The Founders—who wanted no denomination controlled by government—wanted, with all their hearts, God to be involved. God was to have *everything* to do with America, its government, and its covenant, as this book proves beyond a reasonable doubt.

[39] Bennett, *America, The Last Best Hope*, Vol.I, 130.

[40] Linda Monk, *The Words We Live By* (New York: Hyperion, 2003), 119.

[41] Benjamin Franklin, as quoted in James Madison, *Notes on the Debates in the Federal Congress*, 633, available at the Yale Avalon Project, www. Avalon.law.yale.edu/subject_menus/debcont.asp.

[42] Benjamin Franklin, as quoted in William J. Bennett, *The Spirit of America* (New York: Simon and Schuster, 1997), 384-385.

[43] John Fiske, *The Critical Period of American History*: 1783-1789 (Boston and New York: Houghton, Mifflin &Co., 1898), 231-232, emphasis added.

[44] Novak, Michael, and Jana Novak, *Washington's God* (New York: Basic Books, 2006), 3.

[45] Alexander Hamilton, as quoted in Paul L. Ford, *Essays on the Constitution of the United States*, 1892, 251-2, republished (Whitefish: Kessinger Publishing, 2007).

[46] Paul L. Ford, 251-2.

[47] James Madison, as quoted in James D. Richardson, *A Compilation of the Messages and Papers of the Presidents* (Washington D.C.: by Authority of Congress, 1899), Vol. I, March 4, 1815, 561; also available at www.americandestiny.com.

[48] Walter Isaacson, *Benjamin Franklin, An American Life* (New York: Simon and Schuster, 2003), 457-459.

[49] Ben Franklin, as quoted in Meacham, *American Gospel*, 88.

[50] Benjamin Rush, as quoted in Meacham, *American Gospel*, 91.

[51] Jon Meacham, *American Gospel: God, the Founding Fathers, and the Making of a Nation* (New York: Random House, 2006), 99-100

[52] Meacham, 94.

CHAPTER 12

THE CONSTITUTION AS COVENANT

*Our Constitution was made
only for a moral and
religious people. It is wholly
inadequate to the
government of any other....it
is religion and morality
alone, which can establish the
principles upon which
freedom can securely stand.*

—John Adams

Thus far we have demonstrated why and how the Lord inspired the creation of the Constitution. However, up until now we have only pointed out bits and pieces of what it actually says, particularly in the context of its mandate to further the Lord's work. Based on the testimonies of those who were there for its birth, the spiritual offerings of the Constitution must certainly be significant. So what does it say? What are the blessings and safeguards within the document responsible for soliciting such powerful endorsements? How does it fulfill the most profound mission of providing and protecting the liberty necessary for progression unto eternal life? These questions will be answered in the pages below, as we come to see how the Constitution is nothing less than an extension and representation of the American Covenant. In fact, the most prominent blessings of the Constitution are the same American Covenant blessings of *liberty, protection,* and *prosperity.*

The skeptic might argue that things like liberty, protection, and prosperity are the goals of any government, and therefore their existence in the Constitution is not exceptional. However, it must be understood that during the time of the Founders, these constitutional goals were not sought (for the most part) by other governments of the world. The idea was new and revolutionary.

The Constitution (original)
Displayed at the U.S. National Archives.

But more than being unique ideals, these blessings were directly connected to ancient prophecy concerning modern America. For these specific blessings, which the Founders sought after and included in their Constitution, were the *exact* blessings designated by God in the Old Testament for Joseph's posterity. This certainly makes their existence in the Constitution something exceptional. It makes the Constitution a fulfillment of prophecy. Recall that in the history of mankind, less than five-percent ever reaped the blessings of freedom—so few enjoyed the necessary foundation to receive the gospel.[1] No wonder that the ancients, to include Jacob-Israel, Moses, Jeremiah, and Isaiah (see Part I of this book), perhaps received visions of America—even that nation which would usher in unprecedented freedoms in preparation for Christ's Gospel and the advent of His Second Coming. Of such is the importance of the Constitution.

What is more remarkable still is that the Founders *intentionally* sought and received these blessings, for the covenant was, as Jeremiah prophesied, "written in their hearts."[2] Furthermore, the Bible contained everything relating to the national covenant, which is why the Founders used biblical ideas (particularly those parts related to God and country) and applied them to their constitutional government. The connection they felt to the biblical covenants of the House of Israel was so strong that they regularly invoked the national covenant through their authority as the "New Israel," which name they consistently assumed.[3]

That the Founders took seriously their connection to this biblical covenant, particularly in relation to their building the nation and its Constitution, is evidenced in the findings of a 1973 study directed by political scientist Donald Lutz. Dr. Lutz and his team set out to evaluate everything published in America during the time of nation-building (between 1760 and 1805). They sought to settle the long-standing debate about which of the Enlightenment writers most influenced the creation of America. (Was it Montesquieu? Locke? Hume?

Hobbes? Or perhaps it was the more ancient writers, such as Plutarch or Cicero.) The answer stunned them all. It was, overwhelmingly, the writers of the biblical covenant.[4]

Further connecting the Constitution and its blessings to the covenant is the manner in which the Constitution came into being. For, as the Founders themselves readily admitted, these constitutional blessings were not sought after and achieved in a vacuum. They emerged as the fruit of a history overwhelmingly characterized by a miraculous connection to God and covenant. We have seen this through analyzing the truth behind the discovery and settlement of the land, through detailing the history behind the Revolution, and through examining the creation of the Constitution. And now, we will see this once more through exploring the content of the Constitution. Such powerful things should not be trivialized. Let us make no mistake: The Constitution is a direct fulfillment of ancient American Covenant prophecy. In fact, the Constitution is nothing less than the American Covenant codified!

We will begin our discussion of the Constitution's content by detailing the American Covenant blessings found within the document, and then we will outline the American Covenant obligations associated with the document. These obligations, as we shall see, are (fittingly) the same obligations of the American Covenant, as detailed in the Old Testament. As we see that the Constitution does, in fact, carry with it the covenant blessings and obligations of the national covenant (and this is in addition to the many other scriptural and miraculous elements surrounding it, as mentioned above), it will open our eyes to the profound nature of the document. More than just a political paper, it becomes a spiritual text, derived from the Almighty for His eternal purposes.

However, before launching into this discussion, we should note that the mere existence of divine and holy principles within the document did not mean the new nation would necessarily apply them all immediately, or apply them all correctly. Many of these constitutional principles would unfortunately take years—and at times would require blood, sweat, and tears—to fully develop and become the powerful blessings they were intended to be. Notwithstanding America's inability to always apply them in the real world, however, these principles and blessings always had a firm foundation in the Constitution.

Covenant Blessings in the Constitution

In analyzing the great blessings found in the Constitution, we will begin with those outlined in the Preamble.

> *We the People of the United States, in Order to form a more perfect Union, establish Justice, insure domestic Tranquility, provide for the common defense, promote the general Welfare, and secure the Blessings of Liberty to ourselves and our Posterity, do ordain and establish this Constitution of the United States of America.*

Surely, the Preamble should inspire confidence in any person or organization (including Christ's church) desiring to live and prosper unmolested. After all, what else is needed for such progression other than *justice, tranquility, defense, welfare,* and *liberty*? These blessings make fertile ground for man's liberty and thus for his eternal salvation.

The Scene at the Signing of the Constitution of the United States by Howard Chandler Christy. Courtesy of the Architect of the Capitol.

The main body of the Constitution then proceeds to describe how such lofty goals, set forth in the Preamble, are to be obtained. It describes how the new national government will work to eradicate the social ills that obstruct *justice, tranquility, welfare,* and *the blessings of liberty.* First, it explains how it will create public policy through the legislative branch (Article I). Second, it explains how it will enforce this policy through the executive branch (Article II). And third, it explains how it will check the validity of government action through an independent judicial branch (Article III). Subsequent articles include, among other things, certain ground-rules for how states will interact with the federal government, how amendments will be added, and how general ratification of the Constitution will be conducted. The Constitution is rounded out with a list of very specific rights —known as amendments—held by the people, which the government, in administering its duties, is obligated to respect.

Yet the Constitution says so much more. And so, in an effort to present the fullness of the Constitution and to reveal its direct connection to the covenant, we will now analyze its content by exploring eight of its most inspired principles.

Bill of Rights

The Amendments to the Constitution secure liberty for both individuals and for private institutions, such as churches. They guarantee the right to express ourselves freely through word and press (vital to evangelical work); to gather with those we choose (essential for the worship services of many faiths); to be secure against unreasonable searches and seizures; to be free from arrest without probable cause; to have access, if needed, to an impartial jury; and to not be deprived of life, liberty, and property without due process of law. It is easy to imagine the many ways Satan could influence the fight against freedom and against Christ's church if such protections did not exist. But with the existence and proper enforcement of such rights, how could God's work be stopped?

It is perhaps the following clause in the First Amendment, authored by Madison himself, which does more than any of the others to secure God's work on the earth: "Congress shall make no law respecting an establishment of religion, or prohibiting the free exercise thereof." Unfortunately, it would take decades for the nation to fully adopt the principles contained within this amendment. Notwithstanding, the religious freedom eventually born from the amendment would prove to be paramount for the further light and knowledge of Christ's Gospel to find its way into the hearts and minds of modern Christians.

It is important to note that many secularists today try to interpret this amendment's *Establishment Clause*—that there shall not be a government "establishment of religion"—as meaning that God should have no place in government. However, this entire book provides irrefutable evidence that the Founders believed God had (and has) a very *prominent* place in government. *The Establishment Clause* certainly does not take God out of America, but instead, it rightfully prohibits the government from supporting and favoring (i.e. *establishing*) a particular religious domination. Religious favoritism could and probably would eventually be used as a political tool of oppression. And so, in a manner quite the opposite of detracting from God's place in America, this amendment secures our ability to worship Him freely and unobstructed, thus allowing truth to be securely practiced. It truly delivers the liberty God intended for the Constitution to provide.

God certainly reserved this land and government as the designated venue for such blessings unto salvation. For these few constitutional words concerning religious freedom are, as Judge John Noonan put it, an "American invention." He continued, "How foolish it would be to let a false modesty...obscure the originality."[5] It was, in fact, of singular origination. But then again, it was, after all, designed for a singular purpose; to protect liberty in God's promised land so that gospel principles and man's salvation might be realized.

Checks, Balances, and Separation of Powers

Through the constitutional process, the Lord revealed a system of government with separate branches, all with independent powers, and all with clear constitutional responsibilities to keep the others in check. With such a system, one government entity could not easily misapply the inspired constitutional principles, such as the First Amendment, without receiving some form of legal censure from the others. For example, the legislative branch can withhold funds from, or even impeach, a wicked executive and/or judicial branch; the executive branch can veto wicked laws from the legislative branch; and the judicial branch can censure both for violating their constitutional trusts and duties. These are just a few of the built-in checks and balances.

Perhaps the adversary could reasonably gain influence over a segment of the government (say, one of the branches, or at least a part of one). But under this American system, in order for the adversary to have any prolonged negative effect on the political foundations that support God's purposes, he would have to gain all three branches—a highly improbable proposition. Therefore, the system is well safeguarded for liberty; and so, God's church may reside in confidence. As the lawyer, political scientist, and former U.S diplomat, J. Reuben Clark, commented: "It is this union of independence and dependence of these branches—legislative, executive and judicial—...that constitutes the marvelous genius of this unrivaled document....As I see it, it was here that the divine inspiration came. It was truly a miracle."[6]

A Living Document

In 1816, Thomas Jefferson wrote: "Some men look at constitutions with sanctimonious reverence, and deem them like the ark of the covenant, too sacred to be touched."

> They ascribe to men of the preceding age a wisdom more than human, and suppose what they did to be beyond amendment. I knew that age well; I belonged to it, and labored with it...But I know also, that laws and institutions must go hand in hand with the progress of the human mind. As that becomes more developed, more enlightened, as new discoveries are made, new truths disclosed, and manners and opinions change with the change in circumstances, institutions must advance also.[7]

The Constitution is a living document, open to change when such change is needed. Even from the beginning, there were constitutional problems that needed immediate attention. For example, the Constitution placed restrictions on certain segments of the population (based on sex and race), denying millions of Americans full participation in government. Furthermore, Article IV, Section 2 required that all states return fugitive slaves to their original owners, thus tacitly approving the abomination that was slavery. Thankfully, an inspired amendment process was also established (defined in Article V), whereby such immoralities could be purged, as they eventually were.

Though inspired, this amendment process would need to be kept in check in order to prevent an over-zealous (and perhaps less than virtuous) mere majority from getting carried away. Indeed, while it is a living document in many respects, when it comes to the God-ordained freedoms, promised within its pages, the Constitution is a very dead document—unable to be redefined or manipulated in a way that might damage our precious liberty. Knowing some might attempt to amend our freedom and happiness away, the Lord inspired a built-in protection (also defined in Article V) to govern this amendment-making process. J. Reuben Clark explained:

> The Constitution was framed in order to protect minorities...In order that the minorities might be protected in the matter of amendments under our Constitution, the Lord required that the amendments should be made only through the operation of very large majorities—two-thirds for action in the Senate [and the House], and three-fourths as among the states. This is the inspired, prescribed order.[8]

A First Republic

A republican form of government is one whereby the people, through their representatives, remain the source of all power. As Abraham Lincoln put it, it is a "government of the people, by the people and for the people."[9] We live in a day when most nations enjoy such a political structure, and often we take for granted the uniqueness of this concept. But, as few may know, America was the first to implement a republic over such a vast expanse of land and over such a great population. It is true that democratic-republican systems had been tried with relative success over small geographical and demographical regions, such as Greek city-states and Swiss cantons. But nothing like what the Constitution presented had ever been successfully attempted and achieved.[10]

The Old World, even the ever-enduring monarchists, mocked the new document, saying that the people could never govern themselves and that eventually anarchy would emerge and that the states would become separate nations unto themselves. They argued that it was only under strict central control, where power was derived not from people, but from kings and rulers, that the needed discipline for stability could be found. This, critics continued, was necessary, even at the cost of personal freedoms, including freedom of religion. Satan most certainly had blinded the Old World.

But God, through His grace and power during the Revolution, had eradicated such oppressive ideals of governance from America, paving the way for a new order abounding in popular sovereignty. And why was this so important to the Lord? Why inspire the discovery and settlement of a new land, followed by war and nation building, to establish a nation where the power is held by the people? So that inspired laws (like the First Amendment), which were given to the United States, even by God, are well protected. And protected they remain as long as the majority of the people retain the power—as long as the United States remains a true republic—and as long the majority of the people are keeping commandments and serving God.

The idea that such governmental ideas are of divine origin is corroborated by the fact that the national covenant of ancient Israel—equally inspired by God for the same eternal purposes—includes these very principles. The people of ancient Israel were instructed under their national covenant to elect leaders and pass new laws under the common consent of the people (see 2 Samuel 2:4; 1 Chr. 29:22; for the dismissal of a leader, see 2 Chr. 10:16; for the people's approval and consent of new legislation, see Exodus 19:8).[11] Furthermore, the government under Moses boasted of separate branches of government.[12] In 1788, while the Constitution was being debated for final ratification, colonial leaders, including Samuel Langdon and Benjamin Franklin, pointed out how God, through the Constitution, had resurrected the government of ancient Israel in modern America.[13] Indeed He had.

Federalism

The Constitution introduces us to a strange concept we call *federalism*, which is defined as the division of powers between state and federal governments. Today we abide by two separate books of law (state and federal). We elect officers to represent us in two separate capital cities (state and federal). And we pay taxes to two separate jurisdictions (both state and federal). Though we all accept it, as it's the only thing we have ever known, we must acknowledge its uniqueness. We live, work, and play under two governments. And while there is both dependence and independence between them, each functions with its own legislative, executive, and judicial branches. This is unique to America. Some may even argue that it is so unusual that only an outside source—like Heaven itself—could have brought it forth to the minds of men. Yet despite its uniqueness, it would prove to be the best form of government to date, and the nations of the world would even begin to emulate it.

The inspiration behind *federalism* represents itself in the many blessings it produces. For example, two separate types of government facilitate a powerful diffusion of power. While state and local governments can focus on local issues, which they are most familiar with and can best deal with (like crime or pollution in its cities), the federal government can handle broader issues that affect every state (like interstate commerce or foreign policy). Additionally, with two separate concentrations of power, the people have two sources to appeal to. This limits the ability of one single government from becoming overbearing and perhaps oppressive—a common occurrence in the annals of history. This is particularly important for the preservation of liberty.

It is worth noting here that the idea of political protection emerging out of both small, concentrated governmental groups, and simultaneously out of a larger, more centralized governmental head, stems from divine origin. For Moses revealed to ancient Israel that such should be the case for its early governmental structure under its respective national covenant (see Exodus 18: 13-26). Such connections reinforce the Constitution as an embodiment of the national covenant, which God has repeatedly designed and delivered for His gospel purposes.

In terms of the U.S. Constitution, one of the most inspired dimensions to this division of powers is the existence of the Tenth Amendment, which ensures that the state governments focus on what they do best and that the federal government focuses on what it does best. "The powers not delegated to the United States by the Constitution," declares the amendment, "are reserved to the States respectively, or to the people." Here is yet one more check and balance built in for our protection.

However, as beneficial as the Tenth Amendment is, too many have over-interpreted it to mean that unless the Constitution specifically grants a power to the federal government, then the federal government has no right to intervene *at all*. The truth is, the Constitution tempers the Tenth Amendment with certain provisions— for example, the Preamble and the Necessary and Proper Clause in Article I, Section 8—which allows federal intervention on a number of issues, when it is "necessary and proper" in fulfilling the federal government's mandate. An overly strict interpretation of the Tenth Amendment, for example, would have barred the very necessary intervention of the federal government on issues of equal and civil rights. For the Constitution does not explicitly state (only implies) that a national Civil Rights Act, so essential to the protection of minority groups, could be created. But in the cause of civil rights (like in other cases) the individual states were either unable to help or were themselves the problem, which left no other hope than federal intervention. The Constitution's Preamble, after all, mandates the federal government to "secure the blessings of liberty," and civil rights legislation was certainly "necessary and proper" to fulfill that mandate.

Religious minorities (like Jews, Mennonites, Catholics, and Mormons), along with racial minorities, often suffered great and violent persecution by state and local governments. This is one of the dark and sad facts surrounding American history. The federal Civil Rights Act, however, came to the rescue. To this day, if such persecution were to invade any religious organization or racial group, particularly by state and local governments, the Civil Rights Act would serve as their most important tool.

Certainly we must respect and support the Tenth Amendment and states' rights. Through the years (and especially recently) there has, no doubt, been abuses of federal authority over the states. However, as we seek the appropriate balance between the two governments, we must also recognize the many divine fruits that the federal government has produced.

A New Promise of Liberty

As established throughout this book, one of the most significant blessings of the American Covenant is *liberty*. We have seen how this governmental principle is defined in the Scriptures as a powerful element of the covenant. We examined how that most prominent national covenant with ancient Israel promised this same *liberty* (see Exodus 14, Leviticus 26), and provided as its basic tenet: "Proclaim liberty throughout all the land unto all the inhabitants thereof" (Leviticus 25:10). We have also made it clear that all these blessings were given as a support for God's Gospel on the earth.

If such prophecies and promises are really part of the American Covenant, and if the Constitution really is a reflection of this covenant, it follows that an abundance of *liberty*—even a new promise of *liberty*—would be offered through the Constitution. And it would be offered in a way to support God's church. We have already outlined some of these principles of *liberty* found within the Constitution, such as the republican form of government it promotes and the First Amendment protections it offers. Yet there is infinitely more. For the Constitution came equipped with a new and powerful formula for preserving *liberty*.

From the beginning, the inspired Madison knew just how his proposed constitution would supply this formula for *liberty*, and he would strive to teach this formula to his fellow countrymen. After Madison's plan for a new national government was submitted to the congressional delegates, they immediately balked. They argued that conventional wisdom suggested that small governments, like those of the individual states, were better because they were closer to the needs of the people, and permitted more accessibility to government. Though Madison would not have dreamed of scrapping state governments for those very reasons, he did turn conventional wisdom on its head regarding governments that govern over a small geographic/demographic region versus larger governments that govern over vast geographic/demographic regions. Madison stood and boldly asserted that it is only through a comprehensive, national government that a fullness of liberty could ever be secured. The delegates listened in awe as Madison expounded on this new and peculiar political theory.

He explained that every nation on earth was composed of interested parties seeking power over one another. These parties, which he referred to as "factions," are in constant political battle—the rich against the poor, the religionists against the atheists, industrialists against agriculturalists, races against races, families against families, and so on. In a small government, argued Madison, where a lesser population allows for only a limited amount of these "warring factions," there is naturally less political competition. Reduced competition facilitates an eventual victor, who would likely take the political reins and rule tyrannically over the remaining minority factions. The delegates could not deny that, in each of their states, they had seen such a faction do just that, and they had seen the corruption, the dishonesty, and the subversion of minority rights that inevitably follows.

But under this *new* system, Madison explained, there would exist a second government, and one which would include not just the citizenry from one state, but from all states—indeed, from the entire nation. This would naturally open up the playing field for vast participation, allowing so many factions into the political battle, that it would be next to impossible for one or a few oppressive factions to dominate the stage.

An analogy of this concept (popular with my political science students) is as follows. Imagine there are two separate mile-long running races being prepared side by side. Participants are filing in at the two starting lines to run for the reward of political power and control. As the racers are waiting for the gun to sound, you notice that only five people have lined up for one of the races, while five thousand have lined up for the other. Then you look up and notice a familiar face walking up to register for one of the two races. Complete with high-riding jogging shorts and an unsightly tank top, you realize that it is none other than Adolf Hitler! The registrar turns to you and asks, "Which race should I put him in?"

Madison would argue that, under a system of small governments, where only smaller races exist, Hitler must, by necessity, be given the chance to run in the race of five, thus allowing him a good chance to win, wrest control, and then dominate. However, with Madison's concept of an additional and larger national government (where more people create a larger running race) you would have the opportunity to place him in the race of five thousand. This would limit his chances of success and help to secure liberty for the others. "The influence of factious leaders," Madison wrote in his now-famous Federalist No.10, "may kindle a flame within their particular states [the race of five], but will be unable to spread a general conflagration through the other states [the race of five thousand]."

> A religious sect [for example] may degenerate into a political faction in part of the Confederacy but the variety of sects dispersed over the entire face of it, must secure the national Councils against any danger from that source...[and thus], improper or wicked project[s] will be less apt to pervade the whole body of the Union.[14]

We readily observe this principle played out in places like Saddam Hussein's Iraq. Here was a street thug from the streets of Tikrit who became a bodyguard to the then dictator. He convinced his boss to make him a general over the military. Then he just started threatening or killing people above him, including the officials who had promoted him. He eventually became the evil tyrant. There was no process that required the voice of the people, no strong *national councils* to keep such evil in check, and no divine constitutional order that would have held such evil at bay. Saddam represented a faction unto himself with few, if any, serious competing or warring factions to rebuff him. He ran in the race of five, and simply won the race by killing or exiling his few fellow racers. Because of this, Satan has, until recently, been ruling that country for decades—thwarting liberty and prohibiting gospel principles.

Now that we understand Madison's general intention, how do we connect his plan specifically to the Lord's purposes? Or, in other words, if this political theory is in furtherance of God's work, how might that relate to gospel renewal, stability, and growth?

Let us suppose, hypothetically, that within the fifty United States, there exists one state which is highly biased against the relatively large population of red-haired individuals, which, notwithstanding their numbers, make up a minority of the citizenry of that state. The laws in this particular state go so far as to persecute the red-head, prohibiting his ability to freely pursue his righteous desires and goals. Though they have relentlessly appealed to their local governments for help, it is all in vain—for nobody in that state likes the red-head. But what if there were another source of power that could come and liberate the red-heads, even a source which included people from outside this particular state. What if there were a national venue—an all-encompassing "voice of the people"—that included every individual from the other forty-nine states. Certainly among so many added participants in this new forum, there would exist other red-haired individuals and/or sympathizers of the red-head cause who would be willing to act in behalf of their oppressed countrymen. These rescuers would have the *national* legislative, executive, and judicial branches from which to launch their campaign to secure liberty and justice for all.

Let's pause for a moment, jump back into the real world, and ask ourselves, *Where, after all, did black Americans in the South find their defenders? Was it from the state and local governments in South Carolina? Mississippi? Tennessee? Georgia?* No, in every case—from Civil War on through the Civil Rights Act—the reprieve and redress came from the federal or national level, just as Madison might have predicted. There is no clearer or dramatic validation of

Madison's inspired theory than the heaven-induced progress made in black America's fight for equal rights.*

Now, returning to the hypothetical example, let us suppose now that the red-headed people we are talking about throughout the United States happen to be God-seekers, even truth-seekers searching for eternal life. Suppose they are chosen Christian disciples of God, who were raised in the last days to receive, organize, and carry Christ's Gospel to all the world. Thanks to Mr. Madison's Constitution, standing at last in their midst, waving the sword of truth and justice over their local oppressors, is this new national government. It is a new government armed with the God-given laws pertaining to our inalienable rights, ensured by the protections of checks and balances, and tempered by the reasonable and enlightened voice of *all* the people of the land. Now we see, through even

---

* In spite of this constitutional theory and tool which would one day help free black Americans, several criticisms have been launched over the years at the Constitution's seemingly reprehensible compromises over slavery and over black Americans in general. For example, some argue that the Northern non-slave states should never have confederated with the Southern states unless they gave up slavery. Others love to argue that the original Constitution is clearly racist because it only counts blacks as three-fifths of a person. However, there is another side to both these stories. First, the Northern states knew that constitutionally abolishing slavery meant that the Southern states would not join the Union. If this had happened, blacks in the South would have lost a constitutional and societal connection to the Northern factions, who would eventually intervene and help them gain freedom. Keeping the South connected to the North, even at the cost of compromise, was absolutely essential for eventual black liberation. Furthermore, the Northern states at least were able to get the South to agree to constitutionally halt the slave trade after twenty years— not wholly effective, but it lit a dim light at the end of a dark tunnel. And second, it was the abolitionists in Congress who promoted counting slaves as three-fifths of a person (and they would have counted them as less than that if it had been possible). Why? Because members of the lower house of Congress are determined by proportional representation, which means that the more people that were counted in the South, the more representation (or the more delegates) the South would have had in Congress. Had the black man been counted as a "whole" person, there would have been even more racist delegates who would do all they could to maintain slavery. Simply put, the Three-Fifths clause in the Constitution actually assisted efforts toward abolition.

more finely focused lenses, why the Lord inspired a federal/ national government under the Constitution. It was, after all, His work and His glory that hung in the balance.

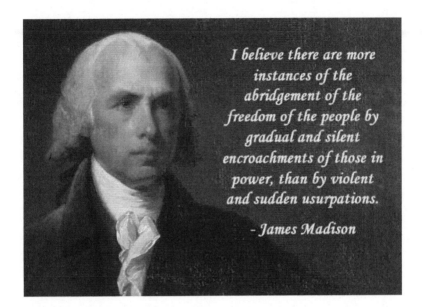

I believe there are more instances of the abridgement of the freedom of the people by gradual and silent encroachments of those in power, than by violent and sudden usurpations.

- James Madison

As moral issues become irrelevant and are struck from public recognition, and as they are replaced with state-endorsed policies encouraging immoralities, two things might happen. First, the God of this land might cease to protect this nation—we may be left alone and at the mercy of the adversary who would seek to destroy us as a people. And second, our ability to worship God according to the dictates of conscience may be hampered, especially if we refuse to acknowledge falsehoods forced upon us by the state, and as we speak out in defense of God's truths. Indeed, there could be serious legal ramifications for Christians who dare to do such a thing. In light of this, it is possible that the federal government will be called upon again (just as racial and religious minorities called upon it in the past), as the last hope, to preserve and protect the freedom of religion that some states have begun to attack.

A New Promise of Protection

Another American Covenant promise discussed throughout this book is that of *protection*. We saw how the Lord established and reestablished this blessing. We outlined how ancient Israel enjoyed this *protection* from its enemies while under the covenant, and we detailed how Jacob-Israel prophesied that this blessing would be bestowed upon his heirs of modern America—that their "bow [would] ab[i]de in strength, and the arms of his hands [would be] made strong by the hands of the mighty God of Jacob" (Genesis 49:24). Such scriptural references demonstrate that the American Covenant blessing of *protection* existed anciently and was foreordained for, and offered to, modern-day America so that wicked oppressors, under the influence of the adversary, could not rock the political foundations that supported God's work.

If such a blessing is truly part of the American Covenant, and if the Constitution is a reflection of this covenant, then it follows that the Constitution should offer this very *protection* required to support liberty and the gospel.

The most direct demonstration of this constitutionally-derived *protection* is found in Article I, Sections 8 and 10 of the document, which charges Congress to raise and support armies, to deal with foreign nations, to declare war, to raise funds, to coin money, and to regulate foreign commerce. Article II, Section 2 charges the president to run the military and foreign policy apparatus (among other things). Before these governing principles existed, the individual states were alone, for the most part, in dealing with any economic or physical threat from overseas. Even if one state decided to place its militias at its borders to stop such threats, all the enemy had to do was approach the land through a neighboring state, which had no such militia. The borders of the United States were thus completely porous to whatever or whoever might do the nation harm. Such weak defenses would make the nation vulnerable to a vast array of threats.

Imagine, for example, if foreign invaders entered the nation in droves and took over the many small state governments and changed the laws to limit personal or religious freedom. Or imagine if these invaders entered the land and posed a constant threat to our infrastructure and physical safety, thus driving us to a constant state of survival. This would severely limit our time, resources, and wherewithal to develop and maintain our individual pursuits of happiness, to include our ability to worship God and build His kingdom on the earth. Satan, knowing what America would mean for the gospel in modern times, would certainly make America a target and thus influence such invaders. How would the United States ever become the Promised Land that the Lord designed it to be, complete with freedoms unto eternal salvation? Fortunately, the Lord would preemptively attack such wickedness by creating the Constitution, which offered the *protection* required for His work and glory in the last days.

For example, the constitutional principles listed above encouraged the creation of a new national military, which set the stage for what would become the largest and most powerful physical force on the planet—a force which would fight and defeat the enemies of freedom and liberty. Without the Constitution, we would be limited to individual state militias, which could never have resembled the massive national military presence we see today and could never have stopped evil in its tracks as the U.S. military has done. It is certainly no coincidence that the very land where God would renew and enlarge His Gospel is also the very land whose military budget (as a percentage of its GDP) is more than double that of any other nation in the industrial world. Furthermore, the military budget of the United States in real numbers is greater than all the other major powers combined, and represents approximately half of what the entire rest of the world spends on defense.[15]

Another one of the very first applications of the Constitution was the creation of the United States Customs Service (1789), which protected the nation and its borders and set the stage for other law enforcement entities. In fact, many agencies and offices we see today like Homeland Security Investigations, Customs and Border Protection (of which the Border Patrol is a part) and the Coast Guard—is directly derived from this constitutional mandate. Today, the government directly targets those people and things that could threaten our indispensable freedoms.

And finally, these constitutional principles direct that the national government maintain a foreign policy, which has allowed the nation to secure its interests overseas and preemptively identify foreign threats. We see the application of these principles through the creation and maintenance of advanced intelligence agencies and effective diplomatic machines, to include embassies around the world dedicated to protecting the United States and influencing freedom everywhere.

It is easy to see that without these protections of the Constitution, our most cherished institutions and ideals, to include freedom of thought and religion, would be threatened by those who, under the influence of the Evil One, would attack and oppress God's children and thus separate them from gospel principles. The Constitution indeed does much to provide the *protection* of the covenant, thus fulfilling the ancient prophecies of this covenant and making the United States a safe-haven for the gospel.

A New Promise of Prosperity

If a nation is to serve God under a national covenant, prosperity and wealth are necessary blessings. They provide the strong military, law enforcement, diplomatic, and other resources necessary to maintain those freedoms that allow God's children to access His Gospel. Furthermore, economic prosperity brings wealth to congregations, which directly increases the financial resources pouring into churches and synagogues all over the country, thus allowing—among other things—more churches and synagogues to be built throughout the *world*.

This is why God blessed His earlier national covenant-makers in ancient Israel with such *prosperity*—even with a land "flowing with milk and honey" (Exodus 3:8). As per the covenant, America has inherited this same blessing. Specifically, Jacob-Israel promised that his American heirs through Joseph would, under the covenant, enjoy the "blessings of the deep that lieth under, blessings of the breasts and of the womb" (Genesis 45:25). Moses blessed this same posterity with the blessings of "precious fruits brought forth of the sun," and for "the chief things of the ancient mountains" (Deuteronomy 33:14-16). Indeed, through these and other scriptural examples, we have established that such blessings are clearly associated with the American Covenant and are intended for modern-day Americans, that God's purposes might be realized.

And once again, if these are blessings of the American Covenant, and if this covenant is represented by the Constitution, then it follows that the Constitution would serve as a support and enabler for the realization of such blessings. And it does just that.

For example, Article I, Section 8 of the Constitution allows for the national government to tax and control money, which secures and maintains the capital market. This constitutional mandate further calls on the national government to foster growth through regulating trade. The Constitution also defines the rights to private property and includes specific protections of those rights. Finally, one of the greatest prosperity inducing principles of the Constitution is its lack of overbearing regulations and controls. The document's relatively hands-off approach represents what history has proven to be the only true wealth-sustaining economic practice—free markets and capitalism. Indeed, one of America's greatest economic assets has less to do with what the Constitution says, and more to do with what it does *not* say. The Fifth Amendment even maintains protections against the temptation to rein in capitalism in exchange for schemes or policies involving radical redistribution of wealth.[16]

One of the earliest examples of how the application of these constitutional principles provided much needed wealth, occurred shortly after the Constitution was implemented. With a national financial crises on the horizon (interest from Revolutionary War loans was piling up uncontrollably, and the states were unequipped to cobble together a financial solution), George Washington, the first president, pooled all the national resources available to him and assigned his Secretary of the Treasury, the brilliant Alexander Hamilton, the task of developing a plan to remedy the situation. The plan included the formation of a national bank, which fostered both domestic investment and growth, and serviced the foreign debt (which debt Hamilton wisely consolidated under the federal government). Hamilton utilized federal powers implied in the Constitution, as described above, to aid all the states and all the people.*

---

* Many people interpreted (and still interpret) the Constitution in a way that would have prevented Hamilton from creating a national banking system among the many states. Critics of Hamilton cited the Tenth Amendment, and argued that since the Amendment states that unless the Constitution specifically charges the federal government with a responsibility, then the federal government must defer to the states. And, as the critics pointed out, nowhere in the Constitution does it specifically state that the national government can create a national bank. The issue was resolved in the case of *McCulloch vs. Maryland* (1819). The Supreme Court pointed out that Article I, Section 8 of the Constitution states that Congress may do whatever is "necessary and proper" in carrying out its responsibilities. In that one of these federal responsibilities was to secure economic stability in the nation, the Court ruled that the national bank was constitutional. Thanks to this decision, the bank stayed, which arguably saved the nation from becoming bankrupt.

Hamilton's plan not only enabled payments on national loans through the new banking system, but also federalized and standardized tariff schedules. He then created the U.S. Customs Service to collect those tariffs. In addition to resurrecting America's good credit, the monies produced under these constitutional programs allowed the country to conduct defense explorations of the West (such as the Lewis and Clark Expedition); to acquire lands (such as those obtained via the Louisiana Territory Purchase); to facilitate infrastructure growth (like the Transcontinental Railroad); and to grow the military.[17]

The nation, complete with these new tools and a flourishing economy, was able to grow from that early point in American history. The economic success achieved by the U.S. system is obvious enough as to not require statistical proof. Notwithstanding, we will mention one interesting indicator here. Recently published data list the wealthiest people that ever lived, beginning from our earliest recorded history. In order to level the playing field, the net worth of the many individuals is calculated and adapted relative to the historical value of commodities at the time in which they lived. The list goes as far back as kings and pharaoh's who lived centuries ago. And yet, of the top seventy-five names listed, an astonishing forty-five were Americans who made their wealth in the United States of America.[18] Americans represent fully sixty percent of the names on the list! And of course, the wealth made by these individuals reflects the vast amount of jobs created and further wealth generated by the entire nation under national capitalism. Indeed, among nations and history, America has been calculably blessed with *prosperity.*

Further proof that this national wealth was connected to God and his plan for a renewal of His Gospel is found in a study of economic prosperity conducted by economist Angus Madison. Madison concludes that the modern prosperity we see today in the world, to include everything from base wealth to advances in science, electronics, and transportation, began approximately in 1820—right at the height of a religious movement, known as the Second Great Awakening, which was occurring right then in America.* Commenting on the study, economist William Bernstein stated that "before that date, growth was essentially nonexistent, and after, sustained and vigorous."[19] Is it just a coincidence that wealth drastically picked up in the middle of a proliferation of religious fervor and Christian enlightenment in America? Or was it all a part of God's plan to begin prospering His children in preparation for greater things on the horizon?

Again, that such *prosperity* directly fulfills ancient prophecies of the American Covenant, and that it does so through the Constitution, is abundantly clear. And that this covenant-based blessing of *prosperity*—along with its sister-blessings related above—has served and continues to serve the purposes of the Lord, by supporting and sustaining His Gospel, is unquestionable.

Covenant Obligations of the Constitution

As explained in previous chapters, the American Covenant requires the American citizenry to keep the commandments and serve the God who resides on the other side of the covenant. Only then will the blessings detailed above be delivered. If the Constitution is truly a reflection of the covenant, then it should promote these covenant obligations. And it does. Much has already been said regarding our obligations under the covenant, in general. For now, however,

---

* The First Great Awakening, detailed in Chapter 7, was also divinely timed to prepare Americans for the Revolution. The Second Great Awakening was no less important in growing Christianity upon the foundation of the Constitution. It was "a Christian revival movement...[which] had begun to gain momentum by 1820...It enrolled millions of new members, and led to the formation of new denominations. Many converts believed that the Awakening heralded a new millennial age." See http://en.wikipedia.org/wiki/Second_Great_Awakening.

we will simply verify and corroborate the idea that the *Constitution* incorporates these obligations—obligations that require national adherence in order to receive national blessings.

The idea that the Constitution incorporates obligations should not be taken lightly. It should compel us to reexamine what the Constitution is. Instead of always asking what the Constitution is doing for us, it makes us ask what we are doing for it—what we are doing for the God that offered it to us. It helps us see it for the covenant it is, and it calls us to action.

The covenant relationship reflects a pattern God uses with His children (individually and collectively). Throughout the Scriptures we observe this type of relationship and how God is able to bless individuals and nations only as they fulfill their obligations to Him. With an understanding of this pattern, we are naturally led to the conclusion that God's blessings, to include those derived from the Constitution He delivered, are activated upon general/national obedience. But, in addition to applying our understanding of how God generally releases blessings through a covenant relationship, there are even more specific reasons to believe that the blessings of the Constitution have been offered as part of a covenant with real obligations. We will now discuss two of them.

The Constitution Maintains Natural Covenant Obligations

The political formula on which the Constitution is based naturally requires obligations to God. For, in light of how the Constitution lays out the governmental system, the only way for the people to access the constitutional blessings listed above, is for the people to live righteously. We see this idea manifested in at least two different ways.

First, as the Constitution allows vast freedoms to the people, it becomes incumbent upon the people to apply virtue

387

to their own lives, thus keeping their passions and desires in check. Only then can the government trust the citizenry to take care of itself, without having to apply oppressive controls to keep order. But if the people fail to keep themselves in check, the government is pressed to intervene, which might help to temporarily bridle the wicked, but ultimately represents a general decline in the ability to acquire the blessings of the Constitution, particularly the blessings of *liberty* and *prosperity*. For once governments begin to grow in influence, too often they grow so large that they begin to impede and stomp on individual and economic freedoms.

We see real world examples of how this works today. Almost twenty years ago the Soviet Union fell. Consequently, Russia began introducing principles of democracy. With the U.S. Constitution as its model, the Russian people sought to gain the same constitutional blessings Americans enjoy. However, after more than a century of virtual godlessness in that region (true freedom of religion was no hallmark of the Soviet Union), the people were ill-equipped to keep themselves in check. With the blessings of freedom came the opportunity to choose good or evil. Sadly, without strong moral and religious traditions, too many citizens chose the latter. Widespread organized crime, government corruption, and the most immoral acts against the innocent have thrived in that country since that time. (I have personally been involved in combating some of these most wicked elements.) With the inability of the Russian people, in the aggregate, to apply morality and religion to their daily lives, the Russian government could not trust the people. Consequently, the government felt compelled to crack down on their freedoms. By 2005, President Vladimir Putin had taken over private industries, rolled back the free elections of Russia's regional governors, and nationalized the media.[20] The country is on the slippery slope that threatens *liberty, protection,* and *prosperity*— even those supports for gospel nourishment. However, had the people adopted national morality, such may not have been the case.

America has struggled with the same problem. The economic hardships we see today have undoubtedly been produced by years of selfishness and greed in the aggregate. Such national immorality has led to national panic, which has led to an increase in governmental control of private affairs. (For example, the government has recently felt inclined to take over more private enterprises and to start making more healthcare decisions for us.) We are witnessing the beginning of that slippery slope that threatens our own constitutional blessings of the American Covenant. Had we stayed spiritually worthy, and bridled our passions and appetites, we would not currently be wondering if our most cherished rights are under attack from within.

We see this same issue applied to our bloated budget and consequent debt. Consider, for example, the overwhelming percentage of taxpayer dollars (e.g. Medicaid and food stamp dollars) that go to support unwed mothers, many of which (to no fault of their own) have been tragically abandoned by the father of their children. By some estimations, over 50 percent of these welfare budgets go to cover these desperate single moms, 90 percent of which are currently on welfare. To make matters worse, recent data suggest that over 50 percent of marriages end in divorce and over 50 percent of children born in the United States are born outside of wedlock.[21] As immorality continues to grow, so will the burden on the individual taxpayer. As it does, our freedoms (to include our financial freedoms as individuals) will continue to diminish. Those who try to distinguish social morality from fiscal policy are very misguided. One affects the other. Again, living the covenant naturally releases blessings. Conversely, violating the covenant naturally sucks away blessings by encouraging the unhealthy growth of the government which, when given the opportunity, will lean ever-more oppressively upon its people in an attempt to "right" the "wrongs" of the citizenry.

We would do well to adhere to the advice of the 18th Century British statesmen, Edmund Burke, who warned, "Men are qualified for civil liberty in exact proportion to their disposition to put moral chains on their appetites."[22] Our own Benjamin Franklin echoed the same warning, declaring: "Only a virtuous people are capable of freedom. As nations become corrupt and vicious, they have more need for masters." This is precisely why Franklin promoted the idea that "nothing is more important for the public weal, than to form and train up youth in wisdom and virtue."[23] Let us consider the wise words of one commentator, who recently explained that we, as a nation, "would not accept the yoke of Christ; so we now must tremble at the yoke of Caesar."[24]

Considering how much the Lord values covenants, and considering that the Lord inspired the Constitution, this system, based on a built-in covenant relationship, is certainly no coincidence. The Lord designed the Constitution to require national worthiness in order for His children to access and maintain the constitutional/covenant blessings.

The second natural, or built-in, covenant system we see in the Constitution is connected to the idea that in order for us, the people, to administer the government in a way that allows us to access the covenant blessings, we must first be worthy to receive proper inspiration from on high. In that the Constitution mandates that the people create their own government and decide how to manage and maintain it, the people are naturally placed in a position of great trust; for the constitutional blessings of the covenant will only be activated to the extent that the people appropriately apply the constitutional principles found within the Constitution. The Constitution allows much wiggle room for proper and righteous interpretation or, conversely, for inappropriate and wicked misinterpretation. The Constitution, as noted above, may even be amended (for good or evil). As such, a sound understanding of what the Constitution says, while necessary, is not always enough. In an ever-changing world, with new problems and issues arising daily, we must be able to appropriately apply the Constitution to things it has never been applied to before—things the Founders did not necessarily foresee. In this quest, we the people, in whom all political power lies, need divine inspiration. A healthy dosage of divine inspiration is the only sure way to properly apply and amend (when necessary) the Constitution and thereby activate and preserve the covenant blessings.

The only way to receive such inspiration, of course, is to live righteously as individuals, that as a nation we might be clean and worthy receptacles of this needed inspiration. And so we see, once again, how the design of the Constitution promotes a natural covenant relationship with the Almighty. Indeed, the covenant pattern again applies— blessings come only as we live righteously under God.

An example of this naturally built-in covenant may be illustrated as follows. Though we read about the mandated principles of free markets in the Constitution, suppose we lose inspiration and begin to misapply the Constitution by allowing the government to dominate commerce or other basic sectors of the economy. We would risk losing our covenant blessings. For not only could this lead to a loss of *prosperity*, but it could also set a bad precedent that places the government on a path to power, thus threatening individual and national *liberty*. Other constitutional rules that need to be followed for the same reasons include those regulating taxation, foreign policy, federalism, and most importantly, the freedom of religion.

On the other hand, if we maintain our righteousness, and thus continue to merit inspiration, we will correctly apply the grand constitutional principles and put them into righteous practice. Then, Christ's Gospel can find its fullness. Thus prophesied Thomas Jefferson in one of the most astonishing statements of any Founding Father. In 1820,

Jefferson declared: "If the freedom of religion, guaranteed us by the law in *theory*, can ever rise in *practice* under overbearing inquisition of public opinion, truth will prevail... and the genuine doctrines of Jesus, so long perverted by his pseudo-priests, will again be *restored* to their original purity." [25] And so we see how important it is under the American Covenant to righteously adhere to constitutional principles by applying and interpreting these principles under the inspiration of Heaven. Only then will righteous *theories* be put into *practice*, thus fulfilling the purposes of God.

Let us ever remember that the Spirit, which reveals the truth of all things, cannot dwell for long in unclean places. Therefore, disobedience among the American citizenry will limit the Spirit and will eventually breed faulty political notions about how things should be. If such notions become accepted by the majority and find their way into policy, the covenant blessings will be diminished.

Thankfully, the Constitution was formulated in such a way that if the majority of us adhere to our spiritual conscience, which is given to all men, then we will have the necessary cumulative inspiration to ensure that constitutional *theories* are put into *practice*. Also, the Constitution's checks and balances protect us from any given executive who has lost his spiritual grip, or from any handful of unenlightened congressmen or judges. But if the majority of the citizenry loses its spirituality and virtue, the American Covenant (the Constitution) will ultimately be breached, and the entire divinely mandated American mission will be jeopardized. Simply put, it is a covenant relationship that *must* be adhered to.

Again, considering how the Lord works in a pattern of covenants, and considering that the Lord inspired the Constitution, this system of natural, built-in covenants was no coincidence. We *must* do His will to receive His blessings.

The Founders Taught of Constitutional Obligations Under God

Based on the above analysis, it is clear that national worthiness is a requirement for the covenant blessings of the Constitution to be activated. The Founders understood this and, as such, taught and admonished the people to live worthily.

James Madison, who was closer to the Constitution than anyone, seemed to comprehend the importance of having a virtuous citizenry in order to reap the blessings of the Constitution. Madison said that there had to be "sufficient virtue among men for self government," and that "republican government presupposes the existence of these qualities in a higher degree than any other."[26] Madison once asked rhetorically: "Is there no virtue among us? If there be not, we are in a wretched situation. No theoretical checks, no form of government, can render us secure. To suppose that any form of government will secure liberty or happiness without the virtue of the people, is a chimerical idea."[27]

John Adams also understood and promoted this concept, declaring, "We have no government armed with power capable of contending with human passions and unbridled by morality and religion...*Our Constitution was made only for a moral and religious people*. It is wholly inadequate to the government of any other."[28] Adams further noted that "Statesmen...may plan and speculate for liberty, but it is religion and morality alone, which can establish the principles upon which freedom can securely stand....Religion and virtue are the only foundations...of all free governments."[29] Adams was resolute in his belief that, as he himself stated, "the highest story of the American Revolution is this: It connected in one indissoluble bond the principles of civil government with the principles of Christianity."[30]

Speaking on the same theme, Samuel Adams added his own testimony, declaring:

393

A general dissolution of principles and manners [meaning standards of morality] will more surely overthrow the liberties of America then the whole force of the common enemy. While the people are virtuous, they cannot be subdued; but once they lose their virtue, they will be ready to surrender their liberties to the first external or internal invader.... [But] if virtue and knowledge are diffused among the people, they will never be enslaved. This will be their great security.[31]

Samuel Adams

In short, without good people in America who adhere to God's commandments, the Constitution, and the covenant blessings it guarantees, will naturally suffer. This divinely designed program built into the Constitution, and the words of the prominent Founders, certainly lend support to the idea that the Constitution is a covenant whose strength lies in righteous adherence to God.

Of course, those inspired leaders quoted above were not the only Founders who believed there was a covenant relationship connected to the Constitution. After all, if it is true that the Constitution was given as part of the national covenant, complete with obligations necessary to access its blessings under God, then surely we would expect that the other Founders who created the document might have known something about it as well. And they did. Historians have commented that these early settlers knew that "God had always dealt with his children by covenant...It was not only individual, between each man and God; it was also public, respecting the formation of churches and civil government."[32] It was due to this "covenant theology" abounding in America that the delegates "incorporated their belief in covenant-making into the Constitution of the United States."[33]

To confirm that the Founders truly understood the importance of seeing the new government as a covenant with God, we need only turn to the Northwest Ordinance. This law and ordinance was not only written and issued by the same Congress that created and signed the Constitution, but was written and issued in 1787—the same year of the Constitution. Article Three of the document states, "Religion, morality and knowledge being necessary to good government and the happiness of mankind, schools and the means of education shall forever be encouraged."[34] In that the Congress felt compelled to write this law in the year it issued the Constitution, shows how clear their understanding was that their new Constitution would be best served by a righteous, God fearing citizenry.

Additionally, many of the state constitutions, which had already been created, or which were in the process of being created or amended, also included a healthy dosage of this same covenant theology.[35]

But why should such an idea surprise us? After all, we have seen how this same concept was reflected in the words and deeds of America's first settlers, who clearly came to this land under what they understood to be a covenant with God. They set up governing documents, such as the Mayflower Compact, which codified this belief. We further saw this covenant theology expressed and acted out among the revolutionary generation, which called on God in the halls of Congress and upon the battlefields of war, and expressed an understanding that God would make them victorious if they but lived worthy of their national covenant. If we have learned anything from this study, it is that Americans have historically understood that "righteousness exalteth a nation; but sin is a reproach to any people" (Proverbs 14:34). Why would the Founders have applied the covenant theology to all aspects of their national life and not to their first national compact?

The most pressing evidence that they did incorporate covenant theology into the Constitution is that, from the day the Constitution was activated, the Founders and leaders of the new nation could not express enough how its success would be contingent upon righteous adherence to God's commands. We have already quoted many of these Founders, who believed and taught this principle. However, above all the rest, there was one who led this call to the covenant under the Constitution, and it was George Washington. We have already seen Washington's relentless invocations of the national covenant throughout the days of the Revolution. Then, as first president of the nation, we see how he continued right where he left off. In his first address to the nation as president, and the first since the Constitution came into force, Washington directly appealed to the American Covenant, calling upon his fellow citizens to live in righteousness so as to merit the constitutional blessings. This was his First Inaugural Address, given April 30, 1789. Toward the beginning of his message, Washington stated:

> It would be peculiarly improper to omit in this first official act my fervent supplications to that Almighty Being who rules over the universe, who presides in the councils of nations, and whose providential aids can supply every human defect, that His benediction may consecrate to the liberties and happiness of the people of the United States.

He then expounded upon the covenant relationship between the American people and the Lord, paying special attention to the people's covenant obligations:

> No people can be bound to acknowledge and adore the Invisible Hand, which conducts the affairs of men more than those of the United States. Every step by which they have advanced to the character of an independent nation, seems to have been distinguished by some token of providential agency. And in the important revolution just accomplished in the system of their United Government, the tranquil deliberations and voluntary consent of so many distinct communities, from which the event has

resulted, cannot be compared with the means by which most Governments have been established, without some return of pious gratitude along with an humble anticipation of the future blessings which the past seem to presage. These reflections, arising out of the present crisis, have forced themselves too strongly on my mind to be suppressed.

Washington then applied the covenant more directly to "the great constitutional charter under which [we] are assembled" by stating that "the foundation of our national policy will be laid in the pure and immutable principles of private morality..."

I dwell on this prospect with every satisfaction which an ardent love for my country can inspire, since there is no truth more thoroughly established than that there exists in the economy and course of nature an indissoluble union between virtue and happiness; between duty and advantage; between genuine maxims of an honest and magnanimous policy and the solid rewards of public prosperity and felicity; since we ought to be no less persuaded that the propitious smiles of Heaven, can never be expected on a nation that disregards the eternal rules of order and right, which Heaven itself has ordained."[36]

Washington ends this first presidential inaugural speech with one final reminder that the Constitution is a covenant with God, declaring that

the benign Parent of the Human Race...has been pleased to favor the American people with... dispositions for deciding with unparalleled unanimity on a form of government for the security of their union and the advancement of their happiness, so His divine blessing may be equally conspicuous in the enlarged views, the temperate consultations, and the wise measures on which the success of this Government must depend.[37]

397

It should be recalled that, in conjunction with invoking the covenant through this speech, Washington had also placed his hand upon the American Covenant Scripture (found in Genesis 49) while entering the oath and covenant of the presidency.

Furthermore, it was clearly understood by the American citizenry that Washington was not invoking the covenant only for himself but for the entire nation. The day was, after all, set aside as a day of prayer and dedication for the whole nation. A proclamation was even sent out in advance to the people so that they might prepare for this historic moment:

> On the morning of the day on which our illustrious President will be invested with his office, the bells will ring at nine o'clock, when the people may go up to the house of God and in a solemn manner commit the new government, with its important train of consequences, to the holy protection and blessing of the Most High. An early hour is prudently fixed for this peculiar act of devotion and is designed wholly for prayer.[38]

After his speech, Washington led a procession down the streets of New York City. The first government, to include the first senators and representatives, followed Washington into the nearby St. Paul's Chapel. There, in one of the very first joint-sessions of Congress, they all bowed together in prayer to the Almighty, Whose land they knew they were consecrating that day.[39]

Washington's inauguration day was a day of covenant-making for the entire nation.

Months later, Washington (reflecting over the entire American Revolution, which had recently culminated with the Constitution), reaffirmed his position on the American

Covenant when he expressed his belief that "[t]he man must be bad indeed who can look upon the events of the American Revolution without feeling the warmest gratitude towards the great Author of the Universe. And it is my earnest prayer that we may so conduct ourselves as to merit a continuance of those blessings with which we have hitherto been favored."[40]

Weeks later, and again reaffirming his position that this new government under the Constitution was firmly based on a covenant with God, Washington would deliver an even more detailed and powerful testimony of this concept. Upon comparing this speech against what we have learned, particularly from the Scriptures, regarding the American Covenant, with its blessings and obligations, his chosen words are phenomenal. For, a close study of it reveals that Washington is telling the nation that it must obey God, be grateful to Him, repent, and implore

George Washington by Gilbert Stuart, oil-on-canvas, 1796

His help; and in return it will receive the constitutional and covenant blessings of *liberty, protection,* and *prosperity.* Declared Washington:

> Whereas it is the duty of all nations to acknowledge the providence of Almighty God, to *obey His will,* to *be grateful* for His benefits, and *humbly implore His protection* and favor....Now therefore I do recommend and assign Thursday the 26th day of November next to be devoted by the People of these States to the Service of that great and glorious Being, who is the beneficent Author of all the good that was, that is, or that will be. That we may then all unite in rendering unto Him our sincere and humble thanks, for His kind care and *protection* of the People

of this country previous to their becoming a Nation, for the single and manifold mercies, and the favorable interpositions of His providence, which we experienced in the course and conclusion of the late war, for the great degree of tranquility, union, *and plenty*, which we have enjoyed, for the peaceable and rational manner in which we have been enabled *to establish constitutions of government for our safety and happiness*, and particularly *the national One now lately instituted, for the civil and religious liberty with which we are blessed*, and the means we have of acquiring and diffusing useful knowledge and in general for all the great and various favors which He hath been pleased to confer upon us.

And also that we may then unite in most humbly *offering our prayers* and supplications to the Great Lord and Ruler of Nations, and beseech Him *to pardon our national and other transgressions, to enable us all, whether in public or private stations, to render our national government a blessing to all people*, by constantly being a government of wise, just and constitutional laws, discreetly and faithfully executed and obeyed, *to protect* and guide…all Nations…and to bless them with good government, peace and accord. To *promote the knowledge and practice of true religion*…and generally to grant unto all Mankind such a degree of *temporal prosperity* as he alone knows to be best. [41]

Washington knew what the nation needed to do in order to activate its blessings. If that were not enough to confirm his invocation of the American Covenant in this speech, he specifically called out, by name, the American Covenant blessings we might gain through our national worthiness: *liberty, protection,* and *prosperity,* even those building blocks required for a fullness of freedom unto eternal salvation. Furthermore, he clearly understood, and thus stated, that this covenant relationship was sealed up by the Constitution "now lately instituted, for the civil and religious liberty with which we are blessed." His understanding of the covenant ran so deep that he even declared that—in addition to religious liberty—the ultimate fruit of this constitutional endeavor would be "the knowledge and practice of true religion." It is simply astounding.

Eight years later, upon delivering his final address to the nation, before stepping down from the presidency, he would make one final plea for Americans to live up to the American Covenant. "Of all the dispositions and habits which lead to political prosperity," declared Washington, "religion and morality are indispensable supports. In vain would that man claim the tribute of patriotism who should labor to subvert these great pillars of happiness."[42]

Washington's repeated calls to the American Covenant —from the battlefields of war to the establishment and application of our Constitution—should not be lost on any one of us. We would do well as a nation to follow his exhortation today. For, if we do not adhere to Him who Washington calls "the Great Lord and Ruler of Nations," then we will—per the running theme of this book—fall into breach of covenant, lose the blessings of the Constitution, forfeit our liberties, and ultimately self-destruct.

Conclusion

In these last two chapters we have outlined how and why God and the inspired Founders of America chose to adopt what would become the U.S. Constitution. We have seen God's hand in the Constitution's creation, and we have seen His national covenant blessings and obligations embedded into the Constitution's content. Thus, we have confirmed yet again a powerful fulfillment of the ancient prophecies surrounding the American Covenant and the divine purposes this covenant represents.

With this historical foundation, perhaps we see more clearly why covenant leaders like Washington took their public oaths to protect and defend the Constitution by placing their left hand upon the Bible, their right arm being raised and forming a square. These gestures symbolize the divine nature of the Constitution and the solemnity with which our leaders entered into their office.

Our own national monuments in Washington D.C. also remind us constantly of this powerful connection between God and country. It is no coincidence that engraved in bronze upon the floor of the entrance to the U.S. National Archives, which houses the original Constitution and the Declaration of Independence, are the words of the famous

Supreme Court Sculptures, Moses.

national covenant obligations—the Ten Commandments.[43] This is a fitting memorial to the final resting place of the original Constitution.

Furthermore, along with other religious imagery decorating the U.S. Supreme Court building (which houses the guardians of the Constitution) we again see prominent

House Chamber, image of Moses

symbolism of the great and ancient national covenant. In no less than four locations in and around the building are depictions of Moses and the Ten Commandments (this imagery is at the center of the sculpture over the east portico of the building, on the bronze doors of the building, inside the courtroom itself, and engraved over the chair of the Chief Justice).[44] Similarly, perched upon the wall of Congress, overlooking the interior of the House chamber (where the Constitution is applied through lawmaking) is a large image of the Prophet Moses. Other ancient law-makers are depicted around the chamber as well, but all have their heads turned to Moses, who is the only full figured image and the only one that hangs directly in the middle of the room.[45] This is no coincidence. With our national covenant perspective, the significance of it all shines radiantly.

Furthermore, as seen throughout this book, and particularly throughout this chapter, the Bible also shines forth as a stunning reminder of the ancient Israelite prophecies of modern America—prophecies which have been fulfilled through the Constitution. Though many may wonder at the inclusion of political principles in the Scripture, the purpose of their existence has become clear to us. For this is the Scripture not only of individual covenants unto salvation, but also of the national covenant that supports them—today's American Covenant. And as we have seen the application of these scriptural-political instructions in the Constitution, we have yet another witness of the Constitution's greatness and divine nature under the covenant.

As a final witness and reminder of the Constitution's grand place in the eternal designs of God, we return to that founder, James Madison—even the Father of the Constitution, who, under God, initiated this building block of the covenant. It was Madison's personal testimony that there is no happiness without virtue.[46] He declared that in our many worldly endeavors, we should not "neglect to have our names enrolled in the Annals of Heaven," and that we should season our lives with "a little Divinity now and then," which he said would make us "more precious than fine gold." And finally, Madison expressed the importance of "always keep[ing] the Ministry obliquely in View whatever your profession be," that we might always be prepared to become "fervent Advocates in the cause of Christ."[47] And this is exactly what Madison was, particularly while playing his indispensable role in the creation of the Constitution. Even as an old and frail man at the age of seventy, he reiterated this testimony, stating that Christianity was the "best and purest religion."[48] He had certainly done his part in ensuring its development through establishing the political foundations that would support and protect it.

All these things, including the above outlined history of the Constitution, from its creation to its content, have truly borne witness of the principal argument of these last two chapters: that God inspired the Constitution as a divine tool of the American Covenant so that the foundations of His church and gospel on the earth might be fortified and that His work and glory might roll forth. Based on all the contributing evidence provided above, it becomes clear that the Constitution holds the distinction of being perhaps the only governmental document in the history of the world with so many endorsements, approvals, and interventions derived directly from the hand of God. Let us never forget this fact, and let us never forget what the Lord has given us through this heaven-sent document.

Indeed, we have now witnessed the details of how God, knowing that Satan's war plan was to destroy the agency and liberty of man (see Revelation 12:7-8), created a powerful defense. This divine defense was the Constitution. More specifically, God provided this defense by lacing, throughout the Constitution, the covenant promises of *liberty, protection,* and *prosperity.* If we live up to our obligations, also put forth in association with the Constitution, then a fullness of these blessings, and thus a fullness of liberty, will be ours. Only then will the ability to access the principles of the gospel forever be secured.

Let us see the Constitution in this gospel light—let us see it as the covenant it is—that we might better adhere to it, sustain it, and promote it. Let it be an ensign to all God's children, both at home and abroad.

On September 17, 1787, after the delegates at the Constitutional Convention had sufficiently prepared their sacred document, they signed it. But, as Article VII of the Constitution required, the states would have to consider it individually, and ratify it for themselves before it could become the "Supreme Law of the Land" (Article VI). The debates abounded in state legislative houses for months upon months. Finally, enough states approved it and ratification was achieved. In light of what we now know concerning the eternal blessings that would flow out of this Constitution, it is quite fitting that the prominent founder, Benjamin Rush, after hearing of its ratification, declared: "I am as perfectly satisfied that the union of the states, in its form and adoption, is as much the work of divine providence as any of the miracles recorded in the old and new testament were the effects of a divine power. 'Tis done! We have become a nation."[49]

ENDNOTES

[1] Chris Stewart and Ted Stewart, *Seven Tipping Points the Saved the World* (Salt Lake City: Shadow Mountain, 2011), 12.

[2] Refer to Jeremiah 31:33; see also Chapter 2 for how this prophecy, and others like it, likely applies to American Covenant-makers.

[3] Bennett, *Spirit of America*, 366.

[4] Feiler, *America's Prophet*, 92-93.

[5] Bennett, *America: The Last Best Hope*, Vol. I, 130.

[6] J. Reuben Clark, as quoted in Dallin Oaks, "The Divinely Inspired Constitution," *Ensign*, Feb. 1992, 69.

[7] Thomas Jefferson, as quoted in Monk, 117.

[8] Oaks, "The Divinely Inspired Constitution," 71.

[9] From Gettysburg Address, as quoted in Bennett, *America: The Last Best Hope*, Vol. I, 368.

[10] Joseph Ellis makes this point in his audio lecture series, *Patriots, Brotherhood of the American Revolution*. Lectures recorded by Recorded Books, Inc, and Barnes and Noble Publishing: 2004. Study Guide lecture 7.

[11] See Cleon Skousen, *The Five Thousand Year Leap* (Washington D.C.: The National Center for Constitutional Studies, 1981), 17.

[12] Feiler, *America's Prophet*, 94.

[13] Feiler, *America's Prophet*, 94-95.

[14] James Madison, *Federalist #10*, as quoted in George C. Edwards III, et al, *Government in America* (New York: Pearson-Longman, 2004), 703.

[15] Mark Steyn, "Helium Diplomacy," *National Review*, May 4, 2009, 56; study also quoted in Mark Hitchcock, *The Late Great United States* (New York, Multnomah Press, 2009), 75.

[16] Refer to Linda Monk, *The Words We Live By, Your Annotated Guide to the Constitution* (New York, Hyperion, 2003), 171-172; See also *Foundations For Teaching Economics: The Constitution-An Economic Document*, available at www.fte.org/teachers/programs/history/lessons/lesson02.htm.

[17] Refer to *History of the U.S. Customs Service at the Port of New York*, available at www.oldnycustomshouse.gov/history/.

[18] A list of the wealthiest persons ranked in history is available at http://en.wikipedia.org/wiki/Wealthy_historical_figures_2008. Details concerning the data can also be found in Malcolm Gladwell, *Outliers, The Story of Success* (New York, Little, Brown and Co., 2008) 56-61.

[19] William J. Bernstein, *The Birth of Plenty* (NewYork: McGraw-Hill, 2004), vii-viii (preface).

[20] Joan DeBardeleben, "Russia," *Introduction to Comparative Politics*, ed. Mark Kesselman, et al (New York: Houghton Mifflin Co., 2007), 372-373; Thomas Remington, "Politics in Russia," *Comparative Politics Today*, ed. Gabriel A. Almond, et al (New York: Longman, 2010), 368.

[21] See Jason DeParle and Sabrina Travernise, "Unwed Mothers Now a Majority Before Age 30," *New York Times*, Feb. 18, 2012, A1; W. Bradford Wilcox and others, "No Money, No Honey, No Church: The Deinstitutionalization of Religious Life among the White Working Class," available at www.virignia.edu/marriageproject/pdfs/Religion_WorkingPaper.pdf.; Jessica Ravits, CNN, "Out of Wedlock Births Hit Record High," CNN, available at http://articles.cnn.com/2009-04-08/living/out.of.wedlock.births;

[22] Edmund Burke, as quoted in Lynn D. Wardle, "The Constitution as Covenant," *BYU Studies* 27, no.3, 1987, 9.

[23] Franklin, as quoted in Skousen, *The Five Thousand Year Leap*, 49, 55.

[24] D. Todd Christofferson, "Moral Discipline," General Conference Address, October 2009, available at www.lds.org/conference/talk.

[25] Jefferson (from letter written in November 1820), as quoted in Cousins, *In God We Trust*, 156. Emphasis added.

[26] Madison, as quoted in *The Federalist No.55*, available at the Yale Avalon Project, www.avalon.law.yale.edu/18thCentury/fed55.asp.

[27] Madison, as quoted in Skousen, *The Five Thousand Year Leap*, 54.

[28] John Adams, as quoted in Charles Frances Adams, *The Works of John Adams, Second President of the United States* (Boston: Little Brown and Company, 1854), Vol. IX, p.229, to the officers of the First Brigade of the Third Division of the Militia of Massachusetts on October 11, 1798, emphasis added.

[29] Adams, as quoted in Peter Marshal and David Manuel, *The Light and the Glory* (Grand Rapids: Revell, 2009), 12.

[30] Adams, as quoted in Newt Gingrich, *Rediscovering God in America* (Nashville: Integrity House, 2006), 92.

[31] Sam Adams, as quoted in Marshal and Manuel, 11.

[32] Nelson Burr, et al, eds, *A Critical Biography of Religion in America*, Vol.4 (Princeton, N.J.: Princeton University Press, 1961), 4:969-70.

[33] Wardle, 9.

[34] Skousen, *The Five Thousand year Lea*, 75-76.

[35] Consider the words from one of the first state constitutions in America, Delaware: *Through Divine goodness, all men have by nature the rights of worshipping and serving their Creator according to the dictates of their conscience.* Or consider the words from the most recent state constitution—that of Hawaii. This document recognizes God in its preamble, expressing how the people are *grateful for Divine guidance.* The state of Washington similarly recognizes God in its constitution, stating that *We the people...[are] grateful to the Supreme Ruler of the Universe for our liberties.* Kansas and Florida agree, both formally extending thanks in their respective constitutions to *Almighty God*, and both recognizing that it is from Him that all blessings of freedom are derived. Such references in state constitutions are certainly not the exception, but the rule. For a complete list of what the many state constitutions say about God as their political foundation, refer to www.undergodthebook.com.

[36] George Washington, as quoted in Bennett, *The Spirit of America* (New York: Simon and Schuster, 1997), 382; also available at www.yale.edu/lawweb/avalon/presiden/inaug/wash1.htm.

[37] George Washington, as quoted in Bennett, *The Spirit of America*, 382.

[38] *New York Daily Advisor*, April 23, 1789, as quoted in David Barton, "The Constitutional Convention," *David Barton's Wallbuilders (blog)*, *July 22, 2010*, *http://davidbartonwallbuilders.typepad.com/blog/2010/07/the- constitutional-convention-by-david-barton.html (accessed June 23, 2011)*

[39] Jonathan Cahn, *The Harbinger* (Lake Mary: Front Line, 2011), 205-206.

[40] George Washington (September 1789), in a letter to Samuel Langdon, as quoted in Janice T. Connell, *The Spiritual Journey of George Washington* (New York: Hatherleigh Press, 2007), 105.

[41] George Washington (October 1789), as quoted in Novak and Novak, *Washington's God* (New York: Basic Books, 2006),144-145.

[42] George Washington, as quoted in *Address of George Washington, Preparatory to His Declination* (Baltimore: George and Henry S. Keating, 1796), 22-23; also quoted in Waldman, *Founding Faith*, 60.

[43] Gingrich, *Rediscovering God in America*, 27.

[44] Gingrich, 87

[45] Feiler, *America's Prophet*, 283.

[46] Madison, as quoted in Skousen, *The Five Thousand Year Leap*, 54.

[47] Waldman, 98.

[48] Waldman, 99.

[49] Benjamin Rush, as quoted in Meacham, *American Gospel*, 99.

One Nation Under God, by Michael Bedard
Courtesy of Bedard Fine Arts.

CHAPTER 13

A CHARGE TO KEEP: LIVING THE COVENANT TODAY

A small child holds a miniature American flag in the air. Together with throngs of people—of differing backgrounds, races, and religions—she watches the Fourth of July parade. An Army band plays *The Battle Hymn of the Republic*. Cheers are heard as United States fighter jets fly close overhead in dramatic and stunning formation. A good-hearted civil servant walks and waves to the crowd. School children march and sing *God Bless America*. Civic and Charitable organizations follow with smiles on their faces. *The Pledge of Allegiance* is recited, even that sacramental symbol of the covenant which bonds us together "under God." An invocation is given in the name of the God of this land, and is received by audible voices declaring reverently, "amen." This is America. A sense that we are an almost chosen people is felt. The Spirit testifies. We believe the sacred truth that the Spirit of God is also the spirit of freedom. But what is at the core of this American spiritualism? Though we seek an explanation, do we comprehend the magnitude of it all?

Do we comprehend that what we feel has its roots in ancient prophecy—prophecy derived from Abraham, Jacob, Moses, Jeremiah, Isaiah and many others? Do we understand that few other lands in the history of the world have been seen so often in vision—have been so long-awaited for—than this land America? Do we oft consider that all of this occurred by the hands of the Almighty, that He might have a place to initiate a marvelous work among *this* people? Indeed, He established this choice land so that *all* His children might achieve eternal life and fill the measure of their creation.

Too often we merely recognize, but only with a glance and nod, this American Covenant story and all that it implies. However, in that the national covenant holds a preeminent place in the scriptural and historical account of God's children on the earth, it should also hold a preeminent place in our hearts. As we read the Scriptures and ponder our history, may we see with new eyes the powerful role this national covenant plays.

Christian scholars have pointed out that the Old Testament "is a book directed to, and recorded for, the Israelite nation in general—not the worthy [followers] who may have been among them. The words of the prophets in it are public pronouncements to their wayward society, not their private teachings to those who had risen above the sins of their generation."[1] Indeed, the Old Testament is the national covenant, which explains why the Founding Fathers of America, while building the nation, quoted it more than any other source (including literature from the Classical and Enlightenment periods). More particularly, the Founders' most quoted book of scripture was Deuteronomy (which does more to lay out the covenant law and obligation, as connected to the "Promised Land," than any other).[2] The New Testament, on the other hand, is a record of gospel principles pertaining to the individual and individual salvation. We need them both!

In that the national covenant element clearly represents a large portion of the Scripture, perhaps it is time we pay closer attention to it. The Old Testament was given to us as a gift from God, to help our nation come unto Him and his covenant. Indeed, it was written for a people (us!) who would live out Old Testament history all over again and would therefore benefit from the lessons learned anciently.

Indeed, what is American history if not Old Testament history? American history, after all, is the story of a chosen people, with ties to the blood and promises of Israel, who were given a promised land by covenant. It is a story of this people's struggle to live righteously as a nation so as to be blessed with the covenant blessings (*liberty, protection* and *prosperity*) required to realize God's work and glory. It is a story of war against evil and oppression. It is also a story of miracles and conversions. It is a story of prophecy and fulfillment, a story of God's efforts to save His people. And at the core of this story is the one thing that ties all elements together, the one thing that, if adhered to, will allow the blessings of *liberty, protection* and *prosperity* to thrive, thus securing the opportunity for salvation for this and future generations. At the core of this story is God's holy covenant.

In many ways, we are *living* scripture. As was the case with the Israelites of old, God is watching, encouraging, and prompting us to choose the right. The question is, *do we realize this?* For years we have gloried in America, celebrating its history as if staring at the image of beautifully splashed colors —red, white and blue—of an autostereograph ("magic eye" image), but only seeing it in two dimensions. This book was written with the intention of encouraging the reader to stare intently enough to realize there is a deeper, multi-dimensional image. Beyond seeing this image, it is hoped that the reader will further realize that he/she is not only looking, but standing squarely inside. Indeed, we are living scripture. Did the Israelites generally understand that they were living scripture when they made decisions that led to their demise? If we fail to realize it ourselves, might our ultimate fate look like theirs often did?

The American Covenant story we have journeyed through—from discovery to revolution to nation building—is not yet over. So what do we, as Americans, do now? We draw on the lessons from the Scriptures, particularly from the Old Testament, and from our own national history, and we *live* the covenant. The lessons are vast and profound, and are left to the reader to flesh out completely. However, we offer here certain principles to be followed.

1. Keep the Commandments and Serve the God of the Land

The Scriptures cannot lay it out any clearer to the nation. As detailed throughout this work, if we keep the commandments, by maintaining a level of righteousness and basic morality, and as we serve God by maintaining the blessings of the Constitution He has provided, we will receive *liberty*, *protection*, and *prosperity* in furtherance of His plan of salvation. This level of righteousness should, at the very least, mean adherence to the Ten Commandments. These are standards easily understood and accepted through the light of conscience, which is given to all men—standards that can be accepted by all, regardless of personal religion.

This is very basic arithmetic. The proof of its function is laid out before us in Scripture and in our own history. We *will* be preserved and blessed, but *only* as we obey. Period. Conversely, Scripture and history also teach that if we fail, and thus lose the blessings, we are at the mercy of evil—evil that influences and utilizes evil men to oppress and drive a gap between us and our Maker. The scourges brought to bear by national unrighteousness in the promised land are as clearly stated in scripture and history as are the blessings for righteousness (read, for example, Leviticus 26 and Deuteronomy 4-6). Promised lands have different standards. Where much is given, much is required. We, of all people, have been given much. We simply cannot risk unrighteousness.

It is our choice.

2. Promote Separation of Church and State, Not Separation of God and State

The one being, above all other beings, who cherishes man's right to choose his own destiny, is God the Eternal Father. Consider what He has done, the sacrifices He has made, for liberty and personal choice to reign. To take Him out of government, for fear that somehow His existence there might threaten liberty (as secularists claim), represents one of the most ironic and wrongheaded political suggestions of all time. Only *with* Him will full liberty exist. Without His blessings and protection, the adversary will take the reins. Then we shall see how the secularist likes his "liberty."

The Founders understood this. They understood that the great constitutional separation had to do with building a wall between government and any one denomination—for any one religion in the hands of the government would certainly prove a useful tool of oppression. However, to misrepresent these constitutional restraints (as secularists do), claiming that it was the Founders' intent to keep God out of government, is simply mindboggling to any honest student of history, and frankly should be embarrassing for the one making such a claim. George Washington accused anyone unwilling to recognize God in American government as "worse than an infidel."[3]

Constitutional scholar David Barton explains how secular jurists' misinterpretation of the First Amendment's *Establishment Clause*—which prohibits the government's "establishment of religion"—is at the root of this problem:

> [The Court] reinterpreted [the First Amendment] without regard to either historical context or previous judicial decisions. The result was that the Court abandoned the traditional constitutional

415

meaning of "religion" as a single denomination or system of worship and instead substituted a new "modern" concept which even now remains vague and nebulous, having changed several times in recent years.[4]

By reinterpreting the word "religion" secularists have blurred the lines. Instead of understanding it how the Founders did—that government cannot establish "religion," meaning the government cannot establish a particular *religious denomination*—secularists have turned the whole thing on its head. Denying what the Founders taught in word and deed, they claim that "religion" means anything and everything up to and including God Himself. This, accordingly, leads them to erroneously (and tragically!) conclude that the presence of God *anywhere* in government means the Constitution has been violated.

In light of the fact that George Washington understood and promoted the *true* meaning of the First Amendment, we should consider the deeper significance of the existence of a little known chapel dedicated to him. *The Washington Chapel*, as it is called, is most relevant due to where it is housed—it sits within the U.S. Capitol Building. The chapel is a private chamber for U.S. legislators for their use in "prayer and meditation." The existence of this chapel within the halls of congress

The Washington Chapel in the U.S. Capitol Building

is the perfect symbolic reminder of what it means to be one nation under God. On the wall of the chapel is a depiction of Washington kneeling in prayer, under the inscription, "This Nation Under God." A prayer is inscribed in the window: "Preserve me, God, for in Thee do I put my trust."[5]

This book need add nothing more here than the enormous amount of evidence already offered with regards to the Founders' belief about God's place in American history and government. To understand it as the secularist does today not only denies history, but represents nothing less than ignorance in its fullness—ignorance that if left to fester will destroy the American Covenant. To fight this ignorance, we must reintroduce God's place in American history books, rather than follow the trend to take Him and His many miracles out. We need to follow the instruction of President Ronald Reagan: "[Americans] must seek Divine guidance in the policies of their government and the promulgation of their laws."[6]

Many readers of this book might have, at one point or another in their lives, wondered how it was possible for the Israelites to have so easily forgotten the wonders and signs that God had blessed them with (such as the parting of the Red Sea). Within a few generations of the miracles (or even within the same generation that witnessed the power), these heavenly signs were somehow cast away and all but lost. We might say to ourselves, *well, I would never have forgotten such miracles.* And yet, how many of us have forgotten our own miracles? How many of us have read accounts in this book wondering why they had never heard them before? The sad truth is, we are forgetting as the ancient Israelites did.

And so, we must fight to put God back into our history where He belongs. For without Him, we have no history—at least not one that makes any sense. Let us follow the example of presidential hopeful, Governor Mitt Romney, who declared, "I will take care to separate the affairs of government from any religion, but I will not separate us from 'the God who gave us liberty.'"[7]

3. Participate in Government

Ours is a living government, just as the Constitution is a living document, able to change for better or worse, per the decisions of the people. Therefore, our righteous political participation is paramount to America's success. Traditionally, voter turnout in America is lucky to reach 40 percent, while other nations find themselves in a much higher range. Good people in America often feel it is their God-ordained duty to go to church, serve their fellowmen, and live their personal covenants according to their faith. But they often feel no such responsibility to their nation. Remember, this is a covenant land. Our participation is recorded in Heaven. In addition to our personal covenant, we are equally responsible under our *national* covenant.

Participation is, of course, bigger than just the vote. It is also about educating ourselves and others, praying for the nation and its leaders, and involving ourselves in a myriad of other activities that lead to sound and virtuous policies designed to preserve liberty and salvation.

As Edmund Burke declared, "When bad men combine, the good must associate; else they will fall one by one, an unpitied sacrifice in a contemptible struggle."[8] Indeed, as has been said so often, all that is necessary for the triumph of evil is for good people to sit there and do nothing.

4. Do Not Legislate Immorality

In order to maintain the freedom to choose, we should not legislate morality, except in cases where *not* doing so puts innocent people in harm's way. Likewise, we should *never* legislate immorality. We should live and let live, of course. But we cannot legislate sin and be in good standing with the Almighty. In the name of liberty and equal rights, many have favored legalizing (and thus recognizing and approving) what the God of this land has deemed sinful behavior. While always careful to supply as much freedom to all Americans as possible, let us be mindful of what happened to the nation the last time we legislated, codified, and slapped our national seal on immoral behavior. It led to the heaven-backed scourge and vexation of civil war.

Abraham Lincoln

Abraham Lincoln understood the American Covenant like few others. And he learned, in no uncertain terms, that the war he presided over was a heavenly-induced calamity to purge the American people of iniquity. "The Almighty has his own purposes," declared Lincoln in his Second Inaugural Address.

> "Woe unto the world because of offenses! for it must needs be that offenses come; but woe to that man by whom the offense cometh." If we shall suppose that American slavery is one of those offenses which, in the providence of God, must needs come, but which, having continued through his appointed time, he now wills to remove, and that he gives to both North and South this terrible war, as the woe due to those by whom the offense came, shall we discern therein any departure from those divine attributes which the believers in a living God always ascribe to him? Fondly do we hope—fervently do we pray—that this mighty scourge of war may speedily pass away. Yet, if God wills that it continue until all the wealth piled by the bondman's two hundred and fifty years of unrequited toil shall be sunk, and until every drop of blood drawn with the lash shall be paid by another

drawn with the sword, as was said three thousand years ago, so still it must be said, "The judgments of the Lord are true and righteous altogether."[9]

Lincoln's solution was as true and real as was his identification of the problem:

> It behooves us, then, to humble ourselves before the offended Power, to confess our national sins, and to pray for clemency and forgiveness... [L]et us then rest humbly in the hope authorized by the Divine teachings, that the united cry of the nation will be heard on high, and answered with blessings no less than the pardon of our national sins, and the restoration of our now divided and suffering country...[10]

This is a God-ordained land. And while He has promised to be forgiving, He will *not* be mocked.

5. Be Slow to Political Wrath

While we need to stand resolute on the principles that should govern our land, let us check our emotions and be slow to wrath against our brothers and sisters of the covenant, who may sit on the opposite side of the political aisle. The building and improving of our nation is not some sort of sporting event where biased and *unfounded* fault-finding and "trash talking" is accepted and encouraged. This is a covenant with the Lord, and should be dealt with respectfully and reverently. At times righteous indignation will be required, but too often we create "straw man" arguments that falsely accuse and incite hate and revenge. We then lay these false accusations upon those we deem political enemies, then we tear our opponents down. This behavior is both dishonest and unhelpful. It never ceases to amaze me that when "our guy" is in office, we are appalled at the wicked slurs laid at his feet, then when "their guy" is elected, we do the same in our turn.

I often tell my political science students that the key to a successful argument (and to an "A" paper) is to get to the root of your opposing argument. Consider what your political opposite would argue, and give that argument a fair and honest try. You will most likely still disagree, which is fine. Our nation was, after all, built on debate. However, you might also realize why the opposition believes the way they do. You may realize that your political opposite ("their guy") is not the evil villain you once thought him to be.

We must work together as brothers and sisters of the covenant, finding commonalties for progress when possible and voting out of office those better suited for different employment. However, let us not obstruct the entire process (as we so often do) simply because we adhere not to the council of James: "Let every man be swift to hear, slow to speak, slow to wrath: For the wrath of man worketh not the righteousness of God" (James 1:19-20).

Contention is of the Devil. The last thing we need as we build upon our national covenant is to invite in the Evil One, who has, since the days of discovery and settlement, been doing all he can to get into the ring. And yet we invite him in daily, as political contention opens his cage. Once free to roam, he will blind us to our covenant purposes.

6. Let Not Your Heart Be Troubled, Neither Let It Be Afraid

When Moses led the Israelites out of bondage, the revolution they were participating in—and the freedom and independence that came with deliverance—began to scare them. Some longed to return to Egyptian slavery (see Numbers 14:2-3). The same has been happening in America, and it represents a tremendous threat to the covenant today.

Professor Michael Walzer explains this concept in his book, *Exodus and Revolution*. According to Walzer, the story of Moses and the Israelites invented the pattern of revolution:

oppression, liberation, social contract (covenant), then new society. Once they entered into the national covenant, which delivered them into freedom, the Israelites realized something: *they now had a responsibility.* They were now required to *live* the

covenant. They were required to *develop* faith in God and His promises. This was more than many of the Israelites wanted to take on. Perhaps it was easier to simply sit back and let the Pharaoh feed them, direct them, and own them. According to Walzer, "The childish and irresponsible slave or subject is free in ways the republican citizen can never be."[11]

The children of Israel refuse to employ simple faith by looking to Moses' staff for healing.

Americans today are backsliding in a similar way. Summarizing Walzer's conclusions, author Bruce Feiler explains how "a near perfect example of [Moses'] revolution occurred in America. In both cases, the moment of liberation—when the Israelites cross the Red Sea; when the Americans win the war—is not a moment of genuine freedom...The newly freed slaves remained trapped in a web of servility...They have the misplaced notion that freedom means lack of responsibility." The recently liberated ones, in both cases, will become free "only insofar as they accepted the discipline of freedom; the obligation to live up to a common standard and to take responsibility for their own actions." Concludes Feiler: "The covenant, in other words, is the linchpin of freedom. The two pillars of the Moses story— freedom and law—have been present in America since the Pilgrims were reconfirmed in America's founding decade."[12]

Martin Luther King Jr.—an American leader who knew a thing or two about revolution and its consequences— perhaps summed it up best: "We usually think of freedom *from* something, but freedom is also *to* something. It is not only breaking loose from some evil force, but it is reaching up for a higher force. Freedom from evil is slavery to goodness."[13]

Like Israelites of old, Americans are fearful. And so, instead of turning to God and covenant, they turn to Pharaoh —they turn to the state. When they do this, there will always be a political faction willing to fill that Pharaoh-like role. There will always be a faction willing to be our "protector," "caretaker," "nanny." They will take us by the hand. But they will not lead us to God and salvation. Instead, they will lead us into the Evil One's trap, even into a world where personal liberty is quashed and where decisions are made for us. Perhaps to some it feels easier, less stressful, but in the end it is damnation, or in other words, it is a cessation of spiritual progression. For, under that system, mankind, placing its trust in the arm of the flesh, is unable to show God its faith and therefore stands unworthy of the covenant blessings. All the while, the state grows and grows. Liberty, in turn, is diminished. Before we know it, we cannot even worship God as we please. The gap between mankind and Deity widens. Personal salvation becomes a scarcity.

We must learn from the mistakes of our ancient cousins of the Old World. We must not be deceived by the Evil One's cunning plan. Instead, we must allow God to bless us through the liberty and law He offers by way of the covenant—it is the only way to salvation. It requires faith and work. But the attendant blessings are worth it. Salvation with our Maker is worth it! Let us heed the council of the Savior Jesus Christ: "Peace I leave with you, my peace I give unto you: not as the world giveth, give I unto you. Let not your heart be troubled, neither let it be afraid" (John 14:27).

7. Deliver the Bible

While we have proven that the national covenant has been written into the hearts of the citizenry, past and present, too many details concerning the covenant blessings and obligations have not yet found access to the populace in general. They need the Bible. Conversion to the Bible, in addition to the blessings of personal salvation, carry also the added benefit of delivering the words of the national covenant.

Let us consider this upon contemplating our missionary efforts. Let us get the Bible into as many hands and hearts as possible, that the Judeo-Christian ideals of the national covenant might be better lived.

8. Take the Blessings Unto Every Nation

In that this book so closely connects gospel blessings to America alone, the critic might feel we are being a bit myopic with our approach to the gospel—for the gospel was not designed for one land only, but for *all* the world. The critic is correct. The nations of the world have a preeminent place in this entire story, though their place falls outside the scope of this particular study. So much could be said of this worldwide story that it is worthy of its own book—a book that should be written. The prophecies and promises of the national covenant do, after all, pertain to all of God's children everywhere.

The prophet Isaiah, as postulated in Chapter 2, perhaps saw and prophesied of the American-Israelites. Indeed, it is possible that he saw a second Promised Land in the New World. If so, perhaps there is something to his great prophecy, wherein he predicted that "it shall come to pass in the last days that the mountain of the Lord's house shall be established in the top of the mountains, and shall be exalted above the hills, and all nations shall flow unto it" (Isaiah 2:2). Could this be America? Even a place in the *last days* where Christ's church could be established, where Christianity could flourish, where the nations of the earth could seek and find salvation? Remember, Jacob-Israel's promise to Joseph/Ephraim (in Genesis 49) included a land of "everlasting hills." Perhaps they *were* talking about

America. If so, the following words of this same Isaiah prophecy (even the words in the very next verse) are profound and telling: "For out of Zion [America?] shall go forth the law, and the word of the Lord from Jerusalem" (See Isaiah 2:3). The Bible—*the word of the Lord*—came from Jerusalem, even the original Promised Land. And *the law*—the Constitution given by God in the *last days* to protect and proliferate *the word*—came from Zion-America, even the second Promised Land!

This sacred law has indeed gone forth from the United States. It has gone forth (and continues to go forth) to South America, to Asia, to Russia, to the Middle East, and everywhere in-between. It has and is filling the earth. And when it enters these nations, history has taught us that it leaves liberty, followed by the advent of Christian principles, in its glorious wake. The law has gone forth through U.S. influence, sometimes by example, sometimes by diplomatic encouragement, and other times by war (when necessary). Some of the most powerful American Covenant experiences are found in the accounts that make up these miraculous events.

Too many fail to see this vision. They fail to understand that the Constitution was created not for America alone, but belongs to all mankind, that it was delivered by Heaven for the rights and protection of all flesh. They fail to recognize that Satan has brought his war over liberty and salvation to the earth, that he has bought up armies and navies to oppress with blood and horror. They do not see that God has, in these last days, called a righteous army (a literal military force) of His own to defeat this spiritual and physical threat to His plan.

Perhaps we do a disservice to ourselves and our covenant by failing to always include the singing of the third verse of the National Anthem:

Oh, thus be it ever, when free men shall stand
Between their loved homes and war's desolation!
Blest with victory and peace, may the heaven-rescued land
Praise the Power that hath made and preserved us a nation!

425

> *Then conquer we must, when our cause it is just*
> *And this be our motto: "In God is our trust!"*

One of our greatest American Covenant leaders was Ronald Reagan. He understood this principle clearly. He manifested his knowledge of the covenant when he declared the following as President of the United Stated before a nationwide television audience:

> How that cry echoes down through the centuries, a cry for all children of the world, a cry for peace, for a world of love and understanding. And it is the hope of heeding such words—the call for freedom and peace spoken by a chosen people in a promised land, the call spoken by the Nazarene carpenter.... Let us then thank God for all his blessings to this nation, and ask Him for his help and guidance so that we might continue the work of peace and foster the hope of a world where human freedom is enshrined.[14]

On another occasion Reagan similarly declared, "I, in my own mind, have thought of America as a place in the divine scheme of things that was set aside as a promised land....I believe that God...has always...kept an eye on our land and guided it as a promised land."* He concluded, "I believe we were preordained to carry the torch of freedom for the world."[15] These verbalized thoughts were certainly not the exception to his normal rhetoric on America's place in the world. He spoke often of this vision. More importantly, he turned his words and vision into action. Utilizing the covenant

Ronald Reagan

---

* During his inaugural ceremony, Reagan raised his arm to square to take his presidential oath of office. He placed his hand upon the following biblical passage: "If my people, which are called by my name, shall humble themselves, and pray, and seek my face, and turn from their wicked ways; then will I hear from heaven, and will forgive their sin, and will heal their land" (2 Chronicles 7:14). See Paul Kengor, *God and Ronald Reagan*, 158.

blessings of the land, he brought freedom to the world. He paved the way, under God and covenant, for the principles of liberty to penetrate lands that had been hijacked for years by tyranny and by the adversary. Unfettered Christianity now flourishes in many of those lands.

Ronald Reagan understood something else about the Promised Land he presided over. He understood that there was one place on earth that needed support like no other. He understood America's divinely ordained obligations to Israel. "The people of Israel and America are historic partners in the global quest for dignity and freedom," declared Reagan in 1987. "We will always remain at each other's side."[16]

One of the first American Covenant-makers who came to the rescue of Israel was President Harry Truman. In 1948, Truman was the first national leader in the entire world to recognize the state of Israel's claim to sovereignty. This prompted other nation-states to follow suite—Israel was then officially recognized, and thus achieved, its national sovereignty. Like Reagan, Truman understood the covenant. "I do not think that anyone can study the history of this nation of ours," declared Truman, "without becoming convinced that Divine Providence has played a great part in it."

Harry Truman

> I have a feeling that God has created us and brought us to our present position of power and strength for some great purpose. It is not given to us to know fully what that purpose is. But I think we may be sure of one thing. And that is that our country is intended to do all it can, in cooperation with other nations, to help create peace and preserve peace in the world. It is given to us to defend the spiritual values—the moral code—against the vast forces of evil that seek to destroy them.[17]

It is interesting to note that those leaders—like Reagan and Truman—who clearly understood the American Covenant were the same leaders who supported Israel. Conversely, those American leaders who clearly *do not* understand the covenant, *do not* support Israel. This is no coincidence. It is imperative that we elect leaders who understand, so that the ancient prophecy can be fulfilled: "And he shall set up an ensign for the nations, and shall assemble the outcasts of Israel, and gather together the dispersed of Judah...The envy also of Ephraim shall depart, and the adversaries of Judah shall be cut off: Ephraim shall not envy Judah, and Judah shall not vex Ephraim" (Isaiah 11:13).

In the biblical account we learn of how Joseph is taken to a foreign land (Egypt). From there, he becomes God's instrument in assisting and restoring his brothers (the other tribes) when they find themselves in deep despair. This is a type and shadow of things to come. The pattern would be repeated. Joseph's seed, in modern times, would likewise be taken to a foreign land (America). From there, Joseph's people have become an instrument in God's hands to assist and restore other tribes and peoples (particularly Israel) who may, from time to time, find themselves in deep despair. May we, like Joseph of old, be willing.

In sum, our covenant, namely the Constitution, is this nation's most important export. Through this export, principles of liberty have created the fertile ground in which the gospel has and will flourish throughout the world, bringing eternal salvation to all mankind everywhere. Let us, therefore, cut through the godless misrepresentations and half truths surrounding American foreign policy—let us support righteous efforts to fight tyranny and export the sacred law, that it might *go forth out of Zion*.

Notwithstanding the existence of the covenant, with all its blessings and obligations, do we have hope that it can be sufficiently lived? Do we have hope that America can be that nation God intended for it to be? Unfortunately, we live in a time of despair. Many good Americans tend to believe that we should just hunker down with our food storage and accept the inevitable: that this nation is in decline, that the end is near. *Let if fall*, they say, and hasten the Second Coming of Christ. But this is wrong! The Lord did not give this land and this covenant with the expectation that we should ever give up. To the contrary, His only commandments relevant to this issue charge us to maintain and build upon the nation—to build upon the covenant.

Let us have hope! After all, despite our many ills, America is still a land worthy of hope. The most recent data suggest that 83 percent of Americans belong to a religion, 59 percent pray regularly, 80 percent are absolutely sure there is a God, and 60 percent are absolutely sure there is a heaven.[18] These statistics, it should be noted, drastically stand out in a world of nations (our European cousins among them) whose numbers in percentages struggle to reach half of those reported for America (as cited above).[19]

In June 2002, when a federal judge ruled that the "under God" clause in the Pledge of Allegiance was unconstitutional, the nation was outraged. Both houses of the U.S. Congress immediately halted important business and drafted a resolution condemning the decision. The resolution was passed unanimously in the Senate, and almost unanimously (with the exception of three members) in the House. But that was not all; members of Congress also immediately gathered upon the steps of the Capitol to recite, with pride, the Pledge "under God." This only reflected the sentiments all around the nation. The ruling was, needless to say, overturned.[20]

Furthermore, statistics are clear that Americans put their faith into action. For example, charitable donations in the United States (not including the colossal amount of service hours offered by Americans) was twice as much as the next most charitable nation (the United Kingdom).[21] And need we even mention the amount of blood and treasure America has spent over the years in fighting world oppressors and delivering freedom to the innocent everywhere, all under God's plan of liberty and salvation? Indeed, there is reason to hope for America's future under the covenant.

★ ★ ★ ★

In conclusion, let us, as a nation, adhere to the American Covenant. May we stand by our covenant leaders, who have throughout our history, admonished us again and again. As a representative sample of such invocations, consider the words from Moses' farewell address to *his* nation under the same covenant (from Deuteronomy 30), which has been repeated for America. In the spirit of all our covenant leaders, these words have indeed been continually repeated by the likes of John Winthrop (while standing in 1630 on the ship that brought the first modern-day covenant-makers to America), by patriots of the American Revolution (particularly after they secured independence), by Martin Luther King Jr. (who repeated these words the night before he was killed in 1968), and by Ronald Reagan (who boldly repeated this covenant language at the base of the Statue of Liberty on its centennial birthday in 1986):

> See, I have set before you this day life and good, death and adversity. For I command you this day to love the Lord your God, to walk in his ways, and to keep his commandments. But if you turn away, you shall certainly perish; you shall not long endure on the soil that you are crossing the Jordan to enter. I have put before you life and death, blessing and curse. Choose life —that you and your offspring shall live. That you may love the Lord your God, and that you may obey his voice, and that you may cleave unto him: for he is your life, and the length of your days: that you may dwell in

the land which the Lord swore unto your fathers, to Abraham, to Isaac, and to Jacob.[22]

If my people...shall humble themselves, and pray, and seek my face, and turn from their wicked ways; then will I hear from heaven, and will forgive their sin, and will heal their land (2 chronicles 7:14).

ENDNOTES

[1] Kent P. Jackson, "Foretelling the Coming of Jesus," Richard Neitzel Holzapfel and Thomas Wayment, ed, *The Life and Teachings of Jesus Christ, Volume I* (Salt Lake City: Deseret Book, 2005), 8.

[2] Bruce Feiler, *America's Prophet, Moses and the American Story,* 92-93.

3 Michael and Jana Novak, *Washington's God*, 126.

4 David Barton, *Original Intent: The Courts, The Constitution, and Religion* (Aledo: Wallbuilders, 2011), 27.

5 See Gingrich, *Rediscovering God in America*, 82.

6 Reagan, as quoted in Paul Kengor, *God and Ronald Reagan* (New York: Regan Books, 2004), 171.

7 Mitt Romney, Speech Given on Religious Liberty, December 6, 2007, available at www.humanevents.com.

8 Edmund Burke, *Thoughts on the Cause of the Present Discontent* (London: J. Dodsley, 1784).

9 Abraham Lincoln, as quoted in Leidner, 113-114.

10 Lincoln, as quoted in Leidner, 107-108; full speech available from Richardson ed, "A Proclamation by the President of the United States of America (March 30, 1863)," *Messages and Papers of the Presidents* (Washington DC: United States Congress, 1897), 164-165; also available at www.showcase.letin.net/web/creative/lincoln.speeches/fast.htm.

11 Bruce Feiler, *American Prophet*, 96-97.

12 Feiler, 97.

13 Feiler, 248.

14 Reagan, as quoted in Paul Kengor, *God and Ronald Reagan*, 181.

15 Reagan, as quoted in Paul Kengor, *God and Ronald Reagan*, 95.

16 Reagan, as quoted in Michael D. Evans, *The American Prophecies* (New York: Warner Faith, 2004), 218.

17 Vaughn E. Hansen, *Whence Came They: Israel, Britain and the Restoration* (Springville: Cedar Fort, 1993), 127.

18 Robert Putnam and David Campbell, *American Grace* (New York: Simon and Schuster, 2010), 7.

19 Chris Stewart and Ted Stewart, *Seven Miracles That Saved America*, 290-291.

20 Richard Ellis, *To The Flag* (Lawrence: University Press of Kansas, 2005), Preface.

21 Chris Stewart and Ted Stewart, *Seven Miracles That Saved America*, 290.

22 From Deuteronomy 30:15-20; as quoted in Bruce Feiler, *American Prophet*, 25-26, and as quoted in Cleon Skousen, *The Majesty of God's Law*, 14-16.

Epilogue:

WINTER 1799

In early December 1799, only two years after having retired from public life, a happy and healthy Washington was fulfilling his quiet dream of farming his beloved Mount Vernon. He suddenly caught what appeared to be a common cold. Then, to the shock of his family and the entire nation, within twenty-four hours of becoming ill, he was dead. (Perhaps due to a premonition of sorts, shortly before becoming ill, Washington had given specific instructions on the construction of his tomb.) While on his deathbed, and with Martha at his side, he declared, "I die hard...But I am not afraid to go."[1] And why should he fear? This was, after all, the man who seemed to walk with God throughout his life, even stating himself that "No Man has a more perfect Reliance on the alwise [sic], and powerful dispensations of the Supreme Being than I."[2] Furthermore, it was Washington who stated years before his death that when the "curtain of separation shall be drawing, my last breath will, I trust, expire in a prayer for the temporal and eternal felicity of those who...extended their desires to my happiness hereafter, in a *brighter world.*"[3]

Upon his death, his beloved Martha would submit, saying "Tis well, all is now over. I shall soon follow him! I have no more trials to pass through."[4] She too was a woman of great faith, a Christian well-versed in the Scriptures.[5] She was

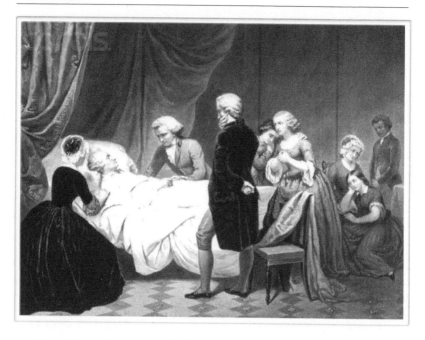

Life of George Washington: The Christian, by Junius Brutus Stearns, 1853

always willing to suffer with the suffering and pray for their wellbeing.[6] Within two years, she would join him in death. Though they were a private couple, they could not hide the fact that they were "soul mates." George would often write to her during the war of his longing to be near her. He would invite her, when he could, to come and stay with him at his ever-changing military headquarters. And she would always come. Furthermore, he loved her children (from a previous marriage), and adopted them as his own, which certainly endeared him to her all the more.[7] The "brighter world," which Washington said he looked forward to in the world beyond, must have become all the brighter if we believe that he and Martha were reunited in heaven.

If Washington had not yet learned what his great sacrifice to God and country had meant in mortality, he most certainly did now. In mortality, he had knowingly entered the national covenant, he had walked with God on the battlefields of war, he had felt His presence, he had incessantly pleaded with the Father on behalf of the nation, and he had repeatedly called his fellow citizens and soldiers to the covenant. Moreover, he had strongly expressed his deep belief that America was part of God's divine plan and that it was meant to secure religious freedom, and he had shown a willingness to put his life on the line time and again for these principles under God.

These principles should be remembered and applied today as we reflect upon the father of our nation. To help us remember, we have been given an awesome monument dedicated to this awesome man. Indeed, the Washington Monument reflects God and covenant just as Washington would have desired. For example, the monument includes inscriptions of prayers for the well-being of the nation, and placed inside its cornerstone is a Bible. Furthermore, engraved upon the monument are the words: "Holiness to the Lord." And upon the capstone of the monument, facing ever-symbolically to the East*, in a place where perhaps only Heaven can see, is the Latin inscription *Laus Deo*, which literally means "Praise be to God."[8]

Washington Monument

In that this inscription would be completely unseen to any mortal eye, we must recognize to whom the monument was *really* dedicated. It is an invocation of the covenant. Indeed, throughout the whole of the Washington Monument symbols of the covenant ring loud and clear, as it

---

*"For as the lightening cometh out of the East, and shineth even unto the west; so shall also the coming of the Son of man be" (Matthew 24:27).

nobly reaches up from the center of our capital and touches, as it would appear, Heaven itself.

But perhaps the most astonishing covenant allusion related to Washington is another national gem—but this one is hiding in plain sight. Gloriously painted onto the ceiling of the U.S. Capitol Building's grand rotunda is a work entitled *The Apotheosis of Washington.* It is a 4,664 square foot

Scene from *The Apotheosis of Washington*
Courtesy of Architect of the Capitol.

fresco that consumes the entirety of the rotunda's massive canopy. The outlaying areas of the fresco are adorned with several scenes reminiscent of the American Covenant. For example, one scene depicts a mythological-type figure that, with raised sword, is destroying other figures representing "tyranny and kingly power." Watching over the victorious freedom fighter is a fierce bald eagle carrying thunderbolts and arrows. The covenant blessings of *liberty* and *protection* are clearly seen within this scene. Other scenes show heavenly messengers (represented by goddesses) providing wisdom to

Americans like Benjamin Franklin, teaching and showing them how to progress in science, commerce, and agriculture. The covenant blessings of *prosperity* are clearly depicted.[9]

Reaffirming the covenant-based symbolism of this work is the fact that other powerful pieces of art depicting great American Covenant moments are also displayed within the grand rotunda. These include the oil-on-canvas paintings entitled *The Landing of Columbus, The Embarkation of the Pilgrims,* and *The Baptism of Pocahontas* (whose symbolic connections to the covenant are described in Chapter 5). Other paintings in this chain of art enveloping the rotunda's interior include depictions of subsequent

Scene from *The Apotheosis of Washington*
Courtesy of Architect of the Capitol.

moments—some of the most powerful moments—of American Covenant history. Present are paintings depicting two of the greatest victories of the Revolutionary War, which, as detailed previously, were won by miracles under the covenant: *Surrender of General Burgoyne* (at Saratoga) and *Surrender of Lord Cornwallis* (at Yorktown). We see depicted another powerful sign of the covenant in the painting *General Washington Resigning His Commission.* And finally, we see the famous painting of the famous signers in *Declaration of Independence.* It is nothing short of the American Covenant story played out around the interior of the Capitol's rotunda.

These giant works seem to support the symbolic power presented by the *Apotheosis of Washington,* not only due to the related and powerful themes carried in all the artistic wonders, but also due to the paintings' position relative to the larger and more prominent work emblazoned upon the canopy. Indeed, the paintings sit upon the base of the rotunda walls, seemingly in support of the canopy on which we see *The Apotheosis of Washington.*

But these symbolisms do not even scratch the surface of the power behind *The Apotheosis of Washington.* For the real power of this work is seen portrayed in a scene placed climactically in the center of the masterpiece: a depiction of George Washington himself, dressed in white robes, ascending on a cloud to heaven with the covenant symbol of a rainbow arch at his feet. Flanking Washington are the goddess Victory and the goddess Liberty, and surrounding him are thirteen maidens, representing the colonies.[10] The principal word in the

Scene from *The Apotheosis of Washington*
Courtesy of Architect of the Capitol.

artwork's title, *apotheosis,* literally means "elevation to the status of a god."[11] It comes from the ancient Greek: *apo* — "to become," and *theos* — "God." To be sure, the scene is nothing less than a depiction of Washington's ascension to the Eternal's presence – receiving personal salvation by virtue of the gospel he worked so diligently for.

The symbolism of it all is overwhelming. Throughout this book, we have documented how Washington was responsible for laying a foundation which would enable principles of salvation to be renewed and enlarged. And so, to stand in the most prominent place of the U.S. Capitol Building and take in what clearly depicts Washington—even he who helped make it all possible—attaining his own eternal salvation is simply breathtaking. Then, to see that imagery supported by so many additional artistic allusions of American Covenant principles, we are presented with the whole picture. We see a full depiction of how America and her covenant truly serve to support God's children and elevate them to their highest potential—even to eternal life. Seen in this light, the U.S. Capitol Building truly becomes a temple of the American Covenant.

As we consider the artwork in the Capitol Building and the notion that Washington received a fullness of all that Heaven has to offer, we can appreciate the full account of this most prominent American Covenant-maker. As a leader of a nation, he lived under a national covenant to bring about *liberty*, *protection*, and *prosperity* – blessings that would enable him, as an individual, to live under a personal covenant which would bring about his own eternal felicity. George Washington's life is the anecdote that tells the full story of the American Covenant.

May we, as Americans, follow this pattern. May we *live* the covenant that God may bless us all beyond measure—that He might lead us all to fill the measure of our creation so that we, like Washington, might find the *brighter world* beyond this mortal existence. May we follow the example of Washington, who once turned to God and prayed, "Accept of me for the merits of Thy son Jesus Christ, that when I come into Thy temple, and compass Thy altar, my prayers may come before Thee." And may we receive the blessing Father Washington once invoked upon a brother, praying that "the Great Architect of the Universe may bless you and receive you hereafter into his immortal Temple."[12]

ENDNOTES

1 Washington, as quoted in Novak, *Washington's God*, 207.

2 Novak, *Washington's God*, 61.

3 Novak, *Washington's God*, 190.

4 Martha Washington, as quoted in Novak, *Washington's God*, 208-209.

5 Meacham, 13.

6 Marshall and Manuel, 404.

7 Novak, *Washington's God*, 26.

8 Newt Gingrich, *Rediscovering God in America* (Nashville: Integrity House, 2006), 38.

9 The facts, descriptions and interpretations of *The Apotheosis of Washington*, as described in this book, can be verified at the following governments official website: www.aoc.gov/cc/art/rotunda/apotheosis; also available at http://en.wikipedia.org/wiki/The_Apotheosis_of_Washington.

10 Ibid

11 Waldman, 56.

12 Washington (January 1792), as quoted in Waldman, 62; Connell, 34-35.

SELECTED BIBLIOGRAPHY

BOOKS AND ARTICLES

Ambrose, Stephen. *To America, Personal Reflections of an Historian.* New York: Simon and Schuster, 2002.

Armstrong, Herbert W. *The United States and Britain in Prophecy.* New York: Everest House, 1980.

Barton, David, *Original Intent*: *The Courts, The Constitution, and Religion* (Aledo: Wallbuilders, 2011),

Bennett, Archibald, "The Children of Ephraim," *Genealogical Magazine*, Vol. 21 (1930), 67.

Bennett, William J. *The Spirit of America.* New York: Simon and Schuster, 1997.

———. William J. *America, The Last Best Hope.* Nashville: Nelson Current, 2006.

Benson, Bobrick, *Wide as the Waters: The Story of the English Bible and the Revolution It Inspired.* New York: Simon and Schuster, 2001.

Bowman, John. *The History of the American Presidency.* North Dighton: World Publication Group,1998.(Revised edition 2008.)

Brookhiser, Richard. *What Would the Founders Do?* New York: Basic Books, 2006.

Brown, Matthew B. *All Things Restored.* American Fork: Covenant Communications, 2000.

Butler, Jon. *Awash a Sea of Faith: Christianizing the American People.* Cambridge: Harvard University Press, 1992.

Carwardine, Richard *Lincoln: A Life of Purpose and Power* (New York: Alfred A. Knopf, 2006)

Childress, David Hatcher. *The Lost Cities of North and Central America.* Kempton: Adventures Unlimited Press, 1998.

Columbus, Christopher. *Libro de las profecias.* Translated by Delano C. West and August King. Gainesville: University of Florida Press, 1991.

Columbus, Ferdinand. *The Life of Admiral Christopher Columbus by His Son Ferdinand Columbus.* New Brunswick: Rutgers University Press, 1959.

Connell, Janice T. *The Spiritual Journey of George Washington.* New York: Hatherleigh Press, 2007.

D'Souza, Dinesh. "Created Equal: How Christianity Shaped the West," *Imprimis,* Volume 37, Number 11, November 2008, 4.

Delaney, Carol, "Columbus's Ultimate Goal: Jerusalem." *Comparative Studies in Society and History,*48, 2006, pp 260-292 .

Edwards, Lester. *The Life and Voyages of Vespucci.* New York: New Amsterdam Books, 1903.

Ellis, Joseph J. *His Excellency.* New York: Alford A. Knopf, 2004.

———. *Patriots, Brotherhood of the American Revolution.* Lectures recorded by Recorded Books, Inc, and Barnes and Noble Publishing: 2004. Study Guide

———. *First Family.* New York: Alfred A. Knopf, 2010.

Entine, Jon, *Abraham's Children: Race, Identity, and the DNA of the Chosen People.* New York: Grand Central Publishing, 2007.

Evans, Michael D. *American Prophecies.* New York: Warner Faith, 2004.

Feiler, Bruce. *America's Prophet: Moses and the American Story.* New York: HarperCollins, 2009.

Ferling, John. Adams vs. Jefferson, The Tumultuous Election of 1800. New York:Oxford University Press, 2004.

Fleming, Thomas "Unlikely Victory," What If? The World's Foremost Military Historians Imagine What Might have been. New York, Penguin Putnam Incorporated, 1999, 162-163.

Ford, Worthington C. and Gaillard Hunt, eds, "Fast Day Proclamation of the Continental Congress, December 11, 1776,"*The Journals of the Continental Congress, 1774-1789.* Vol.6. Washington, D.C.: Government Printing Office, 1904-37, 1022.

Fosdick, Harry Emerson, ed., *Great Voices of the Reformation: An Anthology.* New York: Random House, 1952.

Foster, Marsha, and Mary Elaine Swanson. *The American Covenant, The Untold Story.* Thousand Oaks: The Mayflower Institute, 1981.

Foxe, John, *Foxe's Book of Martyrs,* ed. W. Grinton Berry. Grand Rapids, Mich.: Baker Book House, 2000.

Francis, Richard. *Judge Sewall's Apology.* New York: Harper Collins Publishers, 2005.

Gingrich, Newt. *Rediscovering God in America.* Nashville: Integrity House, 2006.

Grant, James. *John Adams, Party of One.* New York: Farrar, Straus and Giroux, 2005.

Greene, Steven D. *The Tribe of Ephraim.* Springville: Horizon Publishers, 2007.

God Bless America: Prayers & Reflections For Our Country. Grand Rapids: Zondervan, 1999.

Hall, Timothy L. *Separating Church and State.* Chicago: University of Illinois Press, 1998.

Hall, Verna M. *The Christian History of the Constitution of the United States of America.* San Francisco: Foundation for American Christian Education, 1975.

Henry, William Wirt. *Patrick Henry: Life Correspondence and Speeches.* Vol. 1. 1891.

Hinckley, Gordon B. *Standing for Something.* New York: Times Books. Random House, Incorporated, 2000.

Holland, Matthew S. *Bonds of Affection.* Washington D.C.: Georgetown University Press, 2007.

Hosmer, William."Remember Our Bicentennial—1781," Foundation for Christian Self-Government *Newsletter.* June 1981, 5.

Irving, Washington. *The Life and Voyages of Christopher Columbus,* Vol. 6. New York: Peter Fenelon Collier, 1897.

Isaacson, Walter. *Benjamin Franklin, An American Life.* New York: Simon and Schuster, 2003.

Jenkins, Timothy. *The Ten Tribes of Israel.* Colfax: Hay River Press, 2005. Produced by the Ancient American Archeological Foundation. (Originally published 1883).

Jensen, De Lamar. "Columbus and the Hand of God," *Ensign,* October 1992.

Kamen, Henry, *L'Eveil de la Tolerance,* Jeanine Carlander, trans. Paris: Hachette, 1967.

Kengor, Paul. *God and Ronald Reagan.* New York: Regan Books, 2004.

Kennedy, Roger, *Hidden Cities—The Discovery and Loss of Ancient North American Civilization.* Free Press, 1994.

Leidner, Gordon. *Lincoln on God and Country.* Shippensburg: White Mane Books, 2000.

Lester, Edward. *The Life and Voyages of Americus Vespucius.* New York: New Amsterdam Book Company, 1903.

Let Freedom Ring, The Words That Shaped Our America. New York: Sterling Publishing Company, Incorporated, 2001.

Lossing, Benjamin. *Signers of the Declaration.* New York: J.C. Derby Publisher, 1856.

Mann, Charles. *1491-New Revelations of the Americas Before Columbus.* New York: Alfred A. Knopf, 2006.

Marshal, Peter, and David Manuel. *The Light and the Glory.* Grand Rapids: Revell, 2009.

Mathisen, R. *The Role of Religion in American Life.* Washington D.C.: University Press of America.

McCollister, John C. *God and the Oval Office.* Nashville: W Publishing Group, 2005.

McCullough, David. *1776.* New York: Simon and Schuster, 2005.

———. "The Glorious Cause of America," *BYU Magazine* , Winter 2006, 48-49.

———. *John Adams.* New York: Simon and Schuster, 2001.

————. "What the Fog Wrought," What If? The World's Foremost Military Authorities Imagine What Might Have Been. Edited by James Cowley. New York: Penguin Putnam, Incorporated, 1999.

Meacham, Jon. *American Gospel: God, the Founding Fathers, and the Making of a Nation.* New York: Random House, 2006.

Nathanial Greene to Nicolas Cooke, Jan. 10, 1777. *The Papers of General Nathanial Greene.* Vol. 2. Showman, Richard K., and Dennis Conrad, ed. Chapel Hill: University of North Carolina Press, 1980.

Novak, Michael, and Jana Novak. *Washington's God.* New York: Basic Books, 2006.

Novak, Michael. *On Two Wings; Humble Faith and Common Sense at the American Founding.* San Francisco: Encounter Books, 2002.

R, Sergeant. "Battle of Princeton," Vol. 20. *Pennsylvania Magazine of History and Biography,* 1896, 515-16.

Rees, Leslie Pearson, *Ye Have Been Hid: Finding the Lost Tribes of Israel.* New York: Digital Legend Press, 2011.

Reynolds, George, *We Are of Israel.* Salt Lake: Geo. Cannon and Sons, 1895.

Richardson, H.L. "A Most Uncivil War," Vol. 17, No. 1. *California Political Review,* Jan/Feb 2006.

Schweikart, Larry, and Michael Allen. *A Patriot's History.* New York: Sentinel, 2004.

Skousen, W. Cleon. *The Five Thousand Year Leap.* Washington D.C.: The National Center for Constitutional Studies, 1981.

————. *The Majesty of God's Law*. Salt Lake City: Ensign Publishing, 1996.

Sheldon, H., Robert T. Handy, and Lefferts A. Loetscher Smith. *American Christianity, An Historical Interpretation with Representative Documents*. Vol.1: 1607-1820. New York: Charles Scribner's Sons, 1960.

Stewart, Chris & Ted. *7 Miracles That Saved America*. Salt Lake: Shadow Mountain, 2009.

Swanson, Vern, *Dynasty of the Holy Grail*. Springville: Cedar Fort, 2006.

Sweet, Leonard, "Christopher Columbus and the Millenial Vision of the New World, *The Catholic Historical Review,* 1986, pp. 72, 3.

Mac, Toby, and Michael Tait. *Under God*. Minneapolis: Bethany House, 2004.

Thompson, Kenneth W. *The U.S. Constitution and the Constitutions of Latin America*. New York: University Press of America, 1991.

Utah Genealogical and Historical Magazine, Vol.11. July 1920, 107.

Vespucci, Amerigo. *Mundus Novus*. Translated by George Tyler Northrup. New Jersey: Princeton University Press, 1916.

Veit, Hellen, et al., eds., *Creating the Bill or Rights*: *The Documentary Record from the First Federal Congress*. Baltimore: Johns Hopkins University Press, 1991.

Waldman, Steven. *Founding Faith: Politics, Providence and the Birth of Religious Freedom in America*. New York: Random House, 2008.

Wardle, Lynn D. "The Constitution as Covenant," *BYU Studies* 27, no. 3. 1987.

Wasserman, Jacob. *Columbus, Don Quixote of the Sea.* Translated by Delno C. West, and August Kling. Gainesville, FL: 1991.

Watts, Pauline Moffat. "Prophecy and Discovery: On Spiritual Origins of Christopher Columbus' Enterprise to the Indies," *American Historical Review* Feb.1985, 95.

Webster's College Dictionary. New York: Random House, 2000.

Weems, Mason Locke. *A History of the Life, Death, Virtues and Exploits of George Washington.* Philadelphia: Lippencott, 1918.

Wiener, Philip ed., *Dictionary of the History of Ideas.* New York: Scribner's, 1973.

Wilbur, William H. *The Making of George Washington.* DeLand: Patriotic Education, Incorporated, 1970.

Winder, Michael. *President's and Prophets.* American Fork: Covenant Communications, 2007.

Winthrop, John. "A Model of Christian Charity". *Winthrop Papers, 1498-1649.* Vol. 2. Boston: The Massachusetts Historical Society, 282-295.

Wood, Gordon S. *The Creation of the American Republic: 1776-1787.* Chapel Hill: The University of North Carolina Press, 1969.

———. *Revolutionary Characters.* New York: Penguin Press, 2006.

Zagorin, Perez, *How the Idea Religious Toleration Came to the West.* Princeton: Princeton University Press, 2002.

SPECIAL COLLECTIONS AND ONLINE SOURCES

Papers from the Continental Congress, from the Library of Congress *American Memory* collection—memory.loc.gov / ammem / collections / continental / bdsdcoll2.html.

The George Washington Papers, from the Library of Congress *American Memory* collection—lcweb2.loc.gov / ammem / gwhtml / gwhome.html.

The Writings of George Washington, Volume 4, Electronic Text Center, University of Virginia—http:/ / etext.virginia.edu / toc / modeng / public / WasFi04.html.

The Papers of George Washington—http:/ / gwpapers.virginia.edu / documents / constitution / index.html.

The *Avalon Project* at Yale University—www.yale.edu / lawweb / Avalon /.

Joseph J. Ellis, *Patriots, Brotherhood of the American Revolution.* Lectures recorded by Recorded Books, Inc, and Barnes and Noble Publishing: 2004.

Join the author in his fight to end child trafficking

OPERATION UNDERGROUND RAILROAD
Founded by Timothy Ballard.

The O.U.R. Promise:

To the children
who we pray for daily, we say:

Your long night is coming to an end.

Hold on. We are on our way.

And to those captors and perpetrators,
even you monsters who dare offend God's
precious children, we declare to you:

Be afraid. We are coming for you.